Phil McNally:

Now
I work for the company I founded in
businesses, sports teams and students on Winning Mentality and 'Positive Mind power Tools'. I also coach individuals; mostly positive company directors and golfers!

Past
Like any normal boy I played football, watched football, swam, cycled, went to school, read very few books, did homework, watched detective shows and watched business programmes! (OK the last activity is unusual! But the last two activities would influence my future). I developed an interest in business from a young age, reading business press and my Dad's marketing magazines.

Give us a clue?
Growing up I was a big fan of television detectives and I had many heroes like Sherlock Holmes, Chips, Knight Rider and Columbo. I was as interested in business as I was in sport. I watched the evening news, BBC Money Programme and 'Trouble-shooter' at a very young age when other kids just watched sport or cartoons. I looked at business and sport with a curious mind like my detective heroes. My mind kept asking, "How did they do it?" "Why did they succeed?" The answers I found are in here.

At around 19 years of age (1995) I found books I was interested in and started reading them by choice (business books!). In 2000 I read a good book on the mind and have read over 100 books since, as well as many articles and interviews. In 2000 I set over 30 goals including the goal of being a speaker and coach. A year later, that became my top goal. However in 2001 when I looked back at the list I'd written in 2000, I was surprised that 12 months on I had only made progress with two; my previous top goal and one other. I thought to myself "If goal setting is so effective why didn't I achieve any?" The answer popped into my head instantly like a slap on the face. The answer is in here.

After spending 2002 in Australia I came back to Scotland in 2003 and realised a childhood dream by setting up my own company. I soon realised setting up a company is easy (£200), but making a profit is not easy!

I developed over 50 Positive Mind power tools to teach business people. I coached sports people, mainly golfers 'mental skills' in a one hour lesson. Through necessity I fitted the 7 best Positive Mind power Tools into the one hour lesson. In the first lesson with two golfers, I had two hours, so I had to condense it. When golfers, bowlers, cricketers or footballers used the 7 Positive Mind power tools they got incredible results. I soon realised these 7 tools were the most important techniques for 'Winning Mentality' and taught them to business clients as well. So I decided to stop teaching 50 tools and focused my business coaching and book on 7 tools. I knew I could write a great mind book on 'Winning Mentality', better suited for business and sport people than the 100+ I'd read. I used every tool in this book to both write the book (which took over 1 year) and achieve publication. It's an amazing story (but that's another book!)

Using the Positive Mind power tools in this book you can achieve 'Winning Mentality'. With Winning Mentality you can achieve anything. Anything is possible.

Future

I <u>will</u> speak and coach 'Winning Mentality' in Scotland, UK, Ireland, Europe, North America, Australia, Asia and every country in the world. I will have a best-selling book, DVD and CD. I will present a television programme on the subject of 'Winning Mentality' and 'Mind power'. I will help and inspire kids and adults through my charity 'Dreamers'. I will win, achieve goals and enjoy the journey.

Anything is possible!

The author will donate 10% of his profit from this book to the Dreamers Charitable Trust.

Happy with the book?

I am sure you will enjoy and benefit greatly from my book (maybe today, maybe tomorrow, but soon). I hope you are very happy and love this book! If you are not happy and delighted with this book you can return for a full refund (no questions asked). Return the book to the address below, enclosing your address and contact details;

FREEPOST RLTK-LJUG-TGGK
POW
Thainstone Business Centre,
Inverurie,
Aberdeen,
AB51 5TB,
Scotland, UK

WINNING MENTALITY

7 MIND TECHNIQUES USED BY WINNERS

PHIL McNALLY

Lipstick Publishing

Published by Lipstick Publishing.
West Knockenbaird Croft, Insch, Aberdeenshire. Scotland. UK. AB52 6TN.
Website: www.lipstickpublishing.com
E-mail: admin@lipstickpublishing.com
Tel: UK 01464 821954
Fax: UK 01464 821954

First Edition Published UK 2005

Printed and bound by Antony Rowe Ltd, Eastbourne

Dedication

This book is dedicated to my supporters and 'fans' the most important of which have been my Mum and Dad.

I have learnt so much during my life and as my first teachers they taught me all I needed to know to start my journey and chase my dream. I would not be a great teacher if it wasn't for my Mum and I would not have had the courage to chase my dream and go into business if it was not for my first hero and role model, my Dad. I grew up to be so like them both it scared them! There are many other great people who have helped me get where I am today and they are mentioned at the back. I have met many teachers and believers in my life. I am very lucky.

Thanks to all the great open minded clients who use my services and enjoy the great results. Thank YOU for buying my book. I need clients and book buyers to keep me in work.

Contents

Introduction

For over 5 years I have been like a detective obsessed with solving a puzzle. The puzzle to solve was "How do successful sport and business people think to help them succeed?" After years of research, interviews and studying I solved the puzzle. I found the answer was they all used similar 'mind techniques'. I then developed an easy to understand method of teaching the 7 'mind techniques' to others. I began by offering my services to golfers and business people. When I taught business people the techniques, the results were outstanding (one of my clients tripled the company turnover by using them). When I have taught them to sports people, they amazed themselves (several clients won BIG competitions by using them). This book is TOP secret; it contains the secrets of the TOP winners in business and sport today.
Warning: This book is dangerous. In the hands of a talented young athlete, World Number 1 is "just a few years away." In the hands of a talented businessman World Domination is "believable and achievable." Tomorrow there will be more winners than today. And the world will be better for it.
Warning: This book may scare you. The results may startle you. For anyone who is not used to 'thinking big' or 'dreaming' this book will make a Stephen King thriller feel like a comedy! If you have sat back comfortably in your sofa watching dreamers for years achieving great things and never believed you could be one of them, this book will change all that. It will build that belief. When people first start dreaming or start thinking beyond their current ability to a future of possibility, it can scare their socks off! But....
If you are a dreamer this book will be different for you. Anyone who is hungry for his or her dream, or thirsty for improvement will find this book more exciting than a ride at Disneyland! This book won't scare you!
Warning: This book will help you!
Be prepared, this book offers transformation. If you want to translate your dreams conceived into dreams achieved, read on. If you are looking to be the next Branson or Gates, Wilkinson or Woods you've got the right book. This book will show you how to make the jump but doing the jump is up to you. It's an exciting adventure and this book is just the beginning. Hold on to your seat.

STOP!
Do not turn the page until you have a pen beside you. Use it to; Highlight points or quotes and answer the questions. You must write on this book! Your mind works better that way.

Get a notepad or preferably a notebook beside you. Write the word 'ACTION' at the top left hand side. As you read the book write down here any actions you want to take and write your favourite quotes at the back perhaps put a few on your wall later. Writing things helps remember things. On the top right hand side write "WINNING HABIT" and leave the space below it free all the way down the page. You can draw a line down the page from in front on the 'W' if you like.
When you have finished the book review the actions, prioritise them and write the date you will action them by.

Do you need winning mentality?

Winning mentality is essential to win. It is one of four essential 'ingredients' to win. However, winning mentality is the most important! If you think you'll win, you'll win! You also need skills, strategy and action!

The "ingredients" of winning

The "ingredients" of winning in sport and business are very similar. Winning Mentality is one of the essential "ingredients" of winning. The simple formulas I use to show what I believe are the "ingredients" of winning is;
PxAxSxS = Success

P = Positive Belief aka "Winning Mentality"
A = Action
S = Skills
S = Strategy

P.A.S.S.= Success

I will explain this by giving an example. If I was going on a road trip to Austria from Aberdeen I think I need;
P- Positive belief I will get there
A- Start moving towards destination
S- The ability to walk/bike/drive depending on how I'm travelling
S- A plan/map/strategy/knowledge of directions or work it out on the way and ask people directions!

You see what I mean? The formula is the same in business and sport.

This means that if I don't have POSITIVE mentality the result is;
0 x A x S x S = Poor results (ask the golfers and cricketers I coach!)

This means if I don't have ACTION the result is;
P x 0 x S x S = No results! (Going nowhere! The handbrake is on.)

This means if I don't have SKILLS the result is;
P x A x 0 x S = Average results! (Ask the average golfers I coach!)

This means if I don't have STRATEGY the result is;
P x A x S x 0 = Win some/Lose some! (Ask the Portugal football team!)

However if I do have; ACTION, SKILLS, STRATEGY and POSITIVE winning mentality the result is;

P x A x S x S = Winning results! (Ask my clients, any winner or Greece!)

So what I am saying is there is no guarantee you will be 100% successful immediately after using my Positive Mindpower Tools. But I can guarantee you will be MORE successful immediately after using my Positive Mindpower Tools. Adopting 'winning mentality' will improve your performance when you take ACTION with your current SKILLS and STRATEGY.

Zero action equals zero results.
P x A x S x S = Success

If you use 'winning mentality' and already have great skills and strategy you will win! Ask Stoneywood Dyce Cricket Team! After 5 loses in a row they asked me to talk to the team before their next match and they won the match! They won 5 weeks in a row! I am honest and modest enough to admit that if these guys weren't good players, they wouldn't have won. Even with my help.

I can help people become good. I can help good people become great. I cannot help someone become great overnight in any sport.

If you work with me AND work successfully on your skills and strategy you will win! Ask Michael Cheney, of Seniority.co.uk! He increased his turnover 3 fold. I believe Michael has been very successful after working with me because he uses the Positive Mindpower Tools EVERYDAY and because he worked on his skills and strategy. (He did a great 3-day course on business strategy with an amazing company called Develop Succeed Prosper).

I was only one "ingredient" in helping Michael and Stoneywood Dyce succeed. Clients know that after working with me they will achieve greater success, if they use the Positive mental techniques! They also know they need skills, strategy and action for great results! There are FOUR ingredients inside every winning cake. PASS.

Winners don't always have the best skill or strategy,
but they always have the best winning mentality.

Few teams win that believe they will lose.
Many teams win that believe they can win.
What teams believe, teams achieve.
It's the same with individuals.
What people believe, people achieve.

Winning mentality is essential

Winning mentality can bring you success quicker in sport or business. Few winners in sport or business started with winning skills or strategy but they all started with winning mentality and developed their winning skills and strategy. Winning mentality will enhance your skills, strategy and action.

Great winning Mentality will make you run faster than a great pair of trainers. It's not about the trainers.

"It's not about the bike." – Lance Armstrong

Winning mentality beats Goliath

A business or sport person with winning mentality can beat better and bigger opposition. Winning mentality will beat opposition with better skills or better strategy or more money or more brains. It has been proven many times in sport and business and this book includes some amazing examples and tells you how they did it. David can beat Goliath.

Winning mentality beats money

The founders of Seniority.co.uk beat off competition from a company with £10M backing from GE and Prudential. Which was £10M more than they had! They had less than a few thousand spare between them. Dyson, Disney, Microsoft, Virgin, Nike, Apple and IKEA were all started up with less than $10,000. It's the same in sport with many sporting heroes having limited finances in the beginning before reaching great heights and great riches. In fact having it harder is almost an advantage! It makes you hungrier and more resourceful. World record cyclist Graeme Obree built his own bike and beat Chris Boardman who had a £10,000 Locus bike. It's not about the bike. It's about the person on the bike. A business or sport person with winning mentality can beat opposition with a bigger chequebook. This book includes plenty of examples.

Fifty percent of millionaires come from uncomfortable backgrounds. Twenty percent of millionaires were either poor or struggled to survive in childhood. (Tulip Financial Research)

Adversity is an advantage! It makes you hungry.
Great challenges develop great characters.

The most determined and successful football players often come from poor back grounds or "rough" areas.

Winning mentality beats skill

The most talented players do not always win games. Ask Portugal football team, ask Celtic Football Club and ask England rugby team. They will all tell you about times they have been beat by opposition with a greater mindset and not a better skill set. Ask Mohammed Ali

"Champions have to have the skill and the will. But the will must be stronger than the skill." - Muhammad Ali, author, The Soul of a Butterfly – Reflections on Life's Journey

Winning mentality beats brains
Few people with great IQ become millionaires, many people with great 'I Can' do. Few people who are 'smart' achieve great things, many people who are wise do.

Sixty six percent of millionaires were not academic achievers at school, a Tulip survey found.

"I can is better than IQ." -Tom Hunter, Entrepreneur Legend

You need winning mentality knowledge
Knowledge is power. You need to know the 7 techniques of winning mentality in order to have winning mentality. Some winners I've coached came to me during a painful losing streak, like the cricket team after their 5th defeat in a row. (This is similar to many of us who go to the dentist when we are in pain and are reactive rather than proactive!). After our coaching session the 'losers' had the knowledge of the 7 techniques and knew how to get back to their winning game. They did. A five game losing streak was turned into a 5 game winning streak for the cricket team! Winning mentality 'makes' you win. Hindsight can be a beautiful thing! Whether you are being proactive or reactive in learning winning mentality will make you dominate and exterminate your competition! Knowledge is power. Anything is possible using winning mentality.

You need to know the "techniques of winning mentality" and use them to win.

With a closed mind you learn nothing, with an open mind you learn everything.

"I've always had an open mind. I don't see how scepticism helps anybody. When people say 'healthy scepticism', I don't understand. What's healthy about that? All you're doing is blocking. I'd rather someone opened my mind." –Anthony Head, actor, 'Little Britain', 'Buffy The Vampire Slayer'

"The mind is like an umbrella – it only works when it is open". -Scientist Sir James Jeans

"Absorb what is useful, reject what is useless, and add what is specifically your own." – Bruce Lee, Martial Art Legend

"Knowledge is power. What you don't know can hurt you."
-Ivan Misner, founder, BNI & author
'The Worlds Best Known Marketing Secret'

Why YOU need winning mentality;

1. Winning mentality 'makes' you win.
2. Winners use winning mentality in sport AND business
3. You need to know the "ingredients of winning" to win
4. Knowledge is power
5. What you don't know can hurt you.
6. 4 ingredients to win; Winning mentality, action, skills & strategy.
7. Winning mentality is more important than skill and strategy.
8. No action, no results.
9. You need to know the 7 techniques of winning mentality

A business or sport person with winning mentality can beat opposition with better skills or strategy or more money or brains.

David can beat Goliath.
It's been proven many times in sport and business.

"One man that has a mind and knows it can always beat ten men who haven't and don't." - George Bernard Shaw

"Always remember that your success begins inside you: If you can't see it first, no one else ever will."- Chuck Norris

"Winning gold medals today is down to the quality of an athlete's physical and mental preparation, not the quantity of training."
-Sylvester Stein, World Champion Runner, gold medallist and Chairman of Peak Performance Newsletter

"Psychological factors are the most important thing, having the character to win."
-Allan Wells, 100m, Olympic Gold Medallist, Moscow 1980

"I was as mentally strong as I've ever been, where I'd just pick a target and hit it with no swing thoughts at all –I just stood up and let rip because I was in the zone."
–Paul Lawrie, 1999 Open Champion, on winning the Open.

Preview

This book is like an 'Instruction Manual: Owner's guide to using your mind to succeed'. I will tell you how to THINK while you play sport or run your business. I will not tell you how to PLAY sport or RUN your business. This is a book about how to 'run' your mind. The advice and techniques that have helped many winners can help you. I have helped golfers win, students excel, saleswomen sell and business people do amazingly well. Whatever your goal, this book will help you "ready- aim- shoot- score."

Very fast summary of the 4 areas in which winners excel;

1. Positive Belief
2. Energy
3. Goals
4. Sixth Sense (Intuition)

In order to teach people 'how to do it' and how to excel in these areas I developed 7 Positive Mindpower Tools (PMT not PMA) similar to those used by winners. They are described in this book, so that you can also apply the super 7 techniques. The order in which the tools follow in this book are the same winning order my golf clients' use for every shot and my business clients use for every day. They are simple to understand, quick and easy to use. You will see a difference immediately and for years to come. The 7 Positive Mindpower Tools cover the 4 areas; Positive Belief, Energy, Goals and Sixth sense (Intuition) or P.E.G.S. for short. After reading this book you can choose to use the tools and be one of the PEGS (Winners) or you choose not to use them and be one of the NEGS (Negative Losers). It's your choice.

Remembering the 7 tools

You might be thinking "How am I supposed to remember SEVEN tools? Give me a break!" This is where I need a bit of help from your imagination. To help you remember the tools more easily we are going to use an imaginary car. Each of the 7 tools will be associated in some way with your imaginary car, to remind you what the 7 are. It will assist your memory recall. I like to imagine one like Fred Flintstone uses to remind me that it is my feet 'action' that carries me towards my destination and dreams. Before you get in the car you need to decide where you're going!

CHAPTER 1
GOALS

Very fast Summary

To be successful in sport or business you need a dream. What do you really want? Write the answer down. Bingo! That's goal setting. And it works. Big time! (It's like driving a car- you need a destination. Where are you going?)

Included in this chapter;

Where are you going?
Most people order what they don't want
You get what you think about
Think about it
Why goal setting works
How to set goals properly (smart people get it wrong)
Big goals and big guts
Scary goals are good
Little goals achieve little
Thinking, writing and looking at goals (and why it is worth it)
Happy ending and happy journeys
Pictures work
Sacrifices are essential, but sacrificing everything is detrimental
Short term and long term

If you're not excited enough, your goal isn't big enough.

Where are you going?

The starting point for a winner is deciding what they want. They have a goal in mind, a bit like knowing the destination on a car trip, except this is the trip of their life. If you were to stop any car in the street I guarantee the driver can tell you their destination! If you were to stop any winner in the street I guarantee they could tell you their destination! Winners have dreams and goals and they are driving towards it. Few people are working towards their dream, like an Olympic medal or a successful business. These big goal 'keepers' are winners. I believe that we all have goals; it's just that most of the goals aren't very big. Most people are working towards small goals, whether it is a small increase in wages, a holiday or a bigger car next year. Only winners have 'dream destinations'. Most people don't.

Winners have dreams and are working on them or living them.
And loving it.
'Losers' have small goals and are working towards them and hating it.

Shopping list

Having written goals is like having a shopping list and going into a supermarket. Without the list you don't get half the things you want and need. Whereas when you go into a supermarket with a shopping list, you tend to remember, see and get what you want. It's the same with writing goals for your business, sport or life. Your mind works more effectively when you write out a list of goals. It sees the goals on your list and then looks for the goals (and goal opportunities) everyday. Of course not all goals are just found or spotted by your mind so the list also helps you focus your priorities and actions.

Life is like a supermarket, so write out your shopping list.
Or you won't get half the things you want and need.

Your mind needs your help by writing out your goals.
Then you need to help yourself.

Most successful shoppers have their list written down!
Most successful people have their goals written down!

Menu of life

What do you want? What if you woke up one day and were told you could order whatever you like to happen that day. What would you order?

Well today is the day! And I'm the one telling you, you can order what you want. One day you will wake up and believe me. What if the menu today had the choice of either a fun day or a boring day, a lucky day or an unlucky day, a successful day or a slow day, a wonderful day or a wonder-less day; which would you choose?? What

if the menu was unlimited and you could order whatever you want? WHAT IF!
You know, the brain is REALLY that powerful! And it REALLY is that simple!

Mind the Waiter
Your mind is like a waiter. You have to tell it what you want, show it what you want and then it will go looking for it. The waiter will find it or make it!
That's why you need to have a picture of what you want. Either a picture in your mind or in your house! Ever thought about looking for a new house, blouse, car, job or book and it found you?! Ever thought about a friend and then they called you?!

Your mind is like a waiter. What have you been ordering?

If all we have to do is write down our order and the waiter does the rest why aren't we all having successful years or lucky months or happy days? Because only about 1% of people ever write down their order. Is it worth a few minutes of your time to write down your order? Only if you want to succeed! Just 1% do it! It's your choice.

Write down your order. 1% do it and get it. (99% don't get it)

You may not get everything you order. But you will be very surprised at how much you do get when you look back at the end of a day, week, year or years later. Welcome to goal setting.

Remember. If you don't ask you don't get.

Did you order rubbish?
What happens when you order what you don't want?! Do this experiment- I want you NOT to think about a pile of rubbish. Don't think about a pile of rubbish. What did you think about and picture in your mind? That's what the waiter can see too! So don't order what you don't want. A lot of people do.

If people think, believe or say; "I can't lose weight. It's impossible to find a good job. I'm always on my own. I have no money." That's what they get! If they order, "I don't want to mess this up", "I wish I wasn't fat" "I don't want a crap job" "I hope my next partner isn't so bad." That's what they get!

Be careful what you wish for.
Order what you <u>want</u>, not what you <u>don't want</u>!

Show and Tell

Tips for a great meal, day, week or year;

1. Shout out your order or whisper it in your head. Loud. Tell the waiter.
2. Write down your order. Show the waiter.
3. Picture your order in your head or point to the picture. Show the waiter.

What did you show and tell today? If you don't ask, you don't get!

I want to be slim Vs I want to lose weight

Imagine someone heavily overweight wants to get to a healthy weight. If they were to picture themselves slim or say, "I want to be slim" the mind 'sees' the goal and actually keeps working until the goal picture becomes the real picture. Yes, "it is easier said than done." But using the mind to conceive a goal helps you achieve a goal. In fact it's essential to achieve it.

Using the mind to conceive your goal helps you achieve your goal.

However this is the part that 95% of 'scale watchers' get wrong. They don't set the goal correctly. They say, "I want to lose weight." It's a bit like saying "I want to not miss this shot" instead of "I want to score." You can't start winning until you stop thinking about losing! You've got to focus on what you do want, not on what you don't want. The word "slim" is essential because it builds a 'slim' picture in the mind. Most 'scale watchers' are still thinking about their heavy overweight picture in their mind, so the mind compares it to your current self and sees the goal has been achieved! So the mind sits back and does nothing. So do you.

The mind and body work towards the picture in your mind. Fat or slim.

You can't start winning until you stop thinking about losing!
You've got to focus on what you do want, not on what you don't want.
Use winning words not losing words.

Setting Goals for Survival

Humans have been designed for survival. Since cave man days we have been goal setting. When a caveman was hungry he set out with the goal of finding something to eat (like a furry thing on four legs). His mind would help him achieve that goal in order to survive. Humans are really designed to set and achieve goals, but few humans use their capability.

Our minds have been designed to help us achieve our goals.
If you are hungry set yourself a goal!

Humans are designed to set and achieve goals,
but few humans use their capability.

Find it that way, or make it that way
When your mind sees a goal on your wall or in your mind, it then goes looking for it.

Your goal gets your mind to go looking for the goal until it finds it.
Your mind keeps working until the fantasy becomes reality.

Brain VIP Detector
Your brain has a 'very important piece of information detector' which works like a metal detector at an airport. As you know, the 'goal' of a metal detector is to detect metal and when it does, to raise the alarm and bring it to the attention of airport security. The goal of your brain detector is to detect very important pieces (VIP) of information and when it does, to raise the alarm and bring it to your attention. The real name for your 'brain VIP detector' is your Reticular Activating System (I hope you agree that 'brain VIP detector' sounds better!). Your RAS is a 'brain filter' that processes the thousands of pieces of 'incoming' information received every minute by your brain. The RAS ignores the mass amount of non-important information received but will identify important information and bring it to your conscious attention.

Your brain VIP detector needs to know your goals so it can identify
anything relevant to those goals and important to you.

Your mind is like a 'goal detector'
so it needs to know what your goals are!

VIP information
Your eye and mind will see everything, processing thousands of pieces of information a day. To explain how the mind VIP detector tells the difference between non-important information and important information I'll use an example. Let's consider you are driving a familiar car down a very familiar street near your house.

Your brain will ignore the following non-important information it receives;
Car temperature is fine, window is clean, tax disc is still visible, furry dice is still hanging from mirror (great!), hands are a bit dirty but nothing to worry about, the road has no holes, car smells (but nothing unusual!), the street is bright so no need for lights, steering wheel is cold, all the walls and houses are still standing, slates and windows have no smashes, can still taste your toothpaste, neighbours caravan is in drive, you have found second gear ok so just concentrate on the road….

Your brain will not ignore any very important pieces of information it receives and will bring them to your conscious attention (you will then store the info or act on the info);
It's starting to rain (so put on wipers), car coming (don't pull out yet), you're moving now (you've found right gear), Number 10 have curtains closed as usual (sleep addicts), Mr Smith's work van is outside his house, Jenny's Smart car is behind, neighbour's great new car is there and it's the same model as your dream car, watch that kid kicking the ball (without a jacket on!), a car's approaching, it's Brian, the ball's on the road…(stop BRAKE!)

You get the idea. The weather was important. The daylight and road condition weren't. Your neighbours and friend's cars were important. The mind also spotted the car of your dreams, which was very important. The neighbours' caravan wasn't important. The kids' ball was important (the fact the kid had no jacket on surprised you, but shouldn't have!). The houses hadn't fallen down overnight (now that would have been VIP and got your attention!). The cold steering wheel and taste of toothpaste is not abnormal therefore not important. But the ball hitting the road was and you hit the brakes. And you never paused to check any sounds, tastes, feelings, smells or other eye information before you did! Urgent action was requested, focus was required and you delivered. Well done.

Your eyes see everything, your ears hear everything, your skin feels everything, your nose smells everything and your tongue tastes everything and your brain gets sent all this sensory information every millisecond of everyday!
But luckily it only informs you of the VIP important stuff!

The VIP Information List

When you first think about a goal your mind will immediately add the goal to its VIP information list. So, from that moment on, anything related to achieving that goal or connected with that goal is identified by your brain VIP detector as VIP information.

Imagine one day you decide you want a new car, lets say a new Mini! Your brain VIP detector is 'filtering' everything you see and pointing out 'hazards', "goals" and other important information. This includes 'detecting' anything important related to your goal or which could help you achieve your goal. Suddenly from that moment on you notice lots of Mini cars everywhere you look; on the road, television and magazines. Your mind will start looking for VIP and pointing out VIP when you decided on the goal. Rather than filtering and ignoring.

Set a goal and your mind starts looking and pointing.
Without a goal your mind is filtering and ignoring.

'Seek and ye shall find'

Filtering and Ignoring
Your mind must know your goals in order to be able to help you. Which is why you need to regularly look at your goals and remind the mind what to look for! Remember when you first bought a new car or new shoes or new haircut. Suddenly you notice the same car, shoes or haircut everywhere! They were there the day before as well! However they weren't important to you then so although your mind did 'see' them it filtered and ignored them! So you didn't consciously 'see' them! Which meant you weren't aware of them. Like a 'blind spot'.

If your mind isn't aware of your goals,
you won't be aware of the opportunities.

Your mind must know your goals in order to be able to 'start looking'.
Which is why you need to regularly look at your goals
and remind the mind what to look for!

Spotting Opportunities or Being 'Blind' to opportunities
Imagine you have just been shopping in a large supermarket. When you return to the big car park to pick up your car, you scan all the cars and are looking for your car. You may also observe any cars of a person you know or any car models you like (both are VIP information to you). After finding your car, you drive out of the car park. If I was to stop your car and ask you some questions "How many 'black cars' are in the car park? How many estate cars?" You are unlikely to be very accurate. However if I told you before you went to fetch your car that I will ask you those two questions as you drive out I am sure you would observe and 'see' how many black cars and how many estate cars are in the car park. That information is now important to you! Before it wasn't and although your mind did 'see' the cars it just filtered them out! Like a blind spot and you weren't aware of them.

It's the same with goals. If your brain VIP detector knows what your goals are it will look for relevant information and opportunities and make you aware of them, which it would otherwise ignore (and you wouldn't spot it or be made aware of it).

You only consciously see what your mind thinks is important.
If you have a list of goals your mind will spot anything relevant to those goals and make you consciously aware of it.

If you don't have goals your mind will not make you aware when you pass a good opportunity. It will ignore it and 'blind spot it'.

Ignoring goals
If your mind knows what your goal is and brain VIP detector points out useful information and opportunities to you and <u>you</u> ignore them (for several months or years), it will eventually 'drop' that goal from the

important list. You demonstrated to your mind in your actions that the goal and opportunity wasn't important.

If you give up on your goals, your mind will give up on your goals and you will be blind to any future opportunities to achieve your goals.

Mind Recorder

Your mind is like a video camera on 'record' all day. It stores everyday in your mind including all sensory information. This is why it is possible to re-call the feel of the sun, the sound of waves, the taste of chocolate, the sight of your Christmas presents and the smell of dog poo! (I'd recognise that smell anywhere!) The previous sensory information and past experience helps your mind identify new 'incoming' sensory information it receives during every day. Your mind is always recording, even when you're sleeping, hence why it is possible to re-call dreams.

Your mind is like a video camera on 'record' all day
and has a video store full of all the previous days
of your life and all previous experiences.

Does goal setting work?

The powerful 'mind recorder' stores all our thoughts and all our actions everyday. So if you think about a goal or write down a goal just once it is recorded. Is thinking about goals or writing down goals effective for success? I'll tell you the answer.

Think about it

Thinking is something that most people don't do enough of. Positive thinking is something that most people have never heard of! Thinking is not an activity that requires a lot of sweat or a lot of time. Thinking is something that most winners do and most losers don't. You would think that thinking about goals is a lazy mans dream. But the lazy man is too lazy to dream.

Thinking is something that most people don't do enough of.
Positive thinking is something that most people have never heard of!
Thinking is an activity that most winners do and most losers don't.

We actually avoid thinking! From the moment we wake up, we turn the noise up. We are uncomfortable with silence. (As kids we loved it!) After we hit our teens most of us begin to avoid it. As adults we run from it! We 'fill' any silences. It's more a case of "I need to get the music or television on, grab the paper or use my phone quick, because I might need to think for a minute." We switch the 'noise' on and switch ourselves off.

Switch the 'noise' off and let your mind start thinking!
Stop and think for a minute.
Get some silence so you can hear yourself think.
Can you hear yourself think?

Turn off the music
Looking back I remember as a teenager getting picked up by my Dad maybe 10 minutes from our house and driven home. As we drove home I thought to myself, "oh my God, there's something wrong here. What is it? I don't like it...ahhh I've found it. There's no music! Turn on the music!" I needed the music on immediately! I didn't have time to wait around 3 seconds and ask my Dad to do it. Are you kidding? I made a dive for the 'on' switch and had the beats pumping before you could say, "lightening fingers." I even think we were chatting but the music still had to be on! But my point is that thinking was something I didn't do much of, even for 10 minutes. It took me a few years before I realised the old man (a big music lover himself) is a wise man. He must be thinking. He doesn't often have the music on when driving. Whether it's a 5 minute or 5 hour trip. Quality thinking time!

Turn off the music, television, phone, and laptop and stop reading for 10 minutes. Start thinking for a change. It will change your life.

I was just thinking about it
Here is a great story. A good friend of mine Duncan works in the city, in the financial district of London. He was playing golf with a contact of his and the conversation turned to Duncans' job. His playing partner made a comment about how much Duncan should be getting for the kind of job he is doing for the bank. His figure was a lot more than what Duncan was getting at the time! Picking his chin off the ground Duncan thought to himself "I need to look at getting another job." The following week Duncan received a call from a previous client (and contact) and asked if he would be interested in a job. He was offered 'the figure' and took the offer. He told me "I didn't do anything about it. I just thought about it. I'm very lucky. It was amazing. The mind is amazing." Think about it and you're mind will get to work on it. It works wonders. Not all the time, but a lot of the time.

Think about it and your mind will work on it. It's the thought that counts.

Your thoughts can make it happen.

Thinking about goals is a lazy mans dream, but the lazy man is too lazy to dream. Thinking is easy but watching TV is easier.

Writing goals is a great investment

If just thinking about a goal works wonders, why "waste time" writing down goals? Because if you don't write about it, you might not think about it! (And thinking about goals works wonders-as you know!). Secondly, it can assist your focus by establishing your priorities and focus on doing things that are useful or wonderful (and you will know when you are wasting your time). And thirdly writing goals is more effective than just 'thinking' goals. Winners do both!

Writing goals is a great investment.
It pays off bigger than the stock market.
Winners write goals and think goals.

Thailand Appraisal

Once, after giving a talk to some senior executives, an ex HR manager from Shell told me that years ago when she was doing her Annual Appraisal in Thailand she wrote down 'Australia and Argentina' as her 'Personal goals'. A few years later she had lived and worked in both locations! It worked wonders!

A recent evaluation of studies on goal setting showed that it led to performance enhancement in 78% of sport and exercise research studies, with moderate-to strong effects.

Chris Hoy, Michael Phelps and Jonny Wilkinson all set themselves a dream, a HUGE goal when they were younger and now they have achieved their dream! Writing goals works. Winners write down their dreams and then work on their dreams.

"Winning the World Cup fulfilled a promise I made to myself when I was ten. Most children write out Christmas lists for Santa – I wrote out a list of goals I wanted to achieve as a rugby player."
- Jonny Wilkinson, Winner of World Cup 2003

Little goals; little achieved

I have an interesting personal story. I wrote down some goals that I had as part of a CV I designed when applying to two companies in London in December 2000 (St Luke's and Mediacom). I wrote 'Goals; work, travel, learn, yoga, surf, break dance, help, love, smile'. After 12 months working in London I had achieved four goals; work, learn, yoga and smiles. Six months on (18 months after writing the goals) I was in Australia and I came across my old CV and realised I had achieved them all! I wrote the goals for fun. I might not have achieved them if I hadn't written them.

Writing goals achieves goals.

When you write a list of goals your mind records the goals subconsciously and you'll be surprised how effective it can be. If you write down very little goals you will achieve very little goals. You might not achieve goals if you don't write goals.

Writing goals works (if you take opportunities)
Yes, writing goals does work. Some goals will come to you on your plate but you have to grab them! However the above goals were not BIG goals or impossible goals in anyone's book. They were little goals, only a little stretch outside current reality. (In fact, because of the mind's power it even made them look easy to achieve.)

Little goals can land on your plate.
Most big goals won't land on your plate. You have to go looking for them. Little goals may require a little action.
Big goals may require a big amount of action.
(Perhaps years of action).

Your mind will give you opportunities to achieve your little goals and your big goals. But you have to take the opportunities. A big goal may require a big risk- Are you prepared to take it? A big goal may need a big amount of hard work- Are you willing to do it?

"A dream doesn't become a reality through magic;
it takes sweat, determination, and hard work."
- Colin Powell, 67, US Secretary of State

ACTION!
Achieved goals (Did you celebrate success?)
Once you set goals for the future it's easy to focus on them and forget what you have achieved. You have achieved great things already! Some you worked for and some just came to you. Some you thought about once and some you thought about a lot. Think of 7 goals you have achieved and write them down here now.
GO!

Remember what goals you have achieved
when you work towards the goals you haven't.

Did you get 10?
Whether you have got 7 or not I want you to consider three goals that you are unlikely to have put down yet. Talking, walking, cycling! Great

goals and great achievements! Well done. Can you swim? Great! Add these to your list.
GO!

Record Success
Do you make a note of your achievements every week? Every month? every year? Unless we write down our achievements it's easy to miss our progress. You can only see how far you have come if you look back. Have somewhere where you note all your 'success'. Your achievements will inspire you to more greatness. When is the last time you celebrated your achievements? Don't miss your greatness, celebrate your greatness! There are lots of ways to celebrate (some cost money, some don't!). Celebrate with any treat. It will make a stronger memory of it in your mind and boost your self-belief. Celebrate every success (big or small). Success breeds success. But be honest. If you perform well below your ability it's no time to celebrate. It's time to set yourself a goal and give yourself a talking to! Then get on with it and choose a positive attitude to face the future.

Celebrate success. Record success.
"I had a twenty four hour rule to celebrate a victory or bemoan a defeat. Don't get a big head if you win or get too down in the dumps when you lose. Keep things in perspective. Success is not forever and failure isn't fatal."
-American coach Don Shula, most successful NFL coach ever

Make it like Beckham
There is a framed picture in David Beckhams' Dad's house. It holds a picture of David Beckham in a Manchester United strip and within the frame just below the picture is a scrap of white paper. It is a messily written note penned by David when he was young. It reads "Goals; Captain of England, best player in the world, marry a pop star." David is married to his pop star wife Victoria, is Captain of England football team and while not yet the best player in the world, he is valued as one of the best players in the world, playing in one of the best teams in Europe. True story.

"I want to be more famous than Persil Automatic!"
– Victoria Beckham, she achieved her very precise goal

Billionaires do it twice a day
Research in the USA looked at millionaires and billionaires and examined the differences between them. One fascinating difference they found was that millionaires looked at their goals once a day and

billionaires looked at their goals twice a day! They say that 'it costs nothing to look', which is generally correct but the reverse is definitely true in this case. If you don't look it will cost you! This research affirms that writing goals is effective. It also demonstrates that looking at your goals everyday is very effective. And looking at your goals twice a day is VERY very effective!

Billionaires look at their goals 730 times a year! Twice a day.
Out of sight, out of mind.
Looking at your goals twice a day is effective and cost FREE!
Not having goals is very costly!

Millionaire by 30

When Aberdeen businessman Stewart Milne set up in business he said "I set myself the goal of being a millionaire before I was 30" and he achieved it with a few years to spare! It worked wonders. Glasgow based entrepreneur Chris Gorman set up DX Communications with Richard Emmanuel when he was in his twenties. "I had been telling people since I was 21 that I was going to be a millionaire before I was thirty. One month before my 30th birthday I received a cheque for just over a £1M from BT." They both sold a share of DX to BT. A few years later they ended up selling the whole company to BT and have both followed different paths onto bigger things. Chris Gorman is owner and Chairman of The Gadget Shop among other ventures.

Goals- Winners set them, so winners get them.

Never mind

From doing my own informal research I have discovered a difference between Millionaires and Non Millionaires. Most Millionaires actually wrote the goal 'Millionaire' down. Most Non Millionaires never write any goals.

Billionaires look at their goals twice a day, millionaires once a day.
Non-millionaires don't have goals to look at!
Billionaires and millionaires have got what everyone else hasn't.
Guts and Goals.

Dreams with Deadlines

Having a date for your goals is like giving a student a deadline for an assignment- they don't take action until the last minute! Plus you don't get the assignment early and if you didn't set a deadline you'd never get the assignment! Having a date for your dreams and goals is important in the same way. It lets your mind know when to spring into action, when to deliver! If you plan to go on holiday next year and plan to book at the 'last minute' your mind won't suddenly be on the 'look out' for holiday information, travel agents or relevant adverts for you until the date comes closer. In fact it probably won't start looking till a month before if you plan to book 'last minute'. But if you decided to fly somewhere next weekend, your mind will rush into action and start looking for relevant information now.

Writing goals puts your mind on 'look out' for useful 'goal information'.
Writing dates tells it when to go on 'look out' and start looking.
Having a date for your dreams is like giving a student a deadline.
All the action is last minute, you don't get it early and if you didn't set a deadline you'd never get it!

Goals with deadlines are like dreams with delivery dates.

Miss the bus?
Waiting for a goal is like waiting for a bus. If your bus isn't due for an hour you won't start looking for it to arrive now. Your mind will start looking about 5 minutes before it's due. But if you never look for the bus, you'll miss the bus! The same goes for your goals.

'Seek and ye shall find'

Having pictures works
There is a way to further maximise your mind's power and enhance the power of having goals; have pictures of your goals. The mind likes to work in pictures and even when you're thinking or using only words it often translates them to pictures. The words "score a goal", "visit New York", "climb Everest" builds a picture in your mind. The words "kid kicking a ball" built a picture on the previous page. Did you guess it was a girl?! A few words build a picture, but not always the right one. So using pictures for your goals makes sense. It's more accurate. For example if you had written a goal to own a black Porsche and the mind helped you achieve that goal, but you 'receive' a Boxer hard top when you wanted a 911 soft top. (Very unfortunate! If this ever happens to you I suggest you give it away- my number is at the back of the book!).

Pictures help the mind 'deliver' goals accurately.
What it sees is what you get.

Lifetime Dreamers
A lot of adult achievers were childhood dreamers. And they never stopped dreaming. I've heard several sports people say they achieved their childhood dreams by winning an Olympic gold medal (there are several examples included in this book). You will often hear an actor say they achieved their childhood dreams when they collected an Oscar. Why are people who continue, "dreaming" their dream into adulthood continually successful? Your mind accepts any picture you have in your mind as "the way things should be" and it works on helping you achieve that dream.

If you keep dreaming you will keep achieving
- with a little help from your mind.
Adult achievers are grown up childhood dreamers.

Subliminal Advertising

Subliminal advertising is banned. It's banned because it works. Subliminal pictures were used within cinemas before they were banned. A movie picture contains about 24 slides for every second, which to the human eye looks like a continuous and seamless moving picture. Cinemas used to insert pictures of hotdogs and ice cream into the movie, which flashed up on the screen so quickly they were not fully noticed by us consciously but the mind did see them subconsciously. In the good old days half way through a movie an usher would walk down the aisle and serve sweets, popcorn and ice cream (and in the US hot dogs as well). Even people who had finished a 3-course dinner 10 seconds before entering the cinema were climbing over chairs to get some food! (Even if there was no space in their stomach, the throat had spare capacity!) Ok I exaggerate slightly but only to emphasise how effective the technique was. It worked! But it was underhand, so it was banned.

Pictures seen by your mind will influence your thoughts and results.
Pictures seen by your mind will influence your actions.

Subliminal 'Dream advertising'

If you follow a similar process by getting pictures of your dream goals it helps plant the suggestion into your mind and helps you achieve it. One of the best places to plant your pictures is in your bedroom because you will see them before you go to sleep and after you wake up. This time period (before sleep and after sleeping) is when your subconscious is most active, open and dominant due to your relaxed state. The additional benefit of looking at your goals before sleeping is that you may dream up ideas to achieve your goals! If you do write them down as soon as you wake up, even if it's dark outside! Ideas are essential to achieve dreams.

Your mind will achieve some goals for you all by itself.
For some goals your mind may need some help.
Put pictures of your dream goals where your mind will see them
and it will help you achieve them. Subliminal 'Dream advertising'!
Ideas and action make dreams come true.

Popcorn

Once day, while I was in a local town shopping I received a call from my Mum. She asked me to get some popcorn. It was an unusual request (the first time I'd got a call with that request). It later turned out that she had no set plans to watch a movie that night. Don't get me wrong over the years I had bought popcorn for her a few times but only when we were actually hiring a movie, which he hadn't done for a while after getting Sky Movie channel. When I arrived as I walked into the hallway I noticed a pile of old books, which looked like they were about to be given away to charity. I smiled when I noticed the book at the top of the pile. 'Popcorn' by Ben Elton. Because my Mum's mind had seen the word and picture of popcorn on the book cover the idea/goal was planted and my Mum wanted popcorn! It works wonders!

The pictures you see each day influence your mind

Yellow Pages

In 2003 I was talking to a friend of mine called Travis Kennedy, who was the top Yellow pages sales person in Western Australia in 2002. We discussed goal setting and having pictures. Travis said that for the whole of 2002 he had pictures around his desk and computer at work, which were taken in South Africa. He spent most of his working day out at appointments but he would see the pictures when he came back to the office at night. He said that the pictures inspired him especially when he chose to work late at night on paper work. He was the top sales person that year and won the special prize; a trip for two people to South Africa! He achieved his goal. The pictures worked. They worked wonders.

Seeing goal pictures everyday and night helps bring them into sight.

Australia

For many years I thought about going to Australia. I think I became interested because my Dad had been going there for years and talked very highly of the country. I worked in a newsagent called RS McColl from the age of 15 and continued until I was well past my 18th birthday. Old papers were usually thrown out. One day I kept the Financial Times and cut out a small picture of the map of Australia and put it on my wall. I remember thinking to myself 'I'd like to go there one day'. When I was 25 I did.

Sometimes it takes 10 years before you realise
some goals take 10 years.

Snap

The mind is good at recognising things. One of the main reasons goal setting is so powerful is because your mind wants your internal picture (goal) to be the same as your external picture, like a game of snap. It will attract a goal, recognise goal opportunities or work on a goal till you achieve a goal (snap!).

Goal setting is like a game of snap and your mind likes to play!

It will attract a goal, recognise goal opportunities or work on a goal till you achieve a goal (snap!).

Visit your dream

An even more powerful way to 'advertise' your dream to your mind is to visit it! In read life! If it's not possible than in your mind 'visit it' through visualisation. Get a picture of yourself standing beside your dream. Chris Gorman visited the show room of his dream house and took pictures of him and his wife inside and outside and put it on his 'goals board'. He moved in a year later. It get better. He then did the same thing again with an even better house. He moved in a year later. He did it four years in a row with success! I have done this too.

Big Goals

OK, I've outlined why you need to set goals, why you need to write them down, why you need to look at them twice a day and why having pictures of your goals helps (a lot!). Now I would like to emphasise the beauty and benefit of setting BIG goals. There are BIG benefits from having BIG goals!

Number 1 reason to have BIG goals; You might just achieve them!
Number 2 reason to have BIG goals; You won't waste your talents.

The big benefits of working towards big goals: amazing happiness, stretching your ability, increased passion, more energy, infectious enthusiasm, amazing achievement and the life you dreamed of.

Shoot for your goal. If you don't shoot, you don't score.
100% guaranteed.

Big dreams

People who achieve great things had great dreams. Those that achieve big things had big dreams. They are ordinary people like you and I. Those that don't achieve big don't think big. You have got to think big to achieve big.

"It's a story of an ordinary man doing something extraordinary."
-Tom Hunter, Multi-millionaire Entrepreneur
You have got to think big to achieve big.
People who achieve big things had big dreams.
Winners often say,
'I'm just an ordinary person who achieved something extraordinary'.

Be the greatest

There must be one big goal within every business. Every business must have a big goal and every person within the company must know it. It helps if everyone believes it. The method for choosing the big goal for a business is the same as the method for choosing the big goal for a person. Go after your dream goal. Jim Collins states in his book 'Good to Great' that when he looked at companies that went from good to great he found that the company's chosen goal or product had three elements for the company; passion for it, ability to profit from it and possibility of being the best in the world at it. Anything is possible! The same advice could be given to any sport person inside or outside sport; be passionate, be profitable and be the best in the world. Jim found that the goals were always big and he termed them BHAG's; Big Hairy Audacious Goals. I hope Jim's finding has encouraged companies to throw out their SMART goals! Companies setting realistic goals today, won't be around tomorrow, it's as simple as that.

Go after your dreams and profit from it.
Companies setting realistic goals today won't be around tomorrow.
Set yourself a goal; be passionate,
be profitable and be the best in the world.

Victory

In the early years of Nike they had one BIG goal; Crush Adidas and everyone in the organisation knew it, believed it and they achieved it. British Prime Minister Sir Winston Churchill had one big goal during the war "Victory" and the country knew it. Thankfully and amazingly they achieved it. Sir John Harvey-Jones believes that one of the keys to success in a company is everyone knowing the goal. He is not an academic. He has been there and done it. Achieving success in the Navy and upon leaving working through the ranks of ICI to become Chairman.

"The ideal organisation and the one that has the best chance of success is one where, if you were to ask anybody from the chairman down to the newest recruit on the shop floor what the business is trying to do, you'd get the same answer."
– Sir John Harvey-Jones, 'Making it happen'

Dream with deadline

American President, John F. Kennedy set the big goal of being in space in 1961. It was a dream and it had a deadline. He said, "I regard the decision as among the most important decisions that will be made during my incumbency in the office of the Presidency." John F. Kennedy's famous "Moon Speech" the following year (12th September 1962) was brilliant, which made American's fully aware of they were chasing a dream! It's worth reading or hearing his full speech, which includes quotes he like from two great explorers! Great people are inspired by great people. All leaders need inspiration and motivation. Leaders are readers. Here are a few of the comments Kennedy made, "This country of the United States was not built by those who waited and rested and wished to look behind them. This country was conquered by those who moved forward--and so will space. We choose to go to the moon in this decade and do the other things, not because they are easy, but because they are hard, because that goal will serve to organise and measure the best of our energies and skills, because that challenge is one that we are willing to accept, one we are unwilling to postpone, and one which we intend to win, and the others, too. Many years ago the great British explorer George Mallory, who was to die on Mount Everest, was asked 'Why did he want to climb it?' He said, "Because it is there." Well, space is there, and we're going to climb it. Surely the opening vistas of space promise high costs and hardships, as well as high reward. However, I think we're going to do it. And this will be done in the decade of the sixties." He stated that to achieve it "and do it first before this decade is out--then we must be bold." They did achieve it. Those involved in the project became even more motivated and determined to achieve it after he was assassinated. JFK inspired many people including one boy he met called Bill Clinton who set the goal of becoming a Senator like JFK and possibly President! Bill achieved that goal and followed in his footsteps of going from Senator to President.

Have a dream. Have a deadline. Be bold.
Great people inspire great people.
Follow in the footsteps of great people. It is a path to greatness.

Chasing a dream; Changing a dream
Billionaire Oprah Winfrey came from a very poor background. She didn't let that stop her. She says, "One of the defining moments of my life came in the fourth grade, the year I was Mrs. Duncan's student. What Mrs. Duncan did for me was to help me to not be afraid of being smart. She encouraged me to read, and she often stayed after school to work with me, helping me choose books and letting me help her grade papers. For many years after that, I had one goal that I would one day become a fourth-grade teacher who would win the teacher award--because I was going to be the best teacher anyone had ever seen!"

Chasing your dream is essential to achieving your dream,
even if your dream changes.

You can fly
You have no idea what you are capable of. Consider what you think you are capable of. Think big. Really big. Then double it and you're getting close. But you're not even warm. We have to push beyond our limits before we find our limits. Our unused ability is like we all have wings but we've not discovered them yet. It's only if we attempt to fly that we realise we have wings. It's only when we start using our wings that we realise we can fly.

We all have special power under our skin, but we haven't used it yet.

Lazy Goals

I have realised the importance and impact to my life (and my energy) of setting myself some big and exciting goals. I would stop being lazy! I'd stop lying in bed for hours, stop wasting time and stop 'wasting' weekends. To demonstrate to people the impact to our energy of big goals I tell them about what I call 'the Santa Claus effect'.

"There are no lazy people just lazy goals."- Anthony Robbins

Santa Claus effect

Do you remember when you were young how excited you got when Santa Claus was coming? You asked Santa for something you REALLY wanted and you couldn't sleep on Christmas Eve because you were so excited! But on Christmas day you were still the first person up in the country at about 5am! And it was still dark! You were full of excitement and energy the whole day...on less sleep than you'd ever had!

I call this the 'Santa Claus effect'. You CAN capture that same excitement and energy in your life NOW! Decide what you REALLY want. Then take a step towards it. Even a small step each day. In your time off pick something REALLY exciting to do instead. When I don't have something exciting to look forward to, I don't get up early. I don't achieve more and I sleep more!

If you're not excited enough, your goal isn't big enough.

"Winning the World Cup fulfilled a promise I made to myself when I was ten. Most children write out Christmas lists for Santa – I wrote out a list of goals I wanted to achieve as a rugby player."

- Jonny Wilkinson, Winner of World Cup 2003

Realistic goals are too realistic

The world is full of people with big mouths, small minds and no imagination. The place is crawling with Ms Small Goals, Mr SMART Pants, Mr Realistic Haircut, Mrs Achievable Diet, Prof. Impossible and Mr Retirement Planning. Don't be one of them. There are too many people working towards their retirement and not enough people working towards their dream. There is enough evidence and enough stories in this book to demonstrate that impossible dreams are possible. Ordinary people can achieve extraordinary things. If you think you can, you can. If you have got a big dream and you think, "it's impossible" then go over to the mirror now and throw this book at yourself. You need to lock yourself in a room and not come out until you break down the door and tear a path towards your goal. There is

enough advice in this book for you to apply and achieve whatever you want.
By the way, if you come across Ms Small Goals, Mr SMART Pants, Mr Realistic Haircut, Mrs Achievable Diet, Prof. Impossible or Mr Retirement Planning, throw the book at them!

S.M.A.R.T. goals stands for Specific, Measurable, Achievable, Realistic and Time based. S.M.A.R.T. goals stands for small and stupid.
Most people think 'winning a gold medal' is an "unrealistic goal." Yet they give away hundreds of them every four years!

Most people think 'becoming a millionaire' is an "unrealistic goal." Yet, hundreds of people become millionaires every year! Ordinary people can achieve extraordinary things. If you think you can, you can.

"No one jumps out of bed on a Monday morning for a realistic and achievable goal." – Jack Black

Unrealistic People
Have you heard of Lance Armstrong, Henry Ford, Oprah Winfrey, Abraham Lincoln, Sir Richard Branson, John F. Kennedy, Sir Ranalph Fiennes, Winston Churchill, Christopher Columbus, Thomas Edison, Margaret Thatcher, Mohammed Ali, Paula Radcliffe, Walt Disney, J.K. Rowling, Mark Spitz, Michael Phelps, Bill Gates, Tom Hunter, Kelly Holmes or Sir Roger Bannister? Yes, I thought so. The people who achieve truly amazing things are the dreamers; the unrealistic people! The world needs them. There is a shortage of them! None of the heroes above would have become heroes and achieved great things if they were realistic people and not dreamers!

Every year another bunch of unrealistic people achieve their dreams. Some of them have a medal round their neck or a trophy in their hands. The Greek football players and Russian tennis players are a great example to everyone. Anything is possible. If you think you can.

Realistic people achieve nothing, unrealistic people achieve anything. You will never achieve your dream if you are being realistic! You will never win a gold medal being realistic! You will never survive cancer if you are being realistic! You will never live to 100 if you are being realistic!

Scary Goals
Getting a different haircut or buying a new top that isn't black scares some people. Because it's out with their normal 'comfort zone' (or 'comfy chair' as I like to call it). Scary is good. To a teacher teaching

kids is a breeze, to a shopkeeper keeping shop is a breeze. But swap them around and they are desperate to jump back onto their comfy chair! However give them a few weeks in the new job and it's something they are more comfortable with. They have got used to the new 'comfy chair' (comfort zone). If your big goal is scary it's because it's new but you'll get comfy soon enough! Winners set goals and push themselves outside their comfort zone.

Get off your comfy chair and get yourself a scary goal.
Scary is good. You'll soon get comfy.

When we are young we are prepared to take risks and do things we have never done before. When we grow older we can become less comfortable with taking risks and the possibility of failing. The voice in our head can be less positive and more negative. Alternatively we can choose to continue to take risks as we grow up and choose positive thoughts. If we never take risks and stretch our comfort zones we'll never get anywhere.

Winners in business and sport take risks.

Are you comfortable?
Are you a comfortable walker yet? It took a few 'times' doing it before you were comfortable with it. Doing anything for the first time can be an uncomfortable challenge because it is not something you have done several times yet, like walking. If we did presentations or penalties when we were born we'd have no fear of them now! When you're doing it you're improving it. But you can use your mind to do it better.

When you were born you hadn't done anything so everything was a challenge. It was exciting times!

By the time we grow up we are comfortable with anything we have done up to that point and suddenly everything we haven't done is scary not exciting! It's scary times!

If you feel scared, be excited, you are challenging yourself!
Welcome to being a winner. Welcome to being a baby.

If you're not very scared you're goals not very big.

It's good to be aware of your comfort zone and it's great to stretch it.

Scared?
Have you got a dream? Scared? You won't be. It is often like that the first time we do anything new as adults. The techniques in this book

will help you overcome fear. You will actually be excited and feel relaxed! They work for winners and they will work for you.

You don't need to be scared.
You can be excited and relaxed if you use your mind.
It's your mind that is making you scared in the first place!

Stretch Yourself
Sir John Harvey-Jones is also of the view that we are capable of more than we think. In his timeless and classic book 'Making it happen' he stated that people must be stretched within our organisation and we must stretch ourselves. He stated, "The demands made on people always need to be heavy. People at all levels of the organisation can accomplish very much more than they are asked to under contemporary conventions. Look back to what was achieved by people during the war. When occasions have occurred, as they do in all organisations, where it is necessary to take a big risk on a young man whose experience and background we think inadequate for the task, nine times out of ten not only does he rise to the occasion but he does even better than we would expect."

He wisely states, "Not only is it necessary organisationally to stretch others, but it is also necessary to stretch ourselves. How many times have you told yourself you could not do something but when you ultimately faced up and had a go, to your amazement you succeeded? I am firmly of the belief that most people in this world achieve only a fraction of what they are capable."

"I am firmly of the belief that most people in this world achieve only a fraction of what they are capable. Look back to what was achieved by people during the war." — Sir John Harvey-Jones, 'Making it happen'

Necessity is the mother of motivation.
Take a risk. Bet on yourself. You will be amazed at what you can do.
Throw yourself in the deep end.
You will be amazed how well you swim.

Throw yourself at a mountain. You will be amazed how well you climb.
Throw yourself at a marathon. You will be amazed how well you run.
Throw yourself at a challenge. You will be amazed how well you do.

ACTION! (Get pen ready)
What is your big dream? What are your goals?
This is where you write down your dream and goals. Where do you want to drive your destiny to? Grab your pen. Now! Now it's time for you to stop reading and start doing! I want you to take at least 5-10 minutes to write down as many goals as you can in the space below. Yes, you <u>must</u> write on the book! Just do it! (I know years of getting

told off at school for writing in books is holding you back, but this is way too important, so write on the book!)

The best method is to write down as many goals as you can (pick a number between 20-40) and only stop when you have no other goals 'popping' into your head. Before you start writing your goals the first thing you have to do is set a 'goal'! Pick a goal for how many goals you must write before you can stop (the goals can be big, medium, tiny or extra large!). Pick a number now.
Are you ready? On your marks, **GO!**

I said 'go'! Stop everything! Start writing your goals now.
Goal setting is important; for your future,
for your family and for your country.

Think about it
I hope you enjoyed that exercise. I always find it exciting. Now I want you to read the following questions one at a time and think about your answer to each one. You may find these are new goals to add to your goals above or they may be the same. If you are still looking for 'the BIG one' the following questions may help you find your dreams and goals. Write down key words that answer the following questions.
GO!

Describe your 'dream day'?

Describe your 'dream year'?

OK, AFTER you have sat on the beach for a year what would you do?

If you could do anything what would you do?

If you had no fear what would you do?

If you knew you would not fail what would you do?

If you won the lottery what would you do?

If you had only one year to live what would you do with this year? (Let's 'pretend')

What are you waiting for?
I love the question "If you won the lottery what would you do?" Ask anyone how's the job going? And many people will moan about their job or lie and say it's "good" or "OK" when they really mean, "The food is OK but the job is crap." However if you ask a lot of people "If you won the lottery what would you do?" the printable answer is, "Leave my job"! So what are you waiting for?

If you won the lottery what would you do? What are you waiting for?

"I live my dream life." - Annie Lennox, signer and millionaire

If you could do anything what would you do?
There was a period in my life only a few years ago where I didn't know what I wanted to do the following year. I knew I wasn't happy with what I was doing at the time. I asked myself the question 'What do you want to do?' every morning and every night for about two weeks and then came up with an answer and went and did it. What do you want to do?

If you could do anything what would you do?
Now do it.

"A man is a success if he gets up in the morning, goes to bed at night and in between does what he wants to do." -Bob Dylan

BIG Goal
Well done, you are in the top 1% of people that write down goals and think about what they really want. Now look at your list of goals and your answers to the questions above and pick your dream goal, your 'big goal' as I call it. If you could only have one goal what would it be? If it gets your heart racing and gives you 'the Santa Claus effect' you know it's something you really want. Go for it! Highlight your top goal now.
GO!

"You've got to have a dream. If you don't have a dream, how you going to make a dream come true?" - D. Rascal

Motivation
You must find a goal that motivates you. Having a big goal that not only excites you but also motivates you is essential to be a winner. Motivation is so important that I will go into it in more detail in the next chapter.

Finding it
If you are still looking for "the big goal" set yourself the goal to "Find a big goal that I really want" and write any thoughts, ideas, everyday (especially before/after sleeping). Do it everyday until you find a goal which you HUGELY desire. The following groups of questions will help as well.

A big goal gets your heart racing, keeps you up all night and gets you up early! The 'Santa Claus effect'!

Have you found it yet?
Are you thinking, "How will I know if I have found "the BIG one"?" The answer is; "You just 'know'." Here's a tick list;
Is it something you REALLY want?
Is it something you are REALLY passionate about?
Will you do ANYTHING to get it?

If you get three ticks then you know you've struck gold. Really.

Dreamer and doer
If you were to ask any sports person, actor, entrepreneur or any other 'dreamer and doer' the question "If you won the lottery what would you do?" ALL of them would keep doing what they are doing because they ARE doing what they love. The money may give them a few options in their life but not necessarily change it.

*Dreamers do their dream job; no money can stop them doing it.
What do Bill Gates and Tiger Woods have in common?
They are both still working, but could have retired years ago.*

"Find something you love to do and then find someone willing to pay you to do it."- Greg Barnes, Author, 'The Genie Within'

"Choose a job you love and you will never have to work a day in your life." - Chinese philosopher Confucius (551 - 479 BC)

"I want to work, I like working, I don't like supermarkets on Saturday afternoons. I like watching other teams play. I just love football.

But I'm having a break for the first time in 54 years.
I'm not rushing into anything, I'm very fit. I'll do it for the right job."
-71-year old Legend Sir Bobby Robson

Live your lottery dream without the lottery win
One of my friends Elaine lives in France and she told me that she first asked herself the question "If I won the lottery what would I do?" several years ago. She came up with an answer and then worked out what she could do without the money and went and did it! Elaine moved to France. She lives her dream life without waiting for the win. Elaine's philosophy is the same as mine; Decide what you would do if you won the lottery and then work out how to do just that. Decide what you can do without the money, but with some hard work or hard decisions. Don't wait. Just do it.

If you won the lottery what would you do? Start working on it!

ACTION!
Top 7
Look at your now comprehensive list of goals and dreams you have written down in the last few exercises and pick your top 7 goals including "the big goal." Pick the 6 other goals. Now you will write down your 7 top goals in order of importance. Consider the dates you wish to achieve them by. Go with your gut feel but it's important that you put a date against them now. If you are too realistic your big goal might not be quite so big and you lose some of your 'Santa Claus effect' so be careful! Really think about the importance of each but don't spend more than 60 seconds on any goal. You can change the order and make adjustments to priorities and dates later if required (in fact you probably will, I know I do). Ready? **GO!**

DREAM (DESTINATION)	ARRIVAL DATE

Destination
Now you have your dreams and your dates you know where you are going!

If you don't have dreams,
you don't know where you are going to end up!

Twice a day
As you now know you will need to put this book and the page with your TOP 7 where you will see your TOP 7 twice a day (bedside table? bathroom? kitchen?). The first bit of "winners homework" will be to get 7 pictures. The more often you look at pictures of your goals in your mind or on your wall the more effective the mind works. It works for winners!

Write down your top 7 goals and get 7 pictures.
Look at your goals every morning and every night
it's the most effective method for your mind.

One thing at a time
You can't do everything at once, but you can do something at once. I suggest you focus your biggest effort on your dream goal. Most winners have a dream and work on it. They have a priority. Focus on one thing at a time, your dream. The focus and direction of your front wheel will relate to the results you later experience in your back wheel. Where you steer is up to you.

"I was very hungry to make it. That was the only thing on my mind."
-Jelena Dokic, winner of five Women's Tennis Association titles

"For the first 20 years of running the business I never remember a day when I didn't wake up and think about making money that day. And I mean never."
–Tom Hartley, Millionaire founder of 'Tom Hartley', Luxury Cars

"To be successful you need to have a goal and work hard enough and long enough at it." –Tom Hartley Jnr, partner in 'Tom Hartley', left school at 11, became a millionaire at 14,
'the youngest self made millionaire in Britain'

Focus on ONE thing at a time.
You can be a jack of all trades <u>or</u> a master of one.

"My stated ambition remains to be the best No 10 ever.
This is just a goal in my head" -Jonny Wilkinson

'Put all your eggs in one basket and watch that basket'
– Andrew Carnegie

ACTION!
Happy Goals
What makes you happy right now? Write a list of the things that you spend time on during a normal week that you enjoy. Write them down the left hand side below.
GO!

Now re-write them in order of importance on the right of your list.
GO!

All of the activities on this list take up time. Now put down the minimum amount of time per week you think you would need to spend to keep you happy and have time to spend working on your dream goals. You may for example decide "Well for the sake of my dream goal I think I could get by with only one night out a week." But remember without health and happiness you will achieve nothing. Write down the minimum times beside each of them now.
GO!

Ok, now put down the maximum amount of time per week you would love to spend doing these things.
GO!

It's useful for four reasons. One; my definition of 'goals' includes things you haven't got AND things you <u>have</u> got (even if you did acquire your family and cat quite easily it's still a 'happy goal' achieved in my book!) Two: you can set yourself a short-term goal and reward yourself with some Happy Time. Three; it gives you a 'happy goal' target of the minimum amount of time you want to spend on things that make you happy. Four; you don't want to spend all your time in 'goal time', because you'll be less effective and less mentally strong but I'll cover than in the 'energy' chapter. Also spending every hour of every day of every week in goal time is not good for keeping your health and not good for keeping your family. You could reach your goal without your health and without your family, which could make reaching the goal meaning less.

When you strive for the jewels you want,
don't drop the jewels you've got.
Make sure you're on the path towards more happiness not sadness.
Make time for happy time and be happy when you make it.

Working on your goal 24/7 eventually effects your
effectiveness, health, mental strength and your family.

Time

Now consider this question. "Where else are you spending your time?" Are you wasting your time? Write a list of everything you spend time on below including sleep! Calculate your average day and then calculate your average Saturday/Sunday.

GO!

Weekday	**Weekend day**
0000	
0100	
0200	
0300	
0400	
0500	
0600	
0700	
0800	
0900	
1000	
1100	
1200	
1300	
1400	
1500	
1600	
1700	
1800	
1900	
2000	
2100	
2200	
2300	
2400	

Time wasters and Time stealers

Look at the list above and highlight where you could reduce or cut time. Calculate the total amount of time you could spend/invest in working on your dream goal.

GO!

Goal Time

Looking at your happy goal list and your 'time waster' list and calculate the total amount of time you will 'invest' in your big goal. Now consider this question. "What is the most important use of my time?" Do you want to invest it in your 'goal time' or do you want to risk not achieving your goal any time? Time is money. Henceforth evaluate how you spend your time. Ask yourself "Is this a good investment of my time and money or is it a waste of time and money?" Winners invest the majority of their time in their dream, because they don't want to risk not achieving it.

Winners invest almost all their time in their dream
because they don't want to risk not achieving it.

Sacrifice List

To achieve your goal you will have to make sacrifices. But to achieve your happiness you will have to carefully choose your sacrifices.

"Decide what you want, decide what you are willing to exchange for it.
Establish your priorities and go to work."
HL Hunt, American Oil Magnate

"Sometimes, on my day off, I'll be out there practising and I'll be
annoyed with myself because I'd like to be relaxing.
But I know that in terms of priority, that rates way down the list.
I will sacrifice everything for rugby for the next ten years."
– Jonny Wilkinson, World Cup Winner 2003

Happy Goals

Your dream goals are actually 'happy' goals. We pick goals that would make us happy to achieve. The same goes for all your top 7 goals and every goal you've got. But what makes you "really happy" right now? You have to decide which goals would make you happiest whether they are future 'dream goals' or current 'happy goals', which are in your life right now and prioritise time.

Time

To achieve your 'dream goals' you'll need to maximise the use of your 'goal time' while allowing for 'happy time'. Some people make the mistakes of keeping their eye on their goal (what they want) and taking their eye off the ball (what they've got).

A winner will do anything to win and make a lot of sacrifices.

Feeling goals

Do you know what makes you happy? It's not what you've got or what you do that makes you happy but how you feel about what you've got or what you do. Although this book is about striving for more (it's good to stretch yourself- I enjoy it so much I'm over 6ft now!) I want to throw a challenge at you. Consider being happy with less than you have got now. Compare yourself to someone much worse off. The comparison can be beneficial to see your current situation in an even more positive light than I'm sure you already do.

We want much more to make us 'feel' happy but we are surrounded by people who have much less and are much happier.

Some people are happy in a Fiesta,
some people are happy in a Ferrari.
Some people are happy in the sun, some people are happy in the rain.
It's how you think on the inside that makes you happy,
not what's on the outside. Happiness is a choice.

Now

Circle your answer below which most applies to how you feel about your life right now. You can be happy in one area of your life but unhappy in another. Give your overall answer. Be honest. (Don't cheat yourself!)

GO!

How would you describe yourself?

Very Unhappy   Unhappy   OK   Happy   Very Happy

What you need to feel happy

Abraham H. Maslow was a genius who investigated what motivates us to do what we do and live how we live. In other words what it is that makes us happy. In the book he wrote (fifty years ago!) called 'Motivation and Personality' he came up with a 'Hierarchy of Needs' a bit like a ladder motivation; with our survival as the first priority and a challenging purpose as our last priority. Look at the bottom of the ladder, relate it to growing up and then read your way up the ladder.

5th Need- Self fulfilment; Realising potential using creative talents.
4th Need- Self Esteem; Achievement, recognition & success.
3rd Need- Belonging; Love, belonging, affiliation & acceptance.
2nd Need- Safety; Protection against danger, freedom from fear & security.
1st Need- Physiological; Survival needs; Water, food, clothing, shelter & sex.

It's brilliant information and in many cases it's true. Have you met people that 'have it all' but are still not "very happy"? Ever wondered what they need? (Not a good shake!) They need a purpose to use and stretch their talents! We are happy when we have shelter, sex, safe environment, loving friends and family. But we are even happier when we are putting our talent to good use as well. Although the ladder is useful knowledge it is not always true. Everyone is different (I've met a few, have you?!). So we are not all motivated in exactly the same way. For example Mr Joe Bloggs might not care about using his full talent or having a family just show him the money! Or someone else might even be motivated in a way in which the order of the ladder is upside down. Red Cross staff work in dangerous areas (in fear for their safety) and have barely enough food and water supplies to survive but they are motivated to take these risks. Why? Perhaps because they are motivated to help people. They may feel rewarded by being useful, helping others, stretching their talents and making a difference. They have built a hospital rather than a business.

Our first priority as humans is surviving then thriving.

Humans are motivated to be happy. What makes a person happy varies from person to person but most of us need to have Maslows' 5 needs to be happy.

We are motivated to achieve 'goals' that make us happy.
Most goals humans have fall into one of the five areas of our needs.
We get our happiness from climbing up the ladder.

Your goals depend on what you need and how it will make you feel.
All our current and future goals are actually 'feeling happy' goals.
If you're not happy, have a look at the ladder.

The first goal many people write is 'millionaire' or 'win lottery'.
Chasing money is the biggest mistake people make.
It's the doing not the having that provides people most happiness.
If you just chase money you will be unhappy.
Few people can remain motivated on money alone.

The 'way' of making money must provide a level of enjoyment.

Find ways to be happy and look for ways to make money.
Many unhappy people have found a way to make money
and are struggling to find ways to be happy.

Chase happiness and look for richness.
Don't chase richness and expect to find happiness.

Rich or happy? Which would you choose?
Pick your first priority.
Chasing money is a fast way to becoming unhappy.
Do what makes you happy and then find a way to make you rich!

Being happy is a great goal.
Being happy and rich is wealthy goal.

Happy

Let's make an assessment against Maslow's 5 motivating areas for your life now. I've also added 2 measures, which will be useful to calculate. Rate yourself in the following areas out of 10; GO!

NEEDS **0-10**

1.Body; good- health, food, fitness, shelter & sex
2.Mind; safe and in control and relaxed with life; no fear
3.People; belonging, relationship, family, friends, colleagues
4.Self; Self-esteem, self love and admire yourself
5.Job; fulfilling purpose or goal using talent, stimulating
Total out of 50

Winning mentality (Positive, energy, goal driven, intuitive)
Action taker (ruthless, no fear, no analysis paralysis)
Total out of 20

Need Goals

Write down next to the numbers above your goal for the score for each in 1 year's time. Write the date at the top.
GO!

You need a goal to survive

I never expected my interest and research into health and people that live for over 100 years of age to have any connection to goals but it does! I discovered something very interesting. To live a long life you need a goal! Hard to believe perhaps but it's true. Most humans need a goal to survive (there are few exceptions)!

2000

Once, as luck would have it, I came across an article in The West Australian, which interviewed a Funeral Director about his job (bear with me! it's a good story honest!). He talked about his job and said, "I think you choose when you die." He then revealed two stories, which led him to his belief. On average you would think a funeral director would have a steady flow of business throughout the year, perhaps with a slight increase in cold or hot periods (it's not like a flower shop, busy every February). Business actually is not steady over a year for a funeral director, it has an annual peak. They have their 'peak' period after Christmas and New Year. His explanation; older Grand parents have got nothing to look forward to for a whole year apart from the festive period the following year, when they see their kids and grandkids. And there is more. In his twenty plus years in the business the busiest time in their company's history was in January 2000. His explanation; because many older people were 'waiting' until the year 2000 arrived ("the millennium") and then didn't have anything to look forward to.

We need to have a goal for living not just succeeding!
If you don't have a goal you won't make it.

His second story was about a 100 year old centenarian he read about interviewed in the press. He said the reporter was asking the man how he was able to live so long, to which the old man had no answer! However, the reporter didn't spot what was obvious for the Funeral Director to see from the transcript of the interview. The centenarian tended to his plants in his greenhouse everyday (he had a purpose). You can extend your life if you want. Get a goal. Or get a greenhouse.

Have a goal. You need a purpose;
whether it's growing a business or growing a plant.

Crying goals

He also said that there have been occasions when, standing at the back of the church during the service, he has been moved so much about what he has heard and what the person has done that he even shed a tear (even though he didn't know them!). This is a man who has worked in the business for over 20 years, attends funerals every day and has developed a way to cope with them and yet he still gets moved by a stranger's funeral. It must have been some woman! (Or some man!) He even said that some services "inspire" him on how he lives his own life. (Get down to a service today!) What do you want people to say when you die? Who will cry when you die?

When you're born everyone is smiling,
when you die make sure everyone's crying!
(The more the merrier)

"The best way to retire is in a wooden box." - Toni Mascolo, 61, co-founder of 'Toni and Guy', opened first hair salon with brother Guy in 1963, now have 200 Salons in UK and 154 abroad

Get a goal quick

Metropolitan Police discovered a very important trend but a bit of a sad one. They found out that the dedicated and committed Policemen and Policewoman who retire after spending a long career in the force will actually not live more than two years into their retirement unless they find a purpose, goal or activity to occupy their time. Part of the retirement planning of many public and private companies has evolved after this finding to ensure, upon retiring, people "keep busy."

Don't spend more than a year (or a week!) without a goal
Retirement can be fun filled or short lived. You still need to keep busy!

A goal can change your life

One idea, one goal can change your life. Stop dreaming and you stop achieving.

A goal can save your life. A goal can change your life.

It cost me

Colin Montgomerie's goal was to be Number 1 European Tour Golfer. To cut a long story of <u>hard work</u> and <u>determination</u> short, Colin achieved his goal. His goal the following season was to repeat the same performance and be number 1 again. To cut a long, long story of hard work and determination short Colin achieved his goal! This incredible success continued for six years! Colin admitted he was obsessed with being number 1 and thought about it everyday when he got up in the morning (and probably most nights when he went to bed). This is the kind of focus required over a long period to 'win' and achieve goals. It worked. He was the top European Tour golfer 6 years running and wanted it a seventh time. He achieved it. In his eighth year of defending the record he separated from his wife and kids. In hindsight Colin realised the time working on his 'dream goal' cost him his 'happy goal'. With this sad new wisdom his advice to others who wanted his record was "They can have it! But I'd advise them against it. It cost me my marriage. How successful do I have to be?"

Be careful not to throw away what you love, for what you like.

When the benefits outweigh the sacrifices, it's happy days.
When the sacrifices outweigh the benefits, it's sad days.

I sacrificed everything and lived like a monk

When I carried out the above exercise myself recently it reminded me of the chosen sacrifices I had made for my dream goal (best-selling book). Here's an idea of the 'important' things in my life that I have sacrificed;

Health> This is the one thing I chose not to sacrifice (for the benefit of the book), however, I did sacrifice 'competitive fitness' which requires harder and longer training and longer resting and sleeping time, which would cost me working 'dream goal' time

Family> I sacrificed a lot of family time but picked times I would spend with them (this was a 'happy time' reward)

Finance> I sacrificed all the money I had and more for the book, I only made enough money coaching/speaking to pay company costs for 2 years. I chose not to get a high paid busy job or even work elsewhere part time, which wouldn't have been goal or business effective. I stopped spending. No fancy clothes for Phil. In fact no cheap clothes for Phil either!

Work> I kept the business and costs 'lean and mean' including having no assistant or outside help to save money but it cost me more of my time. I had to spend a lot of time on the business in the first 18 months just attracting a little coaching and speaking work which I needed for money, experience and building a reputation. In the last 6 months I worked very few hours on the business and very many hours on the book.

Home/Car> I couldn't afford to own a car or house and chose not to rent either to save 'business/book' money, so even though I was 'too old' to go back home and live at home (I could handle the shame and sacrifice my ego!)

Friends> I have quite a few friends with whom I haven't spent time with in months (for some, possibly over a year and I miss them all). But I have a small network of close friends who live nearby (whom I did spend a little time with)

Social life> What's that?! What social life?! I rarely went out. I stopped drinking completely for many reasons but here are three; to have a more positive mind (alcohol is a depressant), to have more energy (drinking increases sleeping time and costs 'dream book and business time'!) and thirdly I have never felt good the morning after having several drinks! Have you ever felt really good after drinking a lot of alcohol? You mind and body are telling you something. But are we listening?!

Holiday> What holidays? I selected little time off in two years (which in hindsight was a mistake). I went on a snowboarding holiday with parents and sister. I attended a close friends wedding in Italy (I didn't have the time or money but did it). I also went to London to catch up with Australian friends who were in town for a few days on a 'once in a lifetime European tour' and I only spent a few HOURS with them. I didn't have a very positive bank account to spend much time with them. It's not a very happy memory for me but my time schedule and low earning work were my choices! My business and work were risks and gambles, which I believed, would pay off long term.

Partner> You probably appreciate by now that for a long time I was literally 'living like a monk'! I have been on the look out for a partner and met some nice people, and invested some time. However the fact I had almost no disposable income meant it was going to be a challenge, I didn't go out much and I couldn't take anyone out much (even if they did pay half! – I had no half!). A great partner has always been one of my top 7 goals. In the last six months I have been a monk and vaguely remember what a woman looks like! I remember saying to myself a few times in the last year "no dates, no mates" and focused purely on the book and the business for periods. I was having so little fun, who would want to go out with a prisoner?! For two years I was hoping to bump into a busy babe who didn't have much time for me! Snap!

Sometimes winners have to live like monks,
few can, so few are winners!

Pursuing your dream is a risk and gamble, which you believe, will pay off long term; sometimes you just hope it will! But in the short term there are hurdles and painful choices and sacrifices.

Taking it too far

As you can see Colin Montgomerie may have taken it too far, in the pursuit of what he thought was his most important goal. And as shown above I took it very far in the pursuit of my dream goal. But I made a similar mistake to Colin. I took it too far and it cost me. I'll explain later in the book. However not all winners make that mistake.

We must have dreams and chase them. Not just for our greatness but our happiness and the smile on our face! Family and friends will love that smile and might even catch a dream themselves. Wow!

Things that matter least should not be at the expense
of things that matter most.

High bar, low bar

Having a big dream goal to chase is important for the many reasons and benefits already covered. Even if we miss out on the goal we don't miss out on the benefit of the experience. However, there is a way to further maximise our experience and enjoyment of the 'journey' when going for goals; set 'easy' little goals as well. For example; take one step towards goal a day, save £20 towards a dream a week, etc

By setting easy goals we can feel a huge level of achievement and contentment even if we miss out on the big goal. It's useful and beneficial for our happiness to set ourselves some 'easy' goals that will make us happy. For example some goals that might make you happy and be easy to achieve could be; laugh lots, help strangers, smile all day, tell jokes, have fun, sing out loud, write notes, invent dances, etc

Make it easy for yourself to be happy. Set some easy happy goals.

Marathon Runners -Some happy, Some sad!

I know of several marathon runners who have travelled to beautiful parts of the world to run marathons but have ended up "disappointed" on the day. Why? Because they finished a few minutes after their goal time! Don't give yourself that pain! Just completing a marathon is a brilliant feat in itself.

An easier way to be happy would be to have a big goal and some little goals. Or to put it another way, set a high bar and some low bars. The high bar can be winning or finishing with your best ever time. Low bars could be; enjoying, smiling, laughing, finishing, complete under 5 hours, running most of the way, meeting and helping others along the way. Setting high bars and low bars is your route to more joy and happiness. The mind loves to have goals. Beware the goals you choose.

Enjoy your journey whatever the weather.
If you learn to love the wet,
the windy, the hot and the cold you'll be happy all year round.
If you're only happy when it's hot,
you'll be unhappy the rest of the year.

Be one of those people who can sleep in an
airport overnight and still smile.
Don't let your ego get in the way of your happiness.

In Control

Some goals are within your control. Some goals are not. Getting married is a good goal partly within your control. Looking for partners is within your control but getting a woman to say "yes" is not!
Achieving your dream is within your control. When you achieve it is not completely within your control. Kelly Holmes took longer to achieve her dream than she might have thought 4 or 8 years ago. She didn't achieve her dream in Sydney she achieved it in Athens.
Chase a big dream and set big goals but have some goals and 'low bars' within your control. You can play great golf and still get beat by one shot by someone slightly greater on the day. One day it will not be that way. You will achieve your dream some day.

Some goals are within our control.
Some goals are not within our control. Know the difference.
Some things are out with our control. Like the weather. And whether your best is enough to be a winner. You are in control of your thoughts and actions. You cannot control whether someone else has better had some better thoughts and actions and beats you.
You lose some, then you win some.

Short and long

Having short and long-term goals is useful. In golf the long-term goal is to win and the short-term goal on the first tee is to hit a great drive. Paul Lawrie used goal setting to become 1999 Open Champion and even though he missed his target score by one shot he got into the play off and won.

Writing short and long-term goals helps entrepreneurs win. Visualising short and long-term targets helps golfers win. Do both.

Big goal, big steps

Whatever your big goal, it is worth breaking the goal down into steps and put dates against them. Have goals for 1 year and for 1 week. Always work towards a goal and visualise it. This progress will help you successfully step towards your big goal as well as encourage you to use visualisation on your journey. Big goals sometimes require big steps. A big goal will have a few scary moments, but it's not possible to get to your goal with your foot on the brake.

You cannot cross a chasm in two jumps.

Big steps for your Big goal

Look at your big goal and write down the steps and goals you need to achieve to get to your big goal.
GO!

GOALS	**DATE**

Happy future

I think one of the best goals to have is to be happy. Visualise yourself at a future date very happy. Trust that you will have achieved goals to get there. The more detailed the picture the better.

Set yourself the goal of being very happy in future.
Even better picture it.

Women dream, believe, intuitively act and achieve

Most women have a dream and achieve it; to get married, have kids and "be a good Mum." They picture it, believe it, intuitively select the man that can help them, take action and they achieve it. Not all of them pursue further dreams, even though they are likely to be easier and less painful than achieving their first dream! Many women choose to work in the caring professions of teaching and nursing and are living their dream. I wish we all did.

Women dream, believe, intuitively act and achieve.
'Dream. Believe. Plan. Act. Achieve.' – Walt Disney

Hands up

How many men and women would leave their job if they won the lottery?
(Hands up; you're in the wrong job.)
How many men and women have stopped dreaming?
(Hands up; you are not using your potential.)
How many men and women are working on their dream?
(Hands up; you need to read this book and then apply it.)

Very fast Summary

Everyone has a goal. A mother, a father, a cleaner and a CEO.
But most people have a little goal. Few people have dreams.
What do you really want?
That's your big dream.
Work on the first step (short term goal) towards your big dream.
Focus on one thing at a time, your dream goal.
Dreams need deadlines. Every goal needs a date.
Winners are driving towards their dream destination.
Losers don't have a dream destination.
You need a goal for winning and for living.
Write your shopping list.
Look at your top 7 goals twice a day.
Your mind will start attracting and looking for goals (playing snap).
Get pictures of your goals (bedroom ideally).
What seven things make you really happy? Which ones will you sacrifice?
Set some little happy goals with every big impossible goal.

Where do you want to go?
If you've got no goals you'll get no goals.

If you won the lottery what would you do?
If you had no fear what would you do?
What are you waiting for?

Shoot for your goal. If you don't shoot, you don't score.
100% guaranteed.

Your mind will achieve some goals for you all by itself.
For some goals your mind may need some help.

Put pictures of your dream goals where your mind will see them and it will help you achieve them. Subliminal 'Dream advertising'!

Ideas and action make dreams come true.

Winners have Guts and Goals.

If you're not excited enough, your goal is not big enough.

Working on your goal 24/7 eventually effects your effectiveness, mental and physical health and family. Take a break.

"Decide what you want, decide what you are willing to exchange for it.
Establish your priorities and go to work."
HL Hunt, American Oil Magnate

Necessity is the mother of motivation.

Take a risk. Bet on yourself. You will be amazed at what you can do.

CHAPTER 1.5
MOTIVATION

Very Fast Summary

The 'Santa Claus effect' is not just about excitement it is about motivation. If you are not motivated to win, you won't win. Winners are motivated every day of every year. If you're not motivated away from the arena, you won't win in the arena.

Included in this chapter;

Winners are highly motivated.

Four Ingredients + Hunger
What happens when you are up against a winner with Winning Mentality, Action, Skill and Strategy? The difference will be the individual, team or company that wants to win the most. Motivation becomes the most important thing. It's not just about having the goal it's having the hunger to go for goal. The hunger is what gets you to pick up the spoon! I call this hunger motivation. It's what drives your car. Motivation is like the accelerator in the car, if your foot isn't down, you are going nowhere regardless of your skills and strategy. Everyone has the motor but few are using their motivation motor.

It's motivation that gets a winner to use their skills, strategy and winning mentality tools and take the action required to reach their big dream goal. Most people are sitting in a Ferrari with amazing potential but are attempting goals as if they are in a Fiesta. Winners attempt goals as if they are in a Ferrari. Winners believe they can achieve Ferrari potential.

The person who wants to win the most will win the most.

Everyone has the ability to achieve their dream,
but few are motivated to go for it.

Winners are driven by their motivation.

Winners have a goal that motivates them.
Are you hungry for your goal?

Small Difference
The difference between a gold medallist and a silver medallist is less than one second! The difference between a winning team and a losing team is one goal! The difference between a winning company and a losing company is one goal.

There is a very small difference between a winner and a loser.
The difference between a winner and a loser is often motivation.

The battle is won away from the arena.
The battle is won away from the arena. It's easy to work 9 to 5. But how many are prepared to work 5 to 9? Winners are not normal. If they were everyone would be a winner. Winning would be normal. Winners do what everyone else doesn't do. They do the opposite. A winner is motivated to train harder; therefore they can play harder and win. All competitors are motivated to win on the day, but how many are motivated to train every day?

Successful people are prepared to do the things that no one else is prepared to do. Are you prepared?

A winner is motivated to train harder;

therefore they can play harder and win.

All competitors are motivated to win on the day, but how many are motivated to train every day?

Successful people are prepared to do the things that no one else is prepared to do. Are you prepared?

Spot the difference
What is the difference between the thousands of people every year who run a marathon and those that watch? Motivation

What is the difference between the thousands of people every year that set up their own company and those that watch? Motivation

What is the difference between the thousands of sports people who get paid to play sport and those that watch? Motivation

Talent and brains are not essential
Talent and brains are useful but it's motivation that takes you to the top. Without motivation, talent in sport and brains in business are wasted. Winners work with the talent, brains and money they have got and keep working towards their goal until they achieve it.

It's not brains or talent that take you to the top. It's motivation.

Motivation Advantage
The less talent, brains and money that winners have the more motivated they are. Being an underdog brings out the fighting spirit in a winner. Being an underdog increases their motivation. Winners are rarely the most talented which makes success harder to achieve which makes motivation a necessity.

Necessity is the mother of motivation.

"People who are unable to motivate themselves must be content with mediocrity, no matter how impressive their other talents."
-- Andrew Carnegie

Motivation is a choice
You choose everything in life. You choose your motivation. Regardless of whether you're driving towards something you want or not it's you that has your foot on the pedal. Regardless of whether you are doing a job you love or not you can choose how motivated you are. Put any sporting winner in any sport and they will want to win, even if it is a game of table football! Put any entrepreneur in any business and they will want to 'win'.

Motivation wins
If you're not motivated you will not win. You need to help yourself. I'm showing you how to think to win but I will not drive your car for you. You play your sport, you run your business and I will tell you how to run your mind. Find your dream goal and find your motivation.

You need to motivate yourself. You need to drive your car.
To succeed you need a dream and you need motivation.

I work with highly motivated sports people and business people. They want to win. I just show up and help them. I don't make them use the tools, they decide that themselves. I can't make you use the tools. It's your choice.

Winners will do anything to win.
You know you are motivated when you will do anything to win.

Would you pass the cold shower test?
What does World Record Holder Paula Radcliffe and Rugby World Champion's England have in common? Answer- Cold baths. They both take cold baths after competing. Do you think they really enjoy it? No! Me neither but they do it because they are motivated to win and they believe cold baths will help them recover. I think they are right. I heard that it boosts circulation and aids recovery so I gave it a go myself and afterwards I felt physically and mentally fresh. I have a cold shower after every training session because it feels great mentally and physically. Do I enjoy it? I love it! But it took me a few months to enjoy it. I realised that given the choice I would pick a cold shower after training every time because I feel so good after it! It won't kill me. People who are motivated will do what ever it takes to succeed. It's not about feeling great it's about doing great.

Would you pass the cold shower test? Will you do whatever it takes?

Warm beer anyone?
My brother Paul spends several hours every day writing and recording music to achieve his dream of music success and his band Riders of Rebus has already been compared to successful band Underworld (www.ridersofrebus.co.uk). When I last spent some time with him I found out something interesting (but not surprising). When Paul has a drink at a friend's house he drinks warm room temperature beer! Why? Because drinking cold or hot drinks damages the vocal cords (I didn't know that!). He will do whatever it takes to succeed, even if it means working part time, writing full time and drinking warm beer. Paul also avoids milk and chocolate because both are

disadvantageous when it comes to singing and getting the best from your voice.

Would you pass the warm beer test?
Will you do whatever it takes?
It's your choice.

Winners will do anything to win. Winners do whatever it takes.

There are things we know, things we know we don't know
and things we don't know that we don't know.

Have a good weekend Bill

How do you set up and run a successful company for thirty years? How do you become THE richest man in the world? Put in a lot of hours.

"I take it easier on Saturday and Sunday, I only work about 9 hours."
-Bill Gates, Chairman and co-founder, Microsoft

The average worker works 36 hours a week.
The average entrepreneur works 36 hours in 3 days!

Happy Christmas Jonny

How do you become the Worlds most successful rugby kicker? Put in the hours. England kicking phenomenon Jonny Wilkinson practices for hours long after God has switched off the lights. Jonny doesn't leave the practice ground until he has put 6 kicks in a row over the bar from anywhere in the field. Sometimes it takes him hours and he misses social engagements. He even trains on Christmas Day!

Winners are working when it's dark outside.

Happy Christmas Michael

How do you become one of the most successful swimmers ever at an Olympic games? Put in the hours. Olympic gold medal American swimmer Michael Phelps trains every day of the year. "Christmas morning, I'm in the pool", says Michael who won six gold medals and two bronze in Athens Olympics 2004!

How do you become THE most successful swimmer ever at an Olympic games? Put in the hours. "We all love to win, but how many people love to train?" says, Mark Spitz, winner of 7 gold medals at 1972 Munich Olympics. Mark retired from swimming shortly after and is now a top stock broker (with winning mentality!). Why did he stop? His hunger had been fed; he wasn't hungry for swimming anymore. He has now returned to swimming in the master's swimming section.

"We all love to win, but how many people love to train?"
- Mark Spitz, winner of 7 gold Olympic medals, 1976 Olympics

"Christmas morning, I'm in the pool."
- Michael Phelps, winner of 6 gold
- Olympic medals and trains every day.

When choosing a dream follow your heart.

Dreams require some doing.
When you achieve a dream, start dreaming again.
Dreams are motivating.

Underneath we are the same
Underneath, we are all the same. I know plenty of people who could make it in business, sport or other endeavour in which they are talented but they don't. No motivation. A winner is not always the most talented, but they are always the most motivated.

Winners vs. Winners
The Portugal 2004 European Championship opening match was played between Greece and Portugal, with the latter team expected to win. Of course in a match with two teams either could win and so it proved in this match with underdogs Greece the victors.

Evaluation of Motivation + PASS
<u>Greece</u>
Positive Winning Mentality; Yes (The confident Captain talked positive on TV)
Action: Yes (They turned up and went on the pitch!)
Skills: Yes, they had some good players but no top players
Strategy: Yes, their new German Manager had a winning strategy
Motivation: Yes, very motivated. Greeks are highly motivated by personal pride and pride in playing for their country.
<u>Portugal</u>
Positive Winning Mentality: Yes
Action: Yes (They turned up and went on the pitch!)
Skills: Yes, some of the most highly skilled and highly paid players in World
Strategy: Yes, they are one of the best teams in the World
Motivation: Yes, the team is full of players who want to win and hate to lose!
Result;
Greece won the match to the surprise of everyone watching, even most Greeks watching! What was the difference between the two teams in the match? Motivation and Strategy.
The final;
In my humble opinion the Portugal 2004 European Championship final, which was surprisingly between Portugal and Greece, had only one

likely winner, Greece. Their belief and winning mentality was stronger, their strategy was superior and their previous success against Portugal increased their physiological belief.

With motivation a good team can beat a great team.

A highly motivated person can beat a highly skilled person.

"The difference between a successful person and others is not a lack of strength, not a lack of knowledge, but rather in a lack of will." -Vince Lombardi, Green Bay Packers Coach, winner of five NFL championships and Super Bowls I and II.

"Spending time and energy trying to "motivate" people is a waste of effort. The real question is not, "How do we motivate our people?" If you have the right people, they will be self-motivated. The key is not de-motivate them. One of the primary ways to de-motivate people is to ignore the brutal facts of reality." -Jim Collins, 'Good to Great'

Are British hungry?

Tennis player Jelena Dokic originally from Yugoslavia and has won five WTA singles titles, mentioned her theory in 2003 as to why female British tennis players don't have much success. "I think the European girls are much more hungry." the 11th-seeded Jelena said. "I was very hungry to make it. That was the only thing on my mind. That's what I was pushing for. Maybe they're just not hungry enough. Maybe they're not pushed enough. I think the players that have less opportunities are usually the ones that get through because they are so hungry." In 2003 all five British women lost in the first round. It's the first time that Britain didn't have a single female representative in the second round since the Open era began in 1968. The last British born women's winner was Virginia Wade in 1977. It's a similar story for the men and Jelena's answer could also apply to men. Jelena was born in Belgrade but began her tennis career after her family moved to Australia in 1994. Only 21 years old she has now been playing tennis for 10 years and has since left Australia and changed her nationality back to Yugoslavia after negative media coverage. (Another winner and hero attacked by the press. The UK media are no different unfortunately. Build them up and knock them down.)

"I was very hungry to make it. That was the only thing on my mind." -Jelena Dokic, Winning Women, Tennis player

If you are not hungry you won't win.

Russians are hungry

Currently in 2004 seven of the top 15 female tennis players are from Russia! This year's winner at Wimbledon of the women's final was 17-year-old Russian Maria Sharapova. She had to overcome 1999 Champion Lindsay Davenport and 2002 and 2003 Champion Serena Williams. In my opinion Russians and East Europeans are very hungry and motivated and the results speak for themselves.

The next Champion will beat the current Champion.
Maria beat Serena.
David beat Goliath.

"David was the best thing that ever happened to Goliath." - Doug Weed

Winners are very hungry

Lots of people want to win. In sport almost everyone who takes part wants to win. But the individual, team or business that wants to win the most will win, because they have more desire, determination and drive (motivation) to put in more effort. Greece and Portugal both wanted to be the Euro 2004 Champions. But the Greek players were more hungry and motivated to win, so they worked harder.

Winners are driven by passion, desire, fear or determination.

Sylvester Stallone didn't get a day job because "being an unemployed actor kept me hungry." Stallone was knocked back from EVERY addition he went to, but he kept dreaming. He then came up with the idea for the film Rocky when watching a boxing match with the real Rocky. He then refused to sell the movie rights unless he played the role Rocky. He then wrote <u>and</u> directed the follow up films!

Winners are very excited!

People with passion overcome ANY obstacle. Women with babies overcome 1 hours sleep and still handle going to work! I've worked with them. They love their babies and they choose to work. They are motivated by love. You can handle anything with love!

Nothing is impossible. Anything is possible.

There are no limits.

<u>You</u> can handle <u>anything</u> with motivation.

"The only way of finding the limits of the possible,
is going beyond them into the impossible."
- Arthur C. Clarke

"We would accomplish many more things,
if we did not think of them as impossible."
- C. Malesherbes

"As projects get bigger, it just get more exciting." – Carol Ainscow, 46,
Self Made Property Millionaire,
converted first property while teaching at 19

Bob beat fear, beat Thatcher and raised Millions
Bob Geldof came up with the idea of the Band Aid record to raise money for Ethiopia after watching a very moving (and motivating) news report on the BBC about the famine. Although Bob was a singer at the time he was not a confident out going person. Yet he asked huge music stars, record companies, designers, producers, video makers and major media owners like the BBC and The Sun for free help. He had a verbal battle on TV with Margaret Thatcher because the government was taxing the charity record like normal and she wouldn't back down. She is quoted as saying "I am extraordinarily patient, provided I get my own way in the end"! A few weeks later she changed her mind (for about the first time in history!) and the tax was quietly donated back!

Idea + action = success.

Bob Geldof raised millions because he
was fearless and because he was motivated.

"I only think of what must be done, not what might happen."
- The Village

Find a BIG goal and drive towards it
We are all different and we are all motivated by different things. It doesn't matter what motivates you as long as you know what it is. You must be motivated to achieve your goal.

You must be highly driven (motivated) to win or you won't win.

D Stands for Drive
Plenty of people have the desire to be millionaires but not many have the motivation and determination to take more action than just buy a lottery ticket on a Saturday! People who are driven don't just have the desire, they have the determination and motivation to do what ever it takes! Those that have a love and passion for the sport, business or goal will get better results because they an inner drive and will never give up. Many winners love what they do so much they will not give up until they reach their goal.

Winners do whatever it takes.

Love is a create motivator

Passion is a great motivator. Advice I was given when looking for business ideas at 21 years old was: "Find something you are passionate about." It was great advice, as I had taken a holiday to America looking for ideas and the best one I found (online car sales) was not something I was really passionate about. Branson was and launched the idea a year later! It took me three years before I had a business idea I was really passionate about! (The idea and dream of helping people achieve their goals!) Love in its many different forms is a great motivator. Love makes the world go round!

Find something you love and make money out of it.

"Find something you are passionate about."
- Carolyn Maniukiewicz, Founder, Ideas In Partnership

Discovering my Passion and Personality

While I was still at school I remember at a very young age (about 15 years old) I had to decide what I wanted to do for the rest of my life! In particular what I wanted to do after I had finished school and I had no idea. I went and did a degree I didn't like but finished it and worked in 3 different jobs over 4 years before discovering my 'passion'. In total it took me till I was about 25 years old (10 years on) to discover what I really wanted to do was help, teach and coach others to use their mind. However what took me 10 years to work out took Australian coach Greg Barnes less than 10 minutes! While I was working in Australia with ChevronTexaco he went through his four personality cards with fellow employees and myself. I was impressed, surprised and kicking myself that I hadn't seen these 10 years before.

For centuries philosophers identified four broad types of personality. The psychologist Dr Carl Jung further developed this idea in the 20th Century. Jung suggested that all four personality traits (or energies) are present in all of us, with one of them strongest and the different balances between them are what make us unique. Psychologist Myers Briggs also became well known for his work on personality identification. Greg refers to the four personality strengths and calls them 'Analyser, Player, Safekeeper and Carer'.

Every person is unique but the four layers are a useful guide.

Every person is like a different "history book"
with experiences behind them which has shaped them.

Our dominant character quality falls into one of four traits;
Daring Dog, Caring Cat, Building Beaver and Busy Bee.

What kind of animal are you?

For simplicity I will use animals as a metaphor to describe the four personality traits; Daring Dog, Caring Cat, Building Beaver and Busy Bee. See if you can spot the animal traits in you and which trait is the strongest.

Daring Dog (Red)

Commend Strengths;

Challenger, risk taker & showman/woman; vision, creativity, quick decisions, solve problems, impatient

Recommend Improve;

Dislike routine, analysis, focusing is no fun, patience, analysis, team work

Spot a Daring Dog; show man, action and ideas man, loud clothes, transport, bored easily e.g. Donald Trump, Duncan Bannatyne, Chris Gorman

Thinking style; VISUAL, RIGHT BRAIN

Caring Cat (Green)

Commend Strengths;

Caring people person; communication, optimism, enthusiasm, coaching, counselling

Recommend Improving;

Time mgmt, analysis and logic, directness, less soft, less talk, more action, Prioritising

Spot a Dog; listening, caring, intuitive, teacher, nurse, wants to save the world e.g. Mother Teresa

Thinking style; AUDIO, RIGHT BRAIN

Building Beaver (Blue)

Commend Strengths;

Mechanical, analytical & technical; logic, direct, hard, improve performance figures

Recommend Improving;

Communication, people skills, intuition, creativity, networking, public speaking

Spot a Beaver; alone, accountant, technical, computer or car e.g. Bill Gates

Thinking style; LEFT BRAIN

Busy Bee (Yellow)
Commend Strengths;
Organised, Diplomatic & 'Do'er; loyal, patient, consistent, reliable, calm, good listener, worker
Recommend Improving;
Flexibility, prioritising, confidence, assertiveness, openness to change

Spot a Bee; quiet, long serving employees, tidy, organised, doer and follower e.g. personal assistant
Thinking style; KINESTHETIC, LEFT BRAIN

Colourful characters
The use of the animals is a great way to assist understanding and memory recall. The four colours used above also act as useful indicators for the personality traits. The red is for the risky and loud dogs, green is for the caring and environmental cats, blue is for the cool and calculated beavers and yellow is for the bright, friendly and reliable sunny bees.

Remember, each of these personality traits are like 'layers' to our character with one colour strongest on top and the other layers to our character follow. We all have each of these layers and colours within us. Sometimes our strongest behaviour changes to suit the situation for example when we have fun or under stress. For example my own strongest layer is a caring cat, but when I have fun I like to entertain and show off like a cat and under stress I am quieter and less considerate (not like a caring cat).

Our strongest behaviour may change to suit the situation e.g. under stress

This fascinating and insightful information is relevant and useful to 'Winning Mentality' for one main reason. It will help you confirm (or discover) where your passion and strengths are. Which helps us pick our job and pick our dream. When people love what they do, they are great at what they do, because love is a natural motivator! They don't need a carrot or a stick! And it can help you confirm or discover your weaknesses in order to work on them or find someone to 'work in the areas of weakness' for you.

When people love what they do, they are great at what they do! Love is a natural motivator!

ACTION!
Animal Personality
What kind of animal are you? Right down the animal you are most like and then the next three in order of likeness.
GO!

STOP!
Now when you look at your goal does it fit? Dogs do not love money, Beavers do not love taking risks, Bee's do not love sales jobs (or selling themselves!) and Cat's do not love inventing things that take years. I could not work in a job just for the money and not be able to help, teach and coach people! I know that so I work on goals that motivate me and I turn down opportunities that don't. Regardless of money successful people will seldom do a job they don't enjoy. Winners always follow their heart and motivation, but they will do tasks they don't enjoy to achieve success, losers don't. Tim Henman is not a big fan of some of his training routine (like running) but he does it because he knows he has to do it to achieve success in what he does love to do; playing tennis.

If you are unsure take action. I worked in a few jobs and followed a few dream goals (and discovered I didn't really want them). I thought I wanted to be an actor for a while, so I chased the dream and began training in London part time (was told I was good) and realised the main reason I wanted to act was so I could use my fame to go to schools and talk to kids about achieving their dreams! I took a short cut and picked that as my dream job! I think my acting skills and 'show off cat' layer to my personality come in very handy in my current job!

"If we do not change direction, we may end up at the point at which we are heading". - Old Chinese proverb

"Even if you're on the right track, you'll get run over if you just sit there."

When you are up and running it is easier to change direction than if you are standing still. You may be moving in the wrong direction at times but if you're not moving you'll never go in the right direction.

If you live by 'Don't do anything you don't want to do' all the time you will be unhelpful and unsuccessful
If you live by 'Do things you don't want to do' all the time you will be unhappy and unsuccessful

Winners will do whatever it takes to be successful.

Some things they like. Some things they dislike.

Work out what you like, what you don't like and go to work!
Don't do anything you don't want to do, unless you really have to.

Are you working on your dream or someone else's?
Winners work on their dreams.

Pick your purpose

One important point; When people choose a job that is not using their strongest personality trait they are very unlikely to remain motivated or happy or excel in the long term. Modifying your personality long term leads to stress and unhappiness.

Modifying your personality long term leads to stress and unhappiness
Choose a job where your hearts in it.

Choosing a job where neither your heart nor your personality is in it leads to an unmotivated, unhappy and unimpressive worker.

Selecting a Winning Team

Entrepreneurs or team managers that understand how the cats, dogs, beavers and bees think and behave gives them an advantage to identify them, select them and they won't need to motivate them to get the best from them. They are self-motivated. Money will motivate some people but not all people.

Selecting a winning team requires selecting winning personalities.

"People are not your most important asset. The right people are your most important asset. When you have the right people you don't need to motivate them. Get the right people on the bus and the wrong people off the bus." - Jim Collins, author, 'Good to Great'

Are you on the right path? Does you goal really motivate you?
Money alone will motivate some people, but not many people.

"The carrot and the stick doesn't work. Performance based pay doesn't work." - Alfie Kohn, author, 'No Contest' and 'Punished by rewards'

Women with good hearts and Men with good hands

Imagine you were asked to describe the favoured chosen occupation of the 'average man' and the 'average woman'. You might be tempted to say, "the man would choose to use his hands e.g. take care of cars" and "the woman would choose to use her heart e.g. take care of patients". I don't think that statement is wildly inaccurate or untrue. Using the four 'colours' identified by Jung and others, a large proportion of men do have a dominant 'blue beaver' trait in their personality and a large percentage of women have a strong 'caring cat' trait personality. But it's not 100% true for every man or woman. Thankfully there is no such thing as the average man or woman or we'd all be average (and we'd all be the same). We are all different! For example I'm a man and I'm a caring cat that loves to care, coach and teach!

Some men are cats, some women are beavers.
We are all different!

Women have good hearts and Men have good hands
and sometimes vice versa!

'He showed his true colours when he did that.'

'Men are from Mars, Women are from Venus.' – Dr John Gray

Motivation is what winners look for
Motivation (often called 'drive') is what top leaders look for in individuals before considering skills. Why? Because they know that's the most important thing. It's similar to why Southwest Airlines recruitment policy is 'Hire for attitude, train for skill'. I will highlight two examples where team selection for world-class sport teams was made on motivation and <u>not</u> skill or fitness!

The greatest living explorer
Ranalph Fiennes 'The worlds greatest living explorer' selects team members for his gruelling endurance expeditions and competitions based on 'motivation' and not fitness or skill! He looks for 'highly motivated people'. He is also more likely to select someone over 50 years of age than under 50! He considers adults over 30 years old "mentally stronger." Ranalph is almost 60 years old himself.

Action Man
Greg Barnes was responsible for selecting an Australian world beating sailing team that won a gold medal several years ago and one of the members of the team he chose (out of hundreds of applicants) was a lumberjack with no sailing experience. Why? The lumberjack was so highly motivated that he attained the nickname 'action' because of his attitude and work ethic during sailing trials. With motivation you can learn anything and do anything. 'Action' played a big part in winning the gold medal. He then went on to become a millionaire stockbroker but started out with zero knowledge! With motivation you can learn anything and do anything.

'Hire for attitude, train for skill' – Motto of SouthWest Airlines

If you're motivated you can learn anything and do anything.

To be a winner you need to be motivated.
Everything else you can acquire.

What's driving you?
Motivation is like an internal engine! What drives you? What motivates you? These should be your big goals. Now drive towards them! Take action.

"Have your ever noticed that the people who love what they do, do a terrific job?" Alfie Kohn

JD Wetherspoon
Tim Martin, the founder of the JD Wetherspoon pub and restaurant chain called his establishments after a teacher from school. The teacher told him he would never achieve his dream of owning a pub because he came from a poor background and wouldn't be able to do it. He proved his teacher wrong and in the process made a dig at his old teacher by using his name! I personally think that the comment could have helped motivate the entrepreneur even more to achieve his goal. While I don't think it is advantageous for every pupil to be told by every teacher "you'll never achieve your dream" it sometimes can be.

Reverse psychology can work wonders.
"Always listen to experts. They'll tell you what can't be done, and why. Then do it." -Robert A. Heinlein

Best thing that every happened
Larry Ellison is the founder of Oracle Software and one of the richest billionaires in the world. Growing up he would do everything he could academically and athletically to get the approval of his Dad. It didn't matter what he did he never got any praise and anything other than criticism. Larry said "It was the best thing that every happened to me." It drove Larry to show his Dad that he was talented and to be a success in business. It worked wonders!

"I have learned through bitter experience the one supreme lesson to conserve my anger, and as heat conserved is transmitted into energy, even so our anger controlled can be transmitted into a power that can move the world." - Mahatma Gandhi

Anger can be a positive motivator, IF it motivates in a positive way.
If anger is having a negative effect on you, get over it.

"You have undertaken to cheat me. I won't sue you for the law is too slow. I'll ruin you." – Cornelius Vanderbilt

Never

A friend of mine in Secondary School was told by her maths teacher, "You will never get your higher maths." When I found this out I still remember the first thing I thought which was "Great, that could be the best thing her teacher could have said." I knew the strengths of my friend (very creative) and I knew her weaknesses (not very interested or motivated with uninteresting or uncreative subjects). I knew that if she put in little effort she would fail her higher maths. However, I knew that she didn't like any critical comments and the teacher's comment would motivate her to prove her wrong. It did and she passed her higher maths! She proved her teacher was wrong. When someone tells you "you'll never do it", think to yourself, "you'll never believe it when I achieve it"!

Reverse psychology often works. Use it on yourself.
Find people who don't believe in you and make a bet!
They'll never believe it when you achieve it!

A bet can change your life

Ben Fogle is an ordinary 30-year-old man that achieved something extraordinary because he "made a drunken bet"! I love this story. Ben was having a drink with friends who were "talking about enrolling in the London Marathon. I said that everyone runs that one and I'd like to do the Marathon des Sables, if I did anything." The infamous Marathon Des Sables is a gruelling 150-mile run through the Sahara Desert in 6 days! That's like running a marathon every day, in a sauna and across sand, which is much more tiring surface to run on! He enrolled the next day in a hung over state and forgot about it. He says, "Six weeks before the race, I got a call to say that a place had come up. I had never run any distance, never done any sport. I was probably in the worst state. My diet consisted of far too much coffee and food on the move. I wasn't even a gym-goer."

Ben's friends, family, parents AND gym trainers all told him NOT to do it! He says, "I had too much pride to back out. If I make a gentleman's bet, I have to honour it. I'm a stickler for those things. I didn't listen and decided it would make a great documentary. I set up a production company called Rambling Ruminations. The fact that I've managed to strive as an independent and get a commission, what with everything else, is one of the things I'm most proud of."

The punishing race, which takes place every April, involves carrying your own food, rationed water supplies and sleeping in Bedouin tents. People have died during previous events. He was advised by his local gym not to do it and his parents asked him not to do it. He was determined to do it and began running for the first time in his life! He went and did it.

Ben says, "There's one section where you have to run 50 miles in a night. Can you imagine? You follow a big laser in the sky but you're running through 600ft sand dunes. Most runners had been planning for years and took clever, sophisticated food. All mine was bought from Marks & Spencer and weighed about a million pounds. My pack was about 10 times heavier than anyone else's! Because of the heat and the weight of your pack your feet swell to two sizes bigger. Sand goes into your socks and turns them into sandpaper. My feet were the most disgusting thing you've ever seen. A lot of people think that only the mad and fitness freaks take part but there were beauticians, gardeners, secretaries and vets all there to challenge themselves. At the finish line you're all completely broken. I've never seen more tears in my life. I cried - everyone does. I came in the late hundreds, but it's all about finishing, not where you came. Afterwards I spent a day in hospital in Morocco with blood-poisoning from the sand and a week on crutches." Ben was motivated to do it because the pain of not honouring a bet was greater than the pain of doing the bet.

Sometimes we are more motivated by our promises to others than we are by our promises to ourselves.

Motivation can get you through any pain, up any mountain, over any hurdle.
Motivation breeds dedication and determination.

The experience had a big effect on Ben, "When I came back I had more confidence than I've ever had. For 12 hours each day you're out on your own, hurting more than you've ever hurt before. You have no other thoughts - all your worries are gone. You get to clear your mind and reassess everything." For the first time in his life he now has a girlfriend where he made the initial contact, "I'm the shyest person when it comes to girls, practically every girl I've ever been out with has made the first move. It was probably the first time in my life that it was the other way around. That's the sort of profound change The Sand Marathon had on me."

One experience, one book, one quote, one friend or one challenge can completely change your life. Go get them!

Anything is possible.
You are capable of more than you think. About 6 times more!

You will be amazed at what you can achieve when you go for a goal outwith your current ability. Power within you will surface that you didn't know you had. Even if you don't believe in your dreams, attempt them, there is amazing power within you.

You have a top gear, which you haven't used yet.

"Nothing Is Impossible." - Christopher Reeve, 'Nothing is Impossible'

"It's kind of fun to do the impossible." -- Walt Disney

"The difference between the impossible and the possible lies in a person's determination." -Tommy Lasorda, Manager of the Los Angeles Dodgers.

"Within you right now is the power to do things you never dreamed possible. This power becomes available to you just as soon as you can change your beliefs." - Maxwell Maltz, 'Psycho-Cybernetics'

"The good Lord gave you a body that can stand most anything. It's your mind you have to convince." – Vince Lombardi

"Expand your experiences; expand your life." – Anthony Robbins

I bet you can't

I met someone at Robert Gordon University who went to University to do a degree because someone at her school told her she could never go to University! She went to University to prove them wrong! She got her degree and said "I'll do anything to prove people wrong."

Sometimes the greatest motivation is when people don't believe in you. People have achieved some of their greatest achievements after being told "I bet you can't."

I dare you to achieve your dream. I bet you can't.

Almost everyone you know doesn't know what you are capable of. In fact sometimes that includes you. Surprise them all.

Promises Promises

Aberdeen Football Club Player Steve Tosh made a promise to his newborn son "Dad will get a goal for you" and a few hours later in the game against Dundee United he did! He had a goal and a promise to keep! It's easier to break your own promises than it is to break promises made to others. Especially promises made my parent to their own kids!

Have goals and promises to keep!
It's hard to break promises made to others.

It's easy to break promises made to yourself, without motivation.

Make a promise to yourself and hold yourself to it.
Hold it up on your wall.

Make a promise
Write down a promise now.
GO!
Write down a promise to yourself now.

Write down a promise to your family now.

Write down a promise to your friends now.

Write down a promise to your partner now.

STOP!
Better, Worse, Younger, Older
Three motivations for me are these three beliefs I have;

1. There is always someone worse off than me.
2. There is always someone doing better than I am, who started out with less than I have. Whether it is brains, money, talent, health, fitness, contacts or capability.
3. There is always someone who has achieved what I have done or want to do who is much younger and much older.

I have found the latter to be true when it came to writing a book and running a marathon. A came across a young BOY that had written a book and a GRANDMOTHER that was running the same marathon as me!

Motivation is a choice
Being motivated is a choice you can make. Two people can get paid the same but put in different efforts depending on their chosen effort. You don't have to love what you do: you don't even have to get paid for what you do, to be motivated. It's up to you.

Motivation is a choice. Being motivated is a choice.

Losing hurts a winner
When WBO featherweight champion boxer Scott Harrison lost his 'champion belt' when he was beaten in 2003. He was hurt, not physically but mentally! Scott hates to lose. He admits that he had not trained as hard as he should have and had become complacent. Scott became very motivated to win the re match and become Champion again. He began training harder than ever before for the boxing re match against Manuel Medina. He knew his past success had been down to his hard training. So he went back to his winning strategy.

His training included running up mountains with a heavy backpack! He won the match and is Champion again.

Chris Higgens wins gold in 2004

Chris Higgens won silver in the team pursuit in Sydney in 2000 but wanted to win a gold medal in Athens 2004. "The gold medal is something I've wanted since I was 12 years old and watched Chris Boardman in Barcelona. That's when I really knew I wanted to win Olympic gold and that feeling was even stronger after Sydney."

Two years ago he was embarrassingly beaten in Manchester in the Commonwealth games by Brad McGee who lapped him to win gold. He said, "Two years ago Brad sent a message out to the rest of us with his performances and it made me take stock and look at what it would take to get me that far." He decided to enlist the expert advice of Chris Boardman in 2002. Commenting after winning the gold medal in Athens 2004 he said, "We sat down and decided how I was going to win this gold medal and it paid off pretty quickly because I won the world title in Stuttgart last year and this year has been all about this. Chris looked at my training and my mental approach and simplified the pursuit for me and it has brought me success. Today I had very little left with one lap to go so I think that means that I have the pursuit right now and it was a lot sweeter to win beating Brad. I've put everything into this day and I'm just glad it happened."

Seeing other people achieve their dream can inspire you.
Watch your heroes and then go after your dream.

Losing can be a great motivator.

Grit your teeth and go for it and you'll get it.

Very Fast Summary

The person who wants to win the most will win the most.
Winners are motivated every day of every year.
Are you hungry?
If you are very motivated (hungry) you can achieve <u>any</u> goal.
Discover your passion, purpose and personality.
You must love what you do.
People are animals; daring dog, caring cat, builder beaver, busy bee
Can you pass the cold shower test?
Winners are highly motivated.
Winners are driven, by their motivation.
Winners have a goal that motivates them. Are you hungry for your goal?
A winner is motivated to train harder, therefore they can play harder and win.
Successful people are prepared to do anything. Are you prepared?

Your dream must excite you and motivate you.
Motivation breeds dedication and determination.
To others it may look like obsession.

Does your goal give you the 'Santa Claus effect'?
The 'Santa Claus effect' means being excited and motivated.
Will you get up early and take action
tomorrow to achieve a distant goal?

Necessity is the mother of motivation.

All competitors are motivated to win on the day,
but how many are motivated to train every day?

"People who are unable to motivate themselves must be content with mediocrity, no matter how impressive their other talents."
-- Andrew Carnegie

To succeed you need a dream and you need motivation.
Winners will do anything to win. Winners do whatever it takes.

A hungry girl with belief can beat Champions.
David can beat Goliath.

"David was the best thing that ever happened to Goliath." -Doug Weed

Anything is possible.
You are capable of more than you think. About 6 times more!
Everyone has the ability to achieve their dream,
but few are motivated to go for it.

You will be amazed at what you can achieve when you go for a goal out with your current ability. Unknown power within you will surface that you didn't know you had. Even if you don't believe in your dreams, attempt them; there is amazing power within you.

"The difference between the impossible and the possible lies in a person's determination." -Tommy Lasorda, Manager of the Los Angeles Dodgers.

Chapter 2
Sixth Sense (Intuition)

Very fast summary;

When you are making decisions listen to your intuitive gut feeling (sixth sense) and follow it.

Included in this chapter;

How making better decisions separates winners from losers
How your sixth sense increases success
A quick decision is better than a slow decision
Analysis paralysis helps people fail
How your sixth sense can save your life
Following advice from other people is a mistake
The intuitive technique used by winners
How to enhance your sixth sense

What is your sixth sense?
Intuition, hunch, gut feeling or sixth senses are all different names for the same thing. Your intuition is like a guide, which makes you pick one option over another. Somehow you seem to 'feel' confident with one path over another. The decision might be as simple as choosing between 'yes' or 'no' or the option could be open or unlimited e.g. the strategy beat the competition.

Your intuition is like a guide. SShh, Listen.

Decision Time
Decisions are made all day everyday. From the moment you wake up to the moment you decide go to bed and fall asleep you will be making decisions.

Decisions are made every minute of the day.

Every decision you make can influence your success or failure. Some decisions, which at first seem insignificant, can have a big impact. Then of course, there are the glaringly obvious big decisions, which are so significant you can guarantee success or failure. Your sixth sense can guide you when making these decisions. A winner's sixth sense is like a secret weapon when it comes to making big decisions.

A winner uses their sixth sense in every decision they make.
Winners make decisions today that help them win tomorrow.

Listen to your intuition (Don't listen to other people!)
Sir Chris Evans is a very successful multi-millionaire businessman who made his millions through his science company and investing in similar ventures. In an interview he made an enlightening comment:
"I made my own decisions for 10 years, took advice over the last 4 years and that's when some things did cock up. I'm not gonna listen to anyone in the next 4 years."

Listening to others can be a mistake. Listen to your intuition.

European Cup Winners
Alex Ferguson's tactical decisions in Manchester United FC's European Cup final against Bayern Munich were crucial to their success. He made the unusual step of playing David Beckham in central midfield, not right midfield.

Bayern Munich scored in the sixth minute of the game to make it 1-0 and it remained that way for 90 minutes of the game! Alex put on substitute Teddy Sheringham after 77 minutes of the game had been played. In the final few minutes he substituted striker Andy Cole for super sub Ole Gunner Solskjaer. Teddy Sheringham scored just after the 90th minute of the game to make the score 1-1. There were 3 minutes of extra time to be played but 1 minute later Ole scored. The European Cup was won by two subs.

Every little decision can impact upon your success. Every little turn you make can take you on the route to success or failure.

Feel 'it' in his bones
Sir Alex Ferguson has been a very successful manager. He is very experienced but he is also very intuitive. The year after Manchester United won the European Cup they got to the quarterfinals of the competition with the score ending 0-0 in the first leg of the match. The second leg was to be played at home but the manager was worried. Sir Alex said, "I was disappointed and worried. Maybe I was a bit like the old farmer who can divine the weather in his bones, getting pains and funny feelings when the rain is coming. I could feel the rain coming." They lost the second match 3-2 and were out of the European Cup. Alex's hunch was right.

When you get a funny feeling in your body, that's your intuition telling you something, if you choose to listen to it.

Sixth Sense Saves Lisa's Life
I was lucky to talk to a former colleague about intuition. Lisa told me she always followed her intuition and it had actually saved her life. I was keen to hear the story. She told me that when she was 19 years old her Mum and Dad were spending a week away, several miles north of where they lived. Lisa couldn't go with them due to work and exams. However her Dad had to return to their hometown on business on the Friday. He talked to Lisa and asked her if she wanted him to pick her up so she could join them for the weekend before they returned home. She had no plans for the weekend but she told me "I didn't feel like I wanted to go" even though it was normally a fun trip. So she decided not to go. While driving north her Dad was involved in a road accident and the entire passenger side of the car was damaged. Had Lisa been sitting there she would not be around today. Following her sixth sense saved Lisa's life.

Following your sixth sense can save your life.

"I've always been a great believer in trusting your gut instinct and if it doesn't feel right, don't do it."
–Willie Miller, former Captain, AFC, European Cup Winners Cup Winners

Friend or Foe
Naturally since our birth we have instantly evaluated people who have approached us or are situated around us on whether they are a friend (non threat) or a foe (threat). It is our mind's way to defend itself. Your

mind is always looking out for threats. Intuition is like your guardian angel.

Intuition is like your guardian angel,
looking out for and warning you of danger

First Impressions count

Upon meeting someone you will get a 'sense' for the person. You might not trust them, take a dislike to them, or click with them wonderfully. They might not even say anything 'wrong' but you somehow 'sense' whether to like/dislike or trust/distrust them.

Sensing harmful decisions

The same 'phenomenon' of being able to sense potentially harmful people also translates to identifying safe and potentially harmful decisions. You get a 'sense' for what the best decision is. You may have information, which is complementary to your decision, or it may be the opposite. Nevertheless you have a 'feel' for the right decision.

You get a 'sense' for what the best decision is.

Horrors of not following Sixth Sense

An experience of a person I met provides a memorable story. The woman told me that she agreed with my thoughts on intuition. She said it is worth following and said that she had learnt the hard way from personal experience in her relationships. She told me that "My intuition was telling me after four weeks that it wouldn't last. But I didn't listen because I had gone on the Internet and found a site on Horoscopes and I entered our dates of births to see what the site thought of our potential as partners and it said we were a good match." She then told me, "In fact my intuition was telling me within four minutes of meeting him that it wouldn't work out!" I asked her to explain and she said, "He was like an open book the first time we met and told me that all his previous relationships had ended traumatically. My intuition was telling me then to go for the door." But she didn't listen to her intuition she listened to a website! When your intuition tells you to run, run! For your life.

Life can be a horror if you don't follow your intuition.
Don't wait before it's too late.
Ignore Horoscopes but don't ignore your intuition.
'Read the signs'.
Follow your heart and intuition when making decisions.

Facts are fiction

I like the saying 'You can prove anything with statistics' which to me provides a warning that facts can paint a rosy picture particularly when looking into the future. Therefore information and facts can be <u>useful</u>

when considering decisions but they are rarely effective for making decisions.

Information is for considering decisions,
intuition is for making decisions.

Hundreds and thousands

Sir Richard Branson is approached with several ideas every week for new companies to launch. He will be told "I have a great idea" by mail, fax, phone and in person hundreds of times a year. He will bounce some of the ideas off other senior executives or contacts. How does he pick the ones he will take action on and develop into a 'Virgin' company? Answer- Intuition. Sir Richard Branson is a billionaire. It works wonders.

Michael Jackson

There are two Michael Jacksons. The Michael Jackson is a music legend and lives in the USA. However there is another Michael Jackson, a Scottish business legend who shares the same name but lives in Scotland. He set up a successful company called WildDay without performing market research or customer surveys because "my instinct was screaming it was the right thing to do, and I didn't need research to tell me." The company now turns over "a couple of million."

What is your intuition telling you?
(Turn down the 'noise' and you'll hear it!)

Lucky intuition

People that listen to their intuition are luckier according to Professor Richard Wiseman. He set out to scientifically discover the differences between people who are lucky and unlucky. It took him eight years to complete his research into the subject and his book "The Luck Factor" makes great reading. Professor Wiseman found four principle ways of thinking which 'make' people lucky;

Principle One: Maximise Chance Opportunities

Lucky people are skilled at creating, noticing and acting upon chance opportunities. They do this in various ways, including networking, adopting a relaxed attitude to life and by being open to new experiences.

Principle Two: Listening to Lucky Hunches

Lucky people make effective decisions by listening to their intuition and gut feelings. In addition, they take steps to actively boost their intuitive abilities by, for example, meditating and clearing their mind of other thoughts.

Principle Three: Expect Good Fortune

Lucky people are certain that the future is going to be full of good fortune. These expectations become self-fulfilling prophecies by helping lucky people persist in the face of failure, and shape their interactions with others in a positive way.

Principle Four: Turn Bad Luck to Good

Lucky people employ various psychological techniques to cope with, and often even thrive upon, the ill fortune that comes their way. For example, they spontaneously imagine how things could have been worse, do not dwell on the ill fortune, and take control of the situation.

Four tips for being lucky

The four tips could also be worded;

1. Maximise chance opportunities
2. Listen to your intuition
3. Be Positive
4. Put bad experiences into perspective (Be Positive)

When Professor Richard Wiseman gave 'tips' to people to improve their luck, using his principles above, the luck of both lucky and unlucky people improved. As his book points out a lucky decision, a chance opportunity or a bit of luck can change your life, career, fortune or relationship. Winners follow similar ways of thinking, which is why winners are lucky!

Negative people are unlucky

The book is especially useful for any negative and unlucky person that needs to see scientific evidence before they change their negative attitude to a positive attitude! I know a negative attitude ruins your life and I've included plenty of stories and explanations in this book to prove that. Thankfully if you don't believe me, scientist Professor Richard Wiseman has proved the same thing!

Old Wisdom

Although the book is fascinating and provides some new insights, the latter three principles are familiar. However, it's comforting when scientific research proves something, which many winners (ironically) 'intuitively' believed to be true anyway, myself included. Napoleon Hill started telling people 50 years ago that intuitive decision making helps successful people succeed. As did philosophers thousands of years before him. And the wisdom of Henry Ford, Napoleon Hill and Norman Vincent Peale has been preached for over half a century, testifying to 'the power of positive thinking'. The mind can do more than improve your luck. This book in your hands will demonstrate that the mind is even more powerful and useful than most logical left brain scientists believe and have been able to prove. But don't wait for science to catch up.

Winners don't wait for science to prove it before they use it.

If your right brain is telling you something, don't wait 10 years for the left-brain to tell you the same thing.

Be intuitive and positive and you will be lucky.

'It's not what you know, it's who you know'

Blindfold

If you blindfold someone in their own home and ask them to 'get out!' they will still find the right way to the front door (using their knowledge). But if you put them in a strange building and do it (no knowledge), only someone who uses their intuition will get out successfully fast, by using their intuition as their guide. However, if you put someone with a blindfold on into a building they have only visited once before they may quickly 'guess' the right way to get out. But what they think is a guess is actually their 'intuition' guiding them after examining the previous visit recorded in the mind (stored knowledge).

Your intuition helps you make decisions where you have previous experience (knowledge) and where you have no experience.

Decisions which concern the future are 'blind' decisions (where you have no knowledge), therefore use your intuition.

Experience matters

Your mind has been like a video recorder since the day you were born and records all your past experiences, including smell, taste and touch. These experiences, knowledge and recordings can be accessed at any time by your mind. So having lots of experience and a lot of knowledge can be useful and will guide your intuitive decision making subconsciously without you realising it. Your mind is an expert at recognising a 'match' in what you are currently experiencing with a similar previous experience. For example a detective might 'sense' someone is lying because he has seen it all before. A stockbroker might 'sense' a good buy or a time to sell because he has experienced it before. The detective isn't a great stockbroker and the stockbroker isn't a great detective. Experience makes your intuition more effective in situations you've experienced before. But it still works in the dark!

Your mind records everything you experience.
Your mind spots 'matches' with past experiences.

Anything you see, hear, smell, taste, touch now the mind looks for 'matches' with what you've seen, heard, smelt, tasted before.

Experience makes your intuition more effective when making decisions in areas where you have experience.

Information Intuition
The mind stores information and it is used and accessed by your mind to make intuitive decisions. In an experiment people were shown 1000 photographs, one after the other at a speed of about one a second. The psychologist then added 100 new photographs with the original 1000 and mixed them all up. Everyone was asked to identify those they had not seen before and everyone (regardless of intelligent or memory level) was able to identify almost every 'new' photograph and 'old' photograph!

The brain stores all visual and written information but we find it easier recalling images. It can be easier to remember someone's face than their name!

The Paomnnehal Pweor of the Azmanig Hmuan Mnid
Aoccdrnig to rscheearch at Cmabrigde Uinervtisy, it deosn't mttaer in waht oredr the ltteers in a word are, the olny iprmoatnt tihng is taht the frist and lsat ltteer be in the rghit pclae. The rset can be a taotl mses and you can sitll raed it wouthit porbelm. Tihs is bcuseae the huamn mnid deos not raed ervey lteter by istlef, but the wrod as a wlohe.

The mind is good at recognition.
The mind has a good memory!

History helps
One school of thought says that there is no such thing as intuition just past experiences recorded in your mind which your mind will access in order to make decisions. This implies that in a situation where you have to make a decision your mind will examine past experiences and knowledge for guidance and then make an 'intuitive' decision. This is true. Your mind will 'look' at relevant past experiences to help it make the right 'intuitive' decision. Therefore someone highly skilled and experienced in an area can intuitively make highly effective decisions.

However, I believe (and it's been proven) that your intuition also guides your decisions during new 'never experienced before' situations. Your intuition guides you when you get into the unknown. When it is dark. Knowledge is useful. Intuition is very useful!

Knowledge is power. Intuition is super power.
Growing knowledge can enhance your intuition in decision making.
But intuition is more important than knowledge.

Harvard says Intuition is #1
Harvard Business Review stated "intuition and meditation are the two most important tools in business in the 21st century." The reason is that for senior executives one of the most important things they do is make decisions. The best decisions are 'intuitive' decisions.

Meditation is a form of relaxation, which is tool number seven. So not only will you learn seven important tools recommended by Phil McNally but you'll also be using the two most important tools recommended by Harvard business experts!

Intuition and relaxation are the two most important tools for senior execs. The more important the decisions the more important the intuition.

Decision without the full picture

A study on high-ranking corporate executives by Henry Mintzberg detailed in the Harvard Business Review revealed they were "constantly relying on hunches to cope with problems too complex for rational thinking." In his conclusion he stated "Success does not lie in that narrow minded concept called "rationality" it lies in a blend of clear headed logic and powerful intuition."

Knowledge is power. Intuition is super power.

Ford listened to intuition not facts

Successful people are often presented with information to help them make their decision but regardless of what the information proves or shows they ultimately choose what they feel is the right decision, sometimes going against 'expert' advice, information or research! Like Henry Ford.

"If we had asked people what they wanted, they would have said a faster horse." – Henry Ford

Facts fail. Intuition never fails. Experts are not always right. Intuition is a better 'guide'.

Knowledge and intuition enhances sport performance

Knowing where to focus your time every week as a sport or business person is important. Having that 'knowledge' can be the difference between a profitable business and an unprofitable business and a winning athlete and a losing athlete. An individual may have that knowledge intuitively or learn that knowledge either the easy way or the hard way! In golf if you look at the stats of the top 10 drivers you find few winners, but if you look at the top 10 putters you will find many winners (last time I looked there were one and eight respectively!). It's not the power of the start but the skill of the finish. There is a saying in Golf, 'Drive for show, putt for doe'. Business has a similar philosophy, 'Sales are vanity, profit is sanity. Cash is king.' I discovered that a year after starting in business! Better late than never!

Knowledge and intuition is great for business.

Knowledge and intuition is great for sport.
We learn through experience or knowledge
of other people's experience.
'Only a fool learns from experience.
I learn from the experiences of others.' - Otto von Bismarck

Find a way

One of my golf clients is a very motivated and wise golfer and he was looking to improve his game with some "mental skills" knowledge. Like many golfers he was aware that it's not the power of the start (drive) but the skill of the finish (putting) that is important. He was very motivated to find a way to improve his putting and when he didn't find a way he invented a way! Peter didn't see himself as an inventor, more of a problem solver. And he wanted to solve his problem putting! Peter was motivated to find a way.

Find a way or make a way. Or get out of the way.

'We will find a way or make a way.' –Hannibal

'My Road To a Major Putting Improvement'- Peter Royce

"I struggled with putting for years and spent hours and hours on the putting green trying to sort it. I never did in spite of going to golf pros and getting lessons. About 5 years ago I started buying books to help me understand the principles behind the golf swing and putting. Initially it's confusing when you hear too many conflicting views but eventually you start to sort the wheat from the chaff.

Picking up a book by Dave Pelz, (Dave Pelz's Putting Bible) started me on the right track, his research and scientific information about the importance of an "in-line shoulder stroke" made perfect sense to me, I bought his training aids and set about practising with great enthusiasm. At this time I still made little headway, I re-read his book and started practising a drill he showed of practising the stroke standing in a doorway with a shaft across his shoulders to make the shoulders work in a vertical motion. Wow, that felt weird! I then took this a step further by designing the Pro-Putt Laser trainer, with this you can start to putt up and down the carpet and look to see how the laser tracks up and down the wall. Vertical shoulder movement = vertical laser trace. At first it seemed impossible.

Did it work on the course? You bet, shot 69 the next day with a 9 on my card and I haven't ever thought about changing my stroke, not even for a moment. I am 100 % confident my stroke is technically sound. Now it's all down to green reading and visualisation.

I know a lot of golfers who've read the Pelz book and "think" they do an "in-line shoulder" stroke, they don't, they're guessing they do it and an in-line stroke performed correctly is a terrible putting stroke."

"Seeing is believing."

"The fastest way to improvement is to understand and believe the concept and then have someone "show you", I've seen lots of golfers struggle with a vertical shoulder rock yet a "hands on" approach gets them swinging the putter in-line within minutes. The better your putting stroke the more putting comes down to green reading, visualisation and confidence but you have to have the first building block securely in place, it's the foundation and everything else feeds off it. See it, Believe it, Trust it!"

"Initially it's confusing when you hear too many conflicting views but eventually you start to sort the wheat from the chaff."

"The fastest way to improvement is to understand and believe the concept and then have someone "show you." "

"See it, Believe it, Trust it! "Seeing is believing."

All above quotes by Peter Royce, Inventor, Pro-Putt Laser trainer, Putt2win.com. Peter loves golf and he loves to help. He has shared all his 'putting knowledge' and tips on his website 'putt2win.com' which is brilliant.

"It's useful to have the right 'know how', if you use it right!" – Phil McNally

Quick, Slow.

Napoleon Hill identifies Henry Ford as a perfect example of good decision-making. Because he said Ford "makes up his mind quickly and changes his mind slowly." In sport you have to make quick decisions. When you don't make a quick decision in sport, you have just made the wrong decision. If you make a quick decision you will have a chance of being right if you make a slow decision you will have a 100% chance of being slow. Sport is a great 'school' for business people.

Make up your mind quickly and change it slowly.
Avoid 'analysis paralysis'.
Slow decision-making slows you down.

If you snooze, you lose.

60 Seconds

I like the story of how Napoleon Hill came to write the wonderful book 'Think and Grow Rich'. He was interviewing the world's first billionaire, the great Scot Andrew Carnegie. Carnegie had felt for some time that there should be a book written with tips and advice from successful business people on how to be successful so that more people could benefit and be successful also. When he met the young reporter Napoleon Hill, Carnegie intuitively knew that Hill would be a great person to write the book. After Carnegie made his 'pitch' to Hill on the book, he asked if Hill would write the book (Carnegie would not pay Hill any money for the years it would take to write, but would pay for the book's publication). When Carnegie asked the question, unbeknown to Hill, Andrew Carnegie started his stopwatch. Carnegie would give him 60 seconds to say yes or the offer would be withdrawn. The reason being that Carnegie had a strong belief that people who made a quick decision did a great job and those who didn't, didn't. Carnegie had past experience of this proving to be the case. Obviously Hill said yes within the time limit and the rest is history. A great decision and a great book!

Give yourself 60 seconds to make up your mind.
You'll be right 1st time.

Analysis paralysis helps people fail

Making slow decisions can be detrimental to success. By taking a long time to make a decision the competition could sneak ahead and the option and opportunity to make a winning decision is gone. Spending a long time thinking about a decision and the options("analysis paralysis") can damage confidence and the fear of failure may even stop a decision being made at all.

There will be times when postponing a decision is a good decision but for winners this is an exception not the norm. In the words of Sir Winston Churchill "A good plan today is better than a great plan tomorrow."

Delaying a decision or not making a decision can be the worst decision you ever made. Postponing a decision should be the exception not the norm.
"I think the key to success is making quick decisions. If it turns out to be wrong you just make another decision."
– Dr Ian Moir, Successful Entrepreneur, Business Development Advice

The first thought is usually the right one

I was first given the advice 'The first choice is usually the right one' at school but it has proved beneficial in later life. I found that where golf professionals follow this rule they greatly benefit.

The first thought is usually the right one.
If you're wrong, make another decision.

Make it a Quickie

I did a survey of two 18th, 19th, 20th and 21st Century leaders and the survey said 'Make it quick';

Some people need it pointed out to them but we've all got it.

Don't beat yourself up

It's usual that we all on occasion 'beat ourselves up' over our actions or decisions. The key is to live, learn and move on.

Pat yourself on the back

Be positive. Be relaxed. Before you make a decision relax. Tell yourself you WILL make a great intuitive decision.

Make mistakes- they make you great. Learn from mistakes. Tell yourself that there is a small chance you will make a mistake. But mistakes are great lessons. You will get 90% of the decisions you make right. Do not attempt to get 100% of your decisions right.

If you take too long to make a decision you'll miss the bus. Analysis paralysis will make you late. The early bird catches the worm. If you don't make a decision you have no chance of being right or wrong. Look at the positive side of mistakes.

You won't learn if you don't make a mistake.
You don't learn to ride a bicycle by riding a tricycle.

Congratulations

Most people pat themselves on the back when they win. But the path to winning involved lots of losing. Winners win a lot, usually after they lose a lot. I recommend you send yourself a 'Congratulations' card the next time you lose! You're on the path to winning. Start a 'Congratulations' book! You haven't failed, you just haven't succeeded yet.

Praise yourself for making mistakes. You made a decision.
Winners are losers before they are winners.

$10M Mistake

One of my favourite business stories is about a $10M mistake (the story may not be completely accurate but the powerful message is very clear). An employee in IBM was solely responsible for costing the company $10M through a mistake he made. He was called before the head of the organisation. The employee walked into the executives' office and the room was absolutely silent. As he walked towards the seated executive he said "Don't worry I'll clear my desk and leave." The executive replied, "Why would you want to do that?" "Because I have cost the company $10M", the employee responded.The executive smiled and said, "You have learnt a $10M lesson, why would I want you to go and work for someone else to benefit."

Some mistakes are cheap. Some are expensive.
But every mistake is a valuable lesson.

Listen to your intuition

Winners follow their intuition when making decisions and when they reflect back realise that their decisions have proved correct and helped them succeed. They might be called 'lucky' by others through making the right choice (they may even say 'I was lucky' themselves). However their success wasn't down to luck, it was down to their intuition. Your intuition is like your inner voice but it can only be heard if you are listening to it. Are you listening?

Listen to your intuition. Are you listening?

How to use your intuition

I teach business people (and golfers) a quick way to tap into their intuition and make quick decisions with the help of their imagination. I ask them to consider who their biggest hero is. The next time they have to make a decision I suggest they imagine discussing it with their hero and listen to their advice before making a decision. I have used the technique myself successfully on many occasions, as have my business clients. The fact that several of my golf clients have used it and won competitions tell it's own story.

Talk decisions through in your head with a winner,
for winning decisions.

Your Imaginary Passengers

Who would be the best people to coach, consult, mentor, motivate, guide and inspire you to achieve your goals and enjoy your life? They can be alive, dead, real or fictional, male or female, friend or hero you've never met.

It's useful to have a few different heroes in your car to help you on your journey. You can use one or more 'passengers' at any time. You never have to drive to your goal alone.

With heroes in your head you will never walk alone.

Diversity

It is very useful and effective to have a diverse range of passengers with different skills, sex, experience and personality. I have used the likes of Bill Gates, Sir Richard Branson, Billy Connolly (humour is good), my Dad and myself! There is strength in diversity. You could have a comedian, motivator, sports and business hero in your car guiding you on your journey to greatness!

Are you talking to yourself?

One of the best passengers you can talk to is your future self! I have used this passenger and so have several of my clients. Imagine yourself in 5, 10 years time. What advice can that wise and wonderful person give you?

Are you talking to yourself?

ACTION!
Pick your Imaginary Passengers
Who would be the best passengers to help you achieve greatness and happiness? Who comes to mind? Trust the suggestions that come into your head, even if they surprise you. Picture your car in your imagination; it can be as prehistoric or futuristic or big or small, as you like. I like to imagine an open top 'feet powered' car 'Flintstones' style to give me a clear view of the future 'Mental Movie' and remind me through metaphor that I am self propelling or powering myself along the path to my dreams. No one else will carry me there. The passengers power to of course! Imagine you have a few passengers with you who can coach and advise you when you are making your quick intuitive decisions. Trust that you will find the right answer. Write down your passengers now.
GO!

STOP!
If no one comes to mind immediately put the book down, close your eyes, take a few deep breaths and imagine the person(s) will walk towards you or come into your mind. **GO!**

Imagination uses your intuition.
Intuition succeeds beyond your imagination.

Good to talk
The next time you have to make a decision, imagine discussing it with your passengers and listen to their advice before making a decision. When you have to make a big decision, you may find it useful to find a quiet place, relax yourself and consider whose knowledge, experience or advice could help you and trust that you will arrive at the best decision. The more often you use this tool the easier you will find it and the more comfortable you become with it. You may find it helpful to read about your passengers or have pictures of your passengers around you.

Right Destination Slowly
Talking and thinking things through helps make sure you're on the right road. If you're on the wrong road the faster you go, the further away you get. Slow down and check the position and destinations with your passengers.

Stopping to talk and think things through with your passenger's everyday helps you make sure you're on the right road to your dream destination.

It's better to get to the right destination slowly than the wrong destination quickly.

Get on with it

Once, after giving this intuitive tool to one of my clients he used it within a few days. The first time he used it was to consider what to do about a situation within his business. He decided to use this tool while he went out to walk the dog. He said it worked brilliantly and helped him make a decision and achieve peace of mind over the issue. I asked who had helped him and what advice they gave him. He told me that Manchester United manager Sir Alex Ferguson helped him make the decision and he had also told him to "get on with it." And he also 'talked' to John Lennon about it, who told him to "be cool man…relax….it's no big deal."

Take a walk, talk to yourself, take the advice and take action.

How to increase your sixth sense;

Walking, talking, relaxing, exercising, thinking, sleeping and meditating. Increasing relaxation and reducing stress e.g. Baths, showers, washing up, painting, creating, playing and laughing. (The Chapter on Energy and Positive MindpowerTool 7 covers relaxation)

How to decrease your sixth sense;

Lots of stress, lots of noise and lots of work! Lots of time with the television or the computer. No rest, no play, no exercise and no thinking time.

Use the force

One of the ways to describe and understand intuition is to re-call the story of Luke Skywalker in Star Wars. There is a scene where Luke practises fighting with his laser wearing a helmet which is completely blacked out. Unable to see, Luke argues 'I can't see anything, how am I supposed to fight'. He is told to 'use the force' i.e. trust his judgement. After some trial and error Luke begins to relax and trust himself. He successfully fights even though he cannot visually see where the next attack will strike!

Use the force. The force of your intuition

Trust yourself

If you trust your judgement, your 'hunch', gut feeling or whatever you call it you will find yourself making the best decisions.

Trust yourself. You KNOW what to do.

Talk to yourself
From an early age kids will talk to themselves. Especially when playing, sleeping with teddies or making decisions. I remember when I was young I used to talk to my watch a bit like David Hastlehoff in Knightrider. I sincerely wish I still did!

Talk to yourself.

Coach yourself
Spoken self-chat is a very effective way to make decisions, relax, motivate, humour or calm yourself. It's why coaching is so effective in business, sport and life.

Have a word with yourself! Think things through.
Successful people do.

Give yourself a good talking to
A beneficial, therapeutic and profitable way to spend a few minutes everyday is talking to yourself. Perhaps your future self.

Spend a few minutes everyday talking to yourself and your future self.
Give yourself a good talking to.

Fail to Plan, Plan to fail
Plan when you will take time out to talk to heroes in your head and make sure you're going in the right direction. It's the quickest way to get to your destination. If you don't you could be running the wrong way. If you fail to plan it, prepare to fail. Have a meeting with yourself to set your goals, make your decisions and consider your actions at least once a day!

Failing to plan, is planning to fail.

"If you fail to plan, you plan to fail."- Napoleon Hill,
'Think and Grow Rich'

Meetings are magic
Hands up if you have ever thought negatively about 'another meeting'? (I have raised my hand and am typing one handed!) Meetings are magic! A 15-minute meeting with your team can turn around the performance that day. Just ask a football manager! A study found that more goals are scored in the second half of football games than the first half! (Remember Kevin Keegan was losing 3-0 at half time and winning 3-4 by full time!). A meeting can be a turn around. Basketball managers call a 'time out' when they know they need a meeting.

American Football teams have over eighty 30-second meetings and one 30 minute meeting per game! Huddle up! Having a time out with yourself can turn around your performance and turn you on to the right winning path! Have a meeting- with yourself!

Meetings are magic!

Take a 'time out' and have a meeting with yourself.
Meetings can improve your performance and even turn around a losing performance into a winning performance!

Even if you think you might be on the right path, stop and check!

Positive investment
Professor Dennis Tournish of the Aberdeen Business School at Robert Gordon University is an expert on Communication within companies. I like the study he refers to into a poorly performing General Motors Plant that renamed themselves 'New United Motor Company' (positive label!). The plant introduced 25 meetings a month and dramatically improved performance! Here is the changes they made:

1. Weekly team meetings, for one hour
2. Daily meetings of supervisory staff, with union and quality operators involved
3. Monthly meetings between staff and team co-ordinators
4. Regular performance progress reports
5. A weekly plant newspaper

Results;

1. A 100% increase in daily production the first year, 20% the second
2. Warranty claims down 56% in first year
3. A reduction of 50% in controllable costs per engine
4. An increase of 33% in machine uptime
5. Employees contributed ten times more suggestions then rest of GM staff

Thinking and talking is an investment of your time.
Invested positively you will profit positively.
Unless you keep tracking your path to your goal, you lose track.
Winning teams communicate. Winners communicate.
To win have a communication – with yourself.

Begin and End with a goal

Have a meeting with yourself at the start and end of the day. Set your goals. Pick up lessons and ideas from your night and your day. Write them down.

It's good to talk. I sometimes pick up the phone and talk to myself.
He's a real wise guy. I listen as I speak.
I learn and take action. Phone yourself.

Knowledge is power

Learn from your life and your results. Live and learn. Learn from the best sources. Seek out and learn the best information you need to achieve your dream goal. Learn something useful every day. Keep an open mind. The more you learn, the more you know and the better you become. Knowledge is useful! You will improve yourself and you will make better decisions!

Knowledge is power. Live and learn.

"What you don't know can hurt you." –Ivan Misner, founder of BNI

"If you've got a closed mind, you'll never learn anything."
– Brian McNally, co-founder, Dunlaw Engineering

"Leaders are readers." – Anthony Robbins, 'Awaken the Giant Within'

When your mind knows your goals the 'know how' will find you.
You don't choose a book, a book chooses you.

Very Fast Summary
Winners use their intuition to make decisions.
Relax yourself and tap into your intuition.
Have an 'imaginary conversation' with a person you admire then decide.
Give yourself 60 seconds to make a decision.
Make 8 out of 10 of your decisions quickly.
In sport make 10 out of 10 of your decisions quickly.
Make big decisions and sleep on it. Wake up and feel the answer.
Remember being great involves making great mistakes. Get over it.
Record and rejoice your mistakes. Learn from them.
Fail fast. Move fast.

Knowledge is power. Imagination and intuition are super power.

An intuitive decision is one, which turns out to be correct in the future when you are over the horizon but which cannot you see from where you are now.

Avoid 'Analysis Paralysis'. (Frozen and not making a decision).

'Read the signs'. Follow your gut and your heart making decisions.

One of the most important tools for business and sport is intuition.

Take a 'time out' to use your sixth sense for successful decision making.

"I tend to make up my mind about people within thirty seconds of meeting them, I also make up my mind about whether a business proposal excites me within about thirty seconds of looking at it. I rely far more on gut instinct than researching huge amounts of statistics."
– Sir Richard Branson, 'Losing my Virginity'

Stopping to talk and think things through with your passenger's everyday helps you make sure you're on the right road to your dream destination.

It's better to get to the right destination slowly than the wrong destination quickly.

Great companies make great decisions and great mistakes.

If you are not failing fast, you're moving slow.

POSITIVE CHAPTERS

Very Fast Summary

One thing is essential for winning mentality; positive belief! Three techniques used by winners to create positive belief are positive visualisation, positive verbalisation and positive belief building thoughts. Winners have a positive mind, which results in a positive winning performance. The forth Positive chapter 'Positive Mind' covers a fourth technique used by winners that ensures they have a positive mind with positive belief when performing. A positive minds gives a confident performance.

The following 4 chapters show how to build Positive Belief;

Positive Visualisation
Positive Verbalisation
Positive Belief
Positive Mind

Included in these chapters;

Winners are very positive people
Being very positive is a choice
Winners have a positive attitude
Having a positive attitude is a choice
A positive attitude is useful but by itself will not win a gold medal
People with positive belief achieve their goals
Negative people achieve their negative goals
Belief is just a thought
Your thoughts and words create your results
Your are in control of your thoughts and your future
What you believe you achieve
Imagination is more important than knowledge
Being a successful winner is a choice

"I'm an optimist."- Bill Gates, founder, Microsoft & Richest man in the World

"I've just been going out and just believing in myself that I can do it." -Maria Sharapova, 17-year-old Russian, Wimbledon Champion 2004

"Pessimism blunts the tools you need to succeed." -Bruce Lee

CHAPTER 3
POSITIVE VISUALISATION

Very fast Summary

Winners visualise winning. And it works!

Included in this chapter;

Visualisation is very powerful. The results can work in seconds or years.
Mental Movies.
A quick and cheap way to create blockbuster results!
Visualisation is not a guarantee.
Visualisation gives you power when you think you've got none left.
The business is won in the head not in the office.
If you do some Olympic thinking, you will get some Olympic results.
How to influence someone while they sleep.
Mental Movies can heal your body and your friends.
Visualisation is the preparation of champions. Are you prepared?
If you visualise negative, your results are negative!
Focus on the target not the trouble.
Avoid worrying. It works!
The more you fear, the more likely it'll appear.
Visualising while relaxed is more powerful.

Positive Visualisation
Visualisation is one of the most powerful techniques in the world. Visualisation is like a 'mental movie' you direct in your mind of a future event. Positive Visualisation is used by every winner in sport and business. Successful people create an image or 'movie' in their mind of the results they want before they start. Sometimes they have visualised their goals for years.

Visualisation is very powerful.
It helps you achieve your goals a few seconds later or years later, where relevant.

Mental Movie
This powerful technique has been used by famous "greats" like Walt Disney, Mohammed Ali, Nelson Mandela, Jack Nicklaus and Steven Spielberg. If you use this technique too it will be very successful for you. Creating a 'mental movie' can be done with your eyes open or eyes closed. It can be used to win a competition, sink a putt, make a sale or make a great presentation. There are unlimited ways in which it can be used. I'll highlight some of the most powerful and relevant in the following pages. I'll let you use your imagination for the rest. Use your imagination to create a 'Mental Movie' of what you want to happen and what you want to achieve. You are the movie director so make it a very positive successful picture with a happy ending!

Mental Movies are quick and cheap to create but give blockbuster results!

The happy ending
When you are short of time the most important aspect of a 'mental movie' is to create and visualise 'the end'. If you want to succeed picture 'The happy ending' before you begin. All of the successful people I have read about, interviewed or worked with have said something like "I pictured myself winning" or "I had a vision of it before I did it." Before you start, picture the end! Make a mental movie of everything from goals to meetings, to your day ahead. If you can't picture your whole day, just picture the happy ending.

Create a mental movie before you start:
you'll get a happy ending before you stop.

Great first time
The first time you can be scared and below average. The second time you can be nervous and average. The third time you can be excited and good. The fourth time you can be relaxed and great. By doing your improving. But 'doing' does not lead to gold medal performances or everyone would be a winner. Practise does not make perfect. Practise only makes perfect if it's perfect practice.

If you do a positive visualisation several times you will reduce nerves and increase excitement. Visualising your performance or 'first time' at anything will reduce your nerves and improve your performance. You may have used this technique already in your life! But have you used visualisation in your sport or your business?

Practise and 'doing' helps.
When you're doing it you can improve it.
But you can use your mind to do it better.

You can be great the first time if you use your mind.

"Practise does not make perfect. Perfect practise makes perfect."
-Don Shula, Best NFL Coach ever

Faster and Faster

I moved from Aberdeen to London in 2001 and had to change my fitness routine from 'circuit training' and '5-a-side' football with my mates, to running with my mate Martin about 3 times a week. On the first run Martin left me behind when he did a 100-metre sprint half way through the run. From that day on I began to visualise myself sprinting faster than Martin. I would do this several times a week and before every run. By the second week I was matching his speed all the way. On the third week despite his best efforts I was out sprinting him at the half way stage and a sprint at the end. In time my fit body would have adapted to the change in fitness routine anyway. However, I know for sure that I would not have achieved my success so quickly without the visualisation.

Visualisation helps get results faster

Highland games: turn up for the books

Not only do I think visualisation is powerful, I think visualisation is power giving. I ran in the Inverurie Highland Games 10k race in 2003. I had been running regularly and I had recently completed the Edinburgh Marathon so a 10k distance was well within my comfort zone. I had run in my first two 10k races the year before but they had a big field of runners including top national and international athletes. I didn't know what the pace of the runners in this local race would be compared to my pace. But I felt I was a good runner and could win the race. Before the race I had sat and visualised myself winning many times for several minutes. I had also been visualising in the days before the race. I did a gentle warm up and noted the other competitors. Several were doing quite extensive warm ups and from their running clothes you could tell they were regular runners. I did not let this concern me.

Before the start the serious runners' lined up at the front of the line and as soon as the race began shot off at pace. The question of the pace was answered. One small quick runner (who must have weighed less than a loaf of bread!) left everyone standing and shot ahead. Immediately I knew I couldn't keep pace with him at the front so let him go, along with quite a few others who were trailing behind him. And I was behind the trailers! I thought to myself "oh well perhaps I won't win, I'll just enjoy it and see how I get on." I soon found a pace slightly above the comfortable pace that I was used to. Several runners were ahead but I set my goal on just passing the runner in front of me. I succeeded and continued this way of thinking and successfully passed a few runners. By about the 8k mark I found it difficult and the thought of giving up or slowing down entered my head. But I felt I had come too far to give up then and persevered. Ahead of me were the leading female runner and two male runners with running club vests on. By the 9k mark I had passed the female runner and was behind the two male runners. As we entered the Park (about 200 metres from the finish) their pace was really quick and I thought, "I can't go faster I'll just have to sit behind them." However, as we approached the last 100 metres, I somehow felt I had enough power and energy to sprint for the line and as I did I went past them both and crossed the line with my sister cheering me on. Little did I realise that the two runners had been 'fighting' it out for second place, so I was second! (I finished 6 minutes behind the whippet who was already at home having a cup of tea by this time). I did turn up. I did my best. I got 2nd. It did pay off! And I did visualise. It worked quite well!

A mental movie is not a guarantee.
You won't outrun a whippet. (Initially!)
Visualisation gives you power when you think you've got none left.
"80% of success is showing up" -Woody Allen

Fire walking: impossible is possible

A memorable moment in my life and a great learning experience was being taught how to 'fire walk' by Anthony Robbins. A fire walk involves walking across hot coals, which can vary in temperature between 100 to 1,000 degrees centigrade! Can you imagine what an experience that is? Impossible? No! (People have done it before, they LOOKED normal, I think) Easy? No! (Unless you are one of those people that can hover above the ground) Therefore the techniques we used to overcome this 'non-easy' challenge could help anyone overcome their 'non-easy' challenges! We prepared for the "fire walk" using two techniques and doing a few exercises. Do you want to know what the two techniques were? If I can do a 'Fire Walk' using these two techniques imagine what you could achieve using them! You may recognise the two techniques we used: positive visualisation and positive verbalisation! Which built up positive belief! (Before you crank up the BBQ and warm up the coals – get a professional to take you through it. Don't do this at home kids!)

We created a Mental Movie of successfully walking across the hot coals several times in our minds. We 'saw' ourselves being successful in our mind. We also laughed at our fear. We then practised a positive mantra to repeat as we were doing the fire walk which was "cool wet moss, cool wet moss." If those words had feelings they would be good feelings to have walking across hot coals! Don't you think? Colourful words work. I 'postponed' my judgement on whether I was going to be able to do it or not. I wanted to. I lined up and just before it was my turn I seemed to become overcome with power and confidence. I achieved the fire walk and felt "high." We all have an amazing 'power' within us, which we can call upon to achieve amazing things. But we rarely attempt amazing ("impossible") things so we rarely witness our amazing ("impossible") power and achieve amazing ("impossible") things.

Visualisation can enable us to achieve amazing things.

If we attempt so called "impossible" things
with "possible" thoughts, we'll achieve them.

We rarely attempt amazing things,
so we rarely achieve amazing things.
(And we rarely witness our amazing power).

Whisky tour

Once, I had two Danish friends visiting me in Aberdeen for a long weekend just before I left for Australia. They arrived on the Friday and left on the Monday. My intention was to show them as many landmarks and tourist attractions as I could. On the Saturday morning before leaving the house to go to a Whisky distillery, which I'd been to many years ago, I discovered that it wouldn't be open (over the Winter it closed at weekends). However, before we left the house, I went to my bedroom, closed my eyes and visualised someone being at the Whisky distillery and giving us a tour! I will remember the moment for the rest of my life because my friends were in the hall waiting for me and shouted, "Come on Phil!." When we arrived at the Whisky distillery no one was around. So we did a 'peep through the windows' tour and I did my best to explain the equipment and the process of making whisky. Then I heard someone say, "Can I help you?" I turned round to see an employee coming out of a building and walking towards the only car on the site. We explained ourselves and he told us that if we came back on Monday we would get a tour. I told him that my friends were from Denmark and would be flying home to London on Monday. He then offered to give us a tour! Bingo, the visualisation worked! The employee (who was not on duty and had a day off) also said, “I don’t know why I’m here.” I did!

Visualisation does amazing things.
Your visualisation can make others do things.

Winning Business

If you win in your mind, you will win in your business. I worked with successful Aberdeen entrepreneurs Stephen Burt, founder of Motion Software, and Brian Sinclair, founder of Monitor Systems, (one of the fastest growing technology companies in Scotland). Both of these visionary entrepreneurs told me that before giving presentations to prospective clients ‘I see myself getting the contract and shaking hands’. A positive vision of winning! It works wonders for them.

The business is won in the head not in the office.
The deal can be won or lost before it gets to the table.
If you win in your mind, you will win in your business.

Winning movie, winning results (again)

Once, Aberdeen golfer Michael Spence was playing in a tournament at Royal Aberdeen in Aberdeen and performed poorly on the first three holes (3 over after 3 holes). He told me that before he played the fourth hole he imagined winning in his mind, “I pictured myself at the end on the 18th walking up to myself and shaking my hand and saying congratulations Michael you’ve won.” Bingo, the visualisation worked! What a great story. It gets better. He had the same start this year (3 over after 3 holes) did the same visualisation as before and won the competition again! Think the same thoughts, get the same results.

Never change a winning game, always change a losing game.
Think the same thoughts, get the same results.
If you think the way you’ve always thought,
you’ll get what you’ve always got.

Tunnel Vision

To perform at their best, athletes often talk about developing tunnel vision in the moments before competition. Steve Redgrave says, “You’re in your own little world before and during the race. If you can hear people in the crowd you’ve lost it.” The focus helps avoid distractions and keeps an athlete “in a positive state of mind” or “in the zone” as athletes call it. When you are focusing all your power and effort in achieving one big momentary challenge like a match, an Olympic final, a firewalk, or a business deal you are aware of the challenges on the outside but your mind and body are focused on success on the inside. Nothing can stop you.

Get into your world. Get into your zone.
Get into your winning mentality.

Night Vision

I have attended a few important interviews over the years and two of them occurred after I had discovered the power of positive thinking and visualisation. I really feel very strongly that my success was helped substantially if not completely by using visualisation. In an interview it is not just a great performance from myself that I need to be successful, I also need to influence the interviewer into deciding I am the person for the job. This 'night vision' technique has worked wonders for me.

People are most open minded when their (open minded) subconscious is most active and their (closed minded) conscious is least active. Everyone has an active subconscious when they are relaxed or sleeping. It's called dreaming! Therefore one of the best times to influence someone is when you know they will be asleep. Like any visualisation (movie) you are the director and can create/direct a movie with the other person doing exactly what you want. Before you go to sleep tell yourself "I will wake up when X is open to directing." Go to sleep and when you wake, sit up and direct your movie! Have the chat and listen to what they have to say and then get your way. It works wonders! It's not cheating, any more than someone attempting to enhance their chances with nice clothes, cologne or cleavage. You can't get someone to do anything they don't want with directing. Therefore Night vision is not a guarantee. It works some of the time, not all the time.

If you want to influence someone go to bed with them in mind,
affirm you will wake up when they are 'open minded'
and when you wake up direct them.

Go for Gold

In the 2004 Olympics in Athens cyclist Chris Hoy won Gold with an amazing performance in the 1km event. Hoy used visualisation. Chris Hoy is covered in further detail later.

If you do some Olympic thinking, you will get some Olympic results.

Visualising Goals

When you set a goal you will visualise the goal. Show your mind an image of your goal and it will help you get there. Successful goal setting involves regular 'views' of a physical or mental picture of your goal. Winners are visionary goal setters. They have a picture in their mind of where they are going.

Winners have a vision of their goal.
Winners know where they are going.
Visualisation and goal setting are the same thing!

Perfect practice makes perfect performance
When you watch a sports person give a great performance and they 'make it look easy' it is likely that they have been practising, competing and "doing it for years." American coach Don Shula is the most successful NFL coach of all time and he says "Practice does not make perfect. Perfect practice makes perfect." One way to practise perfectly is in the mind. Creating a full 'Mental movie' from start to finish will not only ensure a wonderful performance but will also build confidence. It worked for Ali and may other sport heroes. Create a 'Mental Movie' of yourself giving an amazing and impossible performance.

Picture perfectly in the mind to create a perfect performance.
Anything is possible.
No one is perfect all the time and positive winners accept that.

Winners can make a perfect performance. But it's not luck.

"The more I practice, the luckier I get." – Gary Player, legendary golfer

Perfectionists are not winners
There are few sports where a perfect performance is required to win. Winners in most sports make mistakes but they still win. They get over it! The winners in golf, tennis, football and snooker will all make mistakes. But they give the best performance. Winners in businesses make mistakes. They get back up! They get over it!

If you make a mistake get over it!
Winners make mistakes. They get back up!

Healthy movie, healthy body
In times when you are not in 100% health, building a picture in your mind of your body 100% healthy is one of the most effective ways to return your body to perfect health. Use visualisation for healing, building and slimming.

Mental Movies can heal your body.

Visualise better
If you are ill or injured you can heal yourself and improve yourself using visualisation. Through visualisation you can actually improve when you go back to perform. The UK's top Javelin thrower got injured in the run up to a summer full of competitions. He lay in his hospital

bed and imagined himself throwing in every stadium in Europe. He came back and achieved throws further than he had before his injury.

Your doctor, drugs, plaster or plaster cast don't repair your body. It's your mind and body that repairs your body.

Coma Come Back

A business contact of mine had an unexpected heart attack and was taken to hospital. The news was not good. A couple of my 'open minded' clients and a few others I contacted (who believed in the power of the mind) created a 'healthy mental movie' of him. Only two of us had actually met him and knew what he looked like, so the rest 'made it up'. Did it make a difference? Maybe. He recovered. However, he only survived a few days in hospital, which he spent with his wife and family before he died. He was a very heavy smoker and it was a big heart attack. I think 'mental movies' can help people improve health even from so called 'terminal' illnesses but there will be some people where it's not possible.

It is possible to do a 'mental movie' for anyone you know wherever they live. The more you love them, the more it seems to work. Whether it is a 'cold' or a coma, mental movies will make a difference and help most people.

You can create a mental movie of a friend to improve their health.

Healing power

Dr Andrew Weil author of '8 Weeks to Optimum Health' is another visualisation fan and advocate and states in his book, "In my experience no part of the body or disease process is beyond the reach of these approaches. In some cases, visualisation can produce complete healing responses; in others, it can boost the effectiveness and mitigate the toxicity of conventional therapies."

Slam Dunk

You can also use visualisation for slamming! Basketball slamming that is. Several years ago Reader's Digest included the results of an experiment carried out with a high school group of students. They tested their skill at throwing a basketball through the hoop and split them into three groups of similar ability. They got one group to practise free throwing every day for one hour for a month. One group to do no practice for a month and the third group to practice throwing 'free throws' in their mind for one hour a day for a month.

The group of students who practised with a ball improved by two percent (on average). The group who didn't practise worsened by two percent. The group who practised with their mind improved three and a half percent! Visualisation improved performance seventy five percent better than just physical practise. Imagine if you did both. Use your imagination. It works wonders.

Visualisation helps improve any skill.

Jack Nicklaus

When World Champion Jack Nicklaus talks it's worth listening. Jack revealed one of the techniques he used before competitions. Whenever he was flying in to take part in a competition he would visualise the round in his mind before he got off the plane. Sitting down relaxed is a great time to visualise success in the mind. It was obviously successful for Jack, have a look at his unbeaten records sometime! It worked wonders!

When a winner talks, listen!

Visualisation has major benefits: it helps win major tournaments.

Visualisation is the preparation of champions.
Are you preparing for success?

Be 'in' the movies

Mohammed Ali said, "The fight is won away from the ring." What is he getting at? Preparation! Here is how a winner prepares: Ali revealed that he put his success down to creating in his mind what he called his 'Future History'. In other words, creating a 'mental movie' of himself winning the fight in his mind, which he did after he signed the contract for each fight (a contract was signed several months before a fight). But he didn't call it a 'mental movie' he called it Future History! What a great name to use. It's like he was telling himself "This is the way I will win the future fight and create history!" How's that for solid positive belief! Ali used the same technique and had the same winning belief before every fight. Even when no one else shared his same belief (no one thought he was going to win 'Rumble in the jungle'). He didn't just create short 'highlights' of his Future fight. Ali would find some peace and quiet, relax himself, and picture the entire fight, which is why he used to predict which round he would knock his opponent out in. Not only that but he used all his senses and put himself into the ring and lived it. He said he could hear the crowd, feel the punches, smell the atmosphere and taste the sweat. It worked wonders.

Create a Be movie. Be in it: see it, feel it, hear it, smell it and taste it.

Relax and start directing

As Mohammed Ali and Jack Nicklaus have proved it's not just what you do but how you do it. Both of them were relaxed when doing their

visualisation and they visualised their whole performance. Two important considerations if you are looking for champion success.
Why? (What a great question to ask- I always do)
Visualising when you are relaxed is more powerful than when we are not relaxed.
Why? (What an interesting question to ask!)
Because you have two minds. I hope someone else has broken that news to you before! Otherwise take a deep breath and keep reading. As you now know you have two minds: the conscious mind is the one you use to make decisions (which I'll call the 'manual' mind) and the big subconscious mind is the one that automatically stores skills like talking, eating, walking which we can do without thinking (I'll call it the 'automatic' mind). There is two sides to the conscious mind: left for logical thinking and right for creative thinking. During the day 'manual' mind is dominant with left sided thinking and the 'automatic' mind is working in the background. Unless you have a 'creative' job like an artist, cook or child minder!

The conscious and subconscious in action
Using your 'manual' mind you will think about what to wear in the morning (decisions, decisions!), meanwhile 'automatic' is balancing you on one leg to get your socks on (which is one of many 'learned habits' in your memory), keeping you breathing (which is a 'born habit') and guiding your hands with the shoes laces (another 'learned habits' –clever aren't you!). That was easy wasn't it! Even the automatic brushing of teeth every morning and eating breakfast, lunch at 12 and dinner at 6 are learnt habits (digesting the food is a habit we are born with!).

The power of your subconscious mind
Therefore if we want to show our 'automatic' subconscious mind how to do something we can either do it over and over again or we can visualise it (like the basketball playing students). Visualisation is better! Doing both are brilliant!

Automatic habit
Winning habits become automatic after 30 days. It takes discipline to adopt a new habit. Just like when you first started brushing your teeth. A bit of discipline and reminders from your parents helped you make it automatic.

Winning Habits
Set yourself the BIG goal of adopting Winning Mentality within 30 days and mark your calendar to check. Re-visit your goals every month.

Picturing it and Doing it
Ali and Nicklaus do both! They practise and visualise before they compete. Although they were not learning a new skill, they were showing their subconscious mind how they wanted the body to perform (a brilliant winning performance). Each challenge was 'new' so it was necessary to 'direct' a movie in the mind to 'direct' the body on how they wanted it to behave. It worked wonders for them! It can work wonders for you.

Visualisation shows your mind what you want to do.
It listens better when you're relaxed!
Visualising while relaxed is very very powerful.
Make a habit of visualising winning and you'll make a habit of winning.

ACTION!
Picture your goals
Imagine that your car and your mind need to know exactly where you are going. Setting a goal is not enough. They need a picture of it (like looking for a lost dog). Looking at a picture everyday is great and effective (you know that now). However, a mental movie with you experiencing it is even better (Ali proved that). This is where you will use your imagination to picture the Top 7 goals in your mind. Imagine sitting in your car and let the top open up and windscreen drop down. Watch your mental movie on a big outdoor screen! It is more effective if you are physically relaxed and preferably seated doing long visualisations. Closed eyes seems to work best when visualising for a few minutes but open is effective, especially quick mental movies. Take a few minutes to go through each goal. If you are sitting comfortably then begin!
GO!

Top 1%
That exercise is effective. The more often you go through that exercise the more effective it becomes. You should 'watch' quick mental pictures of your goals every day. 'Watch' a full mental movie of your top goal every day and top 7 every month.'

Winners have winning habits. Visualisation is not a one off.
Winners are visualising on and off everyday.

Winning Habit
Visualise before you take action. This is a winning habit. Use it and you won't lose it. Visualise at the start of everyday and get everyday success.

Verbalise everything to succeed at everything.
Visualise your goals for success.

Habit of losing

Some people are very successful at losing and make a habit of it! You can almost bet on it! They must repeatedly be doing 'something' to have such great success at losing. Most of the golfers, athletes and teams I come across who are losing are losing so successfully because they do the opposite of a winner. They have got losing mentality!

Losing is easy. Do the opposite of a winner. Adopt losing mentality.

The Losing Mentality

When sports people don't follow the 'Winning Mentality' techniques or 'do the opposite' they lose. One of the common mistakes golfers make (and many business people too) is negative visualisation.

Worrying mentality is the opposite of winning mentality!

Negative Visualisation

Golfers are great at negative visualisation. When they have a green fairway ahead of them on the right but a lake to the left of them, they picture their ball landing in the lake! They focus on the trouble not the target! And it lands them in trouble! In the lake! The golf ball is like a magnet to the visualisation. Your mind wants to play 'snap' and match your thoughts to your results. Your fantasy to your reality. Look at the road ahead, not the obstacles ahead. Visualise succeeding, not failing.

If you visualise negative, your results are negative!
Focus on the target not the trouble.
Then you will avoid any trouble.

Are you visualising failing?

Do you use negative visualisation? When you think about the day ahead do you think about what may go wrong or what may go right. If you focus on the trouble not the target it lands you in trouble! Your future results will match your past visualisations. Your mind wants to play 'snap' and match your thoughts to your results. Your fantasy to your reality. Look at the road ahead, not the obstacles ahead. Visualise succeeding, not failing.

Worriers

Visualisation is very powerful as already demonstrated. Worrying is negative visualising. Which is why worrying works well! But visualisation is not 100% guaranteed. It doesn't always succeed in making the disasters or problems you visualised occur. However, even if worrying isn't successful it can still successfully give you an ulcer, headache or sleepless night! People are often happy and relieved when worrying works because they were right! The ulcer was worth it.

Negative mental movies (sometimes called worrying!) work well!
Avoid negative mental movies and avoid the negative results
(and the ulcers!)

Negative thinking is negative visualising
A picture speaks a thousand words. A few words create a picture ("pile of rubbish"). So negative thinking is a form of negative visualising.

I bet
Golfers often worry before they take a shot e.g. "I bet I hit that tree/ bunker/ pond" (insert any hazard here!). Those negative words create a negative picture in your mind. Does it work, you bet. Your mind wants you to achieve your verbal and visual goals, so your ball hits the tree! Bingo, it works. A negative visualisation like "I don't want to hit the tree" would work just as well!
If you want to avoid the tree, avoid talking or thinking about the tree! "I want to hit the green/fairway/flag!" works better. Positive mental movie picture!

Negative words create a negative mental movie and it works well!
Avoid negative words and negative mental movies
and avoid the negative results.

Negative Goal
Negative thinking and negative visualising are negative goal setting. What happens when you visualise what you don't want? You land in the lake! What happens when you order what you don't want? You hit the tree!

Negative thoughts, goals and pictures in the
mind give negative results.
Avoid negative mentality and you avoid negative results.
Be careful what you think about. Think about it.
Order what you <u>want</u>, not what you <u>don't want</u>!

Annual Accident
This story may make you laugh but if you were the person in the story you'd cry. A woman I know crashed her car a year ago and replaced the car with a nice new MG, which actually meant she achieved one of her goals - own an MG. So there was a silver lining in the cloud. However, just before the one-year anniversary of her MG purchase she thought to herself "I'm doing well, I haven't crashed my car yet." The following morning as she was carrying out a difficult reverse manoeuvre in her MG, she said to herself "I'm going to crash my car."

Bingo, it worked. She reversed into a pillar damaging her rear bumper. Negative thinking works!

Negative thinking works! Not all the time, but most of the time!

Redundant thinking

A local business woman had lunch with me to discuss her company and discuss mine. After a brief chat the women had clearly understood my business and told me that her sister was a negative thinker. She explained that she had been this way for years. Amazingly her sister had recently been made redundant... for the third time! I was not that surprised (I didn't drop my fork). I know how amazingly powerful and successful positive or negative thoughts can be! Her sister's negative thoughts and worrying worked.

Here's a wild guess at her sisters thinking process (but wildly accurate I'm sure). The first time she was made redundant she got a second job but worried about 'redundancy' happening again. Bingo, the worrying (negative thinking) worked. The second time she was made redundant she got another job but worried it would happen again. Bingo, the worrying worked. Negative thinking works. Not all the time, just three times in a row!

Worrying works! Avoid it.
Avoid any negative thinking!

Everyday is a Great day to be alive

I know of several people who have been through redundancy and have gone onto bigger and better things. Most took the opportunity to follow their dream and set up their own company. What's the lesson? We are in control of our thoughts - think positive (even in a 'negative' situation!). We are in control of our future- choose it. There is a positive way to look at every situation. I became good friends with my mailman in Perth, Australia and EVERYDAY regardless of bad weather or problems when I asked him "How are you?" he told me "Great day to be alive!" Great attitude. Great minds think alike.

"Great day to be alive!" – Johnny Conway

There is no such thing as a bad day just the wrong attitude.

There is a positive way to look at every situation.
It's better for your health and your future wealth.

If you can't see a positive make one up.
You'll feel better and you could come up with a great idea.

Redundancy can be an opportunity to progress yourself or depress yourself. You choose.

"There is no such thing as bad weather just the wrong clothes." – Billy Connolly

"Nothing happens by chance. We are a part of a universe that is forever giving us definite messages and signals, often in the form of problems. It is not an accident or coincidence that a particular problem is happening to you at a given point in your life; our difficulties are signposts waiting to be read. There are no such thing as problems, only opportunities." -John Kehoe, 'Mindpower'

There is a solution to everything

If you have got a 'challenge' solve it or sleep on it. Use your passengers and your future self. Challenges are great for growing! There is a solution to everything. Every positive and successful person I know and have met will tell you the same thing.

"There is a solution to everything."
–Sir Chris Evans, Millionaire Entrepreneur
When you overcome a big challenge you grow bigger.

Sweet Dreams

Martin Tosh is the Technical Manager in Asia for electronics company Pure Digital. He told me, "When I was working in London the last train I could get home was 11.30 at night. I was working on a problem all day. I couldn't come up with a solution and got the last train home. I had some random dream and came up with a solution! If I'd had a car I would have kept working instead of catching the train." It was a productive nights sleep. (Instead of an unproductive nights work.)

Sleep is good for solving problems and 'dreaming up ideas'.
The subconscious mind is working when you are sleeping.
It's the part of the mind that's keeps you breathing when you asleep.

Everything happens for a reason

There is a lesson in everything. There is a lesson in positive and negative experiences. There is a lesson in people you like and people you hate. The people you most want to change hold a lesson for you. Everything is your teacher. The teacher arrives when the student is ready. I remember being disappointed by the actions of a colleague and then later that night realising I can sometimes be like that as well.

There are 'great teachers' outside books, coaches, lectures and training.

Great teachers are: life, success, failure, problems, kids, history, war, music, quotes, movies, sport, nature, animals, travelling, great people and people you love and hate.

The teacher arrives when the student is ready.

You have no friends, no enemies, only teachers.

You meet people for a season, a reason or a lifetime.

Winners believe in destiny. Winners believe that everything happens for a reason. Every experience and person you meet helps you on your path to your destiny.

"I think he was sent to give me a message:
Don't become an unhappy lonely millionaire."
-Stephen Burt, Founder, Motion Software, who believes he got a timely 'message' from meeting an unhappy lonely millionaire

Everyday is a school day

Your 'teacher' can be a positive or negative experience, a book, a quote, a person or anything. It is only your teacher if you have chosen to learn from it. The teacher arrives when the student is ready. On the path to your dream and greatness you will meet many teachers. Everyday is a school day for a winner. Carry an 'L' plate with you everyday. Visually place it on your car!

Winners learn their lessons. They learn from their 'teachers', which come in many forms. If they make a mistake, where appropriate, they learn from them. Losers don't learn.
They make the same mistakes over and over.

"You will learn lessons. You are enrolled in a full-time informal school called "Life on Planet Earth." Every person or incident is the Universal Teacher. There are no mistakes, only lessons. A lesson is repeated until learned. Others are only mirrors of you. You cannot love or hate something about another unless it reflects something you love or hate in yourself. Your life is up to you. Life provides the canvas; you do the painting. Take charge of your life or someone else will."- Dr. Cherie Carter-Scott 'The Rules for being Human'

'It was a great surprise to me when I discovered that most of the ugliness I saw in others, was but a reflection of my own nature.'

Negative experience again and again

If a person has one negative experience and 'reviews' the negative experience in their mind again, the experience will repeat itself again.

A sports person may do negative visualisation before playing someone who beat them previously. This will 'help' them get beat again! When sports teams do it the opposition become a 'bogie team' and the negative thinking occurs before every game. The same can be said for a golfer who has one bad experience with a course/club/hole. They start to think negatively before a future experience, so they get a negative result! It's all in the mind.

A businessperson may do negative visualisation before presenting to a potential customer who turned them down before. Negative visualisation will work most of the time!

"Winning is a habit. Unfortunately, so is losing." - Vince Lombardi

If negative thoughts are repeated, negative experiences are repeated.

"A lesson is repeated until it is learnt." – Dr Cherie Carter -Scott.

Your current reality was created from your past thoughts and actions.
Your future reality comes from your current thoughts and actions.
Choose positive thoughts and actions.

"I can predict the future. There will be opportunities and difficulties. Sometimes there are more difficulties than opportunities. Sometimes there are more opportunities than difficulties. " - Jim Rohn

There are no problems, only challenges and opportunities.

Disney had a negative start

Walt Disney set up his first company Laugh-O-gram in May 1922 and was bankrupt in 1923! In 1923 he set up Disney Brothers Studio with brother Roy with $200 Roy had saved, $3,000 borrowed from family and for which they had to mortgage their house. Created Oswald the Lucky Rabbit in 1926, which was a great success, and in 1927 he went to New York to secure a new deal for the cartoon. He was told he didn't own the rights to the cartoon and was asked to work for the sneaky business man who did. He refused. Before getting on the train with his wife back to Los Angeles Walt sent his brother Roy a telegram: "LEAVING TONIGHT STOPPING OVER KC ARRIVE HOME SUNDAY MORNING SEVEN THIRTY DON'T WORRY EVERYTHING OK WILL GIVE DETAILS WHEN ARRIVE -- WALT" Walt didn't want to tell his brother the real story but as you can see was very positive considering what had happened. It's not what happens to you, it's what you think about it and do about it. What did Walt do? He dreamed up the idea of Mickey Mouse on the way home! At first Walt thought he'd call his new creation Mortimer. But his wife Lilly didn't like that name. "How about Mickey?" she asked. He took her advice!

Necessity is the mother of invention and motivation!

Disney Brothers lost the rights to best idea.
Lucky Walt Disney was positive!

"Every adversity, every failure, and every heartache, carries with it the Seed of an equivalent or greater Benefit." --Napoleon Hill

It's not what happens to you, it's what you <u>think</u> about it and <u>do</u> about it.

Your thoughts and actions create your destiny.
YOU are in control of your destiny. You can decide your destiny.
Achieving your dream is a choice.

"Once you embrace unpleasant news not as a negative but as evidence of a need for change, you aren't defeated by it. You're learning from it."
Bill Gates, 'Business @ The Speed Of Thought' (1999)

Positive people are lucky
Remember the four tips to be lucky;

1. Maximise chance opportunities
2. Listen to your intuition
3. Be Positive
4. Put bad experiences into perspective (Be Positive!)

Things could be worse.
Always look on the bright side.
Every cloud has a silver lining.

"When one door closes another door opens; but we so often look so long and so regretfully upon the closed door, that we do not see the ones which open for us." -Alexander Graham Bell, Invented telephone at 29, set up Bell business at 30

Lucky Golfer
Have you heard about the Ryder Cup scandal? Golfer Sergio Garcia used a 'performance enhancer' during the Ryder Cup. He also gave one to Lee Westwood and Darren Clarke. However, the players cannot be banned from golf, because the 'performance enhancers' are not actually illegal for golfers to use. They are called 'lucky charm bracelets'! Garcia said, "They're blessed by monks who made them and are very popular in the part of Spain where I come from. I've been wearing one since just after the Masters in April and my fortunes have definitely improved. Golfers are superstitious people and if you believe

something will help it can make you feel more positive. It is like an extra special ingredient."

After the US Masters Sergio Garcia won two US Tour competitions... and one Ryder Cup!

Some golfers are superstitious people.

Lucky or positive?
What does Fantastic Phil think about lucky golfer Garcia and his 'lucky charms'? I think the more positive you are, the more lucky you are! Many successful people I have talked to or studied have said, "I am lucky." Those that didn't said, "I am very lucky"! Or they mention hard work or destiny. However, few winners put luck as the essential ingredient to their success. Sport winners and Millionaires put 'luck' as being a small factor in their success because they know that it was the hard work that was the big factor! But I have not met a winner yet that wasn't positive! Even raffle winners!

You make your own luck. Be positive. Work Hard.
Take Opportunities.

Garcia became "more lucky" and successful after he began wearing the lucky charm because Garcia became more positive. I have worked with many golfers and business people and I've managed to improve their luck and improve their fortunes. How? By using their 'performance enhancing' mind! By getting my clients to think more positively and believe they are lucky: guess what? They get great results and lucky results! Like winning golf competitions and almost every raffle they enter!

If you think, "I am lucky!" you will be lucky.
You mind is a magnet to your thought and your beliefs.

The more positive you are the more "lucky" you are.

"I visualised myself winning something in the raffle and I did."
– Pat McNally

Superstitions are stupid
Am I the only one who laughs at superstitious emails? "Pass this email onto twenty people in the next twenty minutes and twenty pounds will appear in your pocket!" Yeah right. I love black cats, even on my path! Every day is great, even Friday the 13th! I don't touch wood and if I break a mirror - I laugh if it's mine and apologise if it's not! I get a new mirror and don't get a new future with seven years of bad luck! That is stupid! But if you think negative for seven years you're thoughts come true! The best one I heard was if you walk out the back

door of your house it's bad luck to go back in through the front door! It's not going to burn the house down - come on! I am a positive person. I've never had superstitions. I've always had common sense instead.

Don't take my word for it. If you don't believe me, test it! Go and get a mirror and break it and see how much friends, money and jobs you lose! None! (Unless it was not your mirror! You're friend won't be happy!)

It's not what you do it's what you think that's most important!
Seeing is believing.

Thankfully you don't just have to take my word for it. Professor Richard Wiseman has proved it as well. In his book 'The luck factor' Richard states, "Superstition doesn't work because it is based on out of date thinking." It comes from the dark ages! Literally! Is your thinking up to date or out of date? Are you in the dark ages? His evidence must convince you;

1. Survey of lucky people: they said they are not superstitious.
2. Survey of unlucky people: they said they were superstitious!
3. Study on effect of luck: black cats, white cats or no cats: no difference!

Just to recap: Superstitions don't work! Positive thinking does work! This book is full of stories and evidence to prove it! Or test it and prove it yourself! Or read Richards great book for yourself! Get a grip of superstitions. Be superstitious, be UNLUCKY. Be positive, be lucky!

"Superstition doesn't work because it is based on out of date thinking."
- Professor Richard Wiseman
The thing about common sense is it's not so common.
Use your common sense.

Intelligence is over rated. Common Sense is under rated.
I've met plenty of stupid smart people.

Not everyone uses the knowledge they have. Plenty of people smoke.
It's not just what you know, it's what you know and do.

Have you seen the email about Bill Gates giving you $300 if you forward an email? Yeah sure he does! That's how he became the richest man in the world -by paying people to do nothing!

"To be successful - Number 1 you need energy.
But first you need a brain." – Donald Trump

PS BUY 5 COPIES OF THIS BOOK AND PASS IT ONTO 5 PEOPLE IN THE NEXT 5 DAYS AND YOUR FRIENDS WILL BE VERY LUCKY FOR 5 YEARS AND YOU WILL BE VERY LUCKY FOR LIFE!

Very fast Summary

Winners visualise winning. And it works!
Visualisation is very powerful. The results can work in seconds or years.
Mental Movies are quick and cheap to create but give blockbuster results!
A mental movie is not a guarantee. You won't outrun a whippet. (Initially!)
Visualisation gives you power when you think you've got none left.
The business is won in the head not in the office.
Be positive. Be lucky. Be a winner.
If you do some Olympic thinking, you will get some Olympic results.
If you want to influence someone create a 'mental movie' while they sleep.
Mental Movies can heal your body and your friends.
Visualisation is the preparation of champions. Are you prepared?
If you visualise negative results, your results will be negative!
Focus on the target not the trouble and you will avoid any trouble.
Avoid worrying. It works!
Use your head. Use your common sense.

Create a mental movie before you start: you'll get a happy ending before you stop. Avoid negative words and mental movies and avoid the negative results.

Negative thinking works! Not all the time, but most of the time!

"It's not what happens to you, it's what you do about it." -W. Mitchell

Superstitions don't work! Positive thinking does work!
It's not what you <u>do</u> it's what you <u>think</u> that's most important!

"Superstition doesn't work because it is based on out of date thinking."
-Professor Richard Wiseman, 'The Luck Factor'

Everything happens for a reason.
The teacher arrives when the student is ready.

Winners learn their lessons. Losers don't learn.
They make the same mistakes over and over.
Winners visualise winning. And it works!

Winners have winning habits. Visualisation is not a one off.
Winners are visualising on and off everyday.

See success in your mind and you'll see successful results.
Attempt "impossible" things with "possible"
thoughts and you'll achieve them.

You are the director of your thoughts and the director of your future.

Chapter 4
Positive Verbalisation

Very Fast Summary

Positive thoughts and words (internal and external verbalisation) create positive results in sport and business, as well as building belief, which is powerful and works wonders. Negative verbalisation has the opposite affect.

Included in this chapter;

The power of positive thoughts and words.
Verbalising your goals.
Positive words create positive beliefs.
Positive eyes see differently from negative eyes.
The positive and negative voices in your head.
People with a positive mind are more lucky and healthy than negative people
Your mind affects your body and your body affects your mind
Your mind and mood is affected by what you see, hear, read, do, eat & think
Negative verbalisations.
Stopping negative thoughts.
Starting positive verbalisation.

Directing the future with your thoughts and words

Your mind can direct the future a bit like when a Hollywood director is shouting directions when creating a movie. This is the movie of your future history. Instead of visualising the future this time, this technique is about verbalising the future. Your thoughts or words will direct your future. Your thoughts will make things happen. Think positive thoughts, get positive results. Positive thinking works in many powerful ways. Your mind listens to your words and thoughts and brings you what you want, a bit like a magnet. Depending on my audience, I describe the mind as like a servant, genie, waiter, chef or even Santa! Say what you want and you will get it. Not all the time, but most of the time. It's not 100% guaranteed. These are just a few of the many stories I have to show you the power of verbalisation.

Be careful what you wish for. Wishing works.
Your mind will make your thoughts come true.

Think positive thoughts, get positive results.

You can direct the future with your thoughts and words

I'd like a job

Ron Davie is a senior oil executive who was not in employment for a few months in 2003. After hearing me give a talk he told me the story of how he got his current job. He told me he was walking along a city centre street in Aberdeen called Carden Place, which has a mixture of offices and homes on both sides. With the previous companies he'd worked for he had been located in the industrial estates on the outskirts of Aberdeen City centre. Walking along the street he thought to himself, "I'd like to get a job in offices on this street." A few weeks later he did. Bingo, he got what he wished for. Wishing works wonders.

What do you want? Think about it.
Positive thoughts get positive results.

Say what you want and you get it.
Not all the time, but most of the time.

"Make the name Disney famous around the world."
-Walt Disney's goal when he set up 'Disney Brothers Studio' with brother Roy

Wishful thinking Kid

Kids make lots of wishes. Some come true (see Chapter on Goals). Some don't come true (see Chapter on Ingredients of Success). When Steve Redgrave was growing up, his house was a short distance from the letterbox and it was his responsibility to collect the mail and newspaper every day. One day during the Olympics in 1978 he picked up the paper and saw the headline 'Spitz for Six'. It was the story of USA swimming sensation Mark Spitz heading for his sixth gold medal. Steve thought to himself "I'd like to do that. I'd like to win a gold medal." Bingo, he did. He got what he wished for. I am sure Steve Redgrave was not the only person who wished for it, but I'll bet he was the only person who worked for it.

Children wishing rarely works because the dreaming stopped and the action never started.

Kids who have a wish and keep dreaming, grow up and keep believing, take action and keep going: go on to achieve what they believe. Like Steve Redgrave.

Will Power

Will power is stronger than wish power. Wishing starts your mind working and willing starts your mind believing. Belief is very powerful. Willing is a very powerful way of thinking. Your powerful thoughts make great things happen. Positive verbalisations are a bit like a director directing a movie saying to the future "I want this, I will do this, they will do that." You write the script for your future. Your mind directs the future like a director directs a movie. What do you want to happen on this shot/ competition / match/ sale/ presentation/ day/ week? The golfers I coach are encouraged to positively verbalise using 'will power' before playing a shot e.g. "This will go in the hole" and it works wonders! Willing is stronger than hoping or wishing. Golfers have amazed themselves when they have used this technique. From the tee to the hole they will 'direct' what the ball is going to do. Just using this tool I have seen golfers hole amazing putts.

You write the script for your future. Positively direct your future like a director shouting directions on a movie.

"Great things are not something accidental, but must certainly be willed."
--Vincent van Gogh (1853-1890) Dutch painter, worked as art salesman for 7 years before working full time on his dream

Positive verbalisation

A few words create a simple picture. Positive verbalisation can become positive visualisation, as covered in the Visualisation Chapter. The following two stories on positive verbalisation create positive pictures in the mind.

Successful Parking and Successful Shopping
One of my clients found herself on a typical Saturday with lots to do and little time to do it. One of the tasks was to go to the shops, find a birthday present for her daughter's friend and then drop her daughter off at a party. Time was short and as she drove into the city centre out of necessity she practised some very positive thinking. She said loudly, "We will find a parking space. We will find a present quickly." Bingo, it worked. She got what she wished for.

Things will go your way if you will them.
Very positive verbalisation works wonders.
A successful day comes from willing it that way.

This is in the hole
When teaching positive verbalisation to golfers I get them to verbalise the shot they want before they play it. "This is in the hole" works wonders!

This is gonna be my day
American Golfer Phil Mickelson won the US Masters in 2004 and one of the things he said he repeated to himself on the final day in his final round of the competition was "this is gonna be my day." Positive verbalisation! Bingo it worked. He made a come back in the final 9 holes shooting an awesome score! Keep believing and you'll keep achieving.

Winners have a goal.
Verbalisation and goal setting are the same thing!

Winners keep believing, even when they are behind,
so they keep achieving.

"I kept saying to myself the whole way round
'This is gonna be my day.'"
-American Golfer Phil Mickelson, Winner of US Masters 2004

Will the wave
World Champion Surfer Kelly Slater is the best surfer of all time. He has had more success in competitions over the years than any other surfer. The way surf competitions work is that each surfer has a set period of time in which to complete their 'ride' of a wave and get judged and marked. Therefore surfers rely on big waves being available in their time zone. They sometimes find themselves running out of time with the sea almost flat and no big waves to ride on. But Kelly Slater thinks differently from most other surfers and gets different results (high level of success!). How does he do it? He revealed the following secret, which I read. When he is lying on his board in the water and

can see no big waves coming, he said, "I will it in my mind and I don't know how but it always seems to work."

Use your mental will power.
Make orders in your mind of how you want it to happen.

Verbalisation orders are transmitted by the Mind
Positive verbalisation power comes from the mind hearing our words or 'hearing' our thoughts in our head and 'transmitting' the orders out into the world and making them happen. Whether it is getting a job in an Office in Aberdeen or 'creating' a parking space in a shopping centre. Relevant orders are transmitted to the body, such as getting the ball in the hole or getting the body slim! Positive verbalisations use the mind's incredible power. They work wonders.

Verbalisation orders are transmitted by the Big Subconscious Mind
Positive verbalisations have incredible power

Think 'I can' (you're right!)
When winners speak, listen up! Especially if it's a daring positive thinker who changed the world like Henry Ford. His most famous quote should be printed on t-shirts and given to every baby born. By the time they get to reading age they will have done 3 "impossible" things: walking, talking and riding a bike! It's down hill from there without positive parents, positive thinking and positive daring! If most of us had to learn walking, talking or riding as an adult we'd give up!

You are already an amazing winner.
You can talk, walk and ride a bike!
If we had to learn to walk, talk or ride a bike as an adult we'd give up!
"If you think you can, you can.
If you think you can't, you're right."- Henry Ford

Anything is possible
You can achieve amazingly difficult "impossible" things like walking, talking and riding a bike if you think it's possible! 'Impossible' is possible if you don't give up.

"There's not much use in trying", said Alice. "One can't believe impossible things." "I dare say that you haven't had much practice", said the Queen. "Why sometimes, I've believed as many as six impossible things before breakfast."
'Alice In Wonderland' by Lewis Carroll (1865)

Mind Moves Machine
I have a lot of respect and admiration for mind expert Derren Brown whose programme 'Mind Control' features on Channel 4 Television. I

love to watch him and the members of the public he involves in his experiments and demonstrations. One particularly amazing demonstration was at a racetrack. Derren approached a man after a race had been completed and found the man had not won (he wasn't jumping around so it was a give away!). Derren asked if he could have his losing ticket. The man agreed. Derren went up to the bookie inside the Racetrack gave the ticket to the teller behind the glass and said "This is the winning ticket." She put the ticket through the machine and the machine paid out! The man was stunned and couldn't believe it. Using another losing ticket Derren told him how to do the same. He said to hand the ticket over to the woman and say, "This is the winning ticket" and slap the counter. He did and it didn't work. Then Derren stepped forward beside him and said, "This is the one you're looking for" and slapped the protective glass. It worked. The machine paid out. Positive verbalisation gets results, even with machines. I've used it on cars and computers and it works. It still amazes me when I get things working for others using it. (They wouldn't believe me if I told them how I do it). Can you believe it?

Positive verbalisation can get machines to work for you.

Every day and in every way I get better and better

Emile Coue's became well known as one of the first medical practitioners to use the mind to cure his patients. He carried out his own experiment. He gave one group of patients their medicine as normal. He asked a second group of patients to repeat what he called an 'affirmation', when they took their medicine. Every time they took their medication they had to say "Everyday and in every way I get better and better." He discovered that all the patients whom he had asked to do this got better. But only some of those whom he had just given medicine to got better. He then carried out an experiment to give patients a placebo as medication (a placebo is a pill with nothing in it) along with the affirmation and found that all his patients got better even without real medication. Positive verbalisation works wonders!

'Everyday and in every way I get better and better'

Positive verbalisation for other people

I was delighted to come across research about a year ago that studied the health of patients in hospital. A number of people were asked to pray for certain patients, unbeknown to the patients. The research found that the health of the patients who were getting prayed for improved quicker than other patients, who were not being prayed for! Everything is energy. You don't need to live in London to hear the BBC World Service on Radio. You don't need to go to a football stadium to be able to see the match on television. Transmitters will send the waves and your receiver will pick it up. Your mind can send and receive thoughts like a "walkie talkie." A thought is like an energy wave that you can send to anyone.

Positive verbalisation or visualisation for other people works wonders!

Positive thoughts make people positive mentally and physically.

Giving someone unwell a positive comment like "You are unbreakable. You'll bounce back into shape like a spring!" will help them get well.

A positive comment like 'Have a great day!'
will help people have a great day!

Something wonderful will happen today

In 2002 I heard of someone who put a framed sign in their house, which read, "Something wonderful is about to happen"! Aware of the power of positive thinking I realised what a great idea it was. Inspired I put up a sign outside my office door, which read 'Something wonderful will happen today'. (I was in Australia at the time - you get away with those types of things with those types of people - if I had worked in some UK companies they would have called an ambulance!) The sign stopped everyone walking past! "When is it gonna happen?" they asked. The smiles themselves would have justified the exercise. But I knew it would work and felt it was working for me. My eyes were always 'looking' for the wonderful in my day as well as 'willing' it. Inspired a positive open-minded colleague put the same sign outside his office as well.

Get up some signs to will yourself some great moments;
Something wonderful is about to happen!
Something wonderful will happen today!
One idea can change your life.

Today will be a great day

I was giving advice to an entrepreneur client about positive thinking at the start of the day and how it makes a difference to success and results during the day. I mentioned the various ways I thought positively at the start of every day and mentioned, "Something wonderful will happen today." He told me that he already used a similar technique that he found worked for him. Every morning he goes into the bathroom and looks in the mirror and says, "Today will be a great day!" It works wonders. I was already using the bathroom mirror for another fantastic habit (mentioned in the next chapter) and verbalising 'wonderful days' but I liked his idea and copied it.

Have a good day;
Say, "Today will be a great day!" in the mirror every morning!

Create your own horoscope

Horoscopes work in the same way. If your horoscope says you are going to have a great day and you believe it, you'll achieve it! So feel free to create your horoscope everyday and it will work out that way. Have a lucky day! Have a funny day! Have a great day! Create your own day.

Create your own day: what kind of day are you "willing" to have?
Today will be lucky! Today will be a funny day!
Today will be a great day!

Are you having a laugh?

I spoke to a woman who was getting over a separation from her husband. After days of crying she got up one day and said "I'm going to laugh today, I'm not going to cry." She got her wish!

I'm going to laugh today

Positive verbalisation

Positive verbalisation can change your eyesight. If you said, "I'm going to laugh today" your mind will 'make that happen' by making things occur which make you laugh which would not have happened otherwise. However, your mind will also be 'looking for laughs' during the day. It's like when you're going on holiday you suddenly notice all the travel agents because your mind is on the look out for them!

Using your mind can change what your eyes 'spot'.

Setting goals puts the mind on the look out
and puts it into action to achieve that goal.

If you put your mind on the look out for a 'fun' day, it will spot lots of fun things. Some would have happened anyway but some 'fun' is made to happen by your mind and you have an even more 'fun day'!

There is a solution to everything. If you think there is.

ACTION!

Verbally direct your future

I want you to imagine you can positively direct your future like a director shouting directions on a movie. Imagine you are sitting in your car and on the movie screen ahead you can direct what you want to happen. A 'microphone and loud speaker' in the car will transmit the directions to the world. Take a moment now and verbalise your Top 7 goals. 'Will' your future with your Mindpower. Use positive verbalisation to 'direct' your future.

GO!

I WILL…….
I WILL…….
I WILL…….
I WILL…….
I WILL…….
I WILL…….
I WILL…….

You are in control of your thoughts and actions.
You are in control of your destiny.
You are the movie director of your future.

STOP

Verbalise your goals

Verbalise everything you do and you'll get success in almost everything you do. Verbalise at the start of each day when you write down your goals or think about your goals for the day. Adopt this habit in the shower and see your success transform. I use it in the shower and when writing down a goal in my notebook.

Verbalise everything you do and you'll
get success in almost everything you do.
You don't have to verbalise every goal,
just the ones you want to succeed.
Visualise or verbalise your goals for success.

Positive Attitude

If there is one thing that differentiates a winner from a loser it would be motivation. The second thing is positive attitude. You either have it or you haven't (and need to get it). Some people are more positive than others (and some people are more negative than others!). I did an exercise with a very positive and successful entrepreneur and he couldn't think of a negative thought! A positive attitude is important because it means a positive mind. A positive mind is important because it means positive thoughts and a positive vision (or positive glasses as I like to call it!). Winning mentality is more than just having a positive attitude. I have met plenty of people with a positive attitude that were not winning and were not winners. I should know I used to be one.

Winners have a positive attitude.
A positive attitude alone won't help you succeed.

Positive Mind: Positive Eyes

You need a positive mind to win. Your mind impacts in two ways. It affects your results and it affects your eyes. On the first point: a positive mind makes positive things happen and gives positive results. Not all the time, but most of the time.

However, a positive mind also affects your eyes. Having a positive mind is like having positive glasses on! If you have a positive mind you will spot 'the positives' as they happen during your day and remember them and will ignore most of the negative things. However, a negative mind affects your eyes and is like having negative glasses on. If you have a negative mind you will spot the negatives as they happen during your day and remember them and will ignore most of the positive things. Two people can look at a garden (or business) and see two different things: Mr Positive Mind sees the flowers; Mr Negative Mind sees the weeds.

When it comes to dreams or business opportunities a positive mind will be optimistic about it and have a positive vision. Whereas a negative mind is pessimistic and will have a negative rather than positive vision. Put these two people on a bare allotment and they see two different things: Mr Positive Mind sees the potential for flowers, Mr Negative Mind sees the potential for weeds. Negatives have no vision of it working out. They've got different glasses on! (A negative person won't change their negative glasses until they change their negative mind)

A positive mind is more likely to think positive thoughts. Positive people (with positive minds) are 'lucky' which helps success. Note; not all positive people believe in luck. So they're not very lucky! Positive minded people who believe in luck do very well because their mind is on the look out for 'lucky' opportunities, guiding them to make lucky intuitive decisions and attracting lucky events to them.

Having a positive mind is like having positive glasses on!
Your thinking affects your vision. Positive minds have positive eyes.
You need a positive mind to win.
Your mind affects your eyes and results.
Some people have no vision. Meet the negatives!
If you come across a NEG, run!

Positive minded people who believe in luck do very well because their mind looks for luck, guides towards luck and attracts luck.
Positive minded people who believe they will achieve goals, achieve goals, because their mind looks for ways to get to goals, guides towards goals and attracts their goals.

Positive minded people who believe it, achieve it.
Whatever those beliefs may be.
What your mind believes, your life achieves.

Different mind, different vision
Your thinking affects your vision. Positive people have a different vision from negative people. Entrepreneurs have a different vision from non-entrepreneurs. When I see a problem like litter, or kids hanging out on the street, I have a vision of a solution automatically. It took me a while to realise not everyone 'sees' the way I see.

A vision is something not everyone else can see.

Busy Boys
I remember seeing the headline in the local paper, 'Rampage by Vandals. It told of young adults who had damaged local businesses late on a Saturday night. Opposite the article was a picture of local Boy Scouts who had won prizes. I could 'see' both the problem and solution on the front page. But I don't think the editor could 'see' the same solution as me. If you find activities to keep kids' hands and heads busy, they won't have the time or inclination to 'rampage' and vandalise. It's cost effective.

How do you keep positive?
Everyone has a positive and negative voice. I'll tell you how to keep your positive mind and deal with the negative voice.

9 ways to feed the positive voice and keep a positive mind
1. Use positive words. Follow 'Winning Mentality'.
2. Surround yourself with a positive environment; pictures, quotes & mantras.
3. Surround yourself with positive people; family, friends, teachers
4. Find people better than yourself to work with, talk with or train with.
5. Watch great people. Watch, listen and learn. In person, TV, radio or tape.
6. Read inspirational and motivational material; books, stories and interviews.
7. Listen to uplifting music.
8. Relax your mind; a relaxed mind is more positive, creative and productive.
9. Eat healthy food and drink. Eating fruit and vegetables and a varied range of foods in moderate amounts is a good start. When it comes to nutrition, knowledge is power. So power up with some books.
9.5 Have a fit and healthy body; by doing some active exercise your mind produces endorphins and makes you feel good. Quality fresh air helps the mind operate effectively. Remember; Healthy body, healthy mind. A fit <u>and</u> healthy body means a fit and healthy mind. Fit means you can run, cycle, swim etc for 30 minutes. Healthy means your body is in good condition. (No use being fit and smoking, or being a healthy eater and unfit).

Food affects your mood.
Good food, good mood.
See positive, hear positive, read positive; feel positive.
Hear no negative, see no negative,
speak no negative; feel no negative!

I will
Decide now which of the above 9.5 tips you WILL start adopting;
GO!
I will...

Negative thoughts
Negative thoughts are a killer. Negative thoughts are the biggest 'killer' in the world. Negative thoughts kill dreams. Negative thoughts kill health, wealth, success and happiness. Negative thinking works!

The power of negative thoughts
If you are looking for the best way to be unsuccessful I can tell you the secret, start worrying! It works a treat. Negative thoughts work, just ask any golfer. When a golfer worries about hitting his ball 'out of bounds', into water or towards a bunker, you will find that's exactly where they hit the shot! Why? Negative thoughts are negative orders, which are carried out by the mind like a waiter. The golf ball is like a magnet to your negative thoughts. If you think negative before taking action in any sport or business you will get negative results too.

Your future is like a magnet to your thoughts.
If you think negatively before taking action
negative results are almost guaranteed.

Words draw a great picture
Your words create a picture in your mind. Golfers often worry before they take a shot e.g. "I don't want to put my ball into the bunker" but those negative words create a negative picture in your mind. Your mind can see you picturing the ball going into the bunker and it thinks that's your target, so that's where it aims your body and ball. Bingo, it works. In any sport or business if your negative words create a negative picture you will get negative results.

Negative words create negative pictures and
negative pictures get negative results.

Double negative

Two double negatives don't work. Even if you utter the instruction to your mind "I don't want to hit the ball into the bunker" the mind translates the words into a picture of the ball being hit into the bunker. The mind cannot create a reverse picture of the ball not going into the bunker! If you want the opposite you must visualise or verbalise the opposite! For example "I want to hit the ball onto the green grass!" Are you thinking about winning or not losing?

What are you aiming for? Where are your worries taking you?

Some worries don't work

Not all worries and negative thinking works. Most worries people have are about things well into the future and out of their control. Most never happen so the negative worrying was a waste of time.

Most worries never happen so the negative thinking is a waste of time.
Negative thoughts sometimes come true.
Be careful what you wish for.

Don't risk a negative thought

Don't let your mind feed on a negative thought. It's bad for your health and your wealth. Worriers could give you what you didn't want or an ulcer or both.

Worrying is bad for your health and your wealth.
Worrying is a waste.
Spending time worrying is the biggest waste of money in the world!

Negative Killer

I know a true story of a woman who had a friend that owned a motorbike. She knew that he would ride the bike quickly and out of concern and worry for him she would often attempt to encourage him to slow down and change him by saying, "You're going to kill yourself on that bike." I am sure other friends and family would also have had the same concern and maybe even said the same thing. He may even have worried about it himself. Even if he didn't, he had someone else planting the negative thought in his head. Sadly the man died in an accident on his bike. Negative thoughts may not have killed him but they wouldn't have helped him. Negative thoughts are a killer. Get them out your head. Don't let them leave your mouth. If you can't say anything positive, don't say anything. If you can't think of anything positive, don't think.

Negative words could kill people. Don't be a negative verbal killer.

If you can't think of anything positive, don't think.
If you can't say anything positive, don't say anything.

Negative words plant negative thoughts and grow negative results.

Hear no negatives, see no negatives and speak no negatives.

Negative Solider

I spoke to a well-known ex-SAS solider about positive thinking and 'luck'. Andrew Kain, founder of AKE told me "Some people seem to attract trouble. I remember a guy who was shot on his first tour in Northern Ireland. You had to be really unlucky to get shot in Northern Ireland especially on your first tour. On his second tour back after he had recovered he got killed. I used to avoid standing anywhere near people that attracted trouble."

Don't risk a negative thought. A negative thought can hurt you.
Negative thinking creates a negative future. Worrying works. Stop it.
If you meet a NEG run away!

Mr Excuses

B&Q is a successful DIY store in the UK. B&Q was founded by Mr B and Mr Q. They built the business up and when they floated the company on the stock market they became multimillionaires. They both left the company and went off to set up separate businesses. They both failed. Mr B blamed the product, the customers and the economy on the failure (but not himself). He spent all of his fortune on the failed business and the high life. He lost the lot and gave up being an entrepreneur. He withdrew from business with his tail between his legs and now works in health shop Holland and Barrett.

Mr Q was different. He took full responsibility, blaming himself and his product in-experience for his second business failing. He chose to take personal responsibility for the business failing and chose to learn from the experience. And he didn't give up! Mr Q then set up another business, Ritz video chain, which was a great success and he is currently very wealthy. Mr Excuses failed and Mr Responsibility succeeded. Take responsibility for yourself, your actions and your future.

You can take control (and take the blame) or you can lose control (and blame others). If you take control you keep your power or if you lose control you lose your power. Much like driving a car.

Blame gets you nowhere; responsibly gets you everywhere.
If you are looking for someone to blame, look in the mirror.
Take responsibility for yourself, your actions and your future.

Rise every time you fall. Think positively every time you think.
You only fail when you give up. You can't fail if you fail to give up!

"Never give in, never, never, never." – Sir Winston Churchill

The only thing that stops people succeeding is giving up.
You haven't failed. You just haven't succeeded yet.

A winner never comes up with excuses after failing, they get up and have another go.

Beware the loser disease 'excusitis'. It's easy to spot the symptoms – the person will always have a lot of excuses and people to blame for failing and they never look in the mirror.

The only cure to loser disease is to stop negative thinking, start positive thinking, stop blaming and start doing.

Blaming others is a hobby that gets you nowhere.
Taking action is a hobby that gets you somewhere.

Being negative is easy but useless.
Being positive is simple and useful.

It's easier to criticise others than to correct yourself.
It's easier to blame others than to help yourself.

I'll probably top this

Don't joke. A very good golfer was taking a shot near me and before he took his shot he joked "I'll probably top this" (which basically means, "I'll probably mess up!"). Bingo, he did! Your subconscious mind can't take a joke. Negative jokes give negative results. If you say, "I'm rubbish" even as a joke you will be. Your mind won't get the joke. Negative words and negative labels gives negative results, even if you are joking! If jokingly criticise other people and tell them "You're rubbish" they're mind won't get the joke either.

If you think you will, you will!
Your subconscious mind can't take a joke.
Negative words and negative labels give negative results, even if you are joking!

Beaten by Negative thinking

In the Athens 2004 Olympics, the badminton final of the mixed doubles was between World Champions China and wannabe's Great Britain who were seeded 4th and were not expected to reach the finals. Gail Emms and Nathan Robertson represented Great Britain in the final of the badminton mixed doubles to defending Olympic champions Jun Zhang and Ling Gao. The first game went 15-1 against them.

However, they never gave up and battled back to win 15-12. With a huge crowd behind them cheering them on they took the lead in the deciding game 11-8. But Goa and Zhang (who said he went into a "kind of trance" late in the match) came back to win 12-15. Nathan said, "Towards the end they were more positive." They weren't beaten by better players, they were beaten by positive thinking! However, he had not gone into the games expecting to win a medal. They were both seeded 4th and silver is a good result. He went on to say "We gave the performance of our lives. It's something that both of us have dreamed about since we were young. I think we lost control towards the end of the game. The last few points of an Olympic gold medal final are going to be the hardest points of your life. But we did fantastically to put ourselves in the position where we could have won gold." If you think 'it will be hard', it will be hard. Gail Emms said, "I was absolutely gutted. I hate losing. I forgot it was a gold medal match. I was just going out there to win." I think Gail had the better mental approach in the final but I'll let you make up your own mind.

Be a dreamer not a negative thinker.

Don't be beaten by negative thinking.
You don't want to be beaten by yourself!
Positive thinking can win a match.

Be so positive that you know you can only get beaten
by better bodies and not better minds!

Don't risk a negative thought. A negative thought can hurt you.

Negative voice- Giant Goliath

We all have a negative and a positive voice. But for many people the negative voice is big and loud like Giant Goliath and the positive voice is small and quiet like Little David. Your mind hosts a boxing match between the two 'voices' every day throughout the day and for many of us the Giant Goliath wins. If you fight back with positive giant knocking punches you can knock the giant negative voice down. But keep your catapult and positive punches ready.

Your mind hosts a boxing match between your
positive and negative 'voices' every day.

There are two types of people positive and negative.
Winners are always positive and losers are always negative.
Be one of the PEGS don't be one of the NEGS.

Who has been feeding the Giant?
You may be wondering how the giant got so big (how you got so negative or how your negative voice is so loud). Here are some of the possible answers below.

Who's been feeding your negative voice?
1. You: -
Every time you have a negative thought or say a negative word you are feeding your negative voice in your mind. But every time you have failed at something you've given your negative voice a banquet to feed on for weeks, months and sometimes years. Every time you have a great idea, negative thoughts will come to mind, which are unhelpful if you listen. Your job may make you negative. Have you got a 'negative thinking' job? Health and Safety managers, financial advisors and parents can become negative because they are always looking at risks, negatives and worse case scenarios. I know a positive accountant who left his job because he didn't like being negative during the week and only positive during the weekend (as a hockey coach). Indirectly (and probably unknowingly) you have contributed in other ways to feeding your negative voice. Most of the following 'negative voice foods' are within your control.
2. Your parents: -
Kids are very demanding. YOU were demanding growing up. Your parents had to say 'no' to you many times. So many times in fact that it's estimated you will hear the word 'no' around 100,000 times by the time you hit your late teens. I read a quote by a young mother recently say, "She's at the troublesome two's age. She cries every time I say no."
3. Other people: -
Teachers, friends, relations, shopkeepers have all given you their positive or negative opinion on everything. Unfortunately in the UK it's normally the latter.
4. Negative people: -
Negative people or "neg's" as I like to call them, are a dangerous human species growing in epidemic proportions. Because you have been unaware of the danger of getting too close to negative people you have done so and their negativity has infected you.
5. TV: -
Anything on TV between 5pm and 7pm must be avoided. News reports can have as many as nine negative news items and one positive report (this may be due to a questionable belief within media that negative news sells). Soaps on the other hand are written for dramatic effect and any story line will be exaggerated. Most story lines are negative (as TV production companies believe negative stories drive ratings). Therefore each episode will have more negative scenes than positive -the main reason to avoid soaps. Winners don't watch the

news or read the news. They make it. Avoid watching or listening or reading the news for a month. You will miss nothing. It will be the most positive and happy month of your life. Switch off the TV news and do something less boring instead. Read about a winner, watch a comedy or rent a movie. Anything positive, fun or relaxing!

6. Newspapers: -

Newspapers are Negative with a Capital N. Headlines; Crash! Murder! Disaster! Shock! Scandal! This may be due to the (questionable) belief held within the news media that 'negative news sells'. Why do you read it? How much do you get <u>paid</u> for reading the news? Or how much money do you <u>make</u> from reading the news? How many laughs do you get? Negative news makes you negative, kills your happiness, makes you depressed and increases your weight. Is it worth it? Ok, I'm joking it doesn't increase your weight but the rest is true (and you don't lose weight reading news!). It's a habit worth changing. Think about it. The sport and business pages can be inspirational and worth reading. But don't look at the front headlines! Ever. Avoid a newspaper for a month and read a positive book instead. I'm sure you'll see a positive difference (and miss nothing!) and adopt it for the rest of your positive life. Find out about the positive stories happening now or those from previous months and years (history). Invest your time, don't waste your time. Don't feed your mind with negative mental food.

7. Radio news: -

The radio doesn't play all your favourite songs, and contains lots of sad songs and sad news. Every hour on the hour it repeats the same negative news! If you listen in the morning it's not a great start to the day. If you work with the radio on all day you'll get filled with over an hour of negative news before you get home. Not the lift you need before you get into your home time / family time.

8. Stressed mind: -

By being stressed your mind is less resourceful, less energetic and less positive. Short periods of stress are ok, sometimes even good. Long periods stress us out.

9. Unhealthy food, drink and alcohol (stressful nutrition): -

Eating fatty, sugary and processed unhealthy food has a negative (stressful) effect on the mind and body, as does fizzy drinks and coffee. Alcohol is a drug and a known depressant. It is not the best thing in the world for your mind...ever. It is full of 'empty' calories with no energy and no nutritional benefit. Top athletes and winners avoid it when training. That's commitment and sacrifice for you. Good fuel improves the mind and body.

9.5 Stressed (unfit) body: -

Unhealthy body, unhealthy mind. Without some activity, exercise and fresh air the mind does not operate effectively, it operates negatively. Remember; healthy body, healthy mind.

Being a parent can be a negative thinking job!

Healthy body, healthy mind.
Negative food gives you a negative mind and body.
Negative mental food gives you a negative mind and body.

Everything you read, watch, hear, wear, say and do affects your mood.

There are two types of people; drains and radiators.
People who radiate energy and people who drain your energy.
If you meet a NEG run away! Escape from people who drain you!
Escape from BMW's; Bitchers, moaners and wingers.
Search for FORD's; Funny, optimistic, really enthusiastic and driven.

Positive people feed your energy, negative people eat your energy.

Winners don't watch the news or read the news. They make it.
Invest your time, don't waste your time.

Don't fill your mind with useless information.

Henry Ford testified in court that he didn't fill his mind with useless trivial information! It showed how wise and great he was. Copy him.

"Absorb what is useful, reject what is useless,
and add what is specifically your own." – Bruce Lee

If you do what everyone else does, you'll get
what everyone else has got.
An average life. Don't follow the crowd, follow the winners.

Watching the news is not relaxing it's depressing.
Do things that make you money, laugh, healthy, relax, positive
or will help make your future.

How much do you benefit from reading rubbish or watching rubbish?
How much money do you make?

Hear no negatives, see no negatives and speak no negatives.

Hear positives, see positives and speak positives.

You are in control

The great thing about negative people is it's not their fault. Ever. They will love the above list. They will look at the 9.5 excuses above and see 8.5 different things to blame apart from number 1, themselves.

The only reason any of us fail or succeed is because of number 1, ourselves. I fail because of me. I succeed because of me.

Wherever you are now; you drove there with your past thoughts and actions. Blame no one else.

You are in control of your thoughts and actions now; therefore you are in control of your future.

You future is in your control; you've got your hands on the wheel. Wherever you go is up to you. Think about it. Do something about it.

I will
Decide now which of the above 9.5 things you will <u>stop</u> doing and write below what you WILL <u>start</u> doing instead;
GO!
I will...

Positive Thinking Knowledge is Power
After I became aware of the power of negative thoughts, I would watch my words and catch them! Put them in the bin and think positive. With my new knowledge on the power of positive thinking my educated ears would listen with my new awareness to the positive and negative words of others and myself.

New Knowledge; New Awareness
After you gain new knowledge you gain new awareness. When you first discover how to do something, you suddenly become aware of how badly you currently do it and want to improve it. You work on improving it and then you become good at it. After you have become competent at your new skill for a while you start to do it without thinking about it. It becomes automatic. Like riding a bike.
First; you don't 'know' you can't ride a bike. No knowledge.
Second; you get on a bike and realise you can't ride a bike! Awareness.
Third; you start learning and one day you ride without any help. Learning
Fourth; you pedal, balance and ride without thinking about it. Automatic.

Everyone goes through the same process when it comes to learning anything including the knowledge of 'positive thinking'. At first you don't know about 'positive thinking'. Then you 'discover' the knowledge of positive thinking. Then you work on improving your positive thinking. Then one day you automatically 'think positive' without thinking about it!

The stages of learning for anything (like walking) can be described as;
Stage 1; unconscious incompetence (crawler)
Stage 2; conscious incompetence (fallen walker)
Stage 3; conscious competence (walker)
Stage 4; unconscious competence (walker and talker)

When you can walk and talk without thinking about it and concentrating on it you are a natural automatic walker! After I gained my knowledge I worked on being more positive. When I heard people saying a negative word or statement an alarm bell would ring in my head. I still cringe sometimes when I hear people being negative, especially in a group situation where other people are being 'infected' with the negative word as well.

No excuses. Be more positive. It's a choice.
Choose positive thoughts.

There are things we know, there are things we know we don't know and there are things we don't know we don't know.

You can walk and talk winning mentality

Before reading this book on winning mentality there may be knowledge you didn't know. Therefore you couldn't apply winning mentality because you didn't know about it! You were unconsciously incompetent. After reading this book you will know about winning mentality. Some of it or all of it will be new knowledge you didn't have before. You can then choose to apply what you know. It will eventually become second nature and you will automatically think positive and use the tools (and cringe when you hear negative words!). Or you can choose to consciously NOT apply the knowledge. In which case you will be consciously incompetent and crawl about on your knees!

People know what to do, but don't do what they know.

Happy songs; happy people

The BBC did a great study as part of the programme 'The Human Mind' presented by Prof. Winston. They decided to conduct an experiment on two similar people and see the influence external happy or sad stimulus has on a person's mood. They found two identical twins who were almost identical in appearance and personality. The normally inseparable sisters agreed to be separated for a day. Upon waking one sister was asked to listen to a sad song, then watch a sad emotional film (often nicknamed 'tear jerkers') and finally read a sad 'moving' story. Her identical sister upon waking was asked to listen to uplifting music, then watch a happy film (Hollywood style) and finally read an 'inspirational' story. Both sisters (still separated) were then taken shopping in a mall. By watching someone shop psychologists can accurately discover a persons mood.

The 'sad' sister went into several shops, saw little she liked and in total bought only two items of clothing. In the final shop she visited she bought a pair of shoes after a long period of uncertainty. Before buying she inquired, "If I don't like them can I take them back?" (Not a confident comment!) She made the purchase after assurances that she could return the shoes and get her money back if necessary. The camera crew then followed her as she left the shop and went to be reunited with her identical sister. The 'happy' sister eventually appeared weighed down by about 8 bags of clothing! She bounced towards her with a big smile on her face and asked her 'sad' sister how she had got on. She replied that she hadn't seen many things she liked and bought some shoes. She went into one of her bags to get them out and show her sister. Although she had just bought them, when she saw them this time she said "I don't like them, I'm going to take them back"! In contrast the 'happy' sister reflected that she had enjoyed her shopping experience and dived her hand into one of her bags. She removed two identical hats to show her sister, one of which she had bought for her 'sad' sister and she placed it on her head. It was fascinating to see the energy and happiness of the 'happy' sister lifting the mood of her 'sad' sister quickly and transform her face to a smile.

The conclusion; music, movies and stories will influence your mood. A positive stimulus will put you in a positive mood. Positive music will put you in a positive mood. A positive picture will put you in a positive mood. Positive words will put you in a positive mood. You won't get that from news! Words and pictures have feelings attached to them. Surround yourself with positive ones.

Feed your mind with positive stimulus.
Surround your ears and eyes in a positive environment.
What you hear, see and read affects your mood.
Positive 'mind' food will give you a positive mind and happy mood.

If you want to be positive and happy; read, watch and listen to positive and happy words e.g. listen to uplifting music, surround yourself with positive quotes, read and watch positive stories.

You won't become positive from negative news!

Sad stories make you sad

I remember reading a few pages of a book titled 'A child called 'It'' which is a deeply sad true story of a boy who was tortured and poisoned by his own mother. Regardless of the fact that deep down I knew the boy become a man, survived, wrote the book, is living his dream inspiring people and leading a happy life, the story made me sad and physically ill (after only a few minutes of reading). I knew I had to find a powerful way to change my mind mood and lift me back up. So I went for a run and it worked.

Good exercise makes you feel good. Motion creates positive emotion.

Stopping negative thoughts- mental boxing

The previous advice will help you to feed your positive voice and help you to stop feeding your negative Giant. But if a negative thought does arrive in your mind there are ways to deal with it. Imagine you are in a car and you have come up with an idea of a destination (dream) to drive towards. If a negative thought arrives, it's like a red traffic light. It's stopping you getting to your dream. When you think a negative thought imagine a red traffic light and stop the flow of the negative thoughts. Say STOP in your mind. If it's a negative mental movie say CUT! You don't want to keep playing that movie or you will direct your future that way.

Everyone has a positive and non-positive voice in their head and our 'talk in head' is a bit like a boxing match with the positive and non-positive thoughts going back and fourth. Use the red traffic light to STOP your negative thoughts and fight back with positive words and the non-positive voice gets knocked out. Realise that the non-positive thoughts can stop you on the road to success and hold you back. Imagine a green light to keep the mental traffic positive.

If a negative thought arrives, hit the red traffic light!
Red lights are stopping you getting to your dream.
Hit the green light and your positive
thoughts will get you to your dream.

Rubbish thoughts; Rubbish results

I would describe negative thoughts as "mental junk food" which create an unhealthy mind. An unhealthy mind does a lot of damage to our confidence, our health, our creativity, our success and our happiness. Imagine your negative thoughts as garbage and throw them into a garbage bin. If we don't throw out our garbage thoughts, comments and words we will have a mind full of rubbish thoughts and a life full of rubbish results. Put your non-positive wishes in the garbage bin and replace them with positive verbalisation. Phrases like "Not bad", "I'm knackered", "This job/customer is a nightmare", "Miserable weather", "I'll never lose weight" are non-positive words which will give you non-positive success. Don't let your mind become a Garbage bin; Garbage in; Garbage out. GIGO. Think and store only good positive thoughts; Good In; Good Out. GIGO.

Negative thoughts are "mental junk food." Junk food, junk results.

Cut

Imagine your negative verbalisations and mental movies as mistakes when you're directing your 'Future'. Say "Cut" and do the 'take' again. Put the negative words and mental movies in the garbage bin.

Cut the negative mental movies.
Direct your 'Future' towards success with positive mental movie.

Negative thoughts; Negative energy

There is another powerful reason to eliminate negative thoughts and words from your mind. Non-positive words reduce your energy. In his book 'Your body doesn't lie', Dr John Diamond reveals that thinking negative thoughts actually reduces energy. Furthermore your energy also reduces when other people say negative words around you. You can test this for yourself. John uses a volunteer. He asks the person to hold their arm straight out to the side, parallel to the ground. John then tells the person that they will attempt to push their arm down towards the ground with one hand and they must resist and attempt to keep the arm where it is. John goes ahead and attempts to push their arm down for a few seconds, sufficient to test their arm strength (but not so long as to cause fatigue). Most strong people will be able to hold their arm up and resist John. John gives the person a minute to recover before doing the same again. However, this time while John is pushing their arm down he repeats some negative words out loud like "weak", "tired" and "lose" (after all it is like a game with the person wanting to 'win' and keep their arm up). Amazingly this time the person's strength is almost 'zero' and John can push their arm towards the ground and back to the side of their body. It's absolutely amazing to watch or experience this for the first time. Give it a go. You will get the same results when the person silently thinks negative thoughts. So the conclusion is that hearing negative thoughts actually reduces energy. Also thinking negative thoughts reduces energy.

John then does the same again but this time uses positive words like win, strong, love and energy and the volunteer can easily resist. He is actually able to do it easier than the first time and feels stronger.

Positive words increase your energy, negative words reduce it.

Therefore where possible eliminate negative thoughts
from inside your mind and outside your ears.

Watch your words

The words you use and those you hear and see around you will affect you.

Mind your language. Words have feelings or pictures attached to them. Words are energy. Everything is energy.

Choose your words carefully.
Positive words make you positive.
Happy words make you happy.
Energy words give you energy.
The word 'negative' is a negative word! Use non-positive instead!

Words have feelings.
The word cold makes you cold.
The word tired makes you tired.
The word great makes you great.
The word weak makes you weak.
The word angry makes you angry.
The word tense makes you tense.
The word happy makes you happy.
The word stressed makes you stressed.
The words boiling hot makes you boiling hot.

Words create pictures.
Don't push me.
I'm cracking up.
Driving me up the wall.
She's heart broken.
I'm falling apart.
I'm as slow as a tortoise.
I'm as fast as a cheetah.
It's only a scratch.
I am unbreakable.
I'm as strong as an elephant.

I Can't

I want you to answer the following question and write down whatever comes to mind. When you think of the words 'I can't' what comes to mind? What can't you do?

GO!

I can't

STOP!

I Can't RIP

These thoughts are stopping you succeeding. You mind looks up the definition of "can't" in your mind dictionary and then makes sure you fail. You get what you direct! Be careful what you wish for. Negative words give weak negative results. One of the great stories in the book

'Chicken Soup for the Soul' is of a schoolteacher who does this exercise with school kids and then she gets them to take their paper outside and bury it! The kids created a 'grave' for the paper and put the words "I can't RIP" on a piece of wood in the ground when they covered the hole! Powerful message! Put a line through the words above and cut them out of the mental movie mind. Never say "I can't" again! Nothing is impossible. Anything IS possible.
GO!

I Can
In my talks with school kids I go through a similar exercise and get them to throw their "I can't" bits of paper in the rubbish bin. The message is "rubbish thoughts = rubbish results." Start using the word "I can"! Positive words give positive results. Since I spoke at Kemnay Academy two years ago, Physical Education teacher Francis Jones has used the above exercise with pupils. She uses the technique when a pupil thinks they can't do something, like the high jump for example. She shows them the difference between thinking "I can" and "I can't." Every pupil then says "I can" and then they see they can!

If you think you can or say you can, you can.
Positive words give positive results.
"I can is better than IQ." -Tom Hunter, founder of Sports Division, D2 Jeans and West Coast Capital

Stop Negative thoughts
Ever had a negative thought? Me too! We are not alone! Negative thought traffic in our mind can stop our path to success, like a red traffic light. The best way to stop negative thoughts is to imagine a red traffic light! STOP the flow of negative thought traffic, 'cut' the thought from your mind and then see a green GO light ahead. Start positive thinking. The sound of a car horn may help as well! Use it to stop yourself from always stopping yourself! (e.g. "I would love to....but it'll never work.....I'll never do it...It will rain....I can't dance...etc etc). Think positive! Use it to stop yourself from abusing yourself! (Sometimes called "beating yourself up", ouch!). Start positive thoughts!
GO!

Go OTT
I heard about a javelin thrower who had a fault in his throwing action, which he'd attempted to correct but he seemed to naturally revert back to the same faulty habit. So what he did was he deliberately threw the javelin below the perfect line. Then he threw it above the perfect line. He then threw the way he wanted to throw and has done so ever since. Go OTT and then UTT. Then your normal will seem easier to do and be within a new comfort zone. Be really negative for a day. Have fun,

go UTT. Then be really positive for a day. Have fun, go OTT. Then have a 'normal' positive thinking day!

Go Over the top, go Under the top,
then create a winning habit in the middle.
Exaggeration is fun and helps improves the 'normal' habit

Don't worry, be happy

Mothers have a special bond and love for their children. Naturally they want them to be happy, healthy and safe. It goes without saying that when the children are "out" of the house, mothers often think of them and sometimes their thoughts are concern for their safety. This is called worrying! It's almost a natural motherly instinct and I appreciate that it takes effort to change the focus to positive thoughts. The children may be out of sight but they're not out of mind. A mother I know found that as her children got older, they would stay out later and the 'worrying time' became longer. Until one night she changed and decided to stop worrying. She concluded that her worrying was not helping her children to get home safely and even if she stayed up late to wait for them it didn't make one bit of difference. So she decided she would go to bed as normal instead. Henceforth she slept happily ever after. And the 'kids' have grown into healthy and happy adults.

Worrying doesn't make you feel better, and it doesn't help you
or the people you worry about. The opposite in fact!

Worrying is a waste of time. It won't make any positive difference and
won't make you feel better
(in fact you'll feel worse-maybe even get an ulcer)
Either way it's a costly way to spend your time.
Don't worry yourself sick!
Don't worry, be happy!
Sometimes your worrying works.
Your negative thinking can create negative results.

Cut Negative Activities

Over the last few pages I have listed several things people do which reduce their energy and Positivity. Write down everything you do that is reducing your energy or Positivity. Include any negative habits or activities, which you frequently or even occasionally do.

GO!

Cut
Now put a line through every one of the habits you want to 'cut' and say 'cut' as you do so.

Weak words create weak results
If you use negative words you'll get negative results. If you use weak words you'll get weak results. Here are some weak non-positive words and some strong positive alternatives;

Weak Negative	***Strong Positive***
Try	Will or Will not (do or do not)
Nightmare	Interesting
Knackered	Un-energetic
Problem	Challenge
Forget	Remember
Stressed	Not Calm
Sore	Tickle, Body is repairing
Sick	50% Healthy
Weak	Not Strong
Negative	Non-positive
Can't	Can
Should	Could

Here are some weak negative phrases and some strong positive alternatives;

NOT positive!	***Positive phrases (using the word "not")***
I feel terrible	I'm not great
I'm ill	I'm not 100%
I'm useless	I'm not brilliant
I'm starving	I am not fully tanked up and need some fuel
I'm tired	I'm not very energetic
I've got a problem	I have not found a solution to a challenge
I've forgotten	I cannot remember yet
I've got bad news	I've got news and it's not nice
I'm useless at that	I am not brilliant at that ...yet!
I'll never	I could but have chosen not to
I hate...	I am not a lover of....
Horrible weather	Not weather for T-Shirts, could be warmer
I'll try	I will
I should be there	I will be there
I should exercise	I could exercise
I'm not bad	I'm great
I'm cold	I'm not warm

Weak words create weak results.
If you use negative words you'll get negative results.

If you use weak words you'll get weak results.

Positive words create positive results.

Strong words create strong results. Should is a shit word.
"I should" will never happen; 'I will' will always happen.
Using 'I should have' for the past "beats you up"!
Using 'I could' is always better.

Try
For the next exercise I want you to try to pick up your pen now.
GO!

STOP!
I said 'try'! Did you pick it up? Or did you not pick it up? 'Try' and 'tried' are stored in your automatic brain and mean 'attempted but failed'. Therefore using this word before you attempt something will help you fail! Never try. Say you 'will do it' or 'won't do it'.

'Try' is one of the weakest words in the world,
along with 'can't, should and problem '.

"There is 'do and 'do not'. There is no such thing as 'try"
-Yoda, The Empire Strikes Back

Can't is a crap word. Cut the crap!

Cut Negative Words and Thoughts
Write down any words you sometimes use or thoughts you have, which are reducing your energy or Positivity.
GO!

Cut
Now put a line through every one of the words you want to 'cut' and say 'cut' as you do so. Don't try to do this exercise! Do it or don't do it!
GO!

STOP!
Try
Been to a wedding lately? (If not, I guess you are aware of a thing called a 'wedding'!). You know the bit where the minister gives the

vows (this is the bit where he says 'will you love them, kiss them, clean them, etc'). Have you ever heard the bride or groom reply "I'll try" or "I'll do my best"?

No? Me neither. Perhaps it is because it's loser talk! 'Try' is the weakest word in the English language! Show me an Olympic 'try-er' and I'll show you a man/woman without a gold medal round their neck. Weak and negative words give weak and negative results.

Winners use positive strong words. Like 'I WILL win' or 'I WILL score'. It's the same in business. Winners talk about what they 'will do' and not what they 'might do' or 'will try to do'. I'm glad the brides and grooms use positive words! (Unlike the movies they actually say 'I will' rather than 'I do'...'Four Weddings and a funeral' has a lot to answer for.)

Winners talk about what they 'will do' and not what they 'might do' or 'will try to do'.
No one who uses the word 'try' keeps their promise!
Which is why the bride and groom never say 'I'll try'.

How are you?

Your phone is ringing. It's one of your friends. They ask you "How are you?" Write down your answer below

GO!

STOP!

If your answer was "OK thanks" or "Not bad. How are you?" Then you haven't passed the first test! If you said "great" or "awesome" or "amazing" or "I'm super man, how are you?" you have passed! I love the last answer. You will see why later.

Saying 'not bad' will give you 'not bad' energy and 'not bad' performance! Which is not very good!

Do you have a great answer to the question "How are you?"
Most people automatically reply "not bad"
when you ask them how they are.

It's a bad habit that will take about 30 days to 'kick' before the reply "I am great!" becomes automatic. Use a "non-positive" swear jar to help you.

Positive Question

Do you ask loaded questions? Good communicators use these to be positive not pushy. What day can you meet for lunch? How quickly can you do this for me? Have you had a great day today? You look super, how are you?

Positive question. More positive answer.
Ask yourself positive questions.
Ask people positively loaded questions.

Very fast Summary

Your mind will make your thoughts come true.
Think positive thoughts, get positive results.
You write the script for your future.
Seek and ye shall find, ask and ye shall receive, knock and the door will open.
A successful day comes from willing it that way.
Think impossible is possible and it's possible.
Think 'I can' (you're right!)
Create your own day; what kind of day are you "willing" to have?
Today will be lucky! Today will be a funny day! Today will be a great day!
Having a positive mind is like having positive glasses on!
Your thinking affects your vision. Positive minds have positive eyes.
A vision is something not everyone else can see.
You can feed your positive voice (and stop feeding your negative voice)
People with a positive mind are more lucky and healthy than negative people
Your future is like a magnet to your thoughts.
Your mind hosts a boxing match between your positive and negative 'voices'.
Don't worry, be happy!
Negative thoughts kill dreams and kill people.
If a negative thought arrives, hit the red traffic light!
'Cut' negative thoughts and words and increase your energy
Red lights are stopping you getting to your dream.
Hit the green light and your positive thoughts will get you to your dream.

Your mind affects your body and your body affects your mind.
Healthy body, healthy mind.
Your mind and mood is affected by what you see,
hear, read, do, eat & think.
Be careful what you wish for. Wishing works.
Your thinking affects your vision. Positive minds have positive eyes.
Create your own day; what kind of day are you "willing" to have?
If you think you can, you can. If you think you can't,
you're right- Henry Ford
Positively direct your future like a
director shouting directions on a movie.

Be more positive. It's a choice. Choose positive thoughts.

No excuses.

CHAPTER 5
POSITIVE BELIEF

Very fast Summary

Belief and self-belief is essential to be successful at anything. If you don't have it you can 'build' belief and self-belief.

"If you think you can or you think you can't, you're right!"- Henry Ford

Included in this chapter;

Positive verbalisation created positive beliefs
Your beliefs fall into three categories
Fairy Beliefs, One Head Beliefs or Loch Ness Monster Beliefs
Thoughts are powerful. Beliefs are very powerful.
What we see is what we believe
If you don't believe, you don't achieve
Surround yourself with people who believe in you
How to create a belief by using a mantra
You have to be a fan of yourself before you'll believe in yourself
Winners have winning self-belief
A boy with belief and motivation can beat a man with a chequebook.
Negative believers make negative achievers
If you think the way you've always thought, you'll get what you've always got
You have to believe you can do it, before you can do it! Not after!
Negative self-belief can hold you back for months and years
Positive nicknames improve confidence and belief and performance
You are in control of your future.
You're sitting in the driving seat not the back seat!
Start believing and you'll start achieving!
If you think you can, or say you can, you can!
Winners have high self-esteem
Why self-esteem is important

"I am the greatest" – Mohammed Ali

Positive belief

Beliefs are strong thoughts, like thoughts but with bigger muscles! Your thoughts make things happen. Your beliefs can make incredible things happen (like achieving dreams). Also beliefs make things happen again and again (like always winning raffle prizes!).

Gold Winning Beliefs

Many of the stories mentioned already are an example of a belief making incredible things happen. As well as the stories of people like Mohammed Ali and Chris Gorman there are further stories mentioned in this book including Gold medal winners. Against incredible odds they dreamed, believed and achieved.

Dream. Believe. Achieve.
"Whatever the mind of man can conceive and believe, he can achieve"
–Napoleon Hill 'Think and Grow Rich'

Beliefs are like Boomerangs

Beliefs are like Boomerangs. Here are examples of where beliefs make things happen again and again;
If you think 'I think I will win this competition' you probably will.
If you <u>believe</u> 'I am a winner'. You'll win competitions again and again.
If you think 'I feel lucky tonight' you will probably win the raffle prize that night.
If you <u>believe</u> 'I am lucky', you will be lucky and win all the time! It is common for 'lucky people' to win raffles, prizes, enjoy great holidays, find a nice partner, enjoy good health, have a great job and great friends.
If you think 'I will probably catch my colleagues cold' you probably will!
If you <u>believe</u> 'I am always catching a cold every winter' you always will!

If you keep thinking it, you'll keep achieving it.
Beliefs are like boomerangs,
they make things happen again and again.

If you think the way you've always thought,
you'll get what you've always got.

If you've won once you can win again.

"If you win one tournament you can use that
experience when you play next."
Todd Hamilton, 133rd Open Golf Champion, 2004
(Previously won on Singapore Tour)

Where did the thought/belief come from?

Any beliefs you have, started with a thought. Where did the thought/belief come from? There are several possible ways to get a belief from;

Yourself - You may have just created the thought in your own mind,

People - You may have heard the thought from parents, teachers or anyone

Education - You may have got it from a book, television, radio, movie, school.

Experiences- You may have got it after a childhood or adult experience

A belief is born in your thoughts, in your head. It may have been inspired by yourself or other people or education or an experience.

Beliefs –the evidence

After the birth of a belief it is only a thought and usually only grows into a strong belief when you find evidence to support your thought. So your mind goes looking for evidence to support your belief. However, because the mind is focused on finding evidence to support your belief it can overlook evidence which doesn't support your belief. I'll use The Tooth Fairy as an example.

Fairy Beliefs

Most of the thoughts which became beliefs, only did so when you found supporting evidence to support your thought. You thought you believed in The Tooth Fairy. Then a few other friends told you they believed in The Tooth Fairy, so this supported your thought and turned it into a belief. Then when you left a tooth under your pillow and found money the next day you had all the evidence you needed to support your belief for years to come and make it strong! Then one day the evidence was wiped away.

Imagine a belief is like a bag and the supporting evidence is "legs" and strong legs will carry the thought/belief around with you for the rest of your life unless you find conflicting evidence. Then you dismiss the evidence or you dismiss the belief and create another thought/belief. When did you start carrying the 'The Tooth Fairy' belief around with you? It was likely at a young age and your parents created it.

One day we wake up! And change our belief.

We have lots of Fairy beliefs; things we believe in because we found evidence to prove they are right.
We only achieve them if we believe them.

We get most of our beliefs from when we are young;
the age of Tooth Fairy beliefs.

Many beliefs we have now are actually
'Fairy beliefs' -they are not true!
We found some evidence over the years
but if we opened our eyes we'd see they are not true.

If we believed something else we'd achieve something else.

One head Belief

Only a few beliefs (but not many) which you have acquired over the years are actually true. Most of your positive ones are true. Most of your negative ones aren't. A few other beliefs are true, like the ones impossible to change like "I have one head." All other beliefs are not true and are not impossible to change.

Some beliefs are actually true; the 'One head beliefs'.
We found some evidence to prove
them over the years (bathroom mirror)
And they still hold true.

Loch Ness Monster Beliefs

Most of your beliefs found evidence so you kept them. Some of the beliefs we held may not have any evidence e.g. our dreams. We may believe in them but we have no evidence to say we will definitely achieve them. We just believe it to be true. For example some people believe in the Loch Ness monster but there is no recent evidence to prove it to be true but we still believe in it!

Some of our beliefs are 'Loch Ness Monster beliefs',
we've no evidence they are true! But we still believe!

Winners don't have to see before they believe it.
Winners believe in their dream and then achieve their dreams.

Losers have 'Fairy beliefs' - beliefs which are not true.
Losers believe they are useless and can't achieve their dreams
– which is not true -so they never do!

The origin and category of beliefs

So now you know the four main ways which inspired your beliefs (you, others, education or experiences) and you know the three categories your beliefs fall into (Fairy, One Head or Loch Ness Monster).

Impact of Beliefs; Now and Future

Here's an idea of the ways in which beliefs influence our present reality and future reality;

1. Your beliefs will influence how you see the world.

2. What you believe you achieve. Beliefs can limit or stop your success.

3. Some beliefs are not true. Like The Fairy!

4. Conflicting beliefs stop you achieving goals.

5. You can create a new belief anytime and get positive results.

Thoughts are powerful. Beliefs are very powerful.

Positive Glasses

Positive minds have positive eyes. Having a positive mind is like having positive glasses on! If you have a positive mind you will spot 'the positives' as they happen during your day and remember them and will ignore most of the negative things. However, a negative mind affects your eyes and is like having negative dark glasses on. A negative mind will spot the negatives as they happen during your day and remember them and will ignore most of the positive things. Two people can look at a garden (or day) and see two different things; Mr Positive Mind sees the flowers, Mr Negative Mind sees the weeds. In actual fact the garden is full of flowers and weeds!!

"We see things not as they are, but as we are."
-Kant, German philosopher

What we see is what we believe
I believe gardens are full of flowers, so I see flowers.
You believe gardens are full of weeds, so you see weeds.
We are both wrong! Gardens are full of flowers and weeds.

Our beliefs are may differ from reality;
but our eyes will show us what we believe.

Hide and Seek

Your mind plays 'hide and seek' depending on your beliefs. If you are a positive person it will 'seek' the positive and 'hide' the negative. If you're negative it will seek the negative and hide the positive. The mind hides what you don't believe a bit like a blind spot. As soon as you say "I can't" your mind hides possibilities. Whether it is looking for a solution or looking for your car keys!

If you've got you're positive glasses on, you'll see a positive day!

Choose your Attitude

Your beliefs and attitude will influence how you see the world. Our beliefs and attitude are like our glasses through which we see the world. You can choose your beliefs and you can choose your attitude. So you can choose positive glasses.

If you choose a positive attitude your mind wants to play 'snap' so it will search for the positives and you will 'notice' all the positives and your mind will 'hide' most of the negatives!

People can choose to wear bright positive glasses or dark negative glasses.

"Somewhere along the line I made the switch and was able to look at the bright side rather than the dark side all the time. Now I look at everything and think how lucky I am." - Michelle Pfeiffer

Beware of the people on the dark side!

One year belief changed in 4-minutes

Sir Roger Bannister was the first person in the world to run one mile in less than 4 minutes. It's an amazing true story. In 1952, 1953 and 1954 the biggest competition in the world was for the first person to run one mile in less than 4 minutes! In 1952 the fastest runners in the world were John Landy (AUS), Wes Santee (USA) and Roger Bannister (GB). Who was the slowest? Bannister!

13th December 1952 John Landy of Australia ran one mile in 4:02.1
2nd May 1953 Roger Bannister of Great Britain ran one mile in 4.03.6
5th June 1953 Wes Sante of the USA ran one mile in 4:02.4

The American Sante was confident he was the fastest runner and expected to be the first so American crowds flocked to see him every time he raced. As you can imagine the Australians were excited that Landy might do it so big crowds attended his every race as well. However, in 12 months John Landy didn't run any faster;

12th December 1953 John Landy of Australia ran one mile in 4:02

He said that the 4-minute mark was "like a brick wall" and later recalled that in 1954 "I thought no one would break the 4 minute barrier that year." John Landy ran a total of 8 times in one mile races and when each of his times is rounded to the nearest second he got the same time of 4.02 eight times! This by itself provides a great example of the power of a belief to stop success. He didn't believe he could run faster! (And didn't believe anyone else could run faster either). Landy had negative self-belief and got negative self-results! (Negative thoughts = negative results)

However, on a damp and windy morning on 6th May 1954 Roger Bannister was preparing for a race in which he would attempt to run one mile in under 4 minutes. He believed he could do it. His coach believed he could do it and told him "I don't believe in records, I think you can run 3.56." And Bannister had two friends and pacesetters that believed he could do it and would help him by running with him for about 90% of the way.

6th May 1954 Roger Bannister of Great Britain ran one mile in 3.59.4!!

Bannister had positive self-belief and he got a positive self-result! (Positive thoughts = positive results) Landy was shocked! He realised it WAS possible to run under 4 minutes for the mile. That year! A few weeks later…
21st June 1954 John Landy of Australia ran one mile in 3.57.9!

He broke the 4-minute 'brick wall', beat Bannister's time and set a new world record! But it was only because Landy CHANGED his negative self-belief to positive self-belief that he got the positive self result! Note; the positive self-belief comes BEFORE you get the positive self-result.
What results are you getting? What beliefs have you got?
What results do you want? What beliefs do you need?

Start believing and you'll start achieving! (Not the other way round)
Negative self-belief gets negative self-results!
Negative thoughts means negative results.
Positive self-belief gets positive self-results!
Positive thoughts mean positive results.

Within 18 months of Roger achieving the 'impossible' 16 other athletes had managed the feat because they now believed it was possible!

"I confess completely that in 1954 I could not have conceived the mile being run in 3:47. I would have been prepared to bet very big money that that was impossible. So I don't intend to make a prediction for the year 2000." - John Landy

Believers on the outside; non believer on the inside
Colin Montgomerie was leading the British Open in 2001 at Royal Lytham after two days. Everyone in the UK except Colin thought he was going to win. His thoughts came true.

If you don't believe, you don't achieve

Boy with belief and motivation beats Goliath

When Michael Cheney and a few friends developed a website called www.seniority.co.uk in their spare time for 'silver surfers' they spend months on development and then began looking for sponsors. It wasn't until Mike made a cold call to a potential advertiser that he was informed that a similar site had recently been launched aimed at silver surfers called Vavo.

Mike went online and discovered that Vavo had been backed with £10M from GE and Prudential! The Vavo Press Release dated Thursday 30 March 2000 includes the following statement; 'Simon Minshall, President and CEO of Vavo.com, further commented: "With the investment, Vavo can now dominate the e-commerce market for the over 45s in Europe." '

Mike and his friends didn't even have £10K to promote their website! (They had a bit more than £10!). They didn't have a "president and CEO" either! They discussed the competition and Mike decided that he was not going to give up and felt that the site they had developed was better. One year later and the boys with beliefs beat the men with the £10M chequebook! Senority.co.uk was dominating and the other site is no more. Vavo.com RIP.

A boy with belief and motivation can beat a man with a chequebook.
The underdog always has an advantage.

'They have got what money can't buy. A winning team spirit.'
- Defeated Real Madrid manager on the European Cup Winners Aberdeen Football Club (1983)

A person or company with arrogance can be beaten by a more motivated competitor.

Placebo effect

The 'placebo effect' is the name given to the discovery that patients can recover to full health after taking what they thought was medicine (but which had no medicinal quality). However, because they 'believed' that the medicine would help them, they got better. The sole reason this occurs is because the patient believes they are going to get better. The mind has amazing power to heal the body of disease. The power of belief. The 'placebo effect' is well known in medical circles but not commonly practised on patients.

If you believe you'll get better you'll get better.

Everyday I get better and better

Emile Coue's became famous for getting patients to repeat the affirmation "Everyday and in every way I get better and better." The patients that used it all made better improvements in their health than those that didn't, with many of them returning to full health quickly. He even helped patients with an affirmation and without medication. Why did the affirmation work? The patients positive verbalisation (said out loud) helped build up the patient's positive belief.

'Everyday and in every way I get better and better.'
An affirmation can be more powerful than medication.

Pygmalion in Business

An ancient Greek story tells about a sculptor who made a statue of a beautiful woman. He fell in love with the woman statue. He believed in her so much that 'the gods' fired an arrow of 'belief' into the statue and she came to life. The meaning of the story being; If you believe in something enough it will 'come to life'. A term used by physiologists is "the Pygmalion effect." Which is the effect on a child or adult when someone believes in them. In a famous study in the classroom in 1968 they proved that a child significantly improved their performance when their teacher believed they were clever pupils even when (unbeknown to the teacher) they were average pupils. A study reported in Harvard Business Review in 1988 called 'Pygmalion in Management' showed that when a superior believed that an average worker was brilliant they performed brilliantly! They significantly improved their output because someone believed in them, which made them believe in themselves. It's amazingly effective.

The Pygmalion effect describes the improvement on a person's performance when someone believes in them.

"Where it is necessary to take a big risk on a young man whose experience and background we think inadequate for the task, nine times out of ten not only does he rise to the occasion but he does even better than we would expect."
– Sir John Harvey-Jones, author, legend & former ICI Chairman

Believer

Oprah Winfrey said, "In the fourth grade, Mrs. Duncan was my greatest inspiration. In the fourth grade was when I first, I think, began to believe in myself. For the first time believed I could do almost anything. I felt I was the queen bee. I felt I could control the world. In school we had devotions, and I would sit and I would listen to everything the preacher said on Sunday and go back to school on Monday morning and beg Mrs. Duncan to please let me sort of repeat the sermon. So, in the fourth grade, I was called "preacher." The kids used to poke fun at me all the time. It didn't bother me because I was so inspired. And a lot of it was because of Mrs. Duncan. I always wanted to be an actress for most of my adolescent and adult life. I always wanted to be an actress and have taken, I think, a roundabout way to get there because I still don't feel fulfilled as an actress. By the time I entered college, what I really wanted to do was be an actress, but I got hired in television, and so I was never able to make any of the play rehearsals. Story of my life."

We all have a "life story". We all have a destiny.
What happens in the next chapter of our life is written by us today.

Thanks Bill

I have a creative and occasionally unfocused mind. (Which has been a great asset because without it you would not have a book to read!) It did not impress one employee in the first Oil Company I worked with. I was negatively labelled rather than encouraged or constructively criticised. I think it helped motivate me more! He was the only person I can think of that has given me negative criticism in over fifteen years of working from when I washed cars, picked fruit and potatoes and delivered papers as a kid. I positively benefited from the experience (it's a good story for my book!) even though the experience was negative and not enjoyable. Thanks Negative Nigel (not his real name). Luckily everyone else in the company was positive, helpful and constructive. One great colleague called Callum gave me more responsibility than anyone else did and my performance excelled! The responsibility demonstrated clearly that he had confidence in me.

I am lucky I found Nigel and Callum to be my
'teachers' on belief in business!

You have no friends, no enemies, only teachers.
The teacher arrives when the student is ready.

When someone has a problem with you,
they have a problem with themselves.
When you have a problem with someone,
you have a problem with yourself.

Responsibility = Power

I got negatively labelled and I performed negatively.
I was given responsibility and I performed positively.

When someone gives you responsibility they are demonstrating
through their actions that they believe in you.
Actions speak louder than words.

Pygmalion on the Pitch

Arsenal Football Club had a record breaking session in 2002/3 by being the first team to win the league and remain unbeaten all season!

That's amazing! Much of a team's success is down to the manager. Arsene Wenger is a brilliant manager. One of his skills is the way he can spot potential in a player and give players belief in themselves. Player Robert Pires was spotted by Arsene 10 years ago playing for the opposing team. He asked one of the team coaches who the player was and the coach laughed when Arsene said he was going to be a great player. He is now, but only Arsene could see it. Now at Arsenal Robert Pires says, "He is more than a manager for us; he gives us so much confidence and helps us believe in ourselves. The other day against Middlesborough, he told me I'd be coming on, on the right. He didn't seem that worried but he had a way of making me understand that he was asking me for something special. I replied 'Don't worry coach, I'll go on and I'll score.' I went on, I scored, and then I went over to shake his hand." Positive self belief and positive verbalisation!! Assisted by positive belief from the manager. Pygmalion on the Pitch!

Show belief in someone and they improve their belief and confidence in themselves and improve their performance.

Incompetent Sons

A recent television programme followed the great business consultant Brian Robinson. He went into a family hotel business that was run by a father and his two middle aged sons. The father was reluctant to leave his sons in charge because he didn't believe in them. He seemed to have every good reason not too. He was asked to identify faults and he listed a large number for each son including "doesn't take action on agreed tasks", "hates administration", "not good with customers" and a few other essential business and customer service skills. However, the sons were given a task to do (a business plan) and delivered an impressive job. The father was impressed and gave them more responsibility and eventually gave them majority shareholding. After a year working part time the father retired. The sons delivered but only when he believed in them.

If you think they can't, they can't. If you think they can, they will!
Surround yourself with people who believe in you.
Belief can turn incompetent to competent.

"Treat a man as he is, and he will remain as he is.
Treat a man as he could be, and he will become what he should be."
-Ralph Waldo Emerson

Pygmalion works

I have seen the Pygmalion effect work in business and sport. It's very powerful. Show belief in other people and it improves their belief and their confidence which improves their performance.

ACTION!

Beliefs

What you believe you will achieve. So let's see what you believe. Write down whatever comes to mind when you start this exercise and write down as much as you can. What do you believe? Complete this statement as fully as possible; "I believe…

GO!

STOP!

Make sure you have written any beliefs related to work, family, friends, love, health, happiness, success, money, luck, winning, dreams and rich, successful and famous people. If not write down a statement about each. What do you believe?

GO!

STOP!

Cut

What you believe you will achieve. Have a look to see which negative beliefs are giving you negative results. Which beliefs might be holding you back? Now, put a line through any which are stopping you from being successful and winning. You need to 'cut' negative beliefs from your 'future history'. As you do so say 'cut' in your mind or out loud.

GO!

STOP!

Create Positive Beliefs

Cut your negative beliefs and create new positive beliefs! Out with the old, in with the new. You can create a new belief the same way you acquired your old beliefs, with a thought. The last time you had a new belief/thought was because you;

a) Witnessed or had an experience which inspired you to form the thought

b) Discovered information which made you think the thought

c) Just had the thought

We can use the latter route to create a new belief. The process is like creating a mantra.

A mantra builds belief.
A belief is just a thought. Which you like a lot! Only some are positive.

ACTION!
New Mantra - New belief
Think about your number one dream goal. Picture yourself succeeding. How would you describe yourself? Write the words that come to mind down now.
GO!

STOP
How would you feel when you achieve your goal? Write the 'feeling' words that come to mind down.
GO!

STOP
Ok, now write the words "I am" below and choose words from above to include after it. I suggest that three good words to include are 'happy', 'lucky' and 'winner'. E.g. "I am a lucky, happy winner!" Write down your first ever mantra.
GO!

Why Mantras?
Two reasons. A mantra builds self-belief. Secondly a mantra verbalises your goal for your brain VIP detector. You are verbalising how you will feel and how you'd describe yourself. You are verbalising yourself achieving your goal. It's the verbal version of visualising your dream! And it works, as I will explain and demonstrate.

A mantra is the verbal version of visualising your dream.
Repeat a mantra to verbalise your dream come true.

Verbalise your dream in the same way you visualise your dream.
Talk like you have achieved it.
Say 'I am…' rather than say 'One day….'.
Present tense is better than future tense.

New beliefs
To achieve all your Top 7 goals you will need belief. The mantra you have already created may be effective enough for all your goals. However, you may wish to add some extra words or create a second mantra. Think about your other 6 goals. Picture yourself achieving those goals. How would you describe yourself? Write the words that come to mind down now.
GO!

STOP
How would you feel when you achieve your goal? Write the 'feeling' words that come to mind down.
GO!

STOP
Have a look at those words and your first mantra and consider if they are much different. The above words can be added to your first mantra or you can create a second mantra by writing the words "I am" in front of them.

Mantras build beliefs.

Focus on one thing at a time

Put effort into one goal and one mantra every day. Say it several times. I suggest you focus your biggest effort on your dream goal initially. When you want to make one of your goals a priority for a month put more effort into that mantra. For example you may use the mantra; "I am a lucky wealthy winner!" every morning and repeat several times "I am an Olympic champion in 2008!"

"Success demands singleness of purpose." - Vince Lombardi

FOCUS on the step in front

Focus on the goal directly in front of you on a day-to-day basis and think of your dream on a week-to-week basis. You are walking towards your goal. It's like going up a mountain. Some steps are easy and some steps are hard. Some steps require a jump across or bridge across. Each one a step closer to your goal and each one a test. If you look at the top it will appear never ending and a daunting prospect. Focus on the next step, which is an easier challenge then thinking about the many steps ahead! If you watch Tour De France legend Lance Armstrong you will rarely see him lifting his head to look into the distance. Instead he focuses on the man or the road directly in front. The best way to run is like Kelly Holmes from the back and pick people off like targets one at a time. It's how I've set my targets in races. It's the best way to set targets in business. Aim for the big steps one at a time. Just like an 18 hole round of golf. Play one hole at a time. Visualise the big goal often but focus on the step in front of you.

Focus on the step in front. Focus on one step at a time.
"One great cause of failure is lack of focus." – Bruce Lee

Mantra's build great self belief and self esteem

Believing you will achieve your dream is essential. Self-belief is essential too. Most winners have self-belief and self-esteem. The great thing about a mantra is you can use it to build great self-belief and self esteem and achieve great goals. Few people are positive about themselves so few people are winners. Most people don't have positive self-belief or positive self-esteem. (What's that? They say). They need a self-mantra and need self-belief!

Winners have self-belief.
Because they have a self mantra, like 'I am the greatest'!

I am the greatest

Mohammed Ali is famous for being a champion boxer. He is also famous for being a champion talker! Ali was always positive before his fights and was always going to win his fights by delivering a knock out punch! He revealed that he put his success down to visualising himself winning the fight many times in his mind, from the moment he signed the contract for each fight months before. However, Ali's success was also down to his positive talking. He was famous for the mantra he used at every opportunity, "I am the greatest!" That is a very positive way to talk about yourself! It's a great way to build positive self-belief. It worked wonders. Are you the greatest?

"I am the greatest." – Mohammed Ali, born Casius Clay

"I wouldn't say I was the best manager, just the top one."
-Champion manager Brian Clough, former manager of Nottingham Forest, European Cup Winner's Cup Winners

"He was a brilliant football manager, a maverick. He wasn't a coach like Terry Venables, he was a man manager who knew how to play. He managed players impeccably, they were frightened of him but they respected him and gave everything they had. He bought Trevor Francis, the first million pound player, and told him to make the tea I think. Clough could get away with that. He was outspoken but everybody respected his views on football."
-Former England player and manager
Sir Bobby Robson on Brian Clough

I am terrific

Bill Cullen is a very successful multi-millionaire Renault Car dealer from Ireland and he is renowned for his positive attitude. However, he was brought up in the poorest and worst area in Dublin. Luckily, he was brought up in the most positive and best family in Dublin! His grandmother made him look in the mirror and repeat the mantra "I am terrific" everyday before school. It worked wonders.

Look in the mirror and repeat your mantra in the morning.

I am FANtastic
Phil McNally is (soon to be) a very successful author, coach and speaker from Scotland and he is renowned for his positive attitude and self esteem. Every morning he looks in the mirror and repeats his mantra "I am FANtastic Phil!" It worked wonders.

If you want positive self belief look in the mirror;
if you're looking at a FAN your results will be fan-tastic!
You have to be a fan of yourself before you'll believe in yourself.

Mantra's achieve Belief and Beliefs achieve Dreams
Remember Mohammed Ali said many many times "I am the greatest", before he got there! Clients have used "I am a winner" "...number 1" "the best" or "the greatest" and achieved great results. When a client chose to use "I am a good golfer" he never improved his golf. A great mantra would be one that included words like "I am great, lucky and happy." That mantra will increase your success and luck and build your confidence, belief and happiness. Write your mantra down and have it where you will see it daily. Repeating a mantra will help create a belief. Get into the habit of repeating it daily by doing it at the same time as something you already do every morning e.g. brushing teeth. You can add or change your mantra at any time. Have as many as you want. Once you have chosen a belief your mind will keep a 'look out' for goal opportunities and 'make things happen' to create order and 'snap' your belief to your reality. But you have to use the mantra first and then your belief brings you your dream second. Begin it, build it and it will come. Believe and then you achieve.

Mantras build belief and belief builds dreams
Get the mantra going and you'll get going to goal

This is gonna be my day
Remember US Masters winner Phil Mickelson's mantra on the final day in the final round, "this is gonna be my day." I can imagine that in over 4 hours of golf with a lot of walking and thinking time, that he might have said that mantra over 100 times. A great winning mantra! It worked.

Winning Mantra's win dreams. But you have to say it over 100 times.
Winners have winning self-belief.

Faster and Faster

The one tool I strongly encourage clients to make the effort to use is the mantra (and it's so quick and easy it's not asking a lot). It's a great way to build belief and have a great day! I was asked for some 'easy' advice for them to follow to achieve a goal in 4 weeks time. She had to increase her typing speed from 20 words per minute to 40 words per minute. I thought "that's a big ask for anyone, good luck!" I told her to repeat the following mantra over and over everyday, "Everyday I get faster and faster." She said it and wrote it everyday over the next 4 weeks. It was a nail biting 4 weeks but she did it! "How did you do it?!" I asked shocked! "I just did what you said." Music to the ears of any coach!!

Mantras are quick and simple and the results are fast.

Tonight is my lucky night

After giving a talk to members and staff at my previous employer Warehouse Health Club I gave a gift to two friends. It was a 'mantra card' which I wrote out for them on the spot. I wrote, "I am happy, lucky, healthy, loved, great and beautiful!" They were both very well received (sadly I'm well aware of how non positive many women can be about themselves). Upon leaving the venue I drove down the length of Union Street in Aberdeen towards home. Something amazing happened. The first set of lights were green as I drove towards them. Then so was the second set of lights. So too were the 3rd, 4th, 5th, 6th and 7th sets of lights. As I drove towards the eighth and final set of lights I was really excited. They were green as well and changed to amber as I went through them! I think writing out the 'lucky' mantras had a lot to do with how lucky I was with the lights. I was also using positive verbalisation as I drove towards each lights, "Stay green. Tonight is my lucky night! I am lucky!"

Writing out the positive mantra creates belief and creates results.
Think lucky and be lucky.

Winning Homework

Writing out your mantra at least once a week, and filling a page will build your belief and help you achieve. It may not be noticeable at the time. It's like taking a few steps toward your goal. You don't realise your getting closer until a year later when all the individual steps have taken you miles closer to your goal.

Winning Homework; Writing out your mantra
Every time you say your mantra or write it you're taking another step closer to your goal. It's not noticeable at the time until those steps have taken you miles!

How do you feel?

How do you want to feel? Think about your big 7 goals. Imagine you achieve them all. How will you feel? The question is "What is stopping you from feeling that great now?" Remember you choose your thoughts; you choose how you want to feel. Be happy now; don't wait till you get to your goal. By using 'feeling' words your mind will focus on these feelings and give you those feelings now. It also gives your mind a 'feeling' goal. You can change or add to your mantra at any time. Get into the habit of using it.

How will you feel when you achieve your goals?
Choose those feelings now.
Act and feel like you are already there.
Act and feel like a winner on the way to your goals.

'Goal' Words

One client showed me his goal board, which had pictures of all his goals. He had also incorporated his goal words. These words were the 'description' words and 'feeling' words, which he has set for his dream life, like you did when writing your 'description' and 'feeling' mantras. It's a good place to put them as well as in your mantra. They are goals too!

Your 'feelings' and 'description' words of your dream can be put with your goals list or board.

Negative beliefs

Negative beliefs are strong thoughts, like negative thoughts but with big muscles! While your negative thoughts make negative things happen, your negative beliefs will make negative things happen all the time. What you believe you achieve. Negative beliefs have a big impact on your life, sport and business. Negative beliefs hold back more people than the Berlin wall.

Negative believers make negative achievers.
What you believe you achieve.

For example;
If buying a raffle ticket you think 'I won't win, I don't feel lucky tonight' you will not win that night.

If you believe 'I am unlucky', you will be unlucky every day. It is common for 'unlucky people' to never win competitions, be unwell often, have disaster holidays, jobs, partners and ideas and have equipment break down on them.

If you think 'I don't feel well' you will probably be off sick the next day.

If you believe, "I always get a cold in January", you always will!

Negative beliefs give you 'negative success'. What you believe you achieve. Your thoughts create your reality. The following are just a few stories indicating the power of negative beliefs.

If you think the way you've always thought,
you'll get what you've always got.

"Our thoughts create our reality." – Jack Black

You achieve what you belief
Let's take another close look at the beliefs of John Landy and Sir Roger Bannister and the impact they made on history;

13th December 1952 John Landy of Australia ran one mile in 4:02.1
2nd May 1953 Roger Bannister of Great Britain ran one mile in 4.03.6

A year later;
12th December 1953 John Landy of Australia ran one mile in 4:02
6th May 1954 Roger Bannister of Great Britain ran one mile in 3.59.4!!

Note; In 12 months Sir Roger Bannister ran 4 seconds faster and in 12 months John Landy didn't run any faster! (Negative self-belief!) However, look closely at the following dates and times;

29th May 1954 John Landy of Australia ran one mile in 4:02
21st June 1954 John Landy of Australia ran one mile in 3.57.9!

In the space of 5 weeks John Landy had taken 4 seconds off his time! To most smart realistic people they would say that, "that is impossible" and not achievable but he did it. It took Bannister a year to do that! With positive self-belief Landy could have done it months before Bannister! The 'impossible' is only possible if you think it's possible! Believe and then you achieve.

Negative self-belief can hold you back for months and years.
Smash those beliefs!
You have to believe you can do it, before you can do it! Not after!
Don't listen to the 'experts' on what is possible
go out there and prove them wrong yourself.

You achieve what you believe.

Within 18 months of Roger Bannister's doing the "impossible" 16 other athletes had managed the possible. By 2003 a total of 963 athletes had run under 4 minutes. However, one of my recent findings is interesting. In the 1700's men used to run for money. Big money. And time and distance (which could be measured accurately back then) were the elements of bets. Sporting press in 1796 reports that a man called "Weller" won a bet by running a mile in 3 minutes and 58 seconds! They were hungry to win in both senses of the word. They never considered what was and wasn't possible. The time and distance was taken seriously because the betting was taken seriously!

Cricket team

A cricket team in Aberdeen called Stoneywood Dyce Cricket Team asked me to come and talk to the team before their eighth match because they had 5 losses in a row. I coached them in the 7 tools and a few other things over a one hour period on a Saturday morning before they travelled down to Glasgow for a match. They called me at 9:45pm that night to thank me and tell me they had won! I got an email several weeks later saying "5 wins out of 5"! How did I help them win? I changed their thoughts which changed their results. I helped improve their performance but I didn't coach them on improving their skills. I don't know how to play cricket! They were already good players with good skills but with poor thoughts.

Good people with poor thoughts get poor results.
Change your thoughts and change your results.

Teachers; the most important and most dangerous people in the World

Doctors save lives, teachers make lives. Parents are of course 'unpaid teachers'. All teachers have the most important job in the world but negative teachers are dangerous and potentially disastrous. If they say the wrong thing to children they can be affected negatively by it. A friend of mine told me about an experience that she still remembers from when she was a young kid in a classroom. The teacher asked the class a question and she put up her hand to give an answer, which turned out to be wrong. When the teacher heard her answer she commented, "Your brain is so small it's the size of a pea, and it could fall out at any minute." Not very encouraging. The experience had an impact upon her, verified by the fact it was something she remembered years later. I would suggest it had a negative impact.

Negative thoughts create negative beliefs.
Negative beliefs create negative futures.

Clever Kids

In the 1970's a teacher was teaching a class that were upset one morning when they heard that Martin Luther King who had been their 'Hero of the Week' had been shot and killed. The teacher explained that some people don't like people just because of the colour of their skin. In an attempt to show them what it might feel like to be discriminated against she did an experiment with them. She said that everyone with blue eyes was clever and more intelligent than the other children. The brown-eyed children would have to wear a collar round their necks, take a shorter break at lunchtime and could not drink from the water fountain. Other than some 'brown eyes' name calling and fighting, the most amazing lesson came through a simple card test. In groups of four kids the teacher did a test with the class. The brown-eyed kids took 4 min and the blue-eyed kids took 2 minutes. The following day the teacher said she had made a mistake and it was actually the "brown eyed kids who are smart" and they will have to give the collars to the blue-eyed kids. She repeated the test and the results reversed. The blue-eyed kids took 5 minutes and the brown-eyed kids took 2 minutes.

Negative thoughts create negative self-beliefs.
Negative self-beliefs create negative performances.

Positive thoughts create positive self-beliefs.
Positive self-beliefs create positive performances.

Positive personal comments can improve performance by 100%.
Negative personal comments can decrease performance by 100%.

"By the time I was three, I was reciting speeches in the church. And all the sisters sitting in the front row would say, " this child is gifted." And I heard that enough that I started to believe it. Maybe I am. I didn't even know what "gifted" meant, but I just thought it meant I was special." - Oprah Winfrey

Negative label- Nasty Name

Some people get their negative self-belief from being 'labelled' all kinds of nasty things. Remember the saying "Sticks and stones will break my bones but names will never hurt me." Never? Well, I think that "names" WILL hurt you. A negative name is the same as nasty negative criticism. Criticism destroys confidence, which destroys belief, which destroys performance.

Sticks and stones will break your bones but names can also hurt you.
Criticism destroys confidence, which destroys belief,
which destroys performance.

Calamity James

The England Football Team goalkeeper David James is one of the best goalkeepers in England. Like any person he makes mistakes. Unfortunately David James made a few big mistakes over the period of a few games and acquired the nickname 'Calamity James'. That is obviously not a positive label. If you look up the thesaurus under 'calamity' you'll find the words 'disaster' and 'catastrophe'. Which are not encouraging or helpful. He needed a new nickname. What do you think David was thinking after his first big mistake? Possibly - "I hope I don't make a big mistake again." Negative focus. Focusing on what he didn't want to happen created a negative picture in his mind. Bingo, it worked wonders.

Negative names plant negative thoughts.
Negative thoughts hurt your performances.

Stick

One of the most challenging and 'interesting' jobs in the World must be that of a sport referee. All over the world referees get a lot of 'stick' as soon as they make a decision against one of the teams (which they do every time they make a decision!) They get a lot of 'labels' and verbal 'stick' thrown at them. Within professional and amateur football in the UK their job is especially difficult. However, I would suggest that the performance of the referee will actually get worse the more 'stick' he gets. Conversely I believe that a referee's performance would improve if they were given encouragement. Put yourself in their shoes. What do you think? (However- I don't think any sport fans would be willing to test it out though!)

The worse the stick the worse the performance.

The slap and the stick

Scots woman Sandra Gregory spent 18 months in a prison in Thailand after being charged with drug smuggling. The prison where she stayed during that time is so infamous for its horrible state and the physical beatings suffered by prisoners. Inmates sarcastically call it the 'Bangkok Hilton'. She was given a special pardon to spend the final months of her sentence in the UK to be closer to home, friends and family. However, she found the prisons in the UK to be harder to cope with mentally than the 'Bangkok Hilton' because of the verbal abuse she suffered. She said "If I was to punch you on the nose, I might break your nose but in a few weeks time your nose will be healed and you'll more or less forget about it. But if I was to say something particularly unkind to you, and cause you psychological or emotional damage and hurt, that can take an awful lot longer to get over."

Verbal abuse can be worse than physical abuse.
Being hit with a stick can be less harmful than being giving verbal stick.

Non positives

If you have any non-positive labels then you need to remove them. When you put a label on a person they live up to it, positive or negative. You can remove a label any time you want.

The aim of this book is show you positive 'winning mentality' but also point out how to avoid the opposite, negative 'losing mentality'! I have chosen to highlight "the opposite" in case you can identify with where you are going wrong. The opposite of a negative label is a positive label.

Positive label –positive self

Have you ever attended an event or training course where you are given a label with your name on it to stick onto your clothes so other people know who you are? Or when you were young did your Mum ever sew a label with your name onto the inside of your clothes?

These are not the only label that sometimes stick to us. Some people get 'labelled' all kinds of great things. When you put a label on a person they live up to it.

Pele

Have you heard of Pele? One of the best footballers the world has ever seen. So good he won gold. The golden World Cup! Pele is still world famous and world respected. Can you imagine if you were called, "the next Pele"! Wow! Now that would be a HUGE compliment. Well this was the exact compliment given to England football player Wayne Rooney by the England Coach Sven Erikson after a match in the Euro 2004 competition. The following day Pele himself said Wayne played a lot like him in his playing days and he agreed with Sven's comment that he could be the next Pele! That is one of the best verbal compliments you can get in football! I suggest that Wayne would have got a 'boost' when he heard these comments. I also think that if Wayne is called 'Pele' by friends and players in training, it will help too. Why? Because 'Pele' is a very positive compliment. Compliments increase confidence and belief. Confidence and belief increases performance. Pygmalion on the pitch again!

Positive nicknames are like compliments.
Compliments improve confidence and belief.
Confidence and belief improve performance.

Pele Paterson

In Aberdeenshire around 20 years ago, a young kid grew up and was so good at football that his school friends and neighbours nicknamed him 'Pele'. Even his parents began using his nickname! He went on to become a medal-winning player in the Highland League. His name is Steve 'Pele' Paterson. Do you think if he were called 'banana feet' or 'tortoise' or 'jigsaw' it would have helped? No, me neither. (Jigsaw-goes to pieces in the box)

Being given the same nickname as a 'great'
is a belief builder and is powerful for role modelling,
emulating and imagining having the "great's" ability.
Great nicknames ignite great imagination, great confidence and great belief in a kid. Confidence and belief increase performance.
(Ps We are all kids!)
Names can hurt you or help you.

Tiger
I think one of the many things that has helped Tiger Woods become so successful and perform brilliantly is his name, Tiger. How would you describe Tiger Woods? I would describe him as; brilliant, calm, skilful, fit, strong, powerful, fearless, focused, humourous, courageous and hungry to win. How would you describe a Tiger? Impressive, fast, strong, fearless, dangerous and sometimes hungry and focused! Can you see how it may have helped him? By being called Tiger, he may occasionally think and act like a Tiger. I think if he was called Timid Woods he wouldn't play quite as well.

Rocky
The boxing movies 'Rocky' are based on a real boxer called Rocky. The films were inspirational. Rocky's coach often called him "champ" which is a great positive label. The fact he was called Rocky I think helped as well. You influence a person's performance in any sport if you call him "champ."

Energiser
Once, I was lucky enough to get running coaching from a very successful coach in Western Australia. Brian coached many young kids and young adults. Two of his younger runners were especially energetic and fast. I don't know their real names because Brian called them Duracell and Energiser! You would hear him calling their names several times during a training session. After I finished my first ever-10k race I saw 'Duracell'. I asked him how he had got on running the 5k. He told me he had done it in 21 minutes! That was exactly half the time it took me to run the 10k! I told him my time and said that if he keeps that up he'll be brilliant when he grows up.

Reputation
After a person, team or company does something once, or twice they often develop a reputation. They may then be given a nickname.

Super Sub

Super sub Ole Gunner Solskjaer plays for Manchester United Football Club often only as a substitute, but has scored so regularly as a substitute that he is expected to score! Great reputation! He has the nickname 'super sub'.

Come back team

Manchester United under the leadership of Alex Ferguson are famous for coming back from one or two goals down and winning especially in the final minutes of the game. Their reputation was cemented in Europe and the UK after one of the most amazing and most memorable comebacks in history. They were two goals down in the Champions League with minutes to go and they won 3-2. Their past results have instilled the belief and mentality into the players that they can come back and win games when they are getting beat. They often do! It becomes a self-fulfilling prophecy. Positive beliefs work wonders.

Lucky Lynch

One of my clients is Professional Football Player Simon Lynch and when I called him "Lucky Lynch" one day he told me "When I was at Celtic they used to call me "Lucky Lynch"." Helpful? Yes, I think so.

Be careful choosing the name of your baby

In Nigeria they strongly believe that the name you give your baby affects their behaviour so Nigerians take great care and effort choosing a name. I agree with them. Calling someone names will help them or hurt them.

The name of a baby can influence that child.
What names are you calling others?
What names are you calling yourself?

Rock

I can think of a great name, which can on occasions prove a hindrance rather than help. The Gaelic translation of the name Craig is 'rock', which can prove a useful name to have. But when someone called Craig has a challenging time in his life, they may subconsciously feel the need to be strong and solid and deal with everything that is thrown at them rather than get assistance or admit they can't deal with everything for everyone. Accept you can't be a rock every day of the year!

Jolly

Having the nickname 'Jolly' is both a compliment and a helpful label to have. But when someone called Jolly has a sad time in their life, they may subconsciously feel the need to be happy and hide their real emotion and tears, rather than admit honestly they need support and talk it through with someone and deal with it properly. Accept you can't be Jolly every day of the year! We are not robots we have emotions.

Even great people have an off day or make mistakes.
We are humans, we are not perfect.
We are humans not robots
We don't need to live up to our reputation, name or label everyday

New Name
What is your nickname? Are you building yourself up or knocking yourself down? What nickname might help you? Like Fantastic Phil! Choose nickname now!
GO!

STOP!
The stories are a few examples of positive labels. You can influence and improve a child or adults performance in sport just by giving them a positive label, for example calling them "champ" or "magic."

A positive label is like a positive self-belief builder

Beating yourself up
Do you give yourself negative stick? When you make a mistake do you beat yourself up? Do you think negative thoughts about yourself? Are you knocking yourself down? Do you belief in yourself? When you look in the mirror do you think 'I am Fantastic'? Write down any negative words that come to mind.
GO!

STOP!
Cut
Now, put a line through these words above and 'cut' them out from your movie. As you do so say 'cut' in your mind or out loud.
GO!

STOP!
Building yourself up
While in the past it's possible you where knocking yourself down using the mantra will build yourself up. The mantra builds up your self-belief and self-esteem.

The mantra will build up your self-belief and self-esteem.

Positive Fuel

Imagine your car. You know where you are going; you've got your destination. You're passengers beside you are guiding you. You have a mental movie of your destination. And you are directing your future by verbalising your mental movie. Visualisation and verbalisation build up belief. Belief is like the tank of fuel in the car and you need enough belief fuel to get to your dream destination. To add some more fuel to your tank, look in the mirror and repeat the mantra to build up the belief. It's like saying the magic words before the door opens on your road to success!

Belief is your fuel to get to your destination.
A winner has plenty of self-esteem and self-belief in their fuel tank.
Repeat your mantra in the mirror.

Self-esteem is good fuel for self-belief

One simple way to describe self-esteem is 'loving the person in the mirror' and having a positive opinion of your competence. Therefore self-esteem can be the father of self-belief. Because having a positive opinion of your competence is the same as having positive self-belief. So it's useful to know how we got the self-esteem which we have now and how we can boost our self-esteem, which will be fuel (boost) for our self-belief.

Positive self esteem comes from positive thoughts

Positive self-esteem is formed from positive thoughts and words. (The same way positive self-belief is formed). Whatever you think of yourself right now is as a result of previous invested effort to get there. For example if you are positive about yourself it will be because you have thought positive thoughts about yourself (probably hundreds of times over the years). Positive thoughts create positive a person. You've invested a lot of thoughts and time to get positive self-esteem!

Positive thoughts create a positive person.
Confident thoughts create a confident person.

Negative (low) self-esteem comes from negative thoughts

Negative self-esteem (usually called low self-esteem) is created from negative thoughts and words. If you are negative about yourself it will be because you have thought negatively hundreds of times about yourself! Probably comparing yourself unfavourably to friends, models and movie stars, criticising yourself for mistakes and pondering over your faults for hours.

Negative thoughts create negative people. You've invested a lot of thoughts and time to get negative self-esteem!

Negative thoughts create a negative person.

You control your fuel tank

Examining your self-esteem is like examining your fuel tank. Don't expect a positive fuel tank if you haven't been adding any positive fuel! The fuel tank is sometimes full of your negative thoughts and the negative thoughts of other people that you have been carrying round! Carrying a negative thought is like carrying a stone in your fuel tank! Stones drag you down! You have control over what goes in your fuel tank just like your piggy bank. The piggy bank is a great metaphor for self esteem because pigs are beautiful! But not everyone would see it that way. It's the same with you. You are beautiful and wonderful! But not everyone sees it that way. Including you sometimes!

Don't let negative thoughts infect your mind. Cut them out.
Don't let negative thoughts live rent free in your mind.

Carrying negative thoughts is like carrying stones
in your fuel tank, they drag you down!

'Don't let people live rent free in your mind'

You have control over your fuel tank

You are beautiful.

"She wins who calls herself beautiful and challenges
the world to change to truly see her."
Naomi Wolf, The Beauty Myth

"For attractive lips, speak words of kindness;
for lovely eyes, seek out the good in people;
for beautiful hair, let a child run her fingers through it once a day."
-Audrey Hepburn

I am beautiful

"Every woman and girl (men too!) deserves to feel as beautiful as they really are. They deserve to see and embrace their value that is measured in many ways beyond the size of their waist or cascade of their hair. How does this happen? It begins by making a choice. It is a choice to shun the cultural ideal of beauty that is narrow, one-dimensional and distorted and instead to begin to name beauty on your own terms, to claim it and to CELEBRATE it.

Easier said that done? Maybe. But it begins with tiny steps that will lead to an entirely new direction in life. If we can imagine a world in which every woman and girl can proudly proclaim, " I am beautiful!" then we can create it." (Woody Winfree)

'Our mission is simple: to create a world in which every woman and girl can proudly proclaim, "I Am Beautiful!"'
- Woody Winfree and Dana Carpenter

Woody and Dana, are creators of the 'I Am Beautiful' Project and 'I Am Beautiful' book published in 2000. What motivated them? 'A desire to illustrate to our daughters that all women deserve to be embraced as beautiful, whole and worthy human beings.'

Beautiful Woman
Beautiful British female actor Kiera Knightley has starred in 'Pirates of the Caribbean', 'The Phantom Menace' and 'Bend it like Beckham', to name but a few. In 2004 Kiera was voted;

1. The Sexiest Film Star of All Time by Empire magazine poll.
2. The Most Beautiful Celeb by New Woman magazine poll
3. The most Desirable single woman in the UK by Tatler magazine
4. The most Glamorous film actress by Glamour magazine

Kiera has been quoted, as saying she is confident about her body and nudity would not worry her. However, during an interview about receiving the vote for 'The Sexiest Film Star of All Time' she made the quote below;

"I think I look like a man." - Kiera Knightley, Actress,
Pirates of the Caribbean,
The Phantom Menace and Bend it like Beckham
(Voted 'The Sexiest Film Star of All Time' by Empire Magazine)
Unless you focus on all your positive points
you will see yourself negatively.
People without confidence or self-esteem
often can't accept compliments.
They don't see themselves in a positive way.

Some people with low self esteem often 'fish' for compliments. They tell someone 'oh I'm not very good' or something similar, knowing full well that the person they are talking to will say, "Yes you are".

People with confidence and high self-esteem don't fish for compliments.
But they like them accept them and remember them.
It's the last part that is important.

"I know I'm a good golfer, I don't need anyone to tell me that."
-Ian Poulter, European Ryder Cup winning golfer

Who do you think you are?
What do you think of yourself? Do you like what you see in the mirror? Do you believe in the person in the mirror? Self-esteem is like looking in the mirror and liking what you see. Self-esteem is like thinking you are a competent and nice person. Self-esteem isn't bragging about how great you are. It's more like quietly knowing that you're worth a lot (priceless, in fact!). It's not about thinking you're perfect (nobody is!) but knowing that you're wonderfully talented and beautifully presented! It's like looking at a car and saying "hey that's a nice car and I know it can take me where I want to go." Rather than low self esteem which would say "hey ugly useless car, I could never go anywhere or achieve anything with it."

Self-Esteem is the foundation of confidence, self-belief, self-love, self-respect and respect for others.
You are who you think you are.

Confidence is not about appearance
Somewhere between our birth and where we are now many of us have caught the self-appearance bug. Appearance didn't matter when you were young. When have you ever heard a baby ask, "Does my bum look big in this diaper?." We need to be positive about ourselves and accept the things we can control and the things we can't. Accept the things you can't control (like your eye colour, height, size of feet, etc). Accept the things you can control (If you're not fit or don't like the colour of your hair) and do something about it!

Obsession with self-appearance and perfectionism is a virus worth protecting against. High self-esteem is the best protection you can get.
Think like a baby.
Accept the things you can't control and the things you can.

Winners SWOT
Winners do a SWOT of themselves. They are aware of their Strengths, Weaknesses, Opportunities and Threats (SWOT). They will work on their weaknesses or find someone who is strong where they are weak to help them win. In business or sport. Make an assessment of yourself now and as you do evaluate where you need to improve to become a winner or remain a winner. Where are you strong? Where are your weaknesses? What are the opportunities to assist you to achieve your goals? Are there any threats, which could affect your success? Write down whatever comes to mind for each.
GO!

STOP!
Where are you strong? Look at each of these and consider if any are occasionally unhelpful? Where are your weaknesses? Do you need to make improvements in yourself or can you get someone to assist you who is strong where you are weak? Where are the opportunities you need to grasp now to achieve your goals? Are there any threats to your success? If so, look at it positively and decide whether it needs to be handled now or if you only need to take action if the threat does occur (use your intuition to decide). Look at each point you have written and write down a 'tick' if it's OK, a '*' for action and note any relevant actions or ideas.
GO!

STOP!
This is not a time for you to look at your SWOT and give up on your dream! This is a chance for you to evaluate where you need to work on to achieve your dream. There is a solution to everything. Anything is possible.

Put any goal of perfection into perspective; nobody is perfect!
Do a POSITIVE SWOT of yourself and work on the weaknesses.

Work on your weaknesses
Expose your weaknesses and motivate yourself. Arnold Schwarzenegger entered his first body building competition in the UK and lost. The reason was that while his upper body was in great shape, his calf muscles (lower legs) were small. The advice he was given was "don't hide your calf's (with clothes), so you will see them and it will make you work on them" and it did. He went home and ripped the bottom half of the legs of his tracksuit trousers off to expose his calf muscles. Every day when he went to the gym he could see his weakness and he worked on it. Until it was no longer a weakness and the rest is history. He went on to win Mr Olympia six times in a row.

Work on your weaknesses and become a winner.

Surround yourself with Winners
Successful Entrepreneurs like Sir Richard Branson and Chris Gorman are fully aware of their strengths and weakness and rather than be embarrassed by their weakness, they accept them and employ people who are strong where they are weak. It helps you to learn and improve yourself and helps you be successful and it's essential!

"Surround yourself with people better than yourself"
- Robert Morris, Morris Furniture, UK Entrepreneur of the Year 2002

You can't fly like an eagle if you're surrounded by turkeys!

It's very blunt but very true. This super saying could be put another way; "If you want to fly like an eagle surrounded yourself with eagles." I believe this is great advice and here is my evidence. Kelly Holmes, 800m Olympic Gold Medallist in Athens 2004 trained with Sydney 2000 Olympic Gold Medallist Maria Mutola. Athens 2004 Olympic Gold Medal winner Chris Hoy trained with Sydney 2000 Olympic Gold Medallist Jason Queally. I found other examples and came to the conclusion; Top athletes train with top athletes.

I found that top tennis players train with top tennis players, top golfers practise with top golfers and top business people are close to top business people.

You can't fly like an eagle if you're surrounded by turkeys!

Winners learn from winners.

Winners in sport or business spend time with other winners.

If you want to fly like an eagle surrounded yourself with eagles!

"Keep away from people who try to belittle your ambitions. Small people always do that, but the really great ones make you feel that you too, can become great."- Mark Twain

"A single conversation across the table with a wise man is worth a month's study of books." - Chinese proverb

Characteristics of Self Esteem

The National Association for Self-Esteem in America defines self-esteem as "The experience of being capable of meeting life's challenges and being worthy of happiness." Winners meet lots of challenges! While it's beneficial to have a short and snappy definition of self-esteem the full impact is more clearly seen when you examine the characteristics. I think it's easy to understand the importance to Winning Mentality of healthy or high self-esteem when you read NASE President Robert Reasoner's description of the characteristics; "tolerance and respect for others, individuals who accept responsibility for their actions, have integrity, take pride in their accomplishments, who are self-motivated, willing to take risks, capable of handling criticism, loving and lovable, seek the challenge and stimulation of worthwhile and demanding goals, and take command and control of their lives." As you can see it's like reading the characteristics of winners!

Low self-esteem is not a strong winning foundation

Low self-esteem is not a good foundation for strong self-belief or a strong winner. However, high self-esteem is not essential to win in sport or business. But it is worth avoiding! A close relationship has been documented between low self-esteem and such problems as violence, alcoholism, drug abuse, eating disorders, school dropouts, teenage pregnancy, suicide, and low academic achievement. (Worth avoiding!)

Here are some traits of people with low self-esteem;

Low opinion of themselves or high opinion of themselves.
Can't "sell" themselves.
Dislikes giving talks.
Is embarrassed about and feels undeserving of praise or awards.
Often puts themselves down or very boastful (bragger).
Needs compliments from others "fishes" for comments.
Arrogant.
Defensive.
Unassertive.
Need to impress others.
Avoid responsibly
Do not act safely.
Disrespect for others.
Disrespect for their body or health through drink, drugs, and smoking
Disrespect for environment (e.g. drop litter, never pick up litter).
Low confidence for challenges and change like changing jobs.
Blame others for mistakes.
Reluctant to take risks.
Embarrassed at failing.
Incapable of handling criticism
Low learner (does little knowledge reading or studying or "hobbying").
Doesn't like to try new things; food, places, skills.
Can't let young kids win games.
Low 'will power' and confidence.
Over eater or junk food eater.
Over obsessed with body and weight (scale watcher).
Must buy and wear designer clothes.
Spends most money on clothes every month.
Over obsessed with appearance OR does not care about appearance.
Addicted to mobile, text, email.
Very needy.
Loves partner because of need ("I love you because I need you")
Needs partner to make them feel good, important and significant.
Very selfish or very selfless.
Friends have low-self esteem.
Hangs out with "the wrong crowd"

Has few good role models in their life.
Critical of people.
"Hates" a lot of people (even people they don't really know e.g. famous)
Makes comments at people's expense (sarcastic "jokes")
Worries about what other people think of them.

People with low self-esteem don't take responsibility for their themselves, their health or their environment. Have you ever noticed that the trash thrown on the ground is always cola cans, crisp packets, sweet wrappers and cigarettes? Non-healthy food discarded by "not responsible" people. You don't see as many water bottles, healthy food wrappers or banana skins on the pavements. People that look after their health look after their environment. (Of course most healthy foods don't come in a wrapper!)

People with low self-esteem do not feel good about themselves. People with low self-esteem are often needy and "high maintenance". They NEED text messages, phone calls and emails from friends and lovers to make them feel good.

People with low self-esteem do not feel significant or important. They NEED "things" to make them feel significant and important. They need "things" like a lover, expensive clothes, expensive car, etc to make them feel good. Deep down they just want to feel significant and important. Raising their self esteem would be better and cheaper option than the clothes option! They are feeding their natural human need through their love/clothes/car addiction!

"Everyone in this world wears an imaginary button that screams out "I WANT TO FEEL IMPORTANT AND APPRECIATED!"-Robin S. Sharma, 'The Top 200 Secrets of Success and the Pillars of Self-Mastery' (also author of 'The monk who sold his Ferrari' and 'Who will die when you cry?')

Do you have high self-esteem?

To spot someone with high self-esteem look at the list above and they won't demonstrate these traits! They will have 'the opposite' traits, including assertiveness, resilience, being decisive, respectful of others and respecting their body (something all sport winners do and most business winners do). The "high self-esteemers" also have the behaviours mentioned by Robert above including responsibility for their actions, integrity, pride, self-motivated, take risks, capable of handling criticism, loving, seek challenges and demanding goals, and take control of their lives.

"I don't think of myself as a poor deprived ghetto girl who made good. I think of myself as somebody who from an early age knew I was responsible for myself, and I had to make good. "- Oprah Winfrey

Blame gets you nowhere in life. Nowhere!
Blame does NOT improve your performance!

"The superior man blames himself. The inferior man blames others."
-American NFL coach Don Shula, most successful NFL coach ever

Do you have the traits of someone with high self-esteem?
When you look at the list above for 'traits for low-self esteem' how many apply to you? Have a look at the list above and the list below and put a "tick" on the right hand side of all those that apply. Put the words "I am" in front of those below that do not yet apply but you want to acquire and put a date after it. Next time you read this book (at least by this date next year hopefully!) you can tick it off!
GO!

Traits of someone with high self-esteem;
Responsible person.
Takes responsibility for their actions.
Integrity.
Pride.
Self-motivated.
Take risks.
Capable of handling criticism.
Learns from mistakes, advice and criticism.
Friendly, loving, likeable.
Likes challenges.
Stretching goals.
Takes control of their lives.
Healthy opinion of themselves.
No need to impress others OR Likes impressing others.
Assertiveness.
Resilience.
Decisive.
Respectful of others.
Respectful of their body.
Admires winners rich and poor.
Friends have high-self esteem.
Spends time with people better than them.
Does not feel inferior to others.
Unworried about what people think of them who are not family etc.
Can "sell" themselves.
Can give a talk to kids or peers (although nervous)

Accepts praise or awards.
Takes responsibly for things not their fault (e.g. dropped litter)
Accepts blame for mistakes (sometimes even when not their fault e.g. team)
Accepts mistakes and failing.
Learns from other people.
High learner e.g. books, documentaries, Internet, hobbies.
Have lots of interests and skills outside work.
Takes on challenges confidently including new tasks and jobs.
Good with kids.
Acts safely.
Looks out for the safety of others.
Strong 'will power' and confidence.
Healthy eater.
Healthy about looks and weight.
Likes to look good.
Healthy pride about their appearance.
Will occasionally buy clothes.
Comfortable shopping in charity shop or designers shop.
Comfortable asking for discounts and haggling.
Does not like to get bad service and will politely complain (not OTT)
Is forgiving of people and companies that make a rare mistake.
Is comfortable with spending money on themselves and others.
Gives others compliments.
Independent and comfortable with themselves.
Needs partner because of love ("I need you because I love you")
Does voluntary work.
Donates to charity (often anonymously)
Does not make hurtful comments or "jokes" about others.
May jokingly put themselves down.
Will be kind and helpful.
Will not let people take advantage of them.

People with high self-esteem feel good about themselves. They don't need to own expensive things to make them feel significant and important. People with high self-esteem will wear anything and drive anything and still feel confident and good about themselves! I am sure you have seen them around! Perhaps you are one. They are a lot of fun to be around. They don't care what people think about them, what is important is what they think about themselves. If you know you are a good person you don't need to convince anyone.

You can spot people with high self-esteem from the way they act and dress and what they drive. Actions speak louder than words. People with high self-esteem do good things. People with low self-esteem often do bad things.

'The measure of a truly great man is the courtesy with which he treats lesser men'

Confident or Arrogant?
Is it possible to have too much self-esteem? Robert of NASE says, "We don't believe that it is possible to have too much true self-esteem, for having high self-esteem is equivalent to having good health. However, it is certainly possible for individuals to have an over-inflated sense of either worth or competence." Think about Shula's successful 24-hour rule!

"The day you say you've made it is the day you are finished.
I'm always trying to make a better product."
- Robert Braithwaite, founder, Sunseeker International

"Don't get a big head if you win or get too down in the dumps when you lose."
- Don Shula, owner of Shula's Steak Houses, former NFL coach

"I still have my feet on the ground, I just wear better shoes."
- Oprah Winfrey

"People say he is arrogant, I'd say self-confident. He was amazing at Porto. Two league championships, the Portuguese Cup, the UEFA Cup and the Champions League.
He deserves everything that comes his way."
-Former England player and manager
Sir Bobby Robson on manager Jose Mourinho.

Winners admire winners because they admire themselves.
Winners love winners because they love themselves.
But they hate them when they are playing them.

Losers hate winners.
They are jealous of them. But it's actually themselves they hate.
Jealousy gets you nowhere because
it's negative thoughts and energy.
You can only love or hate something about someone,
when it is something you love or hate about yourself.

Rise up and be a winner
Here are the four categories people fit into when it comes to self-esteem. Some kids have high self-esteem, most don't. It's the same with adults. However, it's important to remember that unless you keep topping your positive fuel tank your high self-esteem won't be around every day.

I'm OK, You're OK	High self esteem
I'm OK, you're not OK	Arrogance
I'm not OK, you're OK	Low self esteem
I'm not OK, you're not OK	Negative

To put it another way, there are only two emotions love or fear (hate). Therefore the above information can be represented as follows;

I love me, I love you	High self-esteem
I love me, I hate you	Arrogance
I hate me, I love you	Low self-esteem
I hate me, I hate you	Negative

"There are only two emotions love and fear." - Michael Leunig
"Loving thoughts create a loving person." – John Kehoe

Good to Great
Here is a great example from the business world, which can also apply to sport. In his great book 'Good to Great' Jim Collins details his research into finding companies that went from being 'Good to Great'. Out of 1,435 US companies listed on the US stock market only 11 went from good to great! And every single one of them had a CEO that displayed what Jim refers to as 'level 5 leadership'. One characteristic of level 5 leadership he described was "level 5 leaders look out the window to apportion credit to factors outside themselves when things go well (and if they cannot find a specific person or event to give credit to, they credit good luck). At the same time, they look in the mirror to apportion responsibility, never blaming bad luck when things go poorly."

They have high self-esteem! They are humble and modest but confident. However, he said, "Non level 5 leaders did just the opposite. They'd look out the window for something or someone outside themselves to blame for poor results, but would preen in front of the mirror and credit themselves when things went well." They have low self-esteem!

If you want to go from good to great take responsibility for your mistakes and when you succeed remember the people who helped you. Every winner in every sport or business has a team behind them.

When you fail, look in the mirror
When you succeed, look (at the team) behind you.
Every winner in every sport has a team behind them.
Every entrepreneur has a team of people
who have helped them succeed.

I didn't make a mistake

BBC Television presenter and golf commentator Peter Ellis was commentating at the US Masters in 2004. Ernie Els was in the lead when he finished his final 18 holes and looked like he had won unless American Phil Mickelson in the group behind him sunk an 18-foot putt on the final hole. Phil Mickelson sunk the putt to win and the American crowd went wild. Peter Ellis made the now famous mistake of saying "It's not over yet." He mistakenly thought that he had got the same score as Ernie and would go into a play off. Peter has since denied in interviews that he made a mistake and stated that he was actually talking to the camera crew who would be recording the presentation ceremony. We all make mistakes. When we have low self-esteem we deny mistakes and defend ourselves (and our ego) with excuses. When we have high self-esteem we admit mistakes and sometimes-even laugh at our errors.

When we have low self-esteem we deny mistakes
and defend ourselves and our ego with excuses.
If you need to defend your mistakes then it's a
sign you need to raise your self-esteem.
When we have high self-esteem we admit mistakes
and sometimes even laugh at our errors.
We all make mistakes. Admit and accept them.

There isn't a storm coming

BBC weather presenter Michael Fish made a very famous mistake several years ago. He has since retired and has made a very famous denial that he made a mistake! He presented the BBC weather for the 6pm news on the night of the worse storms in the UK for about 50 years. His words have been repeated many times on television and were even used on a music record! He said, "We have received a call from a concerned viewer in the south west of England saying she has heard that there is a big storm coming. Well I can tell you, that you don't need to worry there isn't." Now retired when asked about the incident he states that he didn't make a mistake! He gives a very weak excuse something along the lines of "I meant that it wasn't going to happen like she thought." Excuses. Excuses.

People with low self-esteem look for excuses
when they make a mistake.

People with high self-esteem look for lessons
when they make a mistake.

Self-esteem is useful but not essential to be a winner.
Not all successful people have self-esteem but they all have self-belief.

Only winners make mistakes and accept it.
Only winners invite criticism and learn from it.

Winners move on and improve, losers look back and defend

The important point in this issue is that winners will accept mistakes and if appropriate learn from them. They will move on quickly after a mistake and progress quickly. They 'keep their power' and use their power to improve performance. When a mistake occurs in a team or between two people the person with the highest self-esteem apologises first. You don't find business winners getting into fights over mistakes.

A loser will deny mistakes and defend themselves with excuses. They avoid responsibility, which means they avoid taking control of the situation. This subconsciously reminds them that making mistakes is a negative situation to be avoided or denied. The impact of that is that in future they focus a lot of energy on avoiding making mistakes. Losers will then progress slowly and carefully when performing or practising in future.

Winners accept responsibly for mistakes and 'keep their power'.
Winners focus their energy on the future and what they can control.

Losers deny responsibly for mistakes and 'give away their power'.
Losers waste their energy on defending the past.

Winners are too busy improving to waste time defending.
Winners don't fight over mistakes.

The person with the highest self-esteem apologises first

Boosting self-esteem

Self-esteem in a nutshell is 'loving the person in the mirror' and having confidence in your own ability. We can boost self-esteem by using the mantra, which is positive and personal, therefore it will develop positive self-belief and positive self-esteem. The mantra is especially effective if we say it when looking in the mirror! Some further detail is included below if required.

If you want positive self belief and self-esteem look in the mirror;
if you're looking at a FAN your results will be fan-tastic!

The mantra will develop positive self-belief and positive self-esteem
I am fantastic!

Copy the 'highs' and avoid the 'lows'!

Further boosts

Another method for boosting self-esteem is to copy the behaviours of people with high self-esteem and avoid the behaviours of people with low self-esteem! The secret is to do good things and remember that you did them. Here are some suggestions for giving yourself a boost.

Write down a list of all the good things you've done for others and here are 7 ways to increase your self-esteem fuel tank;

1. Write a card to a friend.
2. Get a plastic bag and pick up some litter.
3. Send a nice letter to a friend highlighting their qualities, like a reference!
4. Volunteer to help or mentor someone.
5. Do something nice for someone you don't know.
6. Write down a list of all your friends and each week invest time with one of them, either in person, by phone or letter.
7. Spend a few minutes thinking positive thoughts about someone.

Remember all the good things you have done for others and add to your 'fuel tank' each day.

Here are 7 things you can do for yourself to increase your self-esteem fuel tank;

1. Write down a list of your achievements. Look at the list before you perform.
2. Write down your qualities.
3. Write a letter to yourself (or email -if you must!).
4. Do something you really enjoy or are good at.
5. Do/learn something you've never done before.
6. Get a mentor or coach
7. Look in the mirror and love the person you see

"Loving yourself is the most important love of all"
– *Andrew Mathews 'Being Happy'*

Build up confidence by remembering or reliving positive past moments before performance. Create a street of success or window of confidence in your mind. Going down memory lane can improve performance.

If you think positive you feel positive.

Keep reminders of success in your house somewhere so you can look at them when necessary and build confidence. Success breeds success.

Sir Edmond Hillary said that after finding something he was good at (hill waking and climbing) his confidence soared.

How to create a negative low self-esteem fuel tank

Look through this list for things to avoid doing to give yourself negative low self-esteem. See if there is anything you have been doing and need to stop;

1. Compare yourself to others unfavourably
2. Don't believe in yourself or think you are talented
3. Look at magazines and TV and compare your beauty, body, clothes, etc
4. Think of all your PAST mistakes over and over again
5. Gossip, criticise, or dislike others, especially successful people
6. Find faults in people who have achieved great things
7. Laugh at others for their clothes, body, hair, possessions or partners

The key to LOWERING your positive self-esteem fuel tank is to think about yourself a lot, compare yourself to others a lot, consider what you haven't achieved a lot and forget what you have achieved. It's easy to make the last mistake by focusing all your thinking on the future goals (I've done that). The key to avoiding that mistake and avoiding low self-esteem and low self belief is regularly acknowledging your present position and how far you have come and take pride in your achievements.

No ones perfect!
Don't be a perfectionist. (Been there! Achieved nothing!)

You can't raise your self esteem if your negative thoughts are weighing you down.

You won't get to the top if you're carrying all your past mistakes with you.

To be a winner travel light. Leave the baggage behind. Learn from the past and leave it in the past.

Take pride in your present position and achievements. Think about your strengths not your weaknesses.

Stretch your ability and you'll stretch your confidence. Do good things and remember that you did them.

Low Self Esteem and High Spending

Karyn Bosnak is a New York resident who became addicted to buying clothing, shoes, make up and all kinds of what I call "appearance goods" and in the process built up a credit card debt of $20,000 (£12,000)! She used her wages to pay the monthly payments. After losing her job and being out of work for a few months, the debt began weighing on her mind. She cancelled her credit cards and turned them over to a debt consolidation agency, moved to a cheaper flat and kept looking for work. "It got so heavy that I would lay up in bed at night and think, 'What am I going to do?'" Then, one night while lying in bed awake for the "umpteenth night in a row", she came up with an idea. "I thought about Donald Trump, Bill Gates - all those richies in the world. To them, I bet $20,000 was a drop in the bucket. But to me, it was as big as the ocean." Her wild and optimistic idea was that perhaps a couple of rich people could help her and give her some money! She didn't go begging to Bill or Donald but her original idea did help her come up with a great idea.

The lower the self esteem the higher the clothes bill.

Invest time in your self-confidence and you won't have to invest all your money in your self-appearance.

Build up your self-esteem, don't build up your credit card debt.

Build up your savings one drop at a time and eventually you'll have a bucket full of money!

'Ask, and it will be given you. Seek, and you will find. Knock, and it will be opened for you." –Matthew 7:7

The creative idea

In June 2002, 29 year old Karyn Bosnak set up a website called savekaryn.com. It began: "WANTED: $20,000. CREDIT CARDS ARE BAD. Hello! My name is Karyn, I'm really nice and I'm asking for your help! You see, I have this huge credit card debt and I need $20,000 to pay it off. So if you have an extra buck or two, please send it my way... Together we can banish credit card debt from my life."

Karyn cut her spending dramatically (including colouring her own hair) and used eBay to sell the costly designer gear that had got her into debt in the first place. She says, "I learned that it was fine. That I could do without it."

She received a lot of emails. Thousands! Half of the emails were nice and the other half not nice. She was hurt by the "really mean e-mails" she received one even threatening to shoot her. But she decided to reply to most emails nonetheless, using positive sarcasm or kindness. Karyn was always told by her mother to "kill them with kindness". Her reply to one nasty email was simply "Thanks!" Well-done Karyn! Kept her power, energy and positivity!

Five months after she launched the site, she was back in the black. She got $13,000 in donations; the average was between $1 and $5, and the biggest an anonymous donation of $500. People with high self-esteem often make anonymous donations. She got $4,000 from selling her 'appearance goods' on eBay, and the rest she paid off herself. "I never imagined it would actually work," she says. "I prayed it would and I hoped it would, but I had no idea." Karyn's attitude and story are inspiring. She has written a book about her experience called "Save Karyn: One Shopaholic's Journey to Debt and Back" and written a screenplay. A movie is also planned!

We must take responsibility for our past,
present and future to achieve our dreams.

There is a solution to everything.

Keep positive.
'Kill them with kindness'.
What goes around comes around.

The great Martin Luther King never responded to violence with violence and Karyn Bosnak never responded to abuse with abuse. They had a dream. And they used their energy positively to chase their dream. And they achieved it!

Winners are positive about themselves

Winners are rarely insecure. If you are embarrassed to say positive things about yourself or accept positive compliments from others you have low self-esteem. You need to be more positive about yourself. I remember watching businessman Donald Trump on television and when he met a business friend that owned New York Yankies they both said "I love you man." To me it was just one example of how successful people feel comfortable with themselves and can make positive statements. Many without confidence wouldn't make positive statements about themselves or others.

Winners are positive people.
Winners are positive about themselves and others.
Winners are comfortable with themselves and
will be comfortable with others.

If you are embarrassed to say positive things about yourself or accept positive compliments from others you have low self-esteem. You need to be more positive about yourself.

"I know I'm a good golfer, I don't need anyone to tell me that."
– Ian Poulter, European Ryder Cup winning golfer

You are beautiful

Yes, I am talking about you! Some people are beautiful on the outside, some people are beautiful on the inside and some have both! Beauty on the inside is the most important. We can all be beautiful on the inside. Being a beautiful person is not about being perfect. No one is perfect. I am beautiful. But it wasn't until someone told me that I realised it. When someone tells you that you are beautiful it's a very memorable statement! It gave me a smile on the outside and on the inside! It has given me a boost for years just thinking about it! When I thought about it I realised "She's right!" I hope I've helped you realise it! You are beautiful! I'm right! It's a memorable story to emphasise a point that is important to how we think. The point is that positive statements make us <u>feel</u> positive about ourselves because they make us <u>think</u> positive. We can wait years for positive thoughts from others or we can create them ourselves. Or both. The more the merrier. Why wait for positive praise from someone else. Thinking positively about ourselves is important. Winners are positive people. No ones perfect.

Be positive about yourself.
You are beautiful. You are not perfect.
Look in the mirror and see a beautiful person!
We can wait years for positive thoughts from others
or we can create them ourselves.
If you think positive you feel positive.

Give Positive Praise
Give some positive written or verbal praise to people you know, meet, and work with or people who have helped you. Give a boss, colleague or friend 'Positive Praise' verbally or written down. Both are memorable. Trust your intuition. In person can be best. They will feel brilliant and so will you! As they say in BNI 'Givers Gain'. You could also ask one day for some Positive Feedback on you.

What goes around comes around.

Get Positive Praise
Ask your boss, colleague or friend to write a reference for you. Ask for some positive feedback, make up a performance report or send them a questionnaire. I have received some glowing references after leaving a company and wish I had got it sooner! I got a reference from two friends to do voluntary work and what they said was amazing! It gave me a boost!

Give yourself a Boost
Take a note of any positive written or verbal comments you receive. Collect positive comments, memories and photographs. Keep them close so you can boost yourself. Change pictures and trophies round every 6 months because you get used to them and stop noticing them. A new picture is like the new wallpaper after a few days. You stop

noticing it. Rearrange them and you'll notice them. A picture hanging squint will be noticed for weeks!

Positive Praise

I sent a few positive comments to a recent contact (and I am sure future friend). He is a very positive person and not the type of person that needs anyone to send him positive praise. His reply surprised but delighted me, he said, "Thanks for your emails yesterday. I really appreciate what you said in your first email - it lifted me for the whole day." His reply reminded me that everyone gets a boost from positive comments. Positive praise can lift people for days even years. Give people positive praise it makes people positive.

Positive praise can make people positive for a long time.
Positive Praise boosts people's positive self-esteem and positive self-belief.
People' with positive self-esteem and self-belief give a positive performance.

Give people Positive Praise and people give a Positive Performance.
Give people PP and people give a PP.
(Now that's funny! :)
P is the most important letter in the alphabet!
Use it a lot! Share it a lot!

Positive Feedback

The 'Toastmasters International' organisation for improving public speaking and presentation skills has a great method for giving feedback called 'CRC'.

It stands for 'Commend', 'Recommend' and 'Commend'. A person giving feedback will 'Commend' a speaker on their positive points, Recommend ways to improve and then summarise the positive 'Commend' feedback before finishing. Use this method when you want to help people improve. However, with 'Positive Praise' and patience you will find they will improve themselves. It can be useful to do a CRC and SWOT on yourself. If someone does a CRC on you, be positive about your faults and be thankful for the advice! Focus on the Positive points!

Focus on the positive and you will feel and think positive.
As humans when we are given ten compliments and one criticism, we can spend all day thinking about the criticism and not the complements!
Have a better day- think about the compliments!

Focus on 'the Future' and 'the Now'

Winners focus on the future and 'the now'. Winners spend most of their thinking time focused on what they can do, which will help them achieve their future goals. They also spend time thinking about the future. They will think positively about the future usually through some form of visualisation, which they know will practically 'control' their future. Winners focus their thoughts on what they have got control over; the future and 'the now'. A small percentage of their thinking time will be on 'the past'. Winners will consider any lessons that can be learned from past mistakes and consider those in future actions. They will also relive past positive experiences to build self-belief and self-esteem or to get them 'psyched up' for a performance.

Keep your hands on the wheel and your eyes on the road ahead. You will come off the road if you're always looking in the rear view mirror.

Focus on the future. You're going to spend the rest of your life there. You have control of your future. If you focus your energy into 'the now' and your thoughts into 'the future' all your power will be driving you to 'the future'.

If you put your power and energy into 'the past' you'll end up in reverse and going nowhere in the future but in circles.

Relive a past positive experience to get 'psyched up' for a performance and build self-belief and self-esteem.

"My interest is in the future because I am going to spend the rest of my life there." - Charles F. Kettering

Going nowhere

Most losers (and "negative low self-esteemers") focus thinking time on what they don't have control over; the past! Usually going over past mistakes in their mind over and over again (even though the past is gone and cannot be changed). "Lows" focus little thinking time on the future and put little thought into 'the now' because they don't realise the impact it has on the future. Therefore they don't bother taking actions now that would help them achieve their dreams or positive future. They don't have dreams or 'future focused' goals! Losers think the future is "out of my control" but it's not. Losers usually think negatively about the future often visualising what they don't want to happen, and that's what 'future' they get! Every time someone relives a past negative experience they reduce their self-belief and self-esteem and attract a negative repeat performance in future!

Don't focus your thinking time on what you can't control; the past!

Focus your thinking time on what you can control; now and the future!

The past is out of your control- get over it.

Some people think the future is "out of my control" but it's not. They have got their hands on the steering wheel.

Put your power into your thoughts and actions now, they control your future.

Mirror

What do you think of yourself? In general? How would you describe yourself? Imagine you had to describe yourself for a complete stranger who has never met or heard of you what would you say? Let's imagine you are either single or looking for a new job (you want to really impress them because the person/job is hot!). Complete the following sentence writing as much as you can "I am…"

GO!

STOP!

When you are finished make sure you have answered all the following questions and where relevant add the answers to your statement above;

How do you look, think, act, work or spend free time?

What do you like, love, dislike or hate?

What kind of friend, partner, worker, person, relation, stranger, son/sister/mum are you?

GO!

What do you think

OK. What do you think of that person? A positive or negative description will dictate whether you are positive or negative about yourself.

Choose who you want to be

Now I want you to think about the kind of person you want to be. Not just to be a winner but to be the best person you could dream of being. I want you to repeat the above exercise but this time describe an even more fantastic future you! (Hard to imagine you could get any better I

know- but give it a go!). Complete this sentence writing as much as you can “I am…”
GO!

STOP!
Be a Winner
If you look at your description of yourself that opinion is just thoughts and you can choose more positive thoughts. You can replace them now. But remember your self-description is a result of hundreds of remarks you’ve said to yourself in the past. So your new description may take a few days, weeks or months before you begin to accept the more positive remarks. If you were to compare yourself to no one else you can be the greatest, nicest, funniest, cutest person in the world! It would do great things for your confidence and personality! You are the greatest!

You can choose who you want to be.

Very fast Summary

If you don't believe then you don't achieve.
Your beliefs fall into three categories; Fairy Beliefs, One Head Beliefs or Loch Ness Monster Beliefs.
Cut Fairy Beliefs and create some Loch Ness Monster Beliefs.
You can make believe- imagination is more important than knowledge.
A mantra verbalises your dream and builds self-belief and self-esteem. Use it.
Thoughts are powerful. Beliefs are very powerful.
Positive verbalisation creates positive beliefs.
Beliefs are like boomerangs, they make things happen again and again.
If you think the way you've always thought, you'll get what you've always got.
What we see is what we believe.
Surround yourself with eagles and people who believe in you.
Believe in someone and they will give a great performance.
You have to be a fan of yourself before you'll believe in yourself.
You have to believe you can do it, before you can do it! Not after!
A boy with belief and motivation can beat a man with a Goliath chequebook.
Change your thoughts and change your results.
Positive nicknames improve confidence and belief and performance.
The past is out of your control- get over it.
No ones perfect! You are beautiful!
When you fail, look in the mirror. When you succeed, look behind you.

You're sitting in the driving seat to your future!

Most people go through life thinking they are sitting in the back seat but they are in the driving seat and can only blame themselves for where they end up.

You are in control of your future. If you focus your energy into 'the now' and your thoughts into 'the future' all your power will be driving you to 'the future'.
If you put your power and energy into 'the past' you'll end up in reverse and going nowhere in the future but in circles.

"There are only two emotions love and fear" - Michael Leunig

Self-esteem is useful but not essential to be a winner.
Not all successful people have self-esteem but they all have self-belief.
You have control over your fuel tank.

Accept the things you can't control and the things you can.

Do a SWOT of yourself and go to work.

Winners surround themselves with winners. Winners accept mistakes.

Start believing and you'll start achieving! (Not the other way round)

*If you want positive self belief look in the mirror;
if you're looking at a FAN your results will be fan-tastic!*

Repeat a mantra to verbalise your dream come true.

If you think you can, or say you can, you can!

You can choose who you want to be.

Anything IS possible!

No excuses!

CHAPTER 6
POSITIVE MIND

Very fast Summary

Being in a confident mood means giving a confident performance. A positive state of mind is crucial to positive performance.

Included in this chapter;

How to create a positive mind.
Using your imagination to increase your confidence.
How a positive mood improves performance.
How to switch confidence on (like a switch!)
Using your past success for future success.
Why imagination is more important than knowledge.
Why pretending is powerful.
How to copy winners and become a winner.
Modelling winners.

"Without a doubt in 1990 he was the best young player in the world in my opinion, no argument. He oozed confidence."
- Football Legend Sir Bobby Robson on footballer Paul Gascoigne

"I was as mentally strong as I've ever been, I was in the zone."
– Paul Lawrie, on the day he won the 1999 British Open at Carnousite

Positive Mind

A winner with a confident mind will give a confident performance. Therefore; a positive mind means a positive performance. Our mood reflects our mind. As shown already a lot of external stimulus like what we hear, read and see affects our mind and our mood, because they can influence our internal thoughts. However we choose our thoughts. The three positive techniques, I have covered create a positive mind;

Positive Visualisation	Mental Movie
Positive Verbalisation	Directing
Positive Beliefs and Self Esteem	Mantra

Positive thoughts create a positive mind. I include positive 'mental pictures' in the term 'positive thoughts'. If you think positive you feel positive.

1st route to a positive feeling (mood); **Think Positive > Feel Positive.**

Positive Body Language

The other route, which creates a positive mind, is through positive body language. Your mind is closely connected to your body in many ways. As part of your minds' survival mechanism your mind will monitor your body position and facial expression looking for confidence or concern. If it detects a 'concerned' face or body it will start the 'stress response' to prepare the body for battle! If your mind detects a confident face or body it relaxes creating a confident mind and feeling of confidence. Motion creates emotion.

2nd route to a positive feeling (mood); **Act Positive> Feel Positive.**

Positive body language creates positive mind language.

If you can read someone's body you can read someone's mind.
If you don't feel confident you won't look confident.
The best way to look confident (on the outside)
is to feel confident (on the inside).

Using more confident body language does help us feel more confident and look more confident.
The best way to look confident and be confident is to feel confident.

Acting positive on the outside is not as strong as feeling positive on the inside.

Motion creates confident emotion

If you pace up and down like Sherlock Holmes it gives confidence and calmness, helps solve challenges and assists creative thinking. Which is why people do it when they are on the mobile phone! The body motion is linked to the mind emotion. Motion effects emotion.

If you walk confident, you will feel confident.
If you act rushed, you will feel rushed.
If you walk calmly, you will feel calm.
If you act scared, you will feel scared.
If you start dancing, you will start feeling good and improve your mood.

Position effects emotion
Standing up while making telephone calls improves confidence. The body's position is linked to the mind's emotion.

If you lie down, you will calm down.
If you stand up, you will feel confident.
If you're heads down, your confidence will go down.

Keep your chin up and you keep your confidence up.

If you cross your arms you become defective,
negative and retain less info.

If you smile, you will feel more relaxed, positive and happy.
If you frown you will feel stressed and nervous.

Positive Sandwich
A summary of both aspects can be depicted like a sandwich. I like to call it a positive sandwich;
Think Positive > Feel Positive < Act Positive

If we act positive we feel positive; if we think positive we feel positive.

What you will learn
Using what you have learnt so far in this book and in this chapter you are about to discover how to 'switch' into a Positive Mind instantly and perform amazing feats outwith your known ability.

Switching Mood
The moment we create a positive mental movie, use positive directing or repeat a positive mantra we actually 'switch' our mind to a positive confident mood. Using any one of the three techniques creates confidence and produces great results/performances. However, the 'switch' technique you are about to learn can have an even bigger impact on performances. It can be used separately like the other 3 techniques. When all four techniques are used together (which can be done in seconds) the results will amaze you.

As stated in previous chapters visualisation is super power and beliefs are very powerful. Combined they ensure amazing performance. The switch technique powerfully combines both of these elements, with help from your imagination. You will be surprised to discover you have already used this very powerful technique when you were a kid!

Let's Pretend

Kids always play games and pretend to be other people. Whether they are playing 'Cowboys and Indians', 'doctors and nurses' or playing sport they rarely play as themselves. When kids play football they might say, "I'm Ronaldo and you're David Beckham!" When you are acting you can be whoever you want to be. You may be surprised to discover that this technique is very powerful and can be used at any age in any situation.

When you are acting you can be whoever you want to be.
You can be whoever you want to be now.

Acting

I use this technique with every golf client. I ask them who their favourite golfer is and then I ask them to 'pretend' to be their hero when they take their next shot. I say, "Act like them and think like them" and they surprise themselves when they play like them! I have seen amazing results when sports people pretend to be their hero. It can be used brilliantly in any sport and in business too. Think of a 'hero' who has achieved your goal or would perform successful in the situation you are in. Then pretend to be them by acting and thinking like them. Use your imagination! Here's a comment from one of my golf clients after he used the hero technique;

"I always used to play football as someone else, which was probably why I was so good at it." -Ronnie Herd, Entrepreneur

Pretend to be your hero.
If you think and act like them, you will perform like them.
Pretending is very useful and powerful!

Think and act like a hero and you'll feel like a hero!
And you'll achieve heroic results.

Pretending is Powerful

Pretending is very powerful. By pretending to be someone you not only become full of confidence and self-belief (because you are your hero not yourself) but you actually somehow find you have 'taken on' some of their ability by pretending to be them. When you're copying them, you are learning to be like them. It's the fastest way to learn! Three reasons why pretending is very powerful! Belief, ability and fast learning.

Pretending gives amazing confidence and belief and 'hero' ability!
When you want to learn 'pretending' is the fastest route to great skill.

Pretending to be Tiger

I was working with a local golfer on the mental side of his game. We were on a practice green going through some tools. I asked him who his favourite player was. He told me Tiger Woods, so I told him to pretend he was Tiger Woods; think, act and play like Tiger. He went into his golf bag and pulled out a cap to really get into character. He lined up his 15-foot putt, stepped up to the ball, composed himself, hit the ball and sunk it into the hole! It was his best shot so far that day. Imagination is more important than knowledge.

"Imagination is more important than knowledge." – Albert Einstein

Tiger Woods Acting

Like any young person growing up and learning, Tiger looked for great people to copy in order to enhance his golf skills. He said, "When I was young I looked up to a lot of different players for a lot of different reasons. Obviously Jack Nicklaus was the greatest of all time. Ben Hogan was the greatest driver there ever was. Seve Ballesteros probably had the best short game. Ben Crenshaw putted the best. So what I did was analyse every different player's game and try to pick the best out of each and try to look up to that. I wasn't going to look up to just one person." It worked wonders!

When you're growing and learning you look up to people.
Keep looking up as you're growing up.

Jonny Wilkinson's heroes are Walter Payton from NFL, Michael Jordan from basketball and Boris Becker from tennis, Ellery Hanley from Rugby league, Grant Fox and Neil Jenkins from rugby union and Arnold Schwarzenegger.
No wonder Jonny is so great and so strong. Great strong heroes!
Great heroes, great results.

Be a Hero

The main reason Tiger Woods has become a great golfer and achieved success like his heroes is because growing up he pretended to play like his heroes. Tiger grew up and actually became a great hero himself with great ability. He achieved success at a young age because he had been playing since he was three years old and he learnt great skill quickly using the 'pretending' technique. Whatever your goal is you will have to become a hero to achieve it. The best way to achieve your goal and become a hero is to pretend to be a hero now. Find a hero that has achieved what you want to achieve. Think and act like them and you will achieve success like them. You can be whoever you want to be- now! At the flick of a switch.

Find a hero that has achieved what you want to achieve.
Think and act like them and you will achieve success like them.

Pretending is Modelling
This 'pretending' technique is sometimes referred to as 'modelling'. Acting or 'pretending' is very similar to modelling. However 'modelling' can be approached in a more deliberate and methodical way just like Tiger did. You identify what skills or characteristics a hero has and then imagine you have them too! You act like them.

Become a hero
Several years ago Policeman Tim Roberts met a French man who knew how to use imagination and visualisation to achieve great things. The man was called Albert and he had walked four miles to hospital after his car ran out of petrol. The achievement was so amazing because Albert had experienced what he called an 'explosion of pain in his stomach' and continued driving and then had to walk four miles to hospital where he needed emergency surgery. Albert explained that he had achieved this amazing goal by using modelling. "I believe that human beings are broadly similar with a few minor variations. I know with certainty that if something is possible for a human being to achieve then it is theoretically possible for me to achieve. We all have belief, determination, energy, drive, compassion, courage, imagination etc in different amounts at different times. I know of a missionary who was helping children escape from China in the early 1900's when she was shot in the back. Despite the bullet wound she walked for another three days to lead the children to safety. I knew I needed the belief of the missionary that I could make this journey. I needed her determination. I needed to be able to accept the pain I felt without hatred for it, because that would take away my energy. Before I got out my Mercedes I imagined that I was she. I closed my eyes and imagined transferring her courage, abilities and skills to me. Then I made in my mind a picture of me walking safely to the hospital. I visioned my success."

If an another human can do it, you can do it.
If no other human has done it, imagine you can do it and you can do it.
Imagination and visualisation achieve great things.
Believe and achieve.

Model Anyone

Think of a person you admire and would like to perform as well as. How do they act and think? What is their favourite mottos and quotes? What are their skills and characteristics that you want to copy? Use your imagination to act, think and feel like the person. The person can be real, fictional, alive or dead. You can act, copy and pretend to be anyone. If you have to be confident, act confident. If you fake it you will make it. You can model someone just by watching them or reading about them or speaking to them in person (or on the phone!). Use your imagination and then do it!

Increasing your 'knowledge' of the person can make it easier for you to model them. Other than identifying the skills and characteristics of your hero it's useful to know their beliefs, values, qualities and priorities both personally and professionally. However, remember that imagination is more important than knowledge! You don't see a child reading up on a hero before he plays football! He just does it! This tool is very powerful. It works if you know someone well or if you are pretending to be an imaginary person. One way which can assist you to think like the hero is to imagine hitting a switch and you suddenly transform into them.

Pick a hero. Identify their skills and characteristics.
Copy them. Act like them. Think like them.

It's useful to know their beliefs, values, and priorities, but not essential.

You don't see a child reading an instruction manual before he plays Football, he just does it! Just do it.

You can be a super hero. If superman can do it, you can do it.

Knowledge is power. Imagination is super power!

Knowledge is important but imagination is more important than knowledge!

"The unseen energy that was once in Shakespeare or Picasso or Galileo, or any human form is also available to all of us."
– Wayne W. Dyer

Your Switch

Identify qualities that one or more of your heroes have that you need to copy to succeed. Write the qualities down below;

GO!

STOP!
Go back to the SWOT analysis you did earlier and identify what strengths you will need to acquire (which are currently weaknesses).
GO!

STOP!
One essential quality of any sport or business hero is having the courage to take action. Every hero is brave to take risks and follow their dreams. You will need to be brave too.

Be brave. Be a brave hero.

Hero Switch
Using the image of your car picture a 'switch' beside the steering wheel and when you need your 'hero ability' press the 'hero switch'. The qualities of your hero will help your confidence and your performance.

I am a Hero Switch
Think of your dream goal. Imagine you have achieved it. As you visualise this 'mental movie' of yourself in the future what word would you use to describe yourself? How do you feel? How would you act? What thoughts are going through your mind? Start thinking and acting as if you have achieved your dream. You can switch into that state of mind any time you want. Imagine you are your 'I am a Hero' future self every day and imagine the advice you get and the actions you tell yourself you <u>must</u> take to achieve your dream. Listen to the advice and take those actions!

Start thinking and acting as if you have achieved your dream.
"You've got to search for the hero inside yourself."– M People

Already the greatest
This technique above is not to act like one of your heroes but to act like <u>you</u> are the hero now! That is exactly how successful people like Mohammed Ali thought and acted when he stated 'I am the greatest' years before he actually got there. As a small company Hewlett Packard founders said they 'acted like a big company' in the way they spent their time and money and made decisions, because they believed one day they would be. It worked! Act like a big company. Act like you are the greatest now.

Act like you are already the greatest.

You can be whoever you want to be
A shy person I know was about to go on holiday and told me "I'm going to be a different person on holiday." To which I replied "You can be

whoever you want to be now." My instant reply surprised both of us. We both knew it was true.

You can be whoever you want to be.
You can choose to be the bravest, greatest, happiest and most positive person in the world every day.

Tiger, Pele, Edison, Branson

Having the same nickname as a hero has the same power as pretending. It's good to be reminded of your hero and great that you're already a bit like them.

Role Models Parents; Copy Cat Kids

If we have great role models (like our parents) growing up we will become great. As kids we are great 'copiers' so we end up becoming like the people we hang around with or look up to. As adults (big kids!) we can become copiers again and hang around the people we want to be like or get the books out. Watch, listen and copy (that's learning). Successful entrepreneurs Bill Cullen (Glencullen Holdings), Robert Morris (Morris Furniture) and Donald Trump (Trump Empire!) all said that their biggest role models and teachers were their parents.

Great people have great role models.
Having role models is very powerful
Find any great person and you'll find they had a great role model.
Modelling works!

Great people often have great parents.
But there are always exceptions.

"My mother, who taught me to do the right things and my father who taught me to do things right." - Bill Cullen,
who's grandmother taught him self-belief.

Great people have great teachers.
The teachers can be heroes, parents or teachers.

"My mother was the making of me." -Thomas Edison

"We all need to have heroes."- Ally McCoist,
ex Scotland & Ranger FC player

Role Model Henman

Britain's number one tennis player is Tim Henman and his youth coach says that Tim used to 'mimic' top tennis players during training sessions just for fun. It just worked! A great way to develop skill and confidence. Start pretending and have fun!

Raging Bull
Within the acting world one of the well-known 'techniques' is what is called "method" acting. This is basically where an actor will not act like their character but actually 'become' the character. They often do this not just for the camera but off screen as well. This technique is used by Robert De Niro and one famous story is that after the film Raging Bull he actually remained in character for several months after filming finished!

Don't act like a hero, ***become*** *the hero!*

Don't act like them, Be them like them
Oscar winner Ben Kingsley states "I'm in love with the fact that the camera is revolted by acting and in love with behaviour. If I were to go back to stage, I'd be in grave danger of acting. I avoid that at all costs." The lesson here is that to excel you must move beyond acting into 'becoming' and then you will truly model someone.

Amazing people
If you want to be amazing, 'become' someone amazing. The world is full of amazing people you can model. Find someone who has achieved what you want to achieve and think and act like them. Ordinary people have achieved extraordinary things. You can too. Become a collector of great stories. Become a copier, modeller, actor and pretender!

Super power
Aberdeen man Bruce Hosie (30 years old) recently received an award from Prime Minister Tony Blair for rescuing seven-year-old Klay Craig. The boy was pinned under the crushing weight of a Ford Escort estate after an accident near his home. But Bruce heard the boy screaming and ran out his house and managed to single-handedly lift the car off the trapped schoolboy! The hot exhaust pipe was burning his face and the weight of the 1,000lb car was slowly crushing the life out of him. A neighbour pulled badly injured Klay out from under the vehicle. Bruce works offshore and hasn't been to the gym in years! Bruce won the Evening Express Champion of Courage Award and received the Vodafone Life Savers Awards 2004 for the act.

Anything is possible.
Necessity is the mother of invention and motivation.
Everyone has super power but few of us use it.

Don't put ideas in people's head
The only non-positive part to the above story is that so many people who spoke to him weeks later told him "you must have a sore back"

that the thought become reality and he developed a sore back. Plant positive thoughts in people's heads.

Negative thoughts will hurt you. Don't listen to them.
Don't keep negative thoughts in your head. It will hurt you.
Don't put negative ideas in other people's heads. It will hurt them.

Your thoughts and words today make things happen today and tomorrow. And every 'tomorrow' after that.
Thoughts create reality.

Great achievements from great people

Behind any great achievement you will find great people. A great place to find amazing people is the Guinness Book of Records. It's inspiring to just read about the amazing people. Below are just a few of the amazing people.

Ordinary people achieve extra ordinary things.
The difference between ordinary and extraordinary is that little extra.
Behind any great achievement you will find great people.

Brave Skateboarding Legend Never Gave Up

Legendary American skateboarder Tony Hawk did two and a half loops (airborne rotations) off a skateboard ramp at the X Games in 1999. The so-called "900" (as in 900 degree spin) is regarded as one of the most difficult tricks in skateboarding! Hawk remains the first and only person to have achieved it in competition. Tony says he had been dreaming about achieving the 900 for 14 years, and it took him four years of serious practice! Five years after his feat and it is still unbeaten. It took him 11 attempts on the day before he succeeded. Which means he failed 10 times in a row before he succeeded. If Tony only did a little practise once a week for four years he would have 'failed' over 2,000 times! (50 weeks x 10 times x 4 years) But he practised for hours and hours almost every day of every week for four years! So multiply that number by at least 5! Tony Hawk is the Thomas Edison of skateboarding. He never gave up. Warning; the path to success may include a few bumps and scrapes.

You haven't failed, you just haven't succeeded yet.
You only fail when you give up. Never give up. Never.

"Failure doesn't mean you are a failure...
it just means you haven't succeeded yet." - Robert Schuller

"I have not failed. I've just found 10,000 ways that won't work."
- Thomas A. Edison, Serial Inventor who invented the Lightbulb

Tony Hawk is the Thomas Edison of skateboarding.
Tony achieved an airborne 900-degree spin in 1999 after 14 years of dreaming and 4 years of failing! He failed and fell around 10,000 times before he succeeded. But, like Edison, he never gave up.
The path to success can include lots of bumps and scrapes and failing.

Chase your dream.
Anything is possible, with physical and mental practice.
Never give up on your dreams. Keep dreaming.

Super Gran
Jenny Wood-Allen from Dundee in Scotland became the oldest person to complete a marathon in 2002 when she finished the London Marathon aged 90 years 145 days! She was born in 1911, and completed her run in 11 hours 34 minutes! Jenny ran her first marathon aged 71 against her doctor's advice, despite the fact that her heart, lungs and blood pressure were equal to someone half her age. When told of her decision to run, her son said, "Mum, you can't even catch a bus when you run so how are you going to manage a marathon?" As a child, Jenny had never enjoyed athletics and always came last in races. But 30 marathons later she is now a member of the Scottish Veterans Runners Club and continues to run to raise money for the Children's Hospice Association in Scotland (CHAS). At the age of 74 she was hailed the fastest woman over 70 in the 1986 New York Marathon!

It's never too late. Never.
Anything is physically possible.
Doctors aren't always right! Doctors, understandably in today's 'suing culture', have to be cautious and pessimistic.
People, in every culture, have to be daring and optimistic!

You often need to work for at least 12 hours a day to achieve anything great.

Super man
David Huxley pulled a Boeing 747-400, weighing 187 tonnes (184 tons), a distance of 91 m (298.5 ft) in 1 minute and 27.7 seconds on October 15, 1997 at Sydney, Australia. He is since retired from strong men challenges and runs a successful business.

Successful Actor, Body Builder and Politician!
Arnold Schwarzenegger won Mr. Olympia for the sixth time in 1975 and announced his retirement immediately afterwards. He went on to become a very successful movie star and multi-millionaire. In 1980, he came out of retirement to compete in what was the largest Mr. Olympia competition to date with 16 contenders and won! Like Ronald Regan he went from acting into politics. He is now the Mayor of California!

Amazing Woman

Vesna Vulovic, a flight attendant from Yugoslavia, survived a fall from 10,160 m (33,330 ft) when the DC-9 aeroplane she was travelling in blew up over Czechoslovakia (now Czech Republic), on January 26, 1972. She went into the Guinness Book of records for the 'Highest Fall Survived Without A Parachute'. No other passengers survived. Vesna was found with her legs sticking out of the fuselage. Three days after her fall she awoke from a coma in a hospital in Ceska, Karmenice. She says, "I was so lucky to have survived! I hit the earth – not the trees, not the snow, but the frozen ground." Vesna broke both legs and was temporarily paralysed from the waist down.

She suffered no psychological trauma and no fear of flying. Prevented from returning to her job, she forged a new career in administration. "I was able to fly over the world for free," she says. She has positive 'winning' attitude towards life. See her quote below. Humans can achieve amazing things. You can achieve amazing things.

"I believe we are masters of our lives - we hold all the cards and it is up to us to use them right." - Vesna Vulovic

Super power

Remy Bricka walked on water and went without food for eight weeks! He built 'floating skis' and used a paddle to propel himself forward (slowly!). Remy walked across the Atlantic Ocean, starting out from Tenerife in the Spanish Canary Islands on April 2, and ending in Trinidad on May 31, 1998. It's the furthest distance anyone has 'walked on water'. The secret to his super power diet? Fresh air and water! His only nutrition was fresh air, water and a few flying fish that landed on this floating water skier! He said, "Our time goes very quickly. In eternity our time is one second. In this second I will use my time to realise my dream." He was 39 when he broke the record. A self-proclaimed explorer, the thing Remy finds slightly frustrating about his treks across water is the slow pace of it.

"Where you are headed is more important than how fast you are going." -Stephen Covey

"Our time goes very quickly. In eternity our time is one second. In this second I will use my time to realise my dream" - Remy Bricka

Use your time to realise your dream!

With only air and water you will be amazed at how much you can achieve physically and mentally.

We all have super power.

Heroic Pain

A German goalkeeper who played for Manchester City broke his neck during a cup final and played on and won the match for his team! A woman broke her ankle in the 1960's and it wasn't properly diagnosed until recently, 40 years later! She went through 40 years of pain! She said she had to keep mobile because it got worse if she sat around all day!

Anything is possible.

Model Millionaires

Being successful or being a 'winner' in business could be evaluated in many different ways. One obvious way to find a business winner is find a millionaire entrepreneur. A survey of Britains estimated 5,000 self made millionaires by Tulip Financial Research commissioned for a BBC2 series called 'Mind of a Millionaire' found that millionaires have 7 traits;

1. Take risks.
2. Never switch off.
3. Not afraid to fail and keep going.
4. Think Laterally.
5. Belief -that they will be successful.
6. Break the rules.
7. Driven/determined.

The traits of a millionaire are similar to the traits required to be a winner in sport. Have a look at the traits and see if you need to model any of the characteristics to achieve your dream. The traits were the findings of psychologists. In the book 'Think Yourself Rich' there is a survey of the things that millionaires said they believed made them successful. They are in order of importance:

1. Hard Work.
2. Being honest and trustworthy.
3. Enjoyment of work.
4. Getting along with people.
5. Taking opportunities.
6. Being my own boss.
7. Intelligence.
8. Being disciplined and dedicated to success.
9. Being physically fit and healthy.
10. Employing good people.
11. Having a supportive partner.

These are the thoughts and habits of winners and you can model them! Have a look and see what characteristics you need to model to achieve your dream. Believe and achieve. (One thing not mentioned above that I believe a lot of the successful people I meet have –good sense of humour. It helps them through the 'hard work'!)

Rich V. Super Rich
They also compared millionaires with multi millionaires, the rich versus the super rich! The survey found the Super rich are;
More stubborn/self reliant.
More impulsive.
More flash (usually with fast cars)
More likely to save or re-invest money rather than spend.
Super successful people are super stubborn! They never ever give up! It's interesting that the first two traits can relate to making quick decisions and not changing them regardless of the opinion of others. Sounds like an intuitive quick decision maker like Andrew Carnegie! The study also goes to show; Great minds think alike!

Great minds think alike. Think like a great mind.

Come back Curry King
An Indian curry millionaire in UK nicknamed the Curry King has a motto; "RISE, every time after you fall." After his factory burnt down he said, "Things happen, it's how you react that's important." His reaction was to tell staff, "Go home, we'll call you when we're ready, wages will be in your bank as per normal." His banker and accountants told him to lay staff off after the fire. He ignored their advice and looked at ways to get operational again. Three weeks after the factory was burnt down his new factory was operational! Everyone was amazed!

"Things happen, it's how you react that's important.
Rise, every time after you fall." - Curry King

Super motivated
Super rich and successful Entrepreneur Tom Hunter says; "If you don't hate your competitors, you're probably not very good. He's trying to steal your bread from your table. Entrepreneurs are driven by paranoia. They risk 99%." Phil Knight, the founder of Nike, is similarly competitive; "It's a war. If they are not buying Nikes they are buying someone else's."

If you want to be great think like a great mind! Great minds think alike.

You can make believe
You can make believe. Do and 'think' whatever it takes to succeed. Use your imagination as a positive force and you'll get positive results. Imagine yourself as one of the amazing people above and get amazing results.

You can make believe.

Running Power Station
A keen running friend told me of the visualisation he uses when running. He imagines he is a hydro power station full of unlimited energy powered by water up in the mountain but he has to keep running to keep the villagers below alive with electricity! It works for him!

Ice man
I was told a story about a racing driver in the 1960's who won a race in the baking sun (over 100 degree heat) when all his competitors were suffering or had flaked out. He was several laps ahead of everyone. He was asked, "How did you do it?" to which he replied "I imagined that the sweat pouring down my head was ice cold." It helped. He won!

You can't control your conditions but you can control your imagination.
You can make believe- imagination is more important than knowledge.
You can do anything and be anything if you think anything.
You can be a man, you can be a machine, you can be a tiger,
you can be a tree, you can be whatever you want to be.

Faking it
A television programme running in the UK recently called 'Faking It' demonstrated beautifully the possibility of human beings to learn a new skill quickly and execute excellently. The programme makers pick volunteers to learn a skill that is completely different from their job and skills. A lawyer was picked to learn to rap, an architect was picked to learn to surf, and an office worker was selected to learn to sail. The genius of the documentary was including three important elements.

Each person was given;

1. an expert instructor
2. a short period of time to learn the skill (4 weeks)
3. a test at the end of 4 weeks to see if they could pass themselves off as highly experienced and skilled to an expert in that field (who didn't know of the experiment)

Every person without exception was very unskilled when they begun. So much so that all three people and their instructors expressed concerns on being able to 'pass the test'. All of them made good progress over the 4 weeks especially a few days before their test. The architect did not pass the test and demonstrated 'beginners skill' on the surfboard. He was asked how he felt during his 'test' which was a surfing competition; "Panic! I was very, very frustrated - just because things weren't going my way and I kind of knew it wasn't happening so that probably didn't do me any favours and I may have tried too hard. But it was fun all the same. That's just the way the cookie crumbles."

He began negative thinking! Therefore lost belief. Yet had belief at the start. "I did believe I could do it because there would be no point in me even attempting to do it otherwise. Unfortunately though, the surf just didn't go my way." His negative thinking got in the way!

He did have the ability in him even after just 4 weeks and said "I went back to surf about 2-3 days after I'd finished where I had my final day - I wanted to banish some demons which I did by surfing exceptionally well that day, which is just sod's law isn't it?" His didn't use any mind tools to cope with the pressure of the competition and he didn't use positive thinking. I remember reading about the great surfer Kelly Slater winning a competition in the newspaper (but the spectacular picture was of him falling off a wave!) He obviously got back up, kept his head up and went out and won!

The lawyer passed the 'test' rapping expertly in front of an audience and judges. The office manager was a great success passing herself off as a very competent sailor and actually winning a boat race! Her expert coach Emma Richards (the first woman and youngest person to sail solo round the world) was impressed with the performance as she led the boat and crew with some wonderful skill and great decision-making. I found it particularly inspiring and pleasing because I know from experience just how demanding sailing is.

The programme included a few minutes at the end where they visited the 3 people six months on from when they took part in the 'test'. They all spoke about how it had been an amazing and inspiring experience in their life. The lawyer took some time off from his job to visit his relatives in South Africa that he had never seen before. He then went back to his job. For the Architect however it turned out to be a life changing experience, he discovered he loved surfing. He left his job, family and girlfriend in the UK and immigrated to Sydney in Australia so he could surf everyday.

Fake it and you'll make it.
Necessity is the mother of motivation.
It's amazing what you can do when you have to.

Challenge Yourself

The quickest way to learn is to push yourself or learn from a winner or both! Billionaire software developer Larry Ellison expresses the view that very successful people (himself included) complete College or University courses. I heard a story that he put this point across quite bluntly at a College award ceremony in America and had to be escorted from the premises! He has a valid point and is not alone in his view. Several successful people have no college qualifications including; Steve Jobs (Apple Computer and Pixar Animation films), Steven Spielberg (Film Director), Jim Jannard (Oakley Sunglasses), Ralph Lauren (Clothing Designer), Bill Gates and Paul Allen (Microsoft).

Do it

The best way to become a success in sport or business is to do it! Not study it. "Doing" is a great teacher. Do it.

The best way to learn to become a success in sport or business is to do it!
Not study it. Ask Steve Jobs, Steven Spielberg, Ralph Lauren, Bill Gates, Lance Armstrong, Kelly Slater, Pete Sampras or Pele.

Model a hero and become a hero

On the other hand going to University can be a good thing. Warren Buffet went to University to learn from one of his financial heroes who taught at Columbia University. Two years after graduating he went to work for his hero and learn from him. It worked well for Warren! Warren is now a financial legend and is one of the richest billionaires in the world! Learning from and modelling a hero is one of the best ways to learn to be hero yourself. You don't just learn how to do it; you learn how to be great at it! That is one of the reasons this chapter is so important! (The second reason is imagining you are a hero is amazingly powerful! Imagination is more important than knowledge).

Learning from a hero is powerful.
Imagining you are a hero is super powerful.
"If you tell me who your heroes are,
I can tell you how you're going to turn out in life."
- Warren Buffet, Financial investor, 2nd Richest man in the World

What heroes?

I want you to write a list now of who your heroes are and then when you meet myself or Warren Buffet we will ask who your heroes are and take a guess as to how you will turn out! This list may include a person you have admired for years or one you have admired for minutes! Write them all down now.

GO!

Add to this list every time you find a new hero. Put a date beside each new hero. You will be surprised the influence on your life. Write down the date today beside your list above.
GO!

Improve your list; improve your life
You are only as successful as the people you meet, know, hang around and admire. Be aware of that. Improve your list of contacts, friends and heroes and you will improve your life. Fly like an eagle.

Model a champion; become a champion
Tiger Woods is not the only champion that modelled former champions. Champion manager Jose Mourinho's modelled Champion manager Sir Bobby Robson. Sir Bobby has been a successful player and manager with the England football team. Jose has never played professional football! There is a famous quote by Arigo Sacchi "you don't need to have been a good horse to become a top jockey." Sir Bobby says, "It's a fairytale story. When I first went to Sporting (Lisbon) I was met by the president and he spoke no English, and I spoke no Portuguese. He had with him a handsome young boy who spoke very good English. He was a school teacher and acted as an interpreter." The young boy was Jose! He was Sir Bobby's shadow at Porto where they won two league titles in three years before the opportunity to take over at Barcelona came up. He duly took his young protégé with him. They won two Spanish cups and the European Cup Winners Cup before Robson was offered a return to PSV Eindhoven while Mourinho remained at Barca. Sir Bobby says, "We had six years together at Sporting, then Porto, then Barcelona. He learned, listened, wrote things down and remembered. People say he is arrogant, I'd say self-confident. He was amazing at Porto. Two league championships, the Portuguese Cup, the UEFA Cup and the Champions League. He deserves everything that comes his way." Jose is now manager at Chelsea Football Club who are leading the English Championship and could win the title for the first time in years!

"We had six years together. He learned, listened, wrote things down and remembered." - Champion manager Sir Bobby Robson on Champion manager Jose Mourinho.

You don't need to have been a great player to become a great manager! Just model a great manager!

Seve and Willie's Great bubble
The great golfer Seve Ballesteros said that in order to stop the negative thoughts of opponents and opponents' supporters affecting

his mind and energy he would imagine himself in a bubble and all negatives would bounce off and only positive thoughts would get in.

The great footballer Willie Miller said that before each game he would sit in the changing room and get into a bubble where he would picture the match in his mind and see himself playing well. He would imagine himself successfully doing headers, tackles, passes and even scoring goals! It worked! It brought him several medals, including the European Cup Winners medal at Aberdeen Football Club. He told me that when he played against great teams and great players he always thought he was a match for them and never thought they were better. He thought positively. "I can handle it."

Always think positively; "I can handle it."
In the words of a young footballer who uses the bubble
"The bubble's ace"!

Positive Switch

This switch technique is different from the 'hero switch'. Some people have found themselves to be very confident when using it.

ACTION!

Positive Past

Think of a time when you were really confident, positive and 'in the zone'. Put yourself back to that experience. Remember how you looked, felt and talked. Answer the following four questions and note the first answer that comes to mind and trust it;

GO!

What word comes to mind to describe how you felt?
What colour do you associate with that experience?
What sound do you associate with that experience?
What texture/feeling do you associate with that experience?
Which sense is strongest for you the colour, sound or feeling?
We are all different.

STOP!

Bubble Switch

Now imagine that every time you say 'that word' you switch on the positive bubble and you hear the sound, see the colour or feel the texture.

Imagine you are surrounded by a bubble that colour, with that feeling or that sound around you. Imagine the bubble is bullet proof so any non-positive comments, thoughts and energies bounce off.

Positive Tools

The 'hero switch' and 'bubble switch' are powerful techniques to use while performing. Both will give you a Positive Mind and a positive performance. Along with the mental movie, directing and mantra they are winning tools! The later three tools are the best preparation for a brilliant performance in sport or business. For endurance and 'stop start' sports like golf, tennis, snooker and football the tools will be used while playing as well. In business they will also be used during a working day before each meeting, phone call or 'goal' for the day.

What were you thinking?
My first question for any person that has had major success; what were you thinking? Whatever they reply my response is always start thinking like that again and you will start wining again! My second question for any person that has had major success; what were you doing- before and during? Whatever their reply my response is always start doing that again and you will start wining again! Great preparation gives great performances.

Don't change a winning game, always change a losing game.
A winning game does not always win. Know the difference.
You need to spend time with your partner and family to be fit. (Magic 3)
You need to be fit to be a winner.
Keep Magic 5; keep fit.
Return to doing and thinking what you did when you were winning and you will return to winning.

Imagination an easy situation
There is another useful method of pretending, which is slightly different from people just visualising themselves capable in their minds. This is when a person imagines /pretends they are in a situation in which they are 'capable and comfortable' when in fact they are in a situation in which they are either not capable or comfortable or both!

Lets' Pretend
One of the PGA Professional golfers I coach plays better in 'friendly games' than in competitions. So I told him to treat his next competition like a friendly game! A British Olympic athlete in Athens 2004 revealed in an interview that she always ran well in training but not very well in competitions. So she pretended the qualifying race in Athens was just a training run!

Imagine you are
Pretending is powerful. Use your imagination. Whatever emotion you want to feel use your imagination and you will feel it.
Imagine you are confident talking to friends. When you need to speak to someone you are afraid to phone or talk to imagine you are speaking to a friend and feel confident!
Imagine you were really happy a year ago on a certain occasion. Next time you are no so happy imagine you are back at the event or day and feel happy!

Imagine you were really funny, outrageous and confident when you have had a few drinks. Next time you want to be like that (hopefully everyday) imagine you are drunk (perhaps your water or orange is vodka) and you will feel funny, outrageous and confident!

If you imagine you are, you are.

Play to your Advantage

If you want to be confident in a certain situation then imagine it is a situation in which you are relaxed and confident. When winning in competitions imagine you are level or losing to keep you relaxed. Even if it means ignoring the score and who you are playing, just play. You know when you perform at your best so imagine that situation.

Pretend and win

For difficult shots imagine easy shots, when losing imagine your winning or vice versa and for a parachute jump imagine jumping off your front step! Colin Montgomerie often plays better in Match play than he does in an individual event like a Major. He said, "A 10 foot putt for a half is completely different to a 10 footer for par." No it's not! You can pretend it's the same! For business presentations imagine talking to family, for cold calls imagine calling friends and so forth.

Put yourself into a situation in which you are not capable or comfortable but pretend you are. It works!

Pretend Motivation

If you want to be motivated in a certain situation then imagine you're in a situation in which you will be motivated and hungry. Like training with imaginary competitors or training for dinner. Playing against an opponent that is better than you or dislikes you even if it's not true. When winning in competitions imagine you are level or losing to motivate you. You know what motivates you to take action or do your best so imagine that situation.

Motivate yourself by imagining you're in a situation that motivates you.

Positive Advantage

By using the Winning Mentality tools and following the advice you will be in a positive state most of the time. If you also ensure you hear, read and see positive stimulus as well your mood will always be positive (Remember the story of the twin sisters). The following advice can help use the 'switch' and you get into a Positive Mind.

Psych yourself up

People pump themselves up or "psych themselves up" in different ways. It's a useful technique that I've seen other successful people use and I have used myself. I've also used it before firewalking so it is useful! It can combine a number of things like positive words, whispers, shouting, singing, clapping, slapping or punching!

Winner Pumps Himself Up

Razor sharp self made millionaire Bruce Burkett is a very positive, very fit and very successful businessman. He was featured on a television programme on Channel 4 doing a job swap with a car dealer for two weeks. Although he is a very confident person he was outside his normal comfort zone of working within the property market in London. Before he gave a team talk to all the staff within the car dealership (about 30 people) he took a few seconds to 'psych himself up'. Before getting out his car he shouted "Positive, positive, upper cut, upper cut, jab" and then got out his 4x4 BMW and marched towards the office! I thought it was a great insight into how a winner gets 'into the zone' and prepares himself for a performance.

Facing your fear can be a battle, shout some positive words.

Olympic Slap

While watching the Olympics I noticed one of the runners slapping their face before the start of the race!

Talking to

The feelings and emotions behind the words you say to yourself are as important as the words themselves. Whether your emotion is confidence or anger, positive or negative if it will help get you motivated to face a fear. A painful or negative experience or emotion can be a powerful motivator.

Give yourself a pep talk and pump yourself up.

Associate positively

The 'switch' technique can be used with a positive 'prop'. It's more commonly called an 'anchor' or 'trigger'. I like to call it a trigger switch! It can help you to go instantly from stressed to relaxed or from sad to happy. Have you ever had an occasion when you came across a picture; smell, song or location and it immediately brought back memories of a past experience? The smell or song etc was a trigger. We can deliberately switch ourselves into a certain mood if we use the same trigger 'switch' every time. We can use a visually, aurally or kinaesthetically 'switch'.

We can use our memory to create positive states of mind by using a trigger switch.

Aurally

Music can be a powerful 'switch' to change your mood. Select some music that you associate with the emotion you want to create e.g. music that makes you happy and confident. Play this music every time you want to increase this emotion and the 'switch' will become strong and powerful. I love music and I love this tool! Play the same track before you perform and watch the difference. Have a track you listen to when you wake up and take a shower. Before bed slow the music down and turn it down. Classical music is very effective for relaxing or creative thinking. I'm listening to some now writing this book!

Music is a great motivator! Turn it up!

Some music has a positive uplifting energy, some songs have a negative energy.

Music affects your mood and your heart rate.
Choose your music carefully.

Change your thoughts, change your mood.
Change the music, change your mood.

Visually

Think the last time you felt the emotion you want to stimulate, like confidence. Put yourself back in that memory. What picture, colour and visual image have you created? Think of this image, colour or place when you want to 'switch' to that state. It could be a location, picture or colour.

Kinaesthetically

This tool is about creating a 'body switch' either in the position of the body, the clothes on the body or a body feeling. You can do a specific movement with your body before when you think of that memory e.g. clasp hands together, tap your head, pinch arm. You can use a verbal statement simultaneously e.g. tap leg & say/think "calm" or tap head and say "winner"! Alternatively you can create a positive kinaesthetic 'switch' by wearing the same clothing for a performance. The clothing switch can be used in sport or business. Thirdly, Think of the emotion you want to stimulate, like relaxation. When is the last time you felt calm? What feeling do you remember? Use this as a switch, using the memory of when you were relaxed.

Dress for Success

The clothes you wear affect your mind and mood. The style and colour of your clothing and what you use them for are very significant to your mind and mood. For example if you were to go for a run in your beach shorts or leisure clothing you will not perform well. In Australia, even the amateur football team coaches ban players from training in beach shorts. The philosophy is 'having beach shorts means having a beach head'. Even your running shorts should be different from your beach shorts.

Your mind and body build up a strong association with clothes. So even beach style clothing should not be used for running. When you are cooking put on a cooking apron or cooking hat and you'll change into your cooking head and cook brilliantly. When working wear work clothes and change when you finish work in order to separate the time mentally. Do this even if you work from home. I change clothes and having a shower every evening even if I am working late and feel an energy boost from doing so. Whatever clothes you choose dress like the person you want to become. Dress like success. What impression are you making? Imagine you were a complete stranger looking at yourself, what would you think?

You must dress like your hero.
If look like a pro, you start thinking and acting like a pro!
Your mind and the minds of other people will 'make their minds up' about the first time they see you or meet you.

Be prepared. To become a pro you must think, act, practice, prepare, eat and dress like a pro too!

Power Hand

This technique is similar to the bubble and uses your memory of a positive past experience. It is a powerful way to create a positive state of mind and can be used to overcome challenges and fears. Think of a time when you felt confident, calm and happy. Put yourself back in that experience. Remember how you looked, felt, thought and talked. Now write the first answers that come to mind to the following four questions. Put the book down!

GO!

How would you describe yourself? Pick one word.

Now imagine the memory is in your hand. Look down at your hand. What colour do you see and associate with that experience?

Now put your hand up to your ear. What sound do you hear and associate with that experience?

Now look down at your hand. What texture or feeling do you feel and associate with that experience?

STOP!

You have now created a 'Power Hand' which will fill you with confidence. You can use 'the word' with a closed or open hand as the switch. Use it anytime you need it, especially before an important event or facing a fear.

Use it or lose it

Every time you use the 'switch' it gets strong and more powerful. You can turn yourself into a 'hero' every time you play certain songs or see a colourful image or put on a certain top and tap your head!

Winning Music

Olympic gold medal American swimmer Michael Phelps listened to the same music on headphones before he swam in the Olympic games in Athens 2004. It helped him get into the same positive state every time. It helped him win 6 gold medals! He started using this positive trigger in training.

Same actions, same results

Successful rugby kicker Jonny Wilkinson goes through the same routine before every kick, in practice and in matches. He bends forward, holds his hands together, visualises kicking the ball through an imaginary mouth between the posts and then begins his run up. He always scores!

Red Top

Tiger woods always wears a red top on the final day of a golf competition. He is already one of the most successful golfers of all time and he is not even 30 years old! The red shirt may have helped him.

Practical Clothes

Be aware of the practicality of clothes. I turned up to give a young golfer mental coaching during 18 holes and he was wearing jeans. On a hot or cold day jeans are not practical. I also suggested that in summer his clothing should be 'light' colours in order to reflect the sun and not absorb it like dark colours do. All sports have 'practical' clothing applicable to them.

New top, New energy

The World Champion England Rugby Team change their tops at halftime for a new top. It is difficult to prove that this strategy improves their performance scientifically, however, the results speak for themselves! Of course I am not suggesting the only reason they beat Australia in the 2003 final was because they changed their shirts, but I am sure it was one of the many contributing factors. Success leaves clues.

Act confident (Positive body language)

You can choose your thoughts and you can choose your body language. Positive body language sends a signal to the mind that you are moving confidently so it makes your mind feel more confident. Get someone who is sad or crying to look up at the sky and watch the difference!

If you use positive body language you'll feel positive.
Think Positive > Feel Positive < Act Positive

Someone who is thinking positive thoughts will look positive and confident. Someone using positive body language will feel positive and confident. Our mind is affected by our body position. Choose positive body language. It's one of the reasons the 'acting' technique works well.

"Motion creates emotion." – Anthony Robbins

It's amazing that if you pretend to be happy pretty soon you are happy!

"You can read someone's mind by reading their body language"
- Peter Collett, 'The Book of Tells'

Acting confident wins contracts

Entrepreneur Imran Khan founded Picsel Technologies, an international software company based in Glasgow. He said one of the reasons he received contracts and funding from renowned electronic companies like Sony and Toshiba was because he used confident body language. One of his pieces of advice is, "You have got to walk into the meeting confidently."

Walk Tall

If you keep your head up and walk tall your confident body language is spotted by the mind and which in turn makes you feel confident.

Do you walk like a pro?

I spent some time at St Anne's Golf Club this year near Blackpool working with a player wanting to qualify for the European Tour. This tournament had players some of the best up and coming professional golfers from all over Europe and the world playing at it. What was interesting was the body language. In my opinion some players were already walking like the champion professionals you see on television. And some of them were walking like football players out for a round of golf! You could almost guess who you thought was going to hit a good score over the four days by the way they walked. I didn't look at every golfer but a lot of them! You know what? The ones that walked like pros played like pros.

Are you walking like a winner or a loser?

If you are going to become a pro you've got to walk like a pro.
If you act like a pro you will start thinking like a pro.
If think like a pro and act like a pro you will become a pro!
But you have got to practice, prepare, eat and dress like a pro too!

The same goes for becoming a millionaire or a president.
Or becoming a millionaire in any other sport.

Golf Rage

Some where in the world right now a golfer is throwing a golf club! The qualifying tournament for the European Tour was no different. 'Golf rage' as I call it is when a player plays a shot he is not 100% happy with and is so angry he hits his club on the ground, throws it or for good measure screams and shouts and shakes it all about. You are looking at a loser. If you lose your head, you'll lose your game. Winning golfers smile at poor shots and recover from them by keeping positive and keeping positive body language. When things don't go to plan look at the positive and keep taking action. Golf like business is not about being perfect. Perfection does not win in golf, team sport or business. If you don't keep positive after a mistake you won't be positive for your next action. If you think negative the next shot will be negative! Watch Tiger Woods playing well and his body language does NOT change during a winning tournament. Watch Tiger play in a tournament he does not win and every mistake includes 'golf rage'!

If you make a mistake, walk like it doesn't matter and 10 steps later it doesn't matter.

If you fake positive body language on the outside,
you'll keep positive mind language on the inside.
Losing your head loses your performance.

Winners don't do 'mistake rage'. Winners walk like winners.

Winners smile at mistakes

US Masters 2004 Winner Phil Mickelson played the entire last day with a smile. He had never won the US Masters and was not a favourite with the bookmakers. He started the day behind three better players with better scores. He moved up the leader board and was in second place on the second last hole when he hit his shot into a bunker. Kept smiling! He got to the bunker and miss hit his shot back into the same bunker! Kept smiling. Kept positive. He played his next shot out onto the green. He played the 18th hole and sank an 18-foot putt to win the US Masters. Good thing he kept positive and kept smiling!

We ALL make mistakes. Winners keep smiling and keep positive. Losers don't. They get negative and get negative results. Take your pick.

To win, play better than others, don't play perfect like losers.

Keep smiling! Keep positive! Even if you make a mistake. You're next few actions could make you a winner!

Fake it on the outside, feel it on the inside
Even if we do not feel confident about the situation if we choose to use confident body language we will feel more confident.

Fake it, you will make it.

Hero Switch
Use either of the two 'hero' switch methods and model for a successful performance! Combine it with a positive mental movie and positive directing you will be amazed at your performance. It only takes a few moments to do but it's worth it! Using your heroes mantra or your own will boost your positive mind if you use it before, during or after performance. Psych yourself up! The other option is to rush into your performance and get rubbish results!

Be Prepared. Great preparation creates great results.

If you rush into a performance unprepared, you will get rubbish results! It's like going for a run without tying your shoelaces.

Use the mental movie, directing and hero technique and you will be amazed at your performance.

Hero
One quality found in every winner in sport, business and every walk of life is courage. Fear doesn't hold them back. The next chapter talks about fear.

Very fast Summary

Think confident!

Act confident!

If you use positive body language you'll feel positive

Think Positive > Feel Positive < Act Positive

When someone is confident it's down to a positive mind and belief.

If we act positive we feel positive; if we think positive we feel positive.

To be a winner smile at mistakes. Keep positive and keep smiling.

Who is your hero? Pretend to be them. You'll amaze yourself!

Acting is very useful and very powerful!

Think and act like a hero and you'll feel like a hero! (and talk like them too!)

Acting gives amazing confidence, self-belief and 'hero' ability!

Kids don't read books they just do it!

Knowledge is important but imagination is more important than knowledge!

Great people have great role models

Modelling works!

Get into your bubble. Turn on your positive switch

Start thinking and acting as if you have achieved your dream now.

Act like you are the greatest now.

Be Prepared. Great preparation creates great results.
Use the mental movie, directing and hero technique
and you will be amazed at your performance.

When someone is confident it's down to a positive mind and a positive belief.

Imagine a switch; switch to your positive bubble or 'hero'.

Great people have great heroes.

Turn the switch in your imagination and turn on your confidence and power.

*Don't 'act' like a hero, '**become**' the hero!*

Everyone has super power. Use it.

CHAPTER 6.5
FEAR

Very fast summary

There are only two thoughts positive or negative. There are only two emotions love and fear. Fear is a negative state of mind. There is only one emotion stopping you from success; fear. Fear stops action. Stop 'fearing' and you will start achieving.

Included in this chapter;

Identifying your fear(s)
Fear list.
Where fear comes from.
Know fear.
Desire vs. imagination.
Techniques to get over fear.
If you feel fear, great!
If you feel the fear, do it anyway.
What you do is more important than how you feel.
Feel it, accept it and face it.
Do what you fear and death of the fear is certain.
You're not brave and courageous if you're not scared.
Negative thoughts kill dreams. Fear buries dreams.
If you don't bury your fear, your fear will bury your dream.
Action.
Winners take risks.
Heroes are brave, not fearless.
You have 100% control of your thoughts and 90% control of your future.
People prefer to fail to attempt their dream than to fail attempting their dream.
It is less painful to face fear than to live with fear and pain.

"You can't cross a chasm in two small jumps."
David Lloyd George

No action, no wonder

When you examine the ingredients of success where were you lacking? Positive mentality, Action, Skills or Strategy? Or do you not have a goal that motivates you? For most people and most goals the reason they don't achieve them is they don't take action. If you don't take action, it's no wonder you don't win!

Most people don't achieve their goals because they don't take action.
If you don't take action, it's no wonder you don't win!

Fear stops action

We don't take action due to fear. Fear is like a handbrake. Imagine your sitting in your car and you decide on a destination that you really want to go to. You engage first gear and put your foot down but you're realise (perhaps weeks or years later) that you are going nowhere. If you looked down you would realise you have got the handbrake on. Most people don't realise the only thing holding them back is themselves. The foot may be down but the handbrake is up. If you haven't made any action, you have made a fear.

If you are not going anywhere look down.
You have got the handbrake on.
Fear stops people taking action on their dream.
Fear is like a handbrake.
You won't reach your destination with your hand on the handbrake.

Steering Wheel –Pleasure and Pain

Feelings steer decisions. Where you steer your life is decided by your feelings. You will steer towards the things which give you pleasure, and steer away from things which give you pain.

For example most Millionaires value money very highly. "Money is a huge motivator," says Tom Hunter, OBE. And one reason Millionaires are so motivated by money is because many of them come from poor backgrounds which they found a painful experience as a child. "When I was a kid we didn't have much money and we couldn't always afford to get an ice cream (from the Ice Cream van). I remember thinking 'when I grow up I want to be able to have ice cream everyday'" says Duncan Bannatyne. Duncan achieved his goal. Duncan is now a multi-millionaire health club owner, who made his first fortune selling ice creams!

"People will do more to avoid pain than they will to gain pleasure."
- Anthony Robbins, 'Awaken the Giant Within'
You are in control of your future.
Your hands are on the steering wheel.

We are very motivated do things that give us pleasure! But only if they won't give us pain! We are more motivated to avoid pain than gain pleasure. In order to motivate ourselves we need to know what motivates us. In particular what gives us pleasure and what gives us pain. Pen at the ready to answer the following questions. Write the answers down for each.

GO!

Have a look at your 'happy goals'. What feelings do these things give you?

e.g. love, success, power, happy, healthy, honest, freedom, security, passion, connected.

What feelings did you write down related to achieving your dreams (have a look at your mantra)?

STOP!

Now combine both lists below into one list in order of importance, with most important feeling at the top.

GO!

STOP!

Write the answers down for each of the following questions.

GO!

What do you dislike or fear?

Why? What feelings do these things give you?

What feelings do you not enjoy?

e.g. fear, rejection, anger, frustration, loneliness, failure, humiliation, guilt, disappointed, sadness,

STOP!

Now combine the answers for the second and third question into one list in order of importance, with the most painful feeling at the top. Write them down above, on the left hand side of your 'pleasure' feeling list.

GO!

STOP!
This exercise helps you identify what painful feeling is holding you back. All painful feelings are fear. Get over it and you'll progress towards your goals and pleasure! Fear is a hurdle on your path to success. Most people avoid the hurdle and avoid the path to success. The other path is much more painful in the long term.

Fear and pain is a hurdle on your path to success.
Avoid the fear and you avoid the success.
Face you fears. Live your dreams.

Pain is a hurdle on the pleasure path
Here are three examples where 'people are more motivated to avoid pain than gain pleasure'. A person could dislike "going to the gym or pool" because they feel "embarrassed." This means that even if they want to be healthy and happy they will avoid the gym and pool because it is a painful experience and the fear being embarrassed steers them away. If someone really dislikes "getting knock backs from opposite sex" and feels "rejected" or "sad" that person is unlikely to ask anyone out even if they would love a new partner because they are steering away from pain. Likewise if a person has "loneliness" as one of their feelings of pain they may remain in an unhappy relationship because of their fear. A fear of failure affects a business and sport person. Winners have no fear. They accept failure.

All emotions or feelings fall into the category of love or fear.
Pain is a hurdle on the pleasure path.

Chosen Decisions
The most important aspect to understand is the path you are on now is as a result of your past choices and actions you have taken. Your decisions have been steered by your feelings of pleasure (love) and pain (fear). Whatever you have achieved so far will have been motivated by your desire. Either to achieve feelings that give you pleasure or avoid the feelings that give you pain. Do you have a goal or dream, which you have not taken action towards? You will find the reason is that taking action could bring you pain (we subconsciously like to avoid that) so you avoided taking action. This is fear that has held you back. Even though the goal/dream would give you pleasure. We would rather avoid pain!

How you spend your time is driven by your priorities and feelings. For example if you prioritise family above health you will choose to spend time with your family rather than exercise. But if you have a painful fear of losing your job you are may choose to spend time working and not with your family or exercising. We do more to avoid pain than gain pleasure. What priorities and qualities do you need to achieve your goals and enjoy your life? What order do they need to be in? What fears do you need to overcome or face?

Changing your priorities can change your life.

The path

Now you can be more aware of the pleasure and pain that has steered you to your current path. You have identified your fears that have held you back and what you need to overcome in order to steer yourself to pleasure and success.

ACTION! – Get your pen ready

Why?

Write down your top goal. Have a look at your top goal. Why do you want it? List all the reasons below on the left hand side. Write as many as you can but don't stop until you have at least ten.

GO!

STOP!

Now give yourself a few minutes to think about the next question. Write down the answer on the right hand side above. Imagine you DON'T want that goal. Why don't you want it? Write down anything that comes into your mind.

GO!

STOP!

Have a look at what you have written down. These are your fears that are holding you back. Fear is like a hurdle that you must overcome to take the path to your goal. A big enough negative thought will stop you taking any path. You have to knock it down till you are big enough to get over it.

If you weren't able to write any fears down you might not have any fear holding you back which is great. Alternatively you may just not have identified the fear holding you back. Answer the same two questions for your other 6 goals below.

GO!

STOP!
I found this to be a useful question (used by Chuck Spezzano PhD) to identify what is holding us back. Your answer will tell you if you have a fear of success or failure. Do you? If you know you are holding yourself back, you will find it is a fear you're holding onto. Release the fear and you can go forward to the future.

Accept and face the fear and you can go forward to the future.
A big enough why, will overcome anyhow.
Fear is like a hurdle that you must overcome to take the path to your goal.
Do you have a fear of success or a fear of failure?
Some people have a fear of success.
Some people have a fear of failure.
Are you one of them?

ACTION! – Get your pen ready
Fears are fake
All of your fears are untrue. They are fake. They are 'Tooth Fairy' beliefs (fakes!) that you have made up. Look at each of the fears you have written down above and put a line through them.
GO!

STOP!
Now look at each of your fears and write down "the opposite" of that fear. Write down the positive extreme of your negative fear. Do it for each one below.
GO!

STOP!
What you have written down is the new positive belief you need to overcome your fear. For example if your original fear was "money doesn't make you happy", then you will need to write "Money makes me happy" many times before you'll accept it. To build up belief you will need to write them and repeat them many times. Write and say these mantras as often as possible, either every day or at least once a

week. Put it in your diary to say them every Sunday night or Monday morning.

It's always fear

Whatever hurdle and pain you wrote down it is always fear. For example if your original fear was "money doesn't make you happy" your fear may be that if you have lots of money you won't be happy. Fear is always the emotion that holds us back. To overcome fear you need courage. Only if you are brave will you achieve your dream.

Only if you are brave will you achieve your dream.

If you don't ask you don't get

When I first examined what I valued in life and what I feared in life I discovered why I hadn't achieved progress towards one of my goals! I knew I would like to have a girlfriend and I would get more value and pleasure in life. But I was subconsciously avoiding taking action because of a fear of Rejection and embarrassment. I had steered myself away from pain but away from pleasure too! I hadn't realised why I hadn't got a girlfriend was because I had taken no action! Even Colombo could have worked that out! I was silly but I learnt the lesson! I was avoiding pain but I was avoiding pleasure! I knew that in order for me to achieve my goal I had to take action and I had to accept my fear. I did both and I achieved my goal. And there was much more pleasure in my wonderful life. No action, no wonder.

In order to achieve your dream you need to take action.
To take action you need courage.
Be brave and you can achieve anything.
Fear and pain is a hurdle stopping your path to pleasure and success unless you get over it.

Don't be greedy

Once when I was talking to someone who was having financial difficulty (and she had been struggling financially for many years) I told her that repeating a mantra daily would help. I suggested that she use the mantra "I am a money magnet and money makes me happy." She laughed (which can be a reaction of people when they are uncomfortable) and said, "it sounds a bit greedy." Her reply is her evidence for why she subconsciously does not want to be wealthy. She believes that if you want money you are "greedy" and no one likes greedy people so she does not want to be one of them! She believes money would make her unhappy and her mind knows she wants to be happy so she struggles on.

Money doesn't make you happy

I worked through the aforementioned exercise with a client, to examine why she may be holding herself back from achieving success or taking action or both. On the subject of money one of the first 'why don't you' comments was "money doesn't make you happy." With a belief like that her mind will avoid her having money or being successful because her main goal is to be happy and she believes she can't be happy if she's rich so her mind will make sure that richness doesn't happen! Only happiness. Your beliefs must push you towards your goal not push you away from it. A new belief must be created that you can be rich and happy and happy and rich! Anything is possible.

You can be happy and rich!
If you think you can you can, if you think you can't you're right

The same fear appears

The same fear will appear in more than one aspect of your life. A fear of failure will relate to sport, business and personal life. A fear of rejection, money, success, loneliness, embarrassment or any other fear will affect every aspect of your life.

Rejected in life and business

I had to overcome fear of rejection in my personal life before I could take action against my goal. The same fear of rejection had to be overcome in sales as well. I turned it into a positive game. If you don't ask, you don't get. Success is a numbers game!

Fears are expensive

If a fear holds you back from taking action it can be very expensive. A fear can cost you health, wealth, happiness and success. A fear can cost you your dreams.

A fear can cost you dear. Fears only limit us, if we let them limit us.

Don't pass on your fear

Having a fear can limit you, passing it onto others can limit them.

Keep your fears to yourself.

Talk to someone fearless

Find someone without the same fear as you and you'll find someone without the same thoughts and beliefs as you. If choose the same thoughts and beliefs as someone fearless you will become fearless too.

Find someone without the same fear as you and you'll find
someone without the same thoughts and beliefs as you.

If choose the same thoughts and beliefs as someone fearless, you will become fearless too.

She's not rejecting me

One of my clients has no fear of rejection when it comes to talking to members of the opposite sex. Why? He says, "If I get a knock back, it's not because she doesn't like me, it's because she is not single or she's not in a good mood or I'm not her type." He accepts that not everyone can see how beautiful he is! Not everyone can see how beautiful you are.

Not everyone can see how beautiful you are.
You can look at every situation positively if you use your imagination.
It makes every situation easier to deal with.

Don't think of what might happen

There is a great line in the film 'The Village' where a courageous boy is asked why he has no fear like the other boys. He replies, "I just think of what has to be done, I don't think of what might happen." Don't think about it, just do it.

"I just think of what has to be done, I don't think of what might happen."
- The Village
Don't think about it, just do it.
Reverse psychology can work wonders.

Winning is a risk

There is always the risk of failing, but there is also the risk of winning. If you don't risk it, you won't get it. There is a risk and reward to every action and inaction. The risks and rewards are always greater when you take action. You need to speculate to accumulate.

"In order to win, you have to risk losing."
- Matthew Pinsent, 4 time Olympic Gold Medallist

There is a risk and reward to every action and inaction.
The risks and rewards are always greater to those who take action.

There is always the risk of failing and always the risk of achieving.

As a kid you had no fear

Does a kid ever fear to make a sales call because the answer might be no? No! "Mum can I have this? Come on...please...go on, PLEASE...why not? (What ever Mum replies – they will creatively find a way to solve the problem so they succeed!)" Again and again they will not give up. No matter how many times they fail and hear a no!

As a kid you were a determined fearless winner! You never gave up.

Fearless kids or 'Think less' kids

Our former neighbours told us a story about one of their kids Adam. They were at the Lonach Games in Aberdeenshire which Billy Connolly attends every year and Adam saw Billy walking towards him. As he got near Adam went up to him he said "hey Billy" as if he had known Billy all his life! Fearless? Perhaps. Or perhaps he just didn't think! Kids often don't think about it they just do it! We think about it and that's when the negative thoughts start. If an adult saw Billy they would think, "Billy's a big star....I don't want to interrupt his day out......he must get hassled all the time I won't say anything" even if they are a huge fan! A friend of mine was on the same plane as his heroes after their concert and was near them getting baggage at the airport and never said a thing! If he had no fear like Adam I'm sure he would have gone up to them and said "Hi I just want to say I really like your music and the gig was great" or "can you sign my arm please?." You get the idea! (By the way if you ever see me at the airport or want to email me, be fear less! I don't bite! Whatever you have got to say will make my day or will be my lesson for the day - even if you ask the question! There are no stupid questions just 'stupid' people who don't ask a question, so remain ignorant to the answer!)

Kids are probably the most fearless and 'think less' people in the world.
Start thinking less. Be a kid!
Stop thinking. Just do it! Be fearless. Or just don't think!

Stop thinking and jump

There is a great story in Dan Millman's super book 'The Inner Athlete'. Dan Millman is a former world trampoline champion. When he was a young kid Dan climbed up a house under construction with a friend. The friend jumped off the roof onto a pile of sand below. Standing on the roof looking down at the sand Dan froze and couldn't move despite his friend shouting "Come on Dan, you can do it!." He felt almost paralysed by his fear until his friend shouted something, which he will always remember. "Stop thinking and jump!" He found himself moving through the air towards the sand. The words, the encouragement and the experience was to forever change his life.

Around 10 years later at the world trampoline championships he was waiting to do his final routine but some anxiety and fear went through his mind. The last thing he said to himself before jumping to 1st place was "stop thinking and jump." It's a good phrase to remember in moments when we freeze in fear or "analysis paralysis."

If you feel fear, you're thinking fear.

Fearful thoughts create a fearful person.

Brave thoughts create a brave person.

Stop thinking and jump.

"First you jump off the cliff and you build your wings on the way down."
- Ray Bradbury

Be a World Champion- jump

Dan only became a World Champion because he jumped, because he took action. Making decisions and taking action are essential to achieve anything and this story and phrase is appropriate for encouraging a decision or action or both. It might seem contradictory for a book called 'Winning Mentality' which teaches how to think is encouraging you to stop thinking! You're right, but there comes a point when thinking stops and action starts.

There comes a point when thinking stops and action starts.

Stop thinking and jump

Jump, you can build your wings on the way down.

Facing your fear is painful for seconds,
living with your fear is painful for years.

" Regret for the things we did can be tempered by time;
it is regret for things we did not do that is inconsolable."
-Sydney Harris

If you had no fear what would you do?

You need courage to ask yourself this question. When I have asked myself this question I had found answer and taken action. The answers and actions changed my life. I may not be writing this book now if I didn't use that question and act on the answers.

You're not brave unless you are scared.

ACTION!

If you had no fear what would you do?

What fears have you got? What fears have you identified as holding back your dreams and goals? Write down your answers to these two questions. When you have written them all down rewrite the list with the biggest fear at the top and the smallest fear at the bottom and the rest where appropriate.

GO!

STOP!
Now you have a list of your fears start deciding which one you want to over come first and face it. You can start at the top, the bottom or wherever you like. Each time you face a fear you join the Bottle Club.

"If you do what you fear then death of your fear is certain."
"The first and the best victory is to conquer self." -Plato

Bottle Club
Being brave is essential for success. Winners take risks, which by definition means that they take action even where they cannot be guaranteed success.

Being brave and courageous is sometimes referred to as having "bottle." If you look back you will realise that you have faced fears before and been brave. To put it another way "you have joined the bottle club." Take a page in your notebook and write 'Bottle Club' at the top. Then write down all the times in the past where you have shown bottle.
GO!

STOP!
To win and achieve your goals you will need to keeping joining the bottle club.

Face your fear and join 'the bottle club'.
Be brave and be a winner.
Celebrate with a bottle!

"Dare to win." – Mark Victor Hanson, Author, 'Dare to Win'

Brave Bubble

Pick one of your brave experiences above. Think about that time when you were really brave. Put yourself back to that experience. Remember how you looked, felt and talked. Answer the following four questions and note the first answer that comes to mind and trust it;

GO!

What word comes to mind to describe how you felt?
What colour do you associate with that experience?
What sound do you associate with that experience?
What texture/feeling do you associate with that experience?
Which sense is strongest for you the colour, sound or feeling?

STOP!

Brave Bubble Switch

Now imagine that every time you say 'that word' you switch on the 'brave bubble' and you hear the sound, see the colour or feel the texture. Imagine you are surrounded by the brave 'negative proof' bubble!

Our fear is all in the head

If we feel fear it's because we are thinking fearful thoughts. Our thoughts create our feelings. If we changed our thoughts we'd change our feelings.

Our thoughts create our feelings.
Fearful thoughts create fearful feelings.

Fantasy and reality is the same thing

Imagine you are scared of spiders. You will feel scared whether you see a spider in the house, on the television or visualise a spider in your mind because your mind can't tell the difference between fantasy and reality. That is why people get scared watching movies even though it is actors playing out a fantasy. Your fears are a scary mental movie in your mind, to overcome them you need to stop playing them.

Your mind can't tell the difference between fantasy and reality.
Your fears are a scary mental movie in your mind,
to overcome them you need to stop playing them.

Old Movie

Many fears people have relate to a past negative experience and they keep playing the horror movie in their mind!

Stop watching any negative horror movies from your past.
Wipe them and watch positive future histories instead.

Situation>Decision>Response

If we are in a situation we fear, we will make a fearful decision and make a fearful response. We cannot choose the situation but we can choose to *decide* positively and *respond* positively. Any internal or external stimulus works like this; Stimulus>Mind >Response.

In every situation in life, we chose our response.
Whatever the stimulus, we decide the response.
You can look at every situation positively if you use your imagination.
This makes every situation easier to deal with and response to.

Presentation Fear

We can imagine making a presentation and it will scare us. We can make a presentation and it will scare us. We can also imagine that in the future at some point we may have to make a presentation and that will scare us. We can scare ourselves over things that might never happen.

Fears are negative thoughts

Fears are always negative thoughts. We can overcome them by choosing positive thoughts. Fears relate to situations where we have no control.

Even where we have no control what we can control are our thoughts, so we can overcome all fears by choosing positive thoughts.

Fears are always negative thoughts about situations where we have no control. Choose positive thoughts.

We can overcome fear by choosing positive thoughts.
We are always in control of our thoughts.

Fear is only damaging if we let it affect our actions and damage our success.

Fear never stops a successful person from acting so fear is never damaging.

'Fear is the friend of exceptional people.' –Geoff Thompson
"It's not what happens to you, it's what you do about it"- W. Mitchell

When you meet fear

When we come across a fear, we evaluate the situation in our mind and then evaluate and choose a response. Here's an example of two different people in the same situation to achieve one of their goals.

Situation	Evaluation & Decision	Response
Goal Opportunity	If I don't shoot, I don't score	Shoot
Goal Opportunity	I might miss	Don't shoot

Question
Who are you going to be? The shooter or the misser? Decide now who you are going to be.

Our stress and our fears come from our thoughts. Negative thoughts! Positive thoughts can overcome our stress and our fears.

The garage door is open
A car in the garage is safe but that is not what a car is for. Let go of the handbrake and take the road to your dream destination. The garage door is open and has never been locked.

Fear food
You achieved amazing things when you were young. You were brave and you never gave up. Why do we stop being brave and start being scared? Here is a list of some of the things we have done to lose courage and grow fearful;
You did a lot of left-brain 'knowledge' subjects at school like maths, science
You didn't do much 'creative' stuff growing up like drama, music or art
You have done a lot of left-brain logical and realistic thinking for years
You have got a negative thinking /risk management job (like being a parent)
You worry (creative and imaginative negative thinking and visualising!)
You have heard 'No' 100,000 times so you start thinking 'no'
You watch, listen and read doom and gloom news (television, radio, press)
You don't watch, listen or read about winners, heroes and success
You have lost the childhood need for adventure
You have grown a strong need for a sense of control (security)
You left risk taking, dreaming and persistence in childhood
You don't like change
You don't take risks
You are scared of making mistakes
You would be embarrassed to make a mistake
You avoid fear and crave security
You have a risk adverse personality
You are surrounded by turkey's not eagles
You are surrounded by smart left-brain people
You are not surrounded by risk takers or winners
You think too much

Look at the list above put a tick beside the one's which are true for you.
GO!
STOP!
Brave Food
To reduce your fears and develop your courage 'do the opposite'!
Write down below the things you will DO from now on (not what you won't do!)
GO!
I will
I will
I will
STOP!
Feed your courage by doing 'the opposite' every week. Your brave food will help you join the Bottle Club! Keep the 'brave' bottle topped up.

Winners don't watch the news or read the news. They make it.

Desire vs. imagination
When your desire and your imagination are in conflict your imagination wins. Dr Joseph Murphy uses a great example in his book 'The Power of your Subconscious Mind'. Imagine there is a plank on the ground and your desire is to walk across it because of the reward at the other side. The task is straightforward so we could achieve our desire. However, imagine the plank is high up between two buildings and suddenly the task is not so easy! This time your imagination comes into play and the fear created within your imagination is stopping you taking action to achieve your desires. That is the power of imagination.

Fear is your imagination creating a negative picture that will stop you taking action to achieve your desired goals.

Your imagination holds you back. Use your imagination to push you forward. Relax and picture positively over and over again.

Your imagination is good or bad.
If it helps you it's good, if it hinders you it's bad.

It's easy to walk in the woods when it's light during the day.
How many people walk in the woods when it's dark at night?
The only difference is your imagination.
Imagination can hold you back from taking a dark track.

Dream of desires
Millions of people in the UK desire to be a millionaire, they play the lottery. However, few people imagine they could become a millionaire, other than by winning the lottery. Desires don't achieve dreams. Positive imagination and motivation achieve dreams.

Positive imagination and motivation is more important than desire.

Do what you fear and death of the fear is certain

As a wise man once said 'Do what you fear and death of the fear is certain'. Once you do it, you will stop to fear it. The more often you do it the more comfortable you will become with it. You are stretching your comfort zone. You won't regret it! But you might regret not doing it.

"Do what you fear and death of the fear is certain."
You won't regret doing it but you might regret not doing it.

Overcome fear

The winning mentality techniques can help you overcome your fear;

1. Mental Movie
2. Directing (I can do it!)
3. Mantra (I am brave!)
4. Switch to 'Hero' or Positive Bubble
5. Acting fearless
6. Psych yourself up
7. Power hand

Therefore pick one of the techniques and then…just do it!

Negative visualisation's stop people winning

Negative visualisation is the father to a (negative) fear. All fears are negative viewpoints of a situation. Negative fears are the work of our imagination. Fears can be caused by two things; a negative experience or just a negative imagination. We can choose your thoughts therefore we can choose to keep these fears (and keep the negative thoughts) or can choose positive thoughts (and get rid of the fears).

Negative Mental Movie

People sometimes develop a new fear after having a negative experience. A bumpy or turbulent plane trip can be a memorable experience. Frequent flyers can turn themselves into fearful flyers if they choose to replay the negative experience in their mind before future flights. It even stops people flying. They need to focus on their positive experiences and visualise positively. The same can be said for a golfer who has one bad experience with a course/club/hole. It becomes a 'bogie hole' or 'fearful shot' in their golf game. It affects performance. It's the same in business when a 'fear' develops over a presentation. I know business people holding themselves back because of a presentation fear. Presenting is essential in business today.

Negative Experience>Negative visualisation>Negative Fear

*Negative Experience>**Positive** visualisation>**No Fear***

Fears are negative visualisations. People who fear planes, presentations, or putting are all doing negative visualisation in their mind. Play Positive Movie!

When a negative experience is replayed in the mind like a negative 'mental movie' it creates a negative fear. Take out the tape and play a positive one!

Negative Stops

Some people will imagine a negative visualisation so many times that it stops them for taking action. Therefore it stops then from succeeding and in the short-term action it stops them failing. But in the long term inaction is failing. Even if you're on the right road, you'll get run over if you just sit there. Stop negative visualisation before it stops you.

Negative thoughts kill dreams- fear buries them.
If you don't bury your fear, your fear will bury your dream.

Stopping Negative thoughts and fears

You are in control of your thoughts. You are in control of your imagination. You are the director in control of your 'mental movies' so you can "cut" negative ones! Take the tape out of your mind and throw it into the bin and play a positive mental movie. Relax and Play your mental movie and it will 'cut' your fear in 30 days. Then you have to face the fear and have a positive experience to build confidence.

You are the director in control of your 'mental movies' so you can "cut" negative ones! *Relax and Play your positive mental movie*

Positive Visualisation

Overcome fear by doing a positive visualisation. Relax yourself, take some deep breaths and then go through a full experience in your mind. Repeat this every day, preferably at night. Within 4 weeks or 30 days you should face your fear and do it. However, you don't have to wait 30 days to face your fear you could do it in 30 minutes. Picture the positive mental movie several times in your mind. It's very powerful. One other advantage is to use positive verbalisation or a positive mantra at the same time.

Picture them naked

The solution to overcome the fear is to view the fear within your mind in a positive way even humorous way in a 'Mental Movie'. I'm sure you have heard the classic advice overcoming presentation fear, which is "picture your audience naked"! The idea behind this advice is excellent. Create a funny visualisation in your mind instead of a negative one and it will greatly assist your confidence and your mood! Create a 'mental movie' that makes you laugh and laugh away your fear.

ACTION!
Positive Brave Mantra
Through the use of positive verbalisation you can build up confidence and self-belief. The best positive verbalisation is to have a positive mantra. To decide upon your mantra write down the words 'I am' followed by the answers to these two statements. Consider how you feel about your fear now and write down 'the opposite' of those feelings. Secondly imagine you have faced your fear how do you feel?
GO!

STOP!
Simplify your courage building brave mantra to suit you. Write this down several times. Say it, hum it and sing it too. Alternatively you can overcome your fear today using the positive brave mantra and/or positive visualisation.

Anything is possible.
If you say you can, you can.
If you imagine you can, you can.

You can do it!
Whatever gets thrown at you remember one thing - you can do it! "I can handle it!" Is one of the best mantras you can say to yourself.

When you see a challenge think, "I can do it!."
When a challenge sees you think, "I can handle it!"

When you take control of your mind you take control of the situation.
And you CAN then handle it!

Positive thoughts, give you positive power and positive results.

'There are no limits'

Act Fearless
Use positive body language and act fearless. Your mind will read your body and make you feel more confident. Just do it.

Psych yourself up

This technique helps get you in a positive 'state' of mind before you face your fear. However, it doesn't completely eliminate the fear you feel like visualisation can. To put it another way, 'feel the fear and do it anyway'!

Facing your fear can be a battle, throw some positive punches.
Give yourself a pep talk and pump yourself up.
'Feel the fear and do it anyway!' – Susan Jeffers, Author

Power Hand

This powerful technique was covered previously. It is extremely useful for overcoming fear. Your confidence is in your hands.

Get over it

I helped someone overcome a fear of flying. When I got her to visualise herself getting on a plane she was calm and relaxed (she was very uncomfortable and scared minutes before). Afterwards I asked her how she felt about flying now 'I don't feel scared right now, but I know I will'. Don't make the stupid mistake of thinking and talking yourself back into a fear once you get over it.

Don't be surprised when your thoughts get you over a fear.
It was your thoughts that got you into it in the first place!
Don't be stupid and think yourself back into a fear.

In order to succeed like a hero you have to act like a hero. Heroes succeed because they are brave not fearless. For you to succeed you need the same qualities of a hero. Look at the qualities of your heroes and decide what qualities you need to succeed. You did this in the previous chapter. Consider the importance of courage. Now write down the 7 qualities you will need to succeed below on the left hand side.

GO!

STOP!

Now write down your top 7 goals in the middle with the dates on the right hand side.
GO!

STOP!
Above are the 7 qualities you will need to 'model' from your heroes into your character in order to achieve your 7 goals. To succeed you need to 'switch' into a hero and then you can take action in a Positive Mind. Go for it!

To achieve your dreams you will need to make brave decisions and make brave actions.

Passion, Anger, Love, Fear, Pleasure, Pain
Motivation comes in many different forms; passion or anger, love or fear, pleasure or pain. But it always comes down to pleasure and pain. We like to do things that give us pleasure. However, we will do more to avoid pain than to gain pleasure. Fear is one of the biggest pains that everyone avoids. It holds most people back. Nothing holds a winner back.

Change
Winners don't fear change. To achieve dreams people have to change. Most people never change until they have a painful experience. A friend of mine lost 3 stone in 3 months after seeing a holiday photo of himself and deciding to change. That was his motivation. Recently a grand mother from Dundee gave up smoking after she had smoked for 50 years after she was examined about her health. She decided to raise money for the hospital that saved the life of her grand daughter in the process. That was her motivation. Sometimes we need pain to change. Sometimes we get pain and never change. Some people are proactive, some people are reactive and some people never change. Winners can fit into each of the three categories at different times. Winners will change to win.

When the pain of remaining the same is greater than the pain of change, then change will come.
A painful experience can make a person change and achieve a goal.
Some people are reactive. Some people are proactive.
To live happily and successfully you need three things;
Serenity to accept the things you cannot change.
Courage to change the things you can.
Wisdom to know the difference.

Winners Change

Winners do whatever it takes to succeed. Winners change whatever they need to change to win.

If do what you have always done,
you will get what you have always got.
Always change a losing game. Never change a winning game.
Winners don't fear change.
"It's not the strongest, fittest, fastest or smartest that will outlast others and ultimately survive, but those who adapt to change."
- Charles Darwin
"Change or die."
-John Sperling, billionaire entrepreneur, owner of University of Phoenix

"Winners change, losers don't."
– Seth Godin, Business guru and best selling author

"Management is not about preservation of the status quo, it's about managing the highest rate of change that the organisation and people within it can stand." – Sir John Harvey Jones, 'Making it happen'

Mega goal

A service has been launched by bus company Stagecoach this year in the UK called Megabus which offers very cheap fares between the major cities in the UK. A bit like a cheap no frills airline but using buses not planes. The service has gone down a storm. Their competitor may go down. Winners change losers don't.

Companies that don't look at future possibilities could
possibly be beaten in future.
"To be a success. Be bold. Be daring. Be first."
–Ray Kroc, founder of McDonalds
Sometimes being second in business is advantageous.
Look at the success of German, Italian and Japanese cars!

Identify weaknesses

A United Kingdom company that started selling Indian beer called 'Cobra Beer' gets most of their sales through restaurants and on an away day with senior management they did a SWOT session and identified 'wine' as a threat. They set the goal to launch a wine. They developed a range of affordable table wines and developed their business successfully. Winners change losers don't.

Businesses and sports teams that have weaknesses,
could be exposed by their competition.
Dream. Be bold. Be brave.
Be a winner.

Being brave can change your life
To achieve your dreams you need to take action. To take action sometimes you need to be brave. To achieve your dreams you will need to make brave decisions and make brave actions. Heroes are brave, not fearless.

Be brave, be a winner.

To achieve your dreams make brave decisions and take brave actions.

The girl on the train
Sometimes just a few moments of bravery can change your life. I want to tell you a wonderful story that has had a huge impact on my life. A few years ago I began to think about something I wanted..........a girlfriend! I then started to think and investigate why I didn't have a girlfriend. I soon realised the answer- I hadn't spoken to any girls I liked or asked any out! I'd taken no ACTION!

One morning when I was commuting by train into the city, a woman got on and I thought, "that would be the type of girl I would love to go out with." (She was attractive and I could intuitively just 'tell' she was really nice on the inside too). She got a seat near the door. She got off at the same stop but walked off in a different direction. I saw her a few days later get on at the same stop. I was sitting in a bench row of seats facing a bench row of seated commuters. She came in and sat down on the only free seat.....the seat on the left next to me! At first I thought, "What do I say?" and then I didn't say a thing! The whole carriage was in silence! While walking into work and later that day I gave myself a good talking to and thought about the question "If I had no fear what would I do?" The answer of course was talk to her! If that went well ask her out. I thought to myself "If you don't ask, you don't get! I'll never know, she can only say no! If I don't ask I'll still be single but if I do ask and I fail I'll still be single. No difference! But if I succeed big difference!"

I was lucky that one day I saw her again sitting a few seats away and she happened to look across and smiled. I knew I wanted to talk to her and give her my number so I took out a business card and wrote down my mobile on it. She got off the train ahead of me and as I began to walk quickly to catch her up I was full of fear and full of butterflies! I caught her up and said "hi, how you doing?" or similar and we started chatting.

Just as we were both about to walk in different directions I handed over my card and said, "here's my number if you want to go out sometime." And then we both went out off down different streets. I smiled and then a wave of euphoria rushed though me! I felt amazing! In that moment I actually didn't care if she called me I was just overjoyed at facing my fear. It felt wonderful.

But she did get in touch. We did meet up, we did get on and we did go out. It was wonderful. The whole experience has changed my life and the story has inspired many people. I hope it inspires you.

If you had NO FEAR what would you do? What is the "something" that you want? PANIC is good! It means you are stretching yourself, either in your job, relationship, sport or life. No one has "no fear"! If you feel full of fear and full of butterflies, go for it anyway! It's a wonderful feeling and it's a wonderful life.

If you had NO FEAR what would you do?

If you don't act, you don't get! If you do act and fail there is no difference! But if you succeed big difference! It's a numbers game!

Wonderful things can happen when you take action.
No ACTION, no wonder!

'Who dares wins.' – SAS motto

"There are risks and costs to a program of action.
But they are far less than the long-range risks and costs of comfortable inaction."
--John F. Kennedy (1917-1963) 35th president of the U.S.

Pain of Regret

It is more painful to live with fear than to face fear. It is more painful to live with regret than to live with adventurous mistakes.

"Regret for the things we did can be tempered by time; it is regret for things we did not do that is inconsolable." -Sydney Harris

"Twenty years from now, you will be more disappointed by the things you didn't do, than by the ones you did. So throw off the bowlines. Sail away from the safe harbour. Catch the trade winds in your sails. Explore. Dream."
– Inspirational American legend Mark Twain (1835-1910)

Very Fast Summary

There are only two thoughts positive or negative.
To achieve your dreams make brave decisions and take brave actions.
No ACTION, no wonder!
Always change a losing game. Never change a winning game.
Winners don't fear change.
Fear is your imagination holding you back.
Our stress and our fears come from our thoughts. Negative thoughts!
Face your fear and join 'the bottle club'.
Do what you fear and death of the fear is certain.
Dare to win.
There comes a point when thinking stops and action starts.
Stop thinking and jump
You can't cross a chasm in two small jumps.
Just think of what has to be done, don't think of what might happen
Think Positive > Feel Positive < Act Positive
Be brave and you can achieve anything.

We are very motivated do things that give us pleasure! But only if they won't give us pain! We are more motivated to avoid pain than gain pleasure.
Fear and pain is a hurdle on your path to success. Get over it.

If we attempt something and fail there is no difference to our situation than if we made no attempt. But if we attempt and succeed there is a big difference, so always attempt. Success is a numbers game!

People prefer to fail to attempt their dream than to fail attempting their dream.
It is more painful to live with fear than to face fear.
If you had no fear what would you do?
"The first and the best victory is to conquer self." -Plato

Some people have a fear of success.
Some people have a fear of failure.
Are you one of them? Negative thoughts sabotage your success.
Negative thoughts can stop you going anywhere.

"In order to win, you have to risk losing."
- Matthew Pinsent, 4 time Olympic Gold Medallist

Heroes are brave, not fearless.

Be brave, be a winner. Be a hero.

"All of our dreams can come true, if we have the courage to pursue them." - Walt Disney

Chapter 7
ENERGY (Relaxation)

Very fast Summary

Winners need energy. 'Winning Mentality' requires mental energy. Winners need a large reserve of mental and physical energy and one of the ways they achieve this is through relaxation. Relaxing before and after performances is imperative to have the high levels of mental and physical energy necessary for a great performance. In business (and sports like golf) relaxing during performances is also essential to maintain mental energy and concentration.

This chapter includes advice on how to have relaxing "brain breaks" before, during and after performing! To perform brilliantly over a period of a year, longer relaxing "brain breaks" are essential for every business person and almost every sport person.

Included in this chapter;

Winners need mental and physical energy
Being a winner is a challenging and stressful job
Goals require your full concentration and ability
Demanding goals and challenges can be stressful
Stress is great for performance
Too much stress has an adverse affect on performance
Why relaxation is essential in business and sport
Stimulation not relaxation
9 ways in which we increase energy, creativity and decrease stress
9 ways in which we increase stress and decrease energy and Mindpower
How to relax
Deep relaxation improves intuition and energy and reduces sleep required

Winners need energy

Winners need energy. Winners usually have a dream goal beyond their abilities. Therefore they are constantly using every bit of skill and energy they have. Winners need physical and mental energy to achieve their big goal and win.

Being a winner is a stressful job

Winners do challenging tasks and set challenging goals which create stress. Being under stress helps them give a great performance and use their full ability. Winners handle challenging and stressful situations in three ways. They use mind techniques like those in this book. Winners also reduce the stress they experience every week through their habits like those suggested in this chapter. Thirdly winners experience stress but are able to cope because they look after their healthy body and healthy mind.

Winners use their full ability and energy

When winners do things that use their full abilities they experience what Professor Mihalyi Csikszentmihalyi, Department of Psychology at the University of Chicago refers to as 'flow' in his book 'Flow: The Psychology of Optimal Experience'. He says that people enter a flow state when they are fully absorbed in an activity during which they lose their sense of time and have feelings of great satisfaction. He describes flow as "being completely involved in an activity for its own sake. The ego falls away. Time flies. Every action, movement, and thought follows inevitably from the previous one, like playing jazz. Your whole being is involved, and you're using your skills to the utmost." Winners use all of their ability and often all their energy to work on a goal or achieve a goal.

Go with the flow.

Winners stretch

According to Professor Csikszentmihalyi, setting goals is beneficial to attaining a 'state of flow'. If we don't set goals or use our abilities "to the utmost" we become bored. At the other end of the scale he points out that when people do things beyond their abilities they feel 'anxiety' and stress. That is what winners do most of the time! Winners give themselves challenges and stress. This pressure and stress actually helps drive winners to work hard and perform. Everyone needs a little stress and pressure otherwise we would become bored. Winners are always stretching themselves, which is why they need so much energy. In order to have a full tank of energy the relaxation techniques they use are crucial.

Inspired by physiologist Carl Jung, Professor Csikszentmihalyi has devoted his life to the study of what makes people truly happy, satisfied and fulfilled. The detail below shows his theory. If you were to draw a line and join the 'flow' it would be like the shape of the start of a mountain climb. Winners climb mountains;

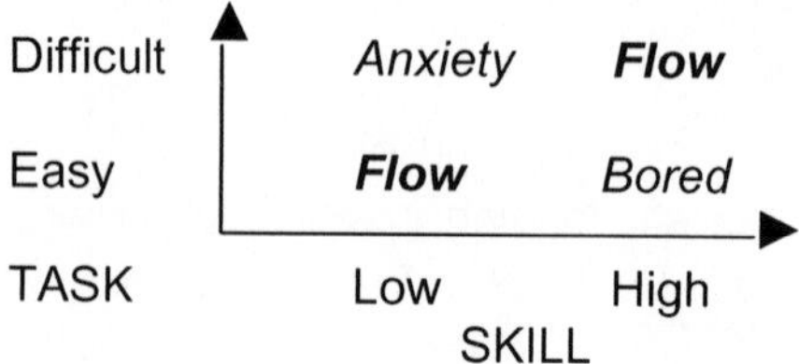

Winners do things that are difficult! Activities in the top right. They set themselves goals that are within and often beyond their abilities! Winners often do the latter to achieve a dream or to stretch their ability and comfort zone. A marathon runner for example might run 30 miles so that a 26-mile race becomes easier. By stretching their ability winners achieve their dreams and get a great feeling of satisfaction from it. Things that are too simple would bore a winner. Easy low skill activities are good for relaxation but are not challenging enough to do all the time. For example reading is an easy activity that requires concentration but is relaxing, and time can fly by because you are in 'flow'. Something often experienced by athletes and referred to as being 'in the zone'. Winning in sport or business requires your full concentration and when you feel it is within your ability you feel 'in the zone'.

Those that use their skills to the utmost experience 'flow'.
Winners do things that are within and often beyond their abilities.
They handle the challenge because they handle the stress.

Winners set challenging goals outwith their ability and stretch until it is within their ability.
Being under stress helps winners give a great performance and use their mind and body fully.

Winners reduce stress by looking after their mind and body.
Being over stressed affects performance.

Winners panic

Winners often do things so outwith their abilities and comfort zone that they panic. I've heard successful actor Pierce Brosnan being really worried before starting his latest film and he has been a successful actor for years! Even James Bond panics! Ask any winner in business and sport and they will have a story to tell. Entrepreneur Michelle Mone's company was three hours away from being closed down by a bank when she secured backing to save the company. Chris Gorman was days away from losing his house and business DX

Communication when he secured funding and went on to become a millionaire. Some even admit to having panic attacks. I've felt it once. You just got for it and it works out fine! I actually looked at the experience really positively because I knew if I was panicking, it meant I was stretching myself!

Winners often stretch themselves well beyond their comfort zone and panic. Even James Bond Panics!
Stretching yourself today and you will be a greater person tomorrow.

Relaxation helps winners win
Winners have lots of energy. They need a large amount of physical and mental energy to succeed. They do several things which give them a bigger tank of energy than most people and one of those is the way they relax. 'Winning Mentality' requires mental energy. Relaxing before and after performances is imperative to have the high levels of mental energy necessary to perform. In business (and sports like golf) relaxing during performances is essential to maintain mental energy and concentration. This chapter includes advice on how to have relaxing "brain breaks" before, during and after performing!

To perform brilliantly over a period of a year taking long "brain breaks" are essential for every business person and almost every sport person. Long brain breaks are fully explained in the chapter.

Relaxation is essential for mental and physical energy.
Winning Mentality requires mental energy.

Why relaxation is essential in business and sport
Mental energy is easier to have for short periods of time than for long periods. A sprinter will find it easier than a snooker or tennis player, for example. Business people have the same challenge as 'stop start' sports like tennis and golf. The period of performance is measured in hours not seconds! Many successful entrepreneurs only work half days-the first 12 hours or the second! In order that mental energy is maintained during a day at the office or during a day on the golf course the individual must include periods of relaxation during their period of performance (even if only for a few minutes over a 2 hour period). Otherwise their mental energy deteriorates, along with their performance, due to the impact on concentration.

Relaxation <u>during</u> performance is essential to win in business.
Relaxation <u>during</u> performance is essential in some sports.

Mental energy can be maintained for hours,
for a few minutes of relaxation every hour

Decreases in mental energy decrease concentration,

which decreases performance.

Relaxation Saves Energy

Even sprinters must be able to relax before competition in order to have the mental energy to give a great winning performance. If sprinters are nervous or stressed in the run up to a performance it will reduce energy both mentally and physically.

Sleeping Wins Olympic Medals

The Australian Freestyle Ski Champion Alisa Camplin won a gold medal in the 2002 Winter Olympics. However, she was so nervous the night before the event that she phoned up her American psychologist in tears. She must have heard what she needed to hear because she went back to bed and the following day she made history and won a gold medal. In my humble opinion the sleep was very useful for her gold winning performance. The following day she woke up as an Olympic gold winner!

A good night sleep can help win medals. So can a good mind coach!
If Olympic contenders sleep well, they'll perform well.

Not Sleeping is Costly

The British World Champion and Marathon Record Holder Paula Radcliffe went to the Olympics in Athens 2004 with a long held dream of winning an Olympic medal. Paula is a 'legend' when it comes to her training, her preparation and her determination for running. Her entire preparation in 2003 and 2004 was targeted at peaking in Athens. The Athens marathon course was going to be a lot harder than the relatively flat courses in London and Chicago where Paula had set records. It was also going to be hotter. Accordingly Paula trained for the conditions and the course, like most other athletes. I sat down to watch the race, as Paula is a hero of mine and a personal running role model. I caught the big build up on television to the race, which included a few aerial shots of the course and the runners warming up. Then the commentator said something, which rang an alarm bell in my mind and caused me a lot of concern. The commentator mentioned that they had found out that "Paula didn't sleep much last night." Oh dear.

Sleep gives the body energy. Adequate sleep before a physically demanding marathon is essential for having high energy levels. Paula may or may not have had adequate sleep. Several other factors can impact a marathon run but I am confident that "not much sleep" would definitely affect performance. I know it affects my energy and the winners I talk to.

Get a good nights sleep. Or it could stop you performing to your best.

"Hindsight is an exact science."

Great performances need great preparation.
And a great nights sleep.

Great Preparation
Great winning performances only come from great winning preparation. A lot is involved in great preparation. Relaxation is one of them. Be prepared.

Be prepared
Winning preparation creates winning results.

"It is a hard event and requires a lot of
physical and mental preparation."
-Paula Radcliffe on a marathon

Poor preparation means poor performance.

Relax before performance to win
A good night's sleep is not the only ingredients of a winning performance. Relaxation before performance is important too to save physical and mental energy. One of my clients told me that he used to drive to golf tournaments listening to comedian Steve Martin on tape. Great way to relax! After our session his "I used to" winning strategy became a "I use it" winning strategy!

Relaxing before performing saves physical and mental energy

Avoiding Stress, Nerves, Worry and Fear
Stress, Nerves, Worry and Fear are all 'mental' challenges and not 'physical' challenges like a twisted ankle. As you know! I have two important points to make. Firstly we need to avoid Stress, Nerves, Worry and Fear because it uses up mental and physical energy. Secondly if the challenge is in the mind then we need to use the mind to resolve it.

A winner finds a way to deal with these challenges because it could cost them the win by thinking too many negative thoughts. And cost them mental and physical energy, which they need to win.

5 Minutes Relaxation won't solve 18 hours of stressful living and eating
A lot of average sports people and business people are costing themselves undue 'stress' unknowingly through their behaviour, mind, eating and lifestyle. Stress reduces their mental and physical energy. Not only that but even if they were to follow the relaxation tool in this chapter for a few minutes everyday it would not be very effective

because their body is under so much stress it doesn't make an impact. It's a bit like not eating for 1 hour every day, it would make no impact whatsoever to a 30 stone man if he was eating for the other 23 hours! So if you live and eat stressfully don't kid yourself if you think this one relaxation tool will give you the energetic, creative, innovate, positive and razor sharp mind you need to win. It won't, although it will help you and it will improve your mind. This tool is very effective in stressful performance periods when your mind and body are being given 'good energy' fuel. This tool is not very effective in stressful performance periods when your mind and body are over stressed by 'stress fuel'.

5 minutes relaxation doesn't solve 18 hours of stressful living and eating!
Relaxation is a very effective tool in stressful performance periods but only when your mind and body are being given 'good energy' fuel every day.

9 ways to increase energy

INCREASE ENERGY	**DECREASE ENERGY**
1. FRESH AIR	1. LITTLE FRESH AIR or BREATHS
2. WATER	2. NO WATER or DEHYDRATED
3. GOOD NUTRITION	3. NO FOOD or NON ENERGY FOOD
4. EXERCISE	4. NO MOVING or EXCESS EXERCISE
5. POSITIVE MIND	5. NON-POSITIVE or STRESSED MIND
6. RELAX 'TIME OUT'	6. NO RELAXATION FOR MIND/BODY
7. SENSES	7. NON POSITIVE STIMULATION
8. SLEEP	8. NO SLEEP or OVER SLEEP
9. SUN/DAYLIGHT	9. NON POSITIVE ENVIRONMENT

More Detail;

1. AIR - FRESH AIR

Fresh air and deep breaths significantly increases energy levels. Best air is located beside forests, rivers, countryside or beside the sea due to the high level of negative ions in the air. The obvious way is to spend time outside; preferable in fresh air or if in the city around sunrise is the best for air quality. Two unique ways to improve air quality in your home is to use an ioniser and vacuum your bed monthly!

Fresh air is good for your mind and body.
"Negative ions are like vitamins in the air." -Patrick Holford
Patrick Holford is the best-selling author of 'Optimum Nutrition Bible', 'Optimum Nutrition for the Mind', 'The 30 day Fat-burner diet' and 'The Holford Diet' and founder of the renowned 'Institute for Optimum Nutrition'.

2. WATER - HYDRATED NOT DEHYDRATED

The body is made up of 70% water and water is an essential requirement for the body and brain to function. The energy of the body is severely affected even with small levels of dehydration. The performance, concentration and memory of the brain are affected by lack of water. Regular intake from morning till night is required for high levels of energy and performance. I drink a pint of water before every meal. I drink a pint of water as soon as I get up in the morning; because the body has had no water for 6 hours and instantly feel more energy. Simple test; if urine is yellow you are dehydrated, if clear you are hydrated. If you are thirsty; drink. If you are hungry; eat (but have a pint of water first). Listen to your body.

Carbonated or fizzy drinks have a high pH and affect stomach acid levels. Water does not have same effect. If the drink also contains sugar there is another reason not to drink it; it will affect your blood sugar and rot your teeth.

Look at what cola does to a dirty coin! Water doesn't have that effect!
Drink one pint before meals and whenever you feel like drinking, drink as soon as you feel thirsty.
Dilute fruit juice with 50% water for steady energy.
If you add a pinch of salt you have got 'cheap mans lucozade'!

Cup of Calm

One of calm expert Paul Wilson's tips is drink a cup a camomile tea. It's calming, relaxing and therefore reduces stress and increases energy. His book 'The little book of Calm' is the best investment you will ever put in your pocket for £2. It is based on the tips included in his other best seller 'Instant Calm' which is classic.

Cut Coffee

Nutritionist Dr Christine Fenn author of 'The energy advantage' makes a 'caffeine challenge' with office and offshore workers after giving her talks and she gets brilliant feedback from those that go for it. No more; headaches, mood swings and tinnitus. And surprisingly better; communication, relationships and sleeping are all common feedback. Chris states,

"Life in the fast lane is.. fast! We eat on the run, trying to pack more and more into each day. Not surprisingly, something has to give and shopping, preparing and eating food gets pushed further down the priority list. The result is that we grab poor quality fast food, gulp it down whilst we text, email or speak on the phone - and then wonder why we feel sluggish, bloated and tired all the time. The end result is that we are overfed but undernourished.

It is time to join the slow food culture, and take time out to eat and enjoy quality food. Making a few small changes to your eating habits can bring large benefits to your energy levels and overall health. Try giving up, or cutting down on caffeine. It is the world's most popular stimulant but far from boosting your brain, it works by stimulating the production of stress hormones (including adrenalin and cortisol). These are released naturally by your adrenal glands every time you are stressed. For most people, this happens many times during a busy day - so you don't need caffeine to add to your stress levels! Caffeine also interferes with your natural sleep cycles - which are important recovery times for your brain and body. Without these your mental energy suffers, you can't think as creatively or make those important decisions. Your immune system is also affected - so that it can no longer fight off bacteria and viral infections. It is interesting that die-hard coffee drinkers are also the ones who tend to suffer regularly from colds, coughs, sore throats and flu.

The energy that you have during the day is a reflection of the quality of the sleep you had the night before. Take caffeine out of your system and feel the difference. However, expect to feel worse before you feel better. After about 3 caffeine free days, expect to feel more alive and energised than you have done in years.

Be all that you can be.. and all that you are. Remember, there are limits to the time you have to live.... but no limits to how you live your time!"

Coffee is not for winners

Volunteers in Japan who took 150mg of coffee took 126 minutes to get to sleep. Non-coffee drinkers took 29 minutes to get to sleep and slept for 444 minutes. Non-coffee drinkers had only 281 minutes sleep.

Liquid lunch

The best liquid for lunch is water. I drink a pint before my meal. Ever felt really good after drinking a lot of alcohol? Your mind and body are telling you something. Few people listen. Everything you eat and drink goes into your blood and your brain. Hence why coffee and alcohol affect the mind. You need to fuel your mind and body with energy. Air and water are essential. The body is 70% water.

Listen to your body.
Studies on kids have shown that when they are given healthy food and water they perform better, concentrate better and behave better.
Eat and drink better food and you get better performance.

3. GOOD NUTRITION - MORE HEALTHY LESS STRESS FOOD

Good food gives us a good mood. Bad food gives us a bad mood. Studies on kids have shown that good food helps their concentration and performance and behaviour. Bad food makes them bad. They perform badly, concentrate badly and behave poorly. Poor quality food gives you poor quality results. In 2002 a British study of young offenders found a 37% drop in violent offence when they were given nutritional supplements! The brain MUST get certain vitamins and minerals from food or it does not perform. Read 'Optimum Nutrition for the mind' by Patrick Holford. He has cured people's mental problems with food. Some people are depressed just because of a lack of niacin or tryptophan in their diet.

You need good food for a good mind.
Bad foods makes boys bad.
Food fall into 3 categories; medicine, poison and neutral.

"Let food be your medicine and medicine be your food" –Hippocrates

"A couple of handfuls of cashew nuts delivers the same dose of serotonin naturally as Prozac does artificially"
– Andrew Saul, author, 'Doctor Yourself'

"How you think and feel is directly affected by what you eat. This idea may seem strange, yet the fact is that eating the right food has been proven to boost your IQ, improve your mood and emotional stability, sharpen your memory and keep your mind young"
-Patrick Holford, author, 'Optimum Nutrition for the Mind'

Brain Food

Good fuel for the brain is carbohydrate. The brain only uses glucose for energy. (Of course love, laughter and positive thoughts are good for the brain too!) However, the brain does need food other than carbs for function and repair. Good food for the brain in order of priority is; air (the fresher the better), water, glucose, carbs, some protein and 'essential fat' (good fat). Ever felt hungry after an exam or several hours thinking and not moving? Your brain has used up the bodies energy and any energy from the food you've eaten therefore you need to feed it. Preferably with the first three priorities first above.

The brain is made of 100% fat so 'no fat diets' are a "no no"! And they give you bad moods. 'Essential fat' is good for the body and the brain and it's found in foods like fish, nuts and cod liver oil.

The brain uses glucose for energy.
The brain uses 20% of the body's energy!
When you eat you are feeding your body <u>and</u> your brain.
Everything you eat and drink goes into your blood stream. Which enters your whole body including your brain. Junk food and drink will give you a junk mind and a junk body. You are what you eat and drink.

Graze all day

I usually eat just fruit for breakfast and feel better and think better. I sometimes have porridge or pancakes mid morning. Good lunch and dinner and plenty fruit and vegetables. I usually eat something like soup and oatcakes for lunch and rice, pasta or baked potato with fish or soya for dinner. I often eat healthy snacks between meals e.g. fruit, pancakes, flapjacks, nuts, dips etc.

Eat light, feel light.
Experiment! If you don't test changes,
you won't see changes in energy.
Eat only fresh fruits for one day and see how you feel.
Eat only meats for one day and see how you feel. (If meat eater!)

"A healthy body wants healthy food, an unhealthy body wants unhealthy food" – Dr John Gray,
'Mars and Venus Diet and Exercise Solution'

Thin Japan

There are almost no fat people in Japan. Outside the Sumo wrestling ring there were no fat people in Japan. But since they introduced McDonald's and Coca-Cola there are now some fat people among the younger generation.

The more overweight you are the more health problems you have and the less energy you have. Someone who becomes overweight may find the quality of their sleep reduced.

Eating breakfast 'wakes up and raises your metabolism which has been asleep while you were in bed and never ate. Every time you eat your metabolism raises slightly. Exercise raises your metabolism for about 24 hours which is why you can exercise every second day and be reasonably healthy. Raising your metabolism burns more calories.

Fat people don't eat breakfast.
Fat people don't exercise.

Grazing is better than gorging. Eating small amounts of food is beneficial because they are easily digested by your body and your blood sugar levels and energy levels are more balanced.

'Eat like a king for breakfast, a prince for lunch and a porper for dinner.' - is a good philosophy for losing weight but is also a good philosophy for losing concentration in the morning and afternoon.

Danger Foods

Processed foods and foods with additives (check the label!) are bad for you. To put it bluntly they are poisonous for the mind and body. Avoid almost all foods with sugar (check the label!). Read Patrick Holford's two 'Optimum' books to find out all the negative effects of sugar. The book 'Sugar busters' gives plenty of good stories on no sugar diet benefits and how borderline diabetics improved health. In countries with no sugar they have no diabetes. In countries with fibre they have low health problems. One spoon of bran a day can save your life according to the great book 'The save your life diet'. Alternatively it suggests eating real foods and not manufactured foods with almost no fibre like white bread and fast food. Small amounts of caffeine, alcohol and chocolate can have a beneficial effect. Medium or large amounts don't. If you don't normally drink coffee or alcohol now, don't start now! You're healthier than 90% of the nation already!

Check the category of the foods you eat.
Food fall into 3 categories; medicine (energy giving and healing), poison (energy stealing and toxic) and neutral (energy giving).

."Let food be your medicine and medicine be your food" –Hippocrates

Energy Food

Processed food, sugar or big meals reduce energy. Junk food and sugar may satisfy cravings but it doesn't satisfy the appetite because it is nutrition-less food and has little fibre and little energy in fact it reduces energy within an hour. The body also uses up a lot of energy to filter junk food. A huge amount of energy is needed by the body if we over eat, even for digesting big healthy meals (hence why a big healthy dinner at Christmas puts you to sleep!) When I began eating a vegan diet (with some fish like the Japanese) my energy went up like a cheetah, I had the strength of an elephant and I stopped sleeping like a lion! Surprisingly my iron levels improved too! I began this 'energy diet' and gave up my favourites foods; steak, chicken and milk shakes after find really powerful health advice. The evidence was so convincing and clear cut about benefits to health, energy and living longer. It had to be for me to give up my favourite foods! Read the book 'Fit for life' by Harvey and Marilyn Diamond for yourself. I eat some soya, quorn, nuts or fish for protein everyday. One of the best nutrition experts in the world that I follow is Patrick Holford, Author of 'The Optimum Nutrition Bible' and 'Optimum Nutrition for the Mind'. The latter one is of more interest for Winning mentality which is why some of the tips are in here. Both books are on nutrition and the second book focuses on the mind and how he's cured mental problems with food! After reading both of their suggestions I don't think either one of them conflicts! Great minds think alike. Read them. Experiment with food. What you eat and when you eat it.

If you do what you have always done,
you'll get what you have always got.
If you test out a few things you might get more of
what you've got! Energy!

Healthy but often low energy

My diet has always been very healthy from the day I was born. I have also kept active (and therefore fit) from the day I was born! After a full medical check at 20 years old my doctor looked at my results and said, "you are going to live forever". I smiled. My Dad was delighted and proud. The only 'fault' in my results was a low iron level in my blood.

Then at 24 years old I changed to an 'energy diet' and began eating fruit in the morning and mostly vegan foods during the day –and my energy shot up! As did my iron levels. (And my farting shot down!) I had been mixing carbs and meat proteins every lunch and dinner which, in hindsight, I discovered was a silly and ineffective thing to do.

Ignorance is useless. Knowledge is power.

The best wisdom for healthy living and eating is to look at those that live over 100 years old. Japan has the highest number of 'centurions' per head of population (and the lowest number of fast food restaurants!) Several books and resources are out there including '100 ways to live over 100' and 'Live well over 100' amongst other gems. At least their advice has been tested over 100 years! How long have people lived following the Atkins?

The Glycemic Index

If you want to understand how some foods give you a rush of energy and than make you feel tired you need to understand the GI index of food. The glycemic index is a ranking of carbohydrates based on their immediate effect on blood glucose (blood sugar) levels. Carbohydrates that breakdown quickly during digestion have the highest glycemic indexes e.g. sweets. The blood sugar kick is too quick and it upsets the balance, which is why it crashes your energy levels. The secret is to eat low GI carbohydrate foods that break down slowly, releasing glucose gradually into the blood stream. The only time to eat high GI foods like jelly beans or a piece of chocolate is immediately before or after exercise when your body will use it or need it respectively. Every food has a GI index so it's worth growing your knowledge in this area. A good health shop, book or Internet site can provide that information. Patrick Holford is one of the best authors around.

Foods that fuel energy for a long time;

Oats, bran, rice crispies
Rye and whole wheat bread
Sweet potatoes
Rice
Fruit and Vegetables

Foods that REDUCE energy long term;

Frosties, sugar puffs
White bread
Fries and Burgers
Colas

Sweets and chocolates
Crisps and cakes

"Eat whole foods- whole grains, lentils, beans, nuts, seeds, fresh fruit and vegetables –and avoid refined, white and overcooked foods."
-Patrick Holford, author, 'Optimum Nutrition for the Mind'

Spoonful of Honey

Scottish pharmacist Mike Innes has discovered that the first four hours of sleep burns more fat than any other activity and that eating two spoons of honey before going to bed assists the process. I think the information is also useful because it could improve the quality of sleep and increase energy the next day. Sleep is important for the brain as well as the body.

"If you go to bed with an empty liver, your body can't get to work because it's desperately trying to sort out your blood sugar levels. So stabilising your blood glucose at night by fuelling up your liver – honey is the key- allows that recovery to take place as it should."
-Mike Innes, pharmacist and founder of Iso Active, Edinburgh

Honey every night keeps the waist tight!
An apple a day keeps the doctor away.
Nature provides the best food and drink.

Hydration; high energy

The first thing I do when I get up every morning is drink a pint a water and then go for a walk. My body has had no water for several hours and is bound to be dehydrated. My mind and body has had no fresh air or exercise for several hours so I go for a walk and my energy is high by the time I come back.

If you don't wake up (using your mental clock of course) and feel energetic after getting six hours sleep you are doing something wrong. You only need more than six hours sleep if you trained very hard the day before or you slept less than 6 hours the night before.

Don't expect to get up every morning with tons of energy. You have not drank, eaten, exercised or breathed fresh air for several hours. Wait until you have a drink (water), a shower and a walk (fresh air and exercise) and you'll feel like superman! I wake up almost every day with a ton of energy- by the time I come back from my walk I've got tons of energy!

Dehydration reduces your energy.
If your pee is yellow; drink water now my fellow!
If your pee is clear you're all clear.

Drink a pint of water before every meal and drink water, juice or tea whenever you are thirsty during the day - you will find you have lot's more energy. And you don't over eat.

The body needs lots of water. You can't over drink water. It can get rid of it easily. Over sip and you'll see.

Fatty foods slow your brain

Eat food that grows. "If it grows eat it. If it does not grow don't eat it." Louise Hay. Growing foods have more energy and the body isn't stressed by any chemicals and over worked to filter them out. Last time I checked crisps and cola don't grow on trees! Research from Sheffield University found that fatty foods slow down the brain and impair mental function! A study found the impact on people who ate a high fat breakfast were worse than those that ate a high fat lunch with people feeling tired, sluggish and easily muddled three hours later! Everything you eat, drink and breathe goes into your blood and your brain. You are what you eat.

Eat light, feel light.
If you want to spend the day thinking, don't spend the day eating.
Eat good, feel good. Positive food, Positive energy.
"If it grows eat it. If it does not grow don't eat it." - Louise Hay.

You are what you absorb

Avoid absorbing chemicals. At Rutgers University researchers compared the mineral quality of organic and non-organically grown foods. It was found that on average organic foods had an 87% higher content of magnesium, potassium, manganese, iron and copper. Organic tomatoes were found to have 500% more calcium than conventional tomatoes. A tomato is not a tomato. A tomato years ago would have had similar nutrients to an organic tomato today. Today; a tomato is not a tomato. Eat organic.

A tomato is not a tomato.
Organic tomatoes have a 500% greater mineral content than a normal tomato today.

Good food V. Organic Food

An article in the December 1999 issue of Positive Health by Dr Joseph Keon is an excellent case in the argument for eating organic foods. Taken from his book 'The Truth About Breast Cancer', he states that every time we choose conventionally farmed foods over organic we are increasing our cumulative exposure to unnecessary chemicals and increasing our risk of disease. It is estimated that if you follow a non-organic diet, you will consume about 150mcg of pesticides each day!

Find a way to get organic food locally and it can be done cost effectively. Where there is a will there is a way!

Egypt 0 - 500 Britain

A recent case cited in the media showed that 500 dangerous man-made chemicals were present in a single fat cell of a seemingly healthy 30-year-old female living in Britain today! By comparison, a single cell of an Egyptian mummy contained none!

Microwave meal

Dr Andrew Weil in his book '8 Weeks to Optimum Health' states, "never microwaves food in plastic containers or plastic wrap, because the microwave radiation can drive plastic molecules into the food; use only glass or ceramic containers and waxed paper or a paper towel for a cover."

Live like a caveman!

Live like a caveman, avoid the cola! Sugar cola is the worst, affecting your blood sugar, your concentration and decreasing your energy. Sugar free cola isn't much better. Fizzy drinks contain carbon dioxide, which raises stomach pH affecting food absorption, it's not natural like water so the body has work to do and it's not as good for you either. Test it. Research it.

Carbonated drinks have been banned in some schools in the UK after a study showed children drinking water performed better. A water bottle has been given to all children in some healthy and open-minded schools (that will soon be 'top performing' schools I'm sure!).

Carbonated drinks have been linked to weaker bones in several studies. There is some evidence to show that teenage girls who drink carbonated drinks are three times more likely to suffer broken bones than those who avoid them. One theory is that phosphoric acid used as a preservative in some fizzy drinks competes with calcium to make bones strong. Although phosphorous and calcium are both needed in equal amounts for bone health, too much phosphorous can prevent absorption of calcium. This can decrease bone strength and increase the risk of bone fractures later in life. The first report I read on this was via the Vitamin Shoppee customer magazine in the USA over 7 years ago! It's been kept quiet in the UK for a long time. Live like a cave woman and caveman.

For good bones absorb calcium. Calcium is food in nuts, seeds, especially sesame, soya, whole grains, vegetables and fish. Essential fatty acids, found in various nut and seed oils and in fish, facilitate calcium absorption and may slow down calcium excretion and bone loss. Limit intake of fizzy drinks, tea, coffee, sugar and bran, which can inhibit calcium absorption and of animal protein and salt which can increase calcium loss in urine.

Cow's milk is for cows! Baby cows! Human's milk is for humans. Baby humans! Drinking animal milk is over rated. Cows milk is not designed for humans and our bodies are not designed to drink it. Read 'Fit for life' to see all the facts. Breast milk is for babies. Dr Robert Mendelssohn says, breast milk is "the best nutrient for babies because it is nature's perfect food". Breast fed babies are 3 times less likely to smoke. Nature provides all the food we need. Test it. Research it.

We all have so many heartbeats. Coffee increases our heart rate and therefore uses some of our heartbeats from tomorrow. Therefore over the long term coffee shortens our life. Or as newspaper 'USA Today' has stated, "Coffee steals energy from tomorrow." People who live long drink tea. See how long you last.

Several studies have shown tea is good for you.
Don't go OTT with coffee and tea!

Cavemen didn't work night shift!

Research shows our bodies need natural light. Even a cloudy day provides Vitamin E to our body if we are outdoors. Sun in moderation is good for the body. When the sun is shining people are happy! Another reason to avoiding working through the night and sleeping during the day is damage to health. A recent study discovered that our bodies need complete darkness while sleeping to repair ourselves and maintain health. Live like a caveman and cave woman.

Our mind and body are designed for our surviving and thriving. If we commit ourselves to a goal our mind looks for ways to make it happen and attracts opportunities to make it happen. Our mind is designed to help us survive and thrive. Commitment is only made when there is no going back. When we have crossed the bridge. Necessity is the mother of invention and motivation.

Avoid Chemicals

Chemicals reduce our energy and are a danger to our health! There are many chemicals to avoid and it is best summed up by a company called 'Green People' who state that; "Our natural ranges are all free from Sodium Laurel Sulphate (SLS), Sodium Laureth Sulphate (SLES), Parabens, Parfum, Colourants, Petrochemicals, Propylene Glycol, PEG's, DEA, TEA and all other unnecessary synthetic additives. Our formulations are biodegradable and environmentally friendly." It is not just those that want to look after their skin that use them, but those that want to look after their health and their energy! Some of these products may cost more but your health is your wealth! It's an investment in yourself and your energy. Researcher Alfred Zam co-author of 'Why Your House May Endanger Your Health' states in the book, "If you can't eat it don't breathe it." He warns against chemical cleaning products and points out that many pre-war household cleaning items were made from foodstuffs e.g. vinegar, borax, lemon juice, beeswax. Watch what you put in your body, what you use on your body and what you use around your body.

Look at the ingredients of what you eat and what you use every day!
You are what you absorb.

Real healthy food and products may cost more but your health is your wealth! You are investing in yourself and your future.

Do you know what your mind and body need for great health?
There is a wealth of information for health. Find the most valuable.
Are you eating what you need to eat or want to eat?
Do the first and it soon becomes both.
Do the last and your body won't get what you need
and you won't want what you get.

During a 3 month long period of 3 times weekly workshops run by Dr John Gray called 'Practical Miracles for Cancer' he had the following results with attendees; 5 died, 5 survived and 15 thrived and had complete remission from cancer! A miracle? No. Thousands of people cure themselves of cancer every year without no drugs or operation.

You are what you eat and you are what you think.
Healthy body and healthy mind can cure cancer.

"What you eat and how much you eat is the single
most important factor in physical and mental health." – Dr John Gray

Eating a large meal can demand more energy from the body than the meal itself provides, even if it's healthy food.
How much energy do you have after Christmas Dinner?

You control your mouth

Dr John Gray states, "A healthy body can endure a little junk food, but a nutritionally deficient person with cancer or any other life threatening disease needs to eat with the same precision as a doctor administering drugs. If you eat too much of the wrong foods, your body's natural ability to heal itself is severely compromised. If a doctor told me that nutrition didn't affect my body's capacity to heal cancer, I know that I would quickly be looking for another opinion."

Many doctors have only received a few hours training in nutrition in medical school and once qualified their full daily diary can make reading up on the latest drugs a priority before the latest alternatives to drugs. They are trained and paid to 'cure' us when we are unwell and not trained and paid to keep us well. There is a difference.

An investment in keeping yourself well is less expensive and painful than the 'cures' when you are unwell.

You get what you pay for.
If you think you're right you're right.

Everything in moderation doesn't work if everything you're eating is junk. Almost everything you eat must be healthy or you will be unhealthy.

If you want to succeed at becoming a millionaire find a method that has worked!
If you want to succeed at curing cancer find a method that has worked.

"People everywhere that eat the most fruits and vegetables, compared to those that eat the least, slash their expectations of cancer by about 50%. Some research shows that eating fruit twice a day, instead of less than three times a week, cut the risk of lung cancer 75%."
– Jean Carper, author, 'Food- Your Miracle Medicine'

Copy Cat

When a winner speaks I listen. When a winner acts I watch. What do you think the 'President' of a country does when he has a problem? Ignore it? Forget it? Or Solve it? You only achieve success at anything if you are a problem solver rather than a 'problem shrugger'. When a winner has a problem one of the first things they do is decide if they can solve it themselves or if someone else can solve it for them! Wise men and women!

If you want to succeed at any goal use your mind, take action and develop your skills and strategy through modelling. In short whatever your goal, find someone who has been there and done that and copy them!

You don't get to the top without being a problem solver.
Winners solve problems, losers shrug them.

Problem Solver

When a President has a family member or friend with cancer who does he call? Answer- A 'winner' that has solved that problem before! Presidents and winners from all over the world call Sir Jason Winters the author of 'Killing Cancer' for advice on how to solve their problem! Here are some facts about Winters' that demonstrate why 'winners' with cancer problems follow the Winters cancer solution;

1. Had terminal cancer in 1977 and was given three months to live.

2. Searched for the herbs mentioned in biblical writings around the world.
3. Invented a herbal tea that improved his health
4. With the assistance of H.R.H. The Prince of Wales and the Archbishop of Canterbury, he recovered completely.
5. His amazing recovery made him famous.
6. Sir Jason Winters' books have sold over 13 million copies.
7. Supported by noted medical practitioners.
8. Won awards from six foreign governments and the U.S.
9. Knighted in Malta.

Winters special teas have helped people all over the world become healthy and cure themselves of diseases including cancer.

To get to the top you have to be a problem solver not a 'problem shrugger'.
When a winner has a problem he calls an expert at solving the problem!

Sounds like common sense? Common sense is not so common.
'Losers' with a 'winning problem' need to copy a winner with the solution.
People with a cancer problem need to copy a cancer winner with the solution.

"If at first the idea is not absurd, then there is no hope for it."
-Albert Einstein

Cancer Heroes

If you want to be healthy model someone healthy. If you want to cure yourself of cancer model someone who has been there and done that. Thousands of people have. Several great books have been written with advice including Patrick Holford 'Say no to cancer', Norman Cousins 'Anatomy of an Illness', Louise Hay 'Heal your body', Sir Jason Winters 'Killing Cancer', Dr Andrew Weil 'Spontaneous Healing', Dr John Gray 'Practical Miracles for Mars and Venus' and Louise Hay 'You can heal your life'. The amazing book by Dr Joseph Murphy 'The power for your subconscious mind' also includes stories on curing terminal dis-ease with the mind. I recommend Louise and John's books because they provide a cure for cancer and provide a cure for the cause of cancer. Which will greatly help to ensure any dis-ease does not reoccur.

"Knowledge is power. What you don't know can hurt you."
-Ivan Misner

Soap

I was shocked when I read about Sodium laurel sulphate and similarly, sodium laureth sulphate (SLS). These are chemicals found in things we use every day and we don't realise it. Companies that make the products don't want you to find out. It's the next tobacco scandal. SLS is a common detergent that is used in most shampoos, bubble baths, shower gels, soaps, face and body washes, toothpaste, washing up & laundry detergents. SLS is also used to clean garage floors and to degrease engines! Research by Dr K. Green into the use of SLS found alarming results: the eyes readily absorb SLS, destroying delicate tissues there. This uptake is also greater in young kids. It can permanently impair the normal functioning of eyes. This may account for why so many children wear spectacles these days. The *American Journal of Toxicology* has found that SLS irritates skin tissue, corrodes hair follicles, and impairs the ability to grow hair. And state it also enters and maintains residual levels in the heart, liver, lungs and brain. (This could explain some of the dangerous chemicals in the 30-year-old woman) Many sufferers of scalp complaints have eased their conditions simply by using a SLS-free shampoo. A company called Simply Soaps makes great soaps that I use. Their website and details on other companies are at the back of the book.

If you see a 'natural soap' look at the ingredients.
If it includes sodium laurel sulphate it includes chemicals!
Avoid the chemical Sodium laurel sulphate
found in soap and toothpaste.
You'll be surprised when you find out how many chemicals
you have been eating and using every day. I was.
ALWAYS read the ingredients of EVERYTHING you buy.

Reduce chemicals, increase energy.

4. EXERCISE or MOVEMENT - EXERCISE 3 TO 7 TIMES A WEEK

Exercise actually <u>increases</u> energy. (When done properly) Sitting or lying all day actually reduces energy. Be active everyday. The body is built to walk & rest. Walk & Rest every day. Exercise at least every second day and notice your energy go up. Experiment with exercise. What you do and when you do it. I have to exercise before my evening meal to be sharp and energetic all night (if I didn't I'd be sleepy after eating). I was out till 1pm at night after my first marathon even though I found finishing very tough! I think my fitness, age and healthy nutrition helps me recover fast. I push myself but I don't usually go over the top. If I am racing or I over exercise, I sometimes find I need a rest afterwards. The key is to experiment and find what feels better during and afterwards. Running a 5k every night will eventually become easy so you have to run further or go faster! If you are training to increase your strength or fitness you will feel your muscles sore (growing) the next day which means you did good! The fitter you are physically and mentally the more energy you will have to think and take action. If you do what you have always done, you'll get what you have always got. Exercise is good for you for several reasons a few of which are;

1. Mind performs better
2. Improves health
3. Stimulates endorphins which create 'feel good' mood
4. Increases energy
5. Reduces stress
6. More positive
7. Improves intuition
8. Boosts confidence
9. Raises metabolism
10. Burns calories and fat

A little exercise is better than no exercise. A new study found that when a group of 'non exercisers' began doing just 7 minutes of stair climbing a day it reduced their risk of some serious diseases by over 50%!

To be physically fit you need strength, endurance and flexibility.
A male body builder can't touch his toes or
run for a bus but he can lift it!
The balance is unhealthy.
The world's strongest men don't live long.

Experiment with exercise.
Health is how you feel not how you look.
Focus on feeling good not looking good.
Do what feels good and you'll look good.
If you focus on looking good you'll always feel bad.
Watch your health not your scales. Don't be a scale watcher!

Test this experiment; next time you feel tired in the evening force yourself to do some exercise for at least 10 minutes and notice the difference in your energy after your shower compared to before your exercise.

The quickest workout I do is dancing around
to a few of my favourite songs.
I feel good, but I knew that I would.
Something is better than nothing.

If you are tired you need fresh air, water or exercise (not sleep!)
If I don't do some form of activity or exercise before dinner every night I will fall asleep just after dinner.

Exercising will keep sharper mentally and physically.
Even if you exercise every second day you
feel the benefit on your rest day.

The fitness advice I currently follow was luckily found by a friend through a recommendation on a Men's Health chat page. Ross Enamait is the author of 'The underground fitness guide to warrior fitness' and founder of warriorforce.com both excellent resources, especially the book which is subtitled 'No gym memberships required'. It requires no weights and no gym and as such the book saves money! At about $9 it includes some of the best routines and exercises I have ever come across (and I have been training and reading for over 8 years!). His attitude is excellent and the advice is sensible and is not just for very fit people. The routines are 'short and sweet; with the emphasis on quality not quantity.

After I followed the Warrior routine the first time I was angry! I realised I'd wasted my time on ineffective exercises in the past particularly for my stomach. The next day after following the Warrior routine I was sore. Excellent! It worked.

"The warrior does not search for the easy way out."
- Ross Enamait, author of 'The underground fitness guide to warrior fitness' and founder of warriorforce.com

However, I do recommend getting a fitness assessment at a gym and doing a few sessions there every now and then to compare your progress. Some amazing weight training advice I have come across which would work for women, men and pensioners is from 'Maximum Contraction Training' by John Little. His advice is quality not quantity! Sound familiar?! Wise John has saved me from wasting time in the gym on a Friday when I can be out having fun. That said, I train hard but train with a smile!

Great knowledge makes you greater.
Lack of knowledge wastes your time.
A little bit of knowledge is dangerous!

My top training tip is; increase your routine every week and change your routine every month. For example do weight training on the even months and warrior training on the odd months. The more outdoor exercise you do the better. I learnt that from being in Australia where they are super fit and super happy and no Aussie's seem to go to gyms. The most I will spend is around one session in a gym a week every second month. Running, swimming and cycling are the best body exercises around. (Walking and swimming are the safest and greatest exercises.)

5. POSITIVE MIND - REDUCE NEGATIVE THOUGHTS /STRESS

Starting and finishing the day with positive thoughts helps energy and results. If you start the day and say 'Today will be a great day' it will! Having a positive mind when working, under pressure and when in a queue reduce stress and increase success. Using all the Positive Mindpower Tools gives you more energy! Positive people have a stronger immune system and are healthier. Keep positive!

Your energy jumps when you have an exciting day ahead.

"Doing a job you hate uses up more energy than the national grid. Doing a job you love gives you more."
-Sharon Maxwell Magnus, 'Think yourself Rich'

Big goals give you the Santa Claus effect.
"No one jumps out of bed on a Monday morning for a realistic and achievable goal." – Jack Black

A positive mental state has a big impact on energy levels as well as physical and mental health. The next chapter focuses on positive and negative energy and emotion.

6. RELAX FOR A FEW MINUTES - BANTER BREAKS

It's important to have small quick relaxation breaks every 60-90 minutes where possible. It helps energy and concentration (always remember relaxation!). Working without breaks isn't working. See relaxation tips further on.

7. SENSES - POSITIVE STIMULATION not OVER STIMULATION

Here are some ways you can increase your energy through your senses;

Eyes - look outside often when you are indoors. Calm colours are calming.

Ears - listen to classical music to increase performance and relaxation, listen to uplifting music in morning or whenever you need to get yourself going

Nose - Research aromatherapy. Lavender on your pillow helps sleep.

Touch - A fresh shower in morning and at night (or after performance) increases energy. Mentally and physically beneficial.

Taste - Giving the taste buds different tastes and foods throughout the day is useful mentally and physically (because different foods have different nutrients). Be aware; taste increases the waist! It's easy to find room for desert even after a huge main course! You don't need the ice cream but the taste is appealing. (Taste 'boredom' helped the survival of cavemen and women because it stopped them eating the same food all day, every day)

Colourful mind
The colours of our clothes and our surroundings will affect us mentally. Psychologically certain colours mean certain things to the brain. As a rough guide;
Red symbolises warmth, energy and stimulation.
Orange; warm, cheering and freeing.
Yellow; awakes, stimulates and inspires.
Green; is the colour of nature and is said to smooth the mind and body.
Blue; cooling, electric and powerful.
Purple; soothing colour. 'Energy' cameras show happy people with a purple aura.
White; perfection, harmony and healing; White combines all colours.
Pink; caring, loving and romance.
Black; seriousness, dark, depression, death, mourning and mystery.
Gold; confidence, creativity, perfection, riches, winning and power.

Colours affect your mind.

Calm your self
When a class of school children had their room painted red it was found that they were more stimulated and creative. When kids or adults are put into a green room they tend to be more calm and relaxed. Calm Expert Paul Wilson is a big advocate of white clothes and surroundings which have a similar affect because white is non-stimulating. I wear white much more often now.

Wear calm clothes, calm your self.

Popular Clothes
Walk down any street in the UK or sit in any pub or club and the most popular colour worn by men and women, especially is black. Do black clothes make you look slimmer? Maybe. Maybe not. I have never seen a 20 stone man in black clothes and thought to myself "he looks about 15 stone with that black top on!." A more important question could be "Do black clothes make you happier?"

Men in Black
A teenager I have known for years went through a stage for about a year of dressing like a 'gothic', wearing black clothes, listening to often depressing and angry music and hanging out with similar friends ("gothic's"). I came across a photo of him during this period and it is the only photo I've seen with him not smiling before or since.

What you wear, what you do and who you hang around,
affects your mood and your attitude.
Angry music creates angry people. Calm down.

8. SLEEP - QUALITY SLEEP NOT OVER SLEEP

The average adult only needs around 6 to 8 hours sleep a day for physical energy and mental happiness, positivity, creativity and energy. Sleeping more than 9 hours a night will reduce energy levels. You only get a good healthy sleep every night if you have got a healthy mind and body every night! Sleep is essential for humans and a great sleep will greatly assist a great performance each day.

Sleeping cycles

You sleep in 90-minute cycles. To improve the quality of sleep use your mind to wake you so you wake up fresh. Sleep in blocks of 90 minutes therefore set your mental clock so you sleep for 4 and half hours, 6 hours, 7 and half hour or 9 hours (if you have trained really hard or not slept much the night before). While you sleep your mind is still working; keeping your lungs breathing, your heart pumping and your mind dreaming! Before I go to sleep I give it something else to work on. I tell my mind that I want to wake up at 5,6,7 or 8 am whenever I want. My mind wakes me up. (I usually give myself 6 hours quality sleep)

Give up coffee or give up having lots of energy.
Coffee affects your sleep.

If you need to wake up in the middle of the night to go to the toilet you are drinking the wrong thing; usually coffee.

'Everything in moderation' is not always a great philosophy to adopt. There are a lot of unhealthy foods and drinks that you could eat all day in moderation!

You wouldn't eat toxic chemicals in moderation and expect to be healthy so don't eat or drink unhealthy nutrition in moderation. Eat healthy nutrition in moderation.

Mental Clock

The best way to increase the quality of your sleep is to stop using your alarm. While you sleep your subconscious 'automatic' mind is still working; keeping your lungs breathing, your heart pumping and your mind dreaming! Before I go to sleep I tell my mind that I want to wake up at 5,6,7 or 8 am whenever I want. My mind wakes me up. I usually give myself 6 hours quality sleep, but I can go through a full day on 3 hours if necessary. Quality is better than quantity, especially where sleep is concerned. This one tool has had more impact on increasing my energy than any other!

You can wake yourself up with your mind.

Quality is better than quantity, especially where sleep is concerned. Britain's first female Prime Minister Margaret Thatcher slept 4 hours a night.

Major Alarm

Do you want to be controlled by someone else? Do you want to be given a shock every morning? Do you want to reduce the quality of your sleep? Do you want to wake up more tired than when you woke up naturally an hour before? If the answer if yes- keep using Major Alarm! If the answer is no stop using an alarm! Get up under your control using your mind, with more energy, without the stressful shock treatment! Use your mind alarm! Do you ever wake up 5 minutes before your alarm goes off? Yes, all the time! The reason is that your subconscious minds knows the time and it knows you want to avoid the loud shock so it gets you up just before Major Alarm even if you are in the middle of a 90 minute cycle!

Your subconscious mind knows the time. Use it to wake up naturally. How many times do you set the alarm but you wake up 5 minutes before it goes off? That's your mind helping you avoid the shock treatment and getting you up just before Major Alarm!

9. ENVIRONMENT - OUTDOOR CALM SURROUNDINGS

Getting a bit of sun or even daylight increases energy and vitamin E. Too much sun and it will reduce energy and increase radiation risk.

Good atmosphere

Living and working in a good environment and atmosphere with fun and no fear helps energy and happiness levels. Whether it be on the sports field or in the office. Good colleagues are great. In an office or home you can 'feel' the atmosphere.

Positive people feed your energy, negative people eat your energy.

Office environment

But if the office is based near a noisy street the external noise pollution will stress the body during the day if you can hear it. Conversely relaxing music throughout the day will be even better than silence to help your performance and concentration. Radio 3 is great (when the news isn't on) but Baroch music at 60 beats per minute is said to be great.

Natures Energy

Every single thing in the world is made of energy. From stones to flowers to running water. There is lots of energy around beaches; rivers, mountains, forests and big parks therefore spend some time there ever day. Use your imagination to "fill yourself" up with energy from the air, trees and water flowing around you. Spending time in the sea, river or even shower surrounds you with energy. I've always found a swim in the sea energising and now I swim in the river nearby too!

Manmade energy

Whether you live in a city centre, busy street or any area of constant traffic your mind is constantly dealing with external 'noise pollution'. Imagine you had a pneumatic drill working outside your home for the whole weekend, it would get to you! The mind likes silence. It is not mentally healthy to be under such conditions. We were not designed to deal with excessive and persistent noise.

Electric Energy

I've seen convincing programmes and research on people living near overhead lines and power stations whose health became adversely affected over time. The number of cases in the same vicinity was quite shocking. Dr Andrew Weil states that it is "not a good idea to live under or next to power transmission lines" and I agree. This is another area not well publicised. There is a lot to be said for living out in the country

Mobile Phones

I advise against putting a mobile phone to your head for any length of period. I was coaching a golfer who had a really sore head using one before he played in a tournament. Big mistake. Using a 'hands free' phone inside or outside the car is best if you have to. Reduce use of a mobile where possible. If you don't believe it, test it! See how you feel after a day on the mobile phone and a day without the mobile.

Mobile phone companies are unlikely to print negative research about their products. Mobile phone companies are protecting their interests just like the tobacco industry did.

Using a mobile 'hands free' is better than having the phone beside your brain.

9 Ways

So now you know 9 easy ways to stress your mind and body or 9 ways to de-stress your mind and body and increase your energy! If you increase your energy you increase your mind!

There are 9 easy ways to stress your mind and body, most people do 8.5!
Reduce stress, increase energy.

Being healthy VIP

Your health is very important. You are very important. Not just to your family but to yourself. To the world you are one person, but to one person you are the World.

Improve your health for yourself. You will also have more energy and time for your family. Being unhealthy takes years off your life and takes a lot off your energy tank. Look after number your body and you can look after any other body! If you don't you won't be able! Look after number 1.

It's not just what you know, it's what you know *__and__* *do.*

A unhealthy person has lower self-esteem, willpower, fitness, life expectancy mental and physical energy.

If you grow your self-esteem you will grow yourself.

Where there is a will, there is a way.
Find the will and you find the way.

Do not blame anyone else for your current wealth, health or happiness.
Blame gets you nowhere in life and gives away your 'power'.
Winners take responsibility for their past, present and future.

Every day people either choose to be a smoker or a non-smoker.

Starting bad habits (like smoking)

Why do we start bad habits like drinking, smoking or bingeing? We choose to because we want to or we choose to because it would be painful not to (being odd one out). People start smoking for many reasons. Kids smoke because they copy adults and want to be cool or they are "in with the wrong crowd" and smoke to fit in. As adults we can make the same mistake. We can always choose to exercise our willpower and choose to be different.

People are copycats. Kids are copycats.
You are only as successful as the people you hang around.

Do you want to stop smoking?

If the answer is yes you are reading the right book! If you do smoke I hope now you see the "impossible" huge challenge of stopping smoking as possible after reading this book and believing in yourself and being positive about yourself and your health. Using the winning mentality techniques you can do it! You need the will (motivation) and the belief you can do it and you will do it. Just like any other goal if you want it and believe it, then you can achieve it. Research proved years ago that smoking decreases your health and fitness but not all smokers listened and "actioned." Any disregard for ourselves is usually down to low self esteem, little self love and little willpower. Where there is a will there is a way. Some smokers were reactive and gave up. Some were reactive to a health scare or death of someone they loved. Painful motivation! But for the last twenty years more people have STARTED smoking than stopped smoking even though the damage to health and fitness is clearly printed on the label! Smoking gives you cancer! Smoking kills! Passive smoking kills! A cigarette is a slow killer and is actually as dangerous as a bullet to our health.

Researchers' recently proved smoking also slightly decreases intelligence! It is not good for you and not good for your brain. When we are unhealthy through the food or drugs we put in our mouths we demonstrate two things every day; we don't love ourselves and we don't love our family.

Not smoking makes you smarter!

Benefits of smoking

Let's have a look at the benefits of smoking;

None!

Two common arguments for smoking are;
It keeps you thin.
It helps you relax.

In actual fact it does neither. If you think you will, you will. If someone thinks they will put on weight when they give up they will! If they think they will relax as soon as they inhale a cigarette they will 'feel' more relaxed! But they will <u>not</u> actually be more relaxed they will be more stressed.

If you don't believe anything, test it.

Test your energy

In his book 'Your body doesn't lie', Dr John Diamond states that any internal or external stimulus physical or mental will affect the body. A negative stimulus will have a negative affect on your energy. A positive stimulus will have a positive affect on your energy. You can test this using a cigarette. Get a volunteer and test the strength of their arm like the previous exercise in the book. Then ask them to put an unlit cigarette in their mouth. Get them to hold their arm straight out to the side, parallel to the ground. Tell the person that you will attempt to push their arm down towards the ground with one hand and they must resist and attempt to keep the arm where it is. Amazingly you will be able to push their arm easily to the ground as the person's strength is almost 'zero'. Any internal stress either physical or mental has a negative affect the body on the body. It's absolutely amazing to watch or experience this for the first time. Give it a go. Test out any food, drink, colour, music, clothes, thoughts or words. Test the words 'love' and 'hate'. It's great fun and will baffle everyone but you!

If you don't believe it, test it.

Any physical or mental stress has a negative affect on your energy.

Physical stress like; cigarettes, coffee, cola, crisps, sugar, alcohol and all junk food all stress the body and reduce your energy.
Junk food gives you junk energy.

Mental stress reduces your energy e.g. negative thoughts, words, worries, music, watching or reading news.
They stress your mind and body.

Love is positive and hate is negative.
One gives energy the other lethargy.
A positive stimulus gives you positive energy.
A negative stimulus gives you negative energy.
"Your body doesn't lie." – Dr John Diamond, author of 'Your body doesn't lie'

How to stop smoking and lose weight
Overcome smoking and lose weight! Here's a tip for you to achieve ANY goal. Including an "impossible" goal like stopping smoking and losing weight! Use winning mentality! Set the goal for 30 days time (your mind takes 30 days to adopt any automatic habit). Use your mind positively not negatively! Follow the 7 mind techniques. Set your goal and get a picture of a no smoking sign and look at it everyday. Repeat your mantra and visualisation everyday. The techniques work.

If you think you will, you will.
The best way to lose weight is with your mind not your mouth.
Being busy is best for being healthy.

Being busy and motivated is the best weight loss diet there is.
If you're over stressed you over eat or forget to eat.
Avoid both because they make you more stressed.

Dream Board
Dream advertising gets your mind working on a goal. With dream advertising it is amazing what can be achieved. Here is a powerful story from Jacinta; "On the dream-board I had the words Gucci time piece, which I now have, but the next day (after making the board) when I arrived home a lady at the gas station dropped her watch in front of me, I bent down and saw it was a Gucci, I laughed and called

the woman and gave it to her as I believe it would not have been good Karma to keep it. Other things of many I achieved was, I put a no smoking symbol on the board I smoked 20 cigs a day for 20 years now I have stopped, its a miracle really. I was also helped with Hypnotherapy, but it was my wish to stop smoking I allowed the way to show up.
Believe it, see it, know it and have it. Life is easier generally now that I take 100% responsibility for my life.

Picture	**Results**
No smoking symbol	I have stopped
Gucci time piece	I now have
De Beers A diamond is forever	I got a present 20.000 Euro diamond
A Picture of two swans	I got a crystal with two swans
An apartment	I bought for 20% under market value With 100% mortgage that was a biggie!!
Health and nutrition	I now go to the gym and eat healthier

I also wanted to change my car I did and got a better one. I believe one can do anything they put their mind to. We only get what we think we deserve so I still have a few things to get which I will get when I allow myself to have them. If its to be its up to me." (Jacinta Anne Hannon, Property Agent, Wealth Creator and Life Coach)

Get pictures of your dreams and goals on your walls. It works!

Changing; to be or not to be
You will need strong motivation and strong visualisation. See yourself achieving it. What if you don't change what will happen? Visualise it and use it as painful motivation. Perhaps the strong positive or negative image may help.

To be or not to be fit and healthy that is the question.
You choose the answer every day.
If it's to be it's up to me.

Why time can be more important than energy
We all have the same time. Twenty-four hours a day, 7 days a week. 24/7. You have the same time as Bill Gates, Bob Geldolf, Richard Branson, Tiger Woods (so no excuses!). You can have all the ability, knowledge, energy and money in the world but it's a waste of time if you waste your time. How you spend your time and focus your energy will dictate whether you win or lose. Spend it wisely. (See Chapter on Action later in the book)

How you spend your time will dictate whether you win or lose.

Spend your time wisely. It's the most important investment you will make.

"The most important thing I ever learnt was the value of my time." -Bill Gates

"Don't say you don't have enough time. You have the same number of hours per day as Helen Keller, Pasteur, Michelangelo, Mother Teresa, Leonardo da Vinci, Thomas Jefferson and Albert Einstein." "Life's Little Instruction Book" by H. Jackson Brown Jr

Time

What if you were given £86,400 pounds to spend every morning and every night any money you hadn't spent was taken off you. What would you do every day? You are given this large sum to spend every day and the currency is called 'time'. You are given 86, 400 seconds (1,440 minutes or 24 hours) to spend every day. How you spend your time is up to you. Any time you waste is lost by the end of the day. Time is money. How you invest it, will relate to how you profit from it.

Get yourself a clock that ticks and listen to time ticking away.
Seize the time. Use it. Don't waste it.
Put your hand on your heart. That is time ticking away. Take action.

Save time; time is money

Find ways to save time. Cut corners. Saving time is like saving money. Time is money. Many millionaires save travel time by working from an office in their home (like Branson, Hartley and McKenzie do) which minimises travel time and maximises working time. Spend your time on what only you can do, value your time. Delegate time consuming tasks you do not need to do. Especially stressful ones.

The CEO of Ryanair bought himself a taxi licence so he could use the quickest lanes to work! Time is money. Be ruthless with your time.

Where energy is more important than time

It looks like we all have the same time. 24/7. But people like Bill Gates, Bob Geldolf, Sir Richard Branson and Tiger Woods have got more time! Because they have got more energy! If you have more energy you can do more with your time and do less with the sleeping. Double hit.

This chapter will show you how to increase your energy. You'll be able to do more and sleep less. Double hit! This chapter will also show you how to increase the quality of your sleep and need less. Triple hit! You will be amazed at the increase in your energy and increase in your time.

Increase your energy and you get more done and need less sleep
Improve the quality of your sleep and you'll need much less sleep
Increase your energy <u>and</u> improve your sleep and
you'll double your time!

"To be successful - Number 1 you need energy.
But first you need a brain." – Donald Trump

Snooze Boy

A guy I know used to sleep for about 9 hours, needed the alarm to go off twice before he got up and took a while to get going. If he got any less than 9 hours the snooze alarm went off three times and the energy was much less positive. Funnily enough with "the Santa Claus effect" and a great morning ahead he managed 6 hours! This boy went from using the snooze alarm to no alarm, from needing 9 hours sleep to needing 6 hours or less and went from low 'a.m.' energy to high energy a.m. and p.m.! I know because the 'snooze boy' was me. You will be amazed at your energy jump when you start getting quality sleep without your alarm and you have Santa Claus effect goals. Some relaxation, quality nutrition and exercise will take your energy to another level too.

More than a third of American adults hit the snooze button every morning an average of three times. What a waste of time and energy. If you snooze, you lose.

Imagine how much more could be achieved in the world if everyone got up early and no one used a snooze alarm or an alarm for that matter!

"If you're from Britain, you have to work harder than the Americans. I did everything I could, giving up an hour of sleep each morning so I could practise before classes. I would love to be a hero to all the kids who follow basketball in England. I'm proof that you can make it to the NBA." - Luol Deng, Chicago Bulls
(Growing up in London his bedroom posters were childhood heroes Ian Wright and Michael Jordan)

7 things that transformed my energy

I did seven things that transformed my energy; eating good energy food and not meat, mental alarm clock, dream goal, positive verbalisation, no negative news, more outdoor exercise. I also expanded my knowledge on food and health. Sounds radical? Every little helps. A few have laughed at or ignored what I eat, how long I sleep or how much energy I have.

"First, they ignore you. Then they laugh at you. Then they fight you. Then you win." -- Mahatma Gandhi

7 changes

My diet was very healthy but I changed it and gave up my favourite animal meats and cows milk. I started looking at 'food' as energy and not as 'food for hunger'. I was shocked at the research on disease and adopted a healthy 'no meat, some fish' diet similar to the Japanese who live till they are 100 years old. I used my mind to wake me up. I used Big goals and 'the Santa Claus effect' to get me up. I increased my positive verbalisation (internally and externally) and 'binned' any 'junk mental food' and non-positive words. I stopped watching, reading or listening to negative news. I did less indoor and more outdoor exercise. I do some outdoor exercise everyday walking, running, cycling, boxing or swimming (but I swim indoors in winter!). I do strength training once a week (usually indoors). I continually increase my knowledge on health and fitness and thereby increase my power. Knowledge is power when it comes to health because 99% of food and drink companies are looking after profits not people.

99% of food and drink companies are looking after profits not people.

I know of a manager of a food company, which makes 'quick cook meals', who doesn't eat his own products because he knows what goes in them!
Do you know what goes in your food? Look at the ingredients!
<u>All</u> high street companies selling 'beauty and body' products have got harmful chemicals in their products.

Great sleep

If someone asked me what "one thing" they could do to get great quality sleep I would say "exercise for at least 30 minutes in the evening and you will sleep like a baby!" Exercise reduces stress and gives you a healthy body and healthy mind, which gives you a great sleep.

Great exercise, great sleep!

Stressed Body

A person with a relaxed healthy mind and body will sleep well. A person with a stressed mind or body will not sleep well! A person, who is worried, stressed or eats stressful food and stressful drinks (like coffee) will not sleep great! In fact they will wake up several times a night! I spoke to a person who is relaxed and competent at work but wasn't sleeping great. She laughed when I said she must be stressed! However, when I asked if she did any exercise and what she ate and drank every day I was almost laughing at her reply! She did little exercise and drank lots of coffee and ate lots of foods that stress the body like crisps and some other junk food! I encouraged her to exercise more and drink water at work and she's sleeping like a log! Even though she still has crisps and chocolate occasionally!

Healthy body, healthy sleep! Healthy mind, healthy sleep!
If you've got a lot of stress, you'll get a little sleep!

"The number 1 health and safety risk in the office is stress."
Greg Harrison, Asset Manager, ChevronTexaco

Signs of Stress

Stress can affect your mind and your body is many many ways. The ways in which stress effects you should not be under estimated. Here are just a few of the ways stress affects you;

Physical

Tired, headache, neck ache, back ache, shaky hands, dry mouth, sleep problems, chest pain

Emotional

Suspicious, paranoid, pessimistic, irrational, poor memory, mood swings, worrying

Behavioural

Overeat, overwork, drive fast, talk fast, eat fast, short tempered, short attention span

With this new 'knowledge' you will be more aware if you or anyone else is stressed.

One sign of stress; throwing things!
One way to eliminate stress; punching or kicking things! True.

Body MOT

People often look after their cars better than their bodies. Get yourself a fitness MOT from your local gym or personal trainer <u>and</u> get yourself a 'full medical' health check. It's an investment. Something highly recommend by founder of The institute for Optimum Nutrition Partick Holford is having your nutritional requirements evaluated, by a qualified Nutritionist. The knowledge you gain from doing these things is powerful. We are all different so my exercise and eating programme may be healthy for me but not as good for you. I had a full medical MOT when I was 21 years old and my local doctor told me two things when he saw my results. One was "you are going to live forever" and the other "you have low iron levels"! Since then I had it checked out and have since made a conscious effort every day to eat iron rich foods. When I was 24 years old I gave up meat and my iron levels improved!

Look after your body better than your car!

Get yourself a fitness MOT and a 'full medical' MOT.
Get an evaluation and advice from a qualified Nutritionist.
Seek advice from experts. It's an investment.

Happy Holland

Having met people from different European countries I was not surprised to see research that stated that the Dutch are the happiest people in Europe. Forty-six percentage of Dutch, forty-five percentage of Danish and forty-two percentage of Irish people describe themselves as "very happy." One of my Dutch friends is typical; she is a really happy and funny person and her clothes are always bright colours or light colours (I have never seen her wear black!). No wonder Brits are not as happy as the Dutch! Our favourite colour is black not orange! The research showed that people in Ireland are almost as happy as the Dutch and are twice as happy as the Spanish! So it's not the sun, which makes the difference! I strongly believe it is the attitude. Having friends from all three countries I can testify to the fact they have a great attitude; very positive, and good perspective. The fact the Irish love a laugh and the colour green may help a little bit too. Laughter is the best medicine.

You can't control or choose the weather any day.
You can control and choose your attitude every day.

"The two best physicians of them all; Dr Laughter and Dr Sleep."
– Dr Gregory Dean

Are you having a laugh?

Have you ever looked at the colour of kid's clothes and the colour of adult's clothes? If you have done a bit of 'people watching' you may have noticed how bright and colourful children's clothes are compared to adults. Kids laugh a lot, smile a lot and they are a lot happier than adults. Their clothes are also a lot brighter! If you brighten your clothes, you'll brighten your mood.

Copy kids. Positive clothes, positive mood. Calm clothes, calm mood.

Positive comedy challenge

You can't bury feelings, but if you express them you can release them. Then you can move onto the next step of looking at all negatives positively. The sooner you imagine your problems positively or comically the quicker you can laugh about them and the better your physical and mental health.

Compare your challenges

When we compare our challenges to others it's easier to put them in perspective and deal with them. Whenever you have a difficult or non-positive day, think of how your challenges could be a lot worse, how other people are in a worse position than you are and put your thoughts into perspective.

Perspective

Imagine getting perspective by looking out a window into the world and see people who are in a worse position than you. See how much better off you are than most; better health, better wealth, safety, freedom, housing, water, work, family, friends and many other things that we all take for granted.

There is always someone worse off than you.
Negative thoughts about yourself
create negative problems for yourself.

Laugh in the face of your fear

Think of something, which you are afraid of. Now put yourself in the scene but add some comic clothes, poses, clowns or music. Use your imagination. If you have to face your fear it's more useful to review this version in your mind than a version which worries and stresses you. There is an old saying that if you've got a fear of public speaking you should imagine the audience naked! Your Grandmother might put you off though. Not a technique I use with all clients! Saying to yourself, "I am really looking forward to doing this for the nation and getting a standing ovation!" is very positive!

When you see fear say hello and wave it goodbye!

Laugh at your "problems"

Worrying solves <u>nothing</u>. Brainstorm a few solutions, but if it's a worry out of your control or in the distant future, stop worrying! Worrying is a waste! Especially for hours every night. Use your imagination and sense of humour to 'imagine the situation positively' and laugh it off and relax. Force yourself in any tough situation. (This technique alone has given been a saviour to me in potentially very negative situations) Now sleep! The last time I checked you don't get more money from your bank by worrying about your money so you may as well laugh. It's better for your 'health' account.

Always look on the bright side of life.
If you can't find one make one up!

Laugh in the face of your mistakes

Think of your mistake and now put a 'Carry on' style humour to it. Feel better?! Don't 'beat yourself up about mistakes in business or life because it deflates your self-esteem. Having a lower self esteem means you are less positive and thereby less successful. Keep positive! There are no mistakes only lessons! ...and laughs! (You will laugh about it in the future so why not start NOW!)

Laugh or smile at your mistakes.
It's better for your health and your performance.

When you make a mistake say "great!"
Then say to yourself "What I have learnt about this mistake is ....?"
"Success is a numbers game!"
When you ask a good question you get a good answer.

Change the subject

This is a mood-changing tool I teach clients, which was inspired by winners I have studied (and parents who use it with young kids). When the kids are angry or upset or fall down and start crying they will distract them by saying something like "hey do you want an ice cream?" or "lets go roll in the mud over there." If you make someone think about something different, they will think different. The same technique will work for stressed or angry or upset adults you meet. If you make them laugh or talk about a funny incident or even make some odd comments like "hey do you want an ice cream?" or "lets go roll in the mud over there", you are sure to make them smile! They can then relax, cool off and review what made them stressed or angry or upset without the heat of the moment 'red mist' reaction. You can use it on yourself too! Very useful and effective. Change the subject and you change the mood! If someone is upset distract them! Or make them laugh!

Change your thoughts and change your mood.
Change someone else's thoughts and you change their mood.
Just like you would do to distract a child
who has fallen over or injured themselves!

Switch to the comedy channel

This is a great tool! Think of a funny memory or something funny. Pick a key word to describe it. When you are angry, sad or stressed switch your thoughts to your funny memory by repeating your key word. It's like switching your TV to the Comedy Channel! If you were to mention the word "carrot muncher" to any of the members of my immediate family they will all smile! The reason is the family dog used to turn up his nose at anything healthy when his was young. He would turn his nose up if a grape landed on the floor. But not long ago my Mum told us that she accidentally dropped a carrot on the floor and she only realised when she heard crunching! The family dog will eat anything it seems including healthy carrots! (He never used to eat anything healthy like fruit or veg!) We call him 'the carrot muncher' now! You can use this tool on other people to change their mood and state of mind when it is "non-positive." You can do this by either stating a key word associated with a funny experience they had or by making a funny statement or asking a odd question like, "I wonder what it's like to pee in space?" or "Did you fart or is it my feet?" or "Why are the Dutch so happy?" This can be used on adults as well as kids.

Whenever you have a "worry" turn it into a positive comedy and see what a difference it makes.
This has kept me healthy and happy on a few occasions!
Worries are a waste of time. Avoid non-positive thinking!

Dance like no ones watching

There were many memorable, inspirational and emotional moments for me during Athens 2004. One took place between events. The camera picked out an athlete in the middle of the track beside the athlete waiting area, near chairs and training bags. It was Sweden's World Champion Heptathlete (and soon to be Olympic Gold Medallist) Carolina Kluft dancing around with headphones on, clearly oblivious to anyone watching and a deliriously happy look on her face. What a relaxing way to take 'time out' between events. Dance like no ones watching.

Olympic Gold Medallists like dancing because it's relaxing.

Sing like no one is listening

If you look at any culture in any part of the world you will see a few things in common. They will gather in groups and talk, sing and dance. All over the world right now people are talking, singing and dancing! We have done it for thousands of years. We have got a winning game going. But sometimes we do not remember to do all three. As humans we need to in order to keep in good health. Talking, singing and dancing are powerful for relaxing, expressing and healing ourselves.

Keep talking, singing and dancing!
Do not underestimate the health benefits of singing.
'Sing like no one is listening,
Dance like no ones watching,
Love, like you've never been hurt before'.

Stress changes you mentally and physically

Stress can give a long list of health problems. I met an entrepreneur that told me that not only did he not feel good when stressed but he also noticed he lot of lot of hair! Stress changes your personality. I have been fortunate to experience myself when I was very stressed in the job I was doing. I was different in the way I acted. I wasn't as nice for a start! I had a bigger bark.

Stress changes your personality.
Stress changes your body.

Losing your sense of humour is no laughing matter.
It's happens to people that are stressed or depressed.

Barking dog
I'll tell you a good story, which I think, makes my point well. A court case was brought in Aberdeen by a family against their next-door neighbours who owned a West Highland Terrier that used to bark "all the time, day and night." The sheriff ordered that unless a suitable home was found for the dog he would need to be put down. A family who lived on a farm came forward and offered to give the dog a home. A few months later a local reporter went to catch up with the dog and his new family. The reporter noted that the dog was very excited but very quiet and asked how the dog had been getting on "He's given porridge in the morning, taken for a big walk everyday and he's never barked since he got here."

Good food + Good walk + TLC = Happy dog!
I think we can all learn a lot from the barking dog! With the same ingredients we can have happier moods! Test it. Remember next time you feel like barking think about the happy dog! Go for a walk! Eat porridge!

Stress can give a long list of health problems.
Stress can change your mentality and personality. It does with me.

"I was nicked named Mr Grumpy by my wife."
-Willie Miller, former AFC manager, was very stressed while manager

Day of Rest
A common mistake to make in business is to plan a stressful weekend to end off a stressful week! Sounds stupid? Two intelligent clients of mine needed to 'learn their lesson' through their mistake. But it was only when the mistakes was understood they learnt the lesson, with a bit of help from myself. The advice on how to avoid it helped them choose if they wanted to avoid making the same mistake again. If you don't know what you are doing, you can't stop doing it! It just so helped that they both made the same mistake! Their jobs had become stressful, one had a new job and the other worked in a department that at the time was in a "mental mess." When they got home every night from work they started another stressful job -working on their house renovations! One was living in the house and extending the other was

living next to the house in a caravan! The 7 days of stress was making them depressed. Even God rested on the 7th day!

Even a super human like you needs to rest!
All work and no play makes a sad boy.
Hard work and play makes a happy boy. Work, rest and holiday.

"Unless you can look at a mirror while you swing a golf club you will always need a coach to help with your swing." Butch Harman, great golf coach, who coached Tiger Woods to greatness

Stimulus>Mind Evaluation>Response

When we come across a situation, we evaluate the situation in our mind and then evaluate and choose a response (which may be to do nothing). Here's an example of two different people in the same situation.

Situation Stimulus	Evaluation	Response
Late for Work	Oh, no	Start stress response, Drive faster
Late for Work	Oh, well	Relax, Drive as normal

The first person evaluated the situation in their mind and chooses to be concerned. The mind noticed the concern and started the body's 'flight, flight or freeze' response, which puts the body under stress. This is OK if we are in real danger but if we think negatively about every situation we'll get stressed at every situation.

If the body is constantly under stress throughout your day, even for the smallest of things that you worry about (like being 30 seconds late for work) then it gets worn out. Stress increases our body energy by using our energy stores. The longer we are stressed the more extra energy it uses from our reserves and eventually our energy crashes or we need drugs like caffeine to artificially stimulate energy. This actually reduces our energy further so that when the caffeine wears off the crash is even bigger. If we constantly use caffeine and drugs to stimulate our energy we are borrowing energy and heartbeats from tomorrow which shorten our life.

Our stress comes from our thoughts. Negative thoughts!
Positive thoughts can overcome our stress.

It's what's on the inside that counts

I once saw a bus bump into the side of a car. The bus was so big (and the car so small) that the bus pushed the car a few metres along the road! It was the bus brakes that stopped the bus, not the car! There was no big bang and none of the bus passengers could see the car because it was below the level of the front window, so only the driver knew there was a crash! The bus was not even scratched but the car was easily dented with the weight of the bus. The passenger door was damaged and the car was not driveable! The bus driver was not bothered and just sat there. The female driver of the car got out and the passenger (a teenage boy) got out. But the boy had to get out the driver side due to the damage to his door. Yet it was the boy that comforted the mother even though his body and head had been about 5 inches from a bus! It gets more interesting.

After the bus had stopped for a few minutes a few annoyed passengers went to the front of the bus to find out if the bus had broken down! Some passengers then got off the bus to see if everyone was OK. Some just sat there for a while and then went to get the next bus, coming 10 minutes behind. Eventually all the passengers including several pensioners got off the bus except for one person. The young boy then left his mother and went off in the direction of where the car was originally heading (and where his mother was taking him). An ambulance arrived. The paramedics get out and go onto the bus to give treatment to the middle-aged woman who didn't get off the bus! Not the boy. Not the bus driver. Not the concerned mother. Not even the pensioners! The middle-aged passenger who was sitting in the middle of the bus!

When someone is stressed it's not what is going on the outside that counts, but what's going on in the inside.

It's not what happens to you, it's what you think about it and do about it.

It's not the stimulus on the outside but the thoughts on the inside that count.

Stress and fear are negative thoughts

Here is some food for thought;

Stress > Fear Stress is caused by fear e.g. negative thoughts Or negative visualisations

Fear> Control Fear comes from having 'no control' over the outcome and having a negative view of outcome.

If someone has a fear of flying it's because they cannot control the plane and cannot control if they will land or crash. Therefore they <u>choose</u> to think negatively e.g. crashing rather than landing, which creates a fear. But everyone else on the plane is in the same situation but they choose to think positively! However, you can control your thoughts.

Control your thoughts, control your fear.
Choose negative thoughts to create fear.
Choose positive thoughts to crush fear.

Everyone chooses to see a situation positively or negatively.
Take your pick.

"All fears are about control." -Dr Phil McCraw
Look at any fearful situations positively instead of negatively.
Tell yourself; 'I can Handle it!'

We do not have complete control over anything but our thoughts.
Get over it.

Fear helped our survival

Like most human features 'fear' was developed to help survival. Just as the caveman found it useful that his mind was 'goal' driven when it came to finding food, another useful feature was the fear factor. A caveman's reaction to a fearful situation (like when he came across a lion or shark) was 'fight, flight or freeze'. The purpose of each one is to assist survival. Our reaction to a fearful situation is 'fight, flight or freeze'. People tend to react in the same way to fear regardless of the situation. For example someone that has a fear of giving a presentation might 'freeze' and if they saw a robber in the street they would have the same reaction ('freeze').

In 1991 in Spain an ecologist found the remains of a jaw in a cave which belonged to a Neanderthal man. The remains of animals were also found including bison, lions, panthers, rhinoceros, hippopotamus and even sharks. Fear helped survival in the caveman days. But in the 21st century the 'fear factor' can be a burden to humans. Like when it's experienced when sitting in a traffic jam or working in an office with an important decision to make.

Our reaction to a situation we fear will either be 'fight, flight or freeze'.

Fight, flight or freeze

Our brain's automatic natural defence mechanism is the 'flight, flight or freeze' response. When we think fearful thoughts our brain responds by starting the defence 'flight, flight or freeze' response. It increases our heart rate, energy level and speeds up our reaction time. Important qualities in a life-threatening situation. But every time we have a fearful thought (feeling stressed indicates fearful thoughts) our mind responds to the 'danger' and activates the body with fight, flight or freeze. The response is the same to a fearful thought about being late for work as it is for a worry about money. If stress is present all day, every day it uses up a lot of energy.

Our stress and our fears come from our thoughts. Negative thoughts!
Our thoughts can overcome our stress and our fears.
Positive thoughts!
We are automatically programmed at birth to survive.

All in the mind

We can actually get as stressed thinking about a problem than actually having a problem. We can be as scared watching a movie of 'Jaws' than if we were actually swimming in the water ourselves with a shark! The stimulus is inside your mind rather than outside. We can choose how to respond to it. You can walk into a dark forest or imagine walking in a dark forest and choose to be relaxed. Between stimulus and response you can make up your mind.

Stress has more to do with your thoughts than your situations.
Not all situations are of your choosing, but all your thoughts are.
Control your thoughts and you control your stress.

'I would die if I had to give a presentation'

Comedian Jerry Seinfeld made a joke about a survey that found that the fear of public speaking ranks higher in most people's minds than the fear of death. "In other words," he deadpanned, "at a funeral, the average person would rather be in the casket than giving the eulogy." It's a funny joke but death is further from business peoples minds than giving a presentation because a presentation is closer time wise and people have more negative thoughts about presentations. Many winners succeed using this communication skill, not just politicians.

Some people love public speaking. Others don't.
People say, 'I would rather die than give a presentation'.
No you wouldn't!

What do you think?

One person can enjoy giving a speech and another may not, so it's not the event itself that affects the person but the way the person thinks about the event. Psychologists Gregory Miller at the University of British Columbia and Suzanne Segerstrom at the University of Kentucky did a study of the 30 years of stress research available, examining over 300 studies involving 19,000 people. They looked at thousands of pages of research in search of common threads and their results were published in the Psychological Bulletin in 2004. Their findings make common sense.

Good stress or Bad Stress?

Long term stress such as unemployment or permanent disability where there is no end in sight will have a negative effect on almost all immune functions if the mind of the person is negative long term.

Stress is associated with negative health including an increase in heart disease. Sheldon Cohen, a professor of psychology at Carnegie Mellon University, found that people suffering long term stress (in jobs or relationships) are at least twice as likely to get sick from a cold or flu. She concluded that the more stress people endure the better their chances of falling ill.
However, short-term stresses like speaking in public actually boost your immune system to cope with the challenge and make you healthier! Short term stress like public speaking has "an end in sight." Therefore it can be beneficial to our health according to the study.

Minimising stress before, during and after performance
As shown above there are many ways to reduce stress and increase energy. Relaxation can help do both and is an essential tool for winners, before and after winning performances (and in business and some sports during). Everything you do everyday affects your performance. In the words of a greater man than me "The fight is won away from the arena." It's the same for you wherever your arena is, on grass or on carpet. Your mental performance and winning performance in any one day is affected by what you do before the event (away from the arena) in the other 24/6.

"The fight is won away from the arena."- Mohammed Ali

Everything you do everyday affects your performance.
What you do during 24/6 affects your
performance during the seventh day.

Relax after performance to win next time!
Relaxation after performance improves mental and physical recovery time and improves quality thinking and positive thinking. This is great preparation for the next performance.

Better and Quicker Decisions
Research quoted in Men's Health stated that when a group of non exercising executives, were put on a plan of exercise involving 3 exercise sessions and 1 weights sessions a week they made better and quicker decisions than a group of executives that did not exercise. Fascinating!

Executives who exercise make better and quicker decision
Healthy body, Healthy mind. Good body, good decisions.

Sharper Millionaire Mind
Bruce Burkett is a successful Estate Agent in London who runs Lynx Homes. He was involved in a TV programme on Channel 4 in 2004, which was watched by millions, and I'm sure inspired millions, myself

included. Bruce goes to the gym every morning before work. He commented about the benefits of his fitness routine; "I'm sharper mentally. I definitely feel I'm better in business. I'm razor sharp and optimistic." It appears that an investment in your health, is an investment in your future wealth.

Exercise is not a "waste of time." It's an investment of your time.
Your performance is more profitable!
Invest in your health and invest in your future wealth. Exercise.
Your health is your wealth.
Exercise keeps the mind razor sharp and optimistic!
Stop and 'sharpen' the body and you 'sharpen' the mind!

Just do it!
How much exercise did you do last week? Find something you like to do and do it. Don't gym it, if you don't enjoy it. However you choose to exercise, enjoy it. Just do it! You'll reap the rewards. And have a razor sharp week!

Swimming Away Problems
I was unable to do my normal exercise routine for two weeks due to a back injury. In the last week, outside of work, I had eight different challenges, as well as coping with not being able to walk, sit or exercise due to my back injury. I do not recall having so many major non-work issues to deal with in a week. One of the things I did which I feel kept my sanity and positivity was exercise! I was unable to run but I was able to swim. So I took time out to go for a swim and it was worth every second.

Keep your sanity and positivity with exercise. No excuses.

No excuses
I had a great excuse to not exercise for two weeks! Back injury! If you didn't exercise last week I'm sure you've got a great excuse. But if you don't exercise this week, you'll reduce your mental performance! If you DO exercise we'll reap the rewards now AND later! Moving your body, improves your mind. (By the way some people take months to recover from back injuries. I healed my back with 'mental movies', mantras and a helpful back specialist).

It's easy to find excuses but in future you won't find it as easy
If you rest, you rust
Moving your body, improves your mind.

Run Away From Drugs
In a controlled study of depressed patients, 30 minutes exercise three times a day had a better success rate than drugs. Short term and long

term. (No surprises there) And it's cheaper too! Walking, running and dancing are all free! Skipping is a great exercise and you need very little space. Positive author Wayne Dyer runs every single day of the year and often he runs up and down the hotel corridor! Exercise. No excuses.

Drugs are for mugs.
Walking, running, dancing and laughing are the best drugs in the world.
Fifty percent of all working days lost are due to work related stress.
If you think and eat positively, take time out to relax and exercise at least every second day you will be more successful than 50% of sick people.

Thinking Energy

You need physical and mental energy to think. Whether it is doing creative thinking, positive thinking or using Positive Mindpower Tools. Creative guru Dr John Park says, "Creative thinking is hard work. You physically need the energy. I spent a whole day recently working on something and got nothing. My tank was empty. I got a good nights sleep and in half a day I achieved more than I did the previous day. Creative thinking is quite strenuous. In one session I did with a group in an afternoon they could only handle one creative exercise. They were wiped out. They didn't have the energy. I had prepared two." What did they eat for lunch? Were they very fit and healthy? Guess!

Relax and solve your problems

Relaxation is important because it not only increases energy it also increases opportunity to come up with ideas or solve problems. A few minutes relaxation can beat hours of stressful problem solving.

"The significant problems we face cannot be solved at the same level of thinking we were at when we created them." - Albert Einstein

Feed it and free it

I like the advice of Creative guru and former Proctor and Gamble Head of Research and Development Dr John Park. He says, "Feed your mind and then free your mind. Ideas won't just come by being focused. Feed it and free it. For example look at different magazines and different television channels. I've got a few bloody good ideas from watching television. As soon as I hear Iraq I switch off." One of the tips from the creative people at the company 'What? If!' is; 'Do something different every weekend'. The tip to 'do something different' is one that I have followed many times. According to Professor Richard Wiseman doing new and different things makes you more lucky. Which is one of the reasons my goal is to visit a different country every year.

"Feed it and free it." - Dr John Park, Creativity Guru, Lecturer at Aberdeen Business School, Robert Gordon University

"To invent, you need a good imagination and a pile of junk." -Thomas Edison, Inventor

Do something different. It improves creativity, knowledge and luck.

Ideas and awareness

I suggest spending time thinking of ideas and then go about your day or weekend or holiday and write down any ideas that come to you. When your subconscious mind knows what your goals are and knows ideas are important to you it will find and attract hundreds of ideas! Be prepared. Take a pen or voice recorder everywhere. Yes, everywhere! You relax when you're in the shower or on the toilet so be prepared! By actively looking for things and being more aware you will come up with more ideas. John says, "People aren't looking for ideas that's the problem. Ideas just come to me."

Be a detective

Find a successful person and you'll find a successful idea and strategy. Copy them. Some of the richest people in the UK have taken ideas from the USA. Autotrader and Kwik Fit are American ideas. Some of the most successful products and companies in the USA have been with ideas from the UK. Sometimes because American funders are more optimistic. Many Successful UK ideas and inventions come from a small country of only 5 million people called Scotland! Japanese companies actually look up UK patents and wait to see if the inventor lets the patent expire or pays to extend it. If they don't they use it. If you snooze, you lose. Some of the best athletes are using ideas and tips they have learnt from the best athletes!

Do your detective work. Success leaves clues. Look for them Travelling to another country can be a very profitable experience.

When to use the relaxation techniques

The following relaxation techniques are a must before and after and in some sports like golf during performance. In any business they must be used during the day or don't expect a winning performance (there's no way). And the techniques are useful for relaxation before sleeping. It's so important that people sleep well so they perform well.

Energy and relaxation is an essential part of Winning Mentality. Winners that sleep well, perform well.

Relaxation; Recharging brain boost

These relaxation techniques will actually recharge mental and physical energy. Making the effort to take a "brain break" is like a Formula 1 car taking a pit stop. If you don't take a pit stop you won't win the race! In fact, you won't even finish that race! In order to think positively, creatively and intuitively you need to control stress by having relaxation breaks. Relaxation boosts positivity, creativity and intuition, as well as increasing concentration and mental and physical energy. Take a few minutes break every hour to give yourself a boost.

Use one of the five 'B's;

1. Breathing; big and slow breaths, start counting!
2. Banter; with the people you're with, have a laugh. Have a 'banter break'! If you're laughing, you're relaxing.
3. Body moving; dancing, singing, playing. Body motion creates emotion, so dancing is great. A favourite song can lift you up. Especially if you sing it! Humming a song or playing a game boosts your brain. The minds emotions is not just linked to motion but body position (language). The mind associates a smile with 'happy', a frown with 'sad' and in between with 'concern or danger'. Sit and smile for a few minutes. A big smile relaxes the brain and body. Keep smiling! More smiles>less stress.
4. Boring tasks; like walking round the block, counting the stairs, doing the dishes, repeating the word 'relax' over and over with your eyes closed, etc
5. Build belief by repeating your mantra several times or writing it out several times (Bart!) Powerful exercise!

Relaxation boosts positivity, creativity and intuition, reduces stress and increases concentration and mental and physical energy.
Taking a "brain break" is like a Formula 1 car taking a pit stop.
After the 'time out' you come back with more energy in your tank.
If you don't take a pit stop you won't win the race!
In fact, you won't even finish the race!

Keep smiling.

'There are over 100 languages in the world but a smile speaks them all.'
'If you see someone without a smile give them one of yours.'

Take a deep breath in now

Large breaths or slow breaths slow the heart rate down. Air is your body and brains number 1 priority. How long can you last without breathing? Drinking? Eating? (About 3 minutes, 3 days and 3 weeks respectively?) Prioritise your brain and body food in that order. Take a deep breath now.

GO!

If your chest moves when you take a deep breath
you're not breathing right!
A deep breath moves your stomach not your chest, lie on the ground
and breath or watch someone sleeping, you see the
stomach move not the chest.

Relaxation not stimulation
They can be used at any time and should be used everyday to reduce stress and increase intuition. Everyone needs R&R! There are hundreds of ways to relax and recharge. One advantage is knowing the things which are not actually relaxation but stimulation. For example watching television, listening to loud music, playing computer games, drinking alcohol, smoking or eating actually only distracts your mind rather than relaxing it and reduces your energy rather than increasing it. To supercharge the mind and body quickly the best way is to reduce the stimulus rather than change the stimulus. Relax and recharge several times a day.

Silence is golden. Stimulus is stressing.

Relaxation before visualisation
Relaxing the body and mind will give direct access to the subconscious mind. Therefore being relaxed before you begin visualisation will greatly assist the impact. Take 7 slow deep breaths before you visualise your car and movie screen and visualise your Top 7 goals! Use this method at the start of the day for visualising things you want to go well. See yourself at the end of the day happy!

Use relaxation before visualisation.
Relaxation is the friend of creative and intuitive thinking.
Stress is the enemy.

Relaxation improves Imagination
We are naturally more relaxed before going to sleep and after waking from sleep so our subconscious mind is most open. Therefore this is a good time to visualise. You will also find yourself at your most creative. This is one reason why many people can find it tricky to get to sleep at night. Your mind can be very creative with 'problems' and worries by creative negative thinking! Control your thoughts and you'll control your future and get back to sleep! When you're relaxed is the best time to use your mind. Use your passengers to solve problems. Solve it or set it as a goal to solve it and the answer will come to you. Usually after a good nights sleep! Don't worry!

Comedy car
A golf client told me that he used to listen to Steve Martin tapes on the way to tournaments. What a great way to spend your drive time.

Never change a winning game
When I am giving tips to a sports 'winner' who is losing I often hear them say "I used to do that" but they stopped doing it and they stopped winning! If you have won in the past I'd ask you; what were you doing? What were you thinking? Now Do it.

My philosophy can be summed up in one slightly misleading generalisation; Never change a winning game. Always change a losing game.

There are few exceptions to this. A winning game can occasionally lose but a losing game will always lose. Spot the difference.

A winning game will need to continually evolve and improve to outclass competition, which is how it became a winning game in the first place!

In other words don't stop improving, when you start improving. Winners change losers don't.

Sense of humour essential
I have done some informal research over the past 4- 10 years observing businessmen, sports men and women and inventors and millionaire entrepreneurs and I have found that they all had a good sense of humour. The best winners always had a great sense of humour. Why is this useful and important? Below are just a few of the benefits.

Laughing is good for your health
Laughing has the following health benefits;

1. Boosts immune system
2. Reduces stress
3. Stimulates endorphins which create 'feel good' mood
4. Increases energy
5. 100 laughs are as good for your health as 10 minutes rowing!

As a result of these benefits winners feel better (are better) and perform better! They cope with the demands of being a winner and demands of stress through humour and relaxation. Healthy body, healthy mind.

Humour is great in the office
Keep up the banter at work! It's good for you and makes you happy! It is also proven to improve productivity, as well as give the associated health benefits for those involved. And happy campers are more loyal! Humour is essential in some jobs!

Jokes are good for building relations
Humour between people you don't know well or don't know at all helps strengthen communication and relationship. It's funny because all the people I get along really well with have a great sense of humour!

Humour is good for personal relationships
Keep the jokes flowing at home and at the pub! It's good for you! It also increases the level of happiness within individuals and relationships. Many entrepreneurs and sports winners have a supporting partner behind them, which keeps them happy and healthy. There are many benefits other than the banter including having someone to talk to and fulfilling the human need for sex and exercise!

Sense of humour essential
All of the above prove why a sense of humour is essential for winners to be winners. Most forward thinking businesses actually state in their recruitment adverts "Sense of humour essential"! Even top companies that don't mention 'humour' in their adverts normally look for it in their interviews!

Laughter is the best medicine. Learn to laugh- a lot.

Motion creates confident emotion
Pace up and down like Sherlock Holmes it aids thinking, helps solve challenges and assists creative thinking. Which is why people do it when they are on the mobile phone!

Pace up and down when you are thinking.

State of Mind
Your brain operates on different wavelengths depending on what you are doing and what you are thinking. The wavelengths are measured in Hz from 0.5Hz when you are sleeping to 40Hz when you are excited or frightened. This is one reason to avoid using an alarm clock. Your alarm sounds off at 50Hz (look at the bottom of the alarm to confirm) and your brain is operating at 0.5Hz!! Alarms start the day in a stressful way and interrupt you in a 90-minute cycle.

Beta = Alert Concentration

Beta waves range between 13-40 HZ. When you are in this state you are wide-awake and alert. You are so alert that a few seconds can feel like a long time, like when you are under stress in competition or in danger. Your mind is sharp and focused. It makes connections quickly, easily and you're primed to do work that requires your full attention. In the Beta state the brain is fully fired up with peak mental concentration. You will be in beta when taking an exam, playing sport, giving a presentation, analysing information, and other activities where mental alertness and high levels of concentration are key to your success. Quick problem solving is possible and often necessary in this state. Beta is associated with heightened alertness and peak concentration and hand eye co-ordination.

In Beta the brain is fully alert in peak concentration for as long as you are stimulated and have the mental and physical energy available.

Alpha = Calm and Creative

Alpha waves range between 7-12 HZ. This is when you are relaxed, but not quite deeply relaxed. In Alpha your creativity flows, which is excellent for problem solving and finding new ideas. This is why relaxed thinking is more effective for creativity than alert or stressed thinking. In alpha you are more calm and confident and less focused and less fearful. Periods of 'alpha' relaxation are essential for having the mental energy and concentration required for the Beta State which you will be in when playing sport or doing business.

When you are relaxed in an Alpha state
your creativity flows and energy grows.

Theta = Deeply Relaxed and Intuitive

Theta waves range between 4-7 HZ. When you are deeply relaxed your brain will operate at Theta state where brain activity slows almost to the point of sleep, but not quite. Theta is a deeply relaxed brain state excellent for talking to your heroes in your head (passengers in your car) and visualising the best strategy to achieve a goal/win! This state is like when time 'floats by' and an hour feels like a minute. In was in this state that Newton and Einstein were said to have come up with their famous discoveries (while lying under trees on a summer day!).

Theta is an ideal state for directing your mind, super-learning, re-programming your mind and new habits. Theta has also been identified as the gateway to learning and memory. You may find it's when you are relaxed that you remember something you were meant to do yesterday! (When this happens write it down and continue relaxing for a few more minutes –you may remember something else!) Theta relaxation increases creativity, enhances learning, reduces stress and awakens intuition and other extrasensory perception skills.

When you are fully focusing your attention on something you will be in a trance like state e.g. reading, watching, learning or goal setting! This is similar to being 'in the zone' when you shut out external noise (like people shouting or talking).

It is when you are relaxing in an Alpha/Theta state that you have amazing ideas! I'm sure you have discovered that when you have engaged your conscious in a simple activity like walking, washing, cycling or driving you will have great ideas. Entrepreneurs are infamous for having their best ideas while on holiday. If you don't relax, take holidays or engage in activity away from your desk you are in danger of coming up with zero great ideas! You won't be solving problems you'll just be creating them.

"The significant problems we face cannot be solved at the same level of thinking we were at when we created them." - Albert Einstein

If you don't relax or take holidays or get away from your desk, you are in danger of coming up with zero great ideas and solutions!

People often have their best ideas while engaging in an activity like washing, walking, driving or sight seeing!

Delta = Dreaming, Sleeping and Sorting (Semiconscious)

Delta waves range between 0-4 HZ. Some waves in the Delta range trigger the release of Human Growth Hormone necessary for healing and regeneration. This is why quality deep sleep is so essential for recovering, recharging and healing. As you are semiconscious in the Delta state, the only part of the brain operating is the subconscious. It is said that it is while we are sleeping that the subconscious will organise knowledge, solve problems, create dreams and make up ideas.

I believe sleep is useful to the learning process. One study showed a higher recall of knowledge the day after being taught than after the lesson itself. It is also brilliant for creativity. I heard about an ingenious student who deliberately took a nap or went to sleep when they were unable to solve a complex problem ('sleep on it'). If you 'will' yourself to come up with a solution to a challenge while you sleep you will be surprised at how often you wake with ideas. You can sleep more effectively and productively with Winning Mentality! Finally I believe sleep is essential for every human being to operate effectively. Quality sleep translates to quality performances.

There are exceptional circumstances when we can survive and thrive without much long periods of deep sleep. Sailing sensation Emma Richards sailed round the world single handed and lasted periods of up to 30 days between ports on around 4 hours of sleep a day, which consisted of twelve 20 minute naps! Which just goes to show what is humanly possible and achievable, despite the fact that most of the world thinks they can't live without 8 hours a night! There is definitely something powerful having 20 minute periods of deep relaxation or sleep.

While we sleep our subconscious organises knowledge, solves problems, creates dreams and makes up ideas. Sweet Dreams! When it comes to solving problems and making decisions it can be useful to 'sleep on it'.

Quality deep sleep is so essential for recovering, recharging and healing. Quality sleep translates to quality performances.

By following the relaxation recommended in this chapter you will be in relaxed 'alpha' state. It's essential that you have periods of relaxation for mental health and physical health. It's the antidote to stress. It's the opposite to stress!

In Alpha your brain activity slows down from the alert Beta state. The brain often flows between the Alpha and Theta state. If Alpha can be summarised as 'relaxed' then theta would be summed up as 'deeply relaxed'. They are so close there is no definitive line between them. Theta taps into your subconscious and is associated with the deepest levels of relaxation and meditation. Periods of relaxation are not just beneficial for using your visualisation, intuition and creativity techniques. Deep relaxation has other major benefits.

Deep relaxation is beneficial for using visualisation, intuition and creativity techniques.

Deep relaxation is powerful

Deep relaxation has two major benefits. If you use the deep relaxation techniques in this chapter you will find yourself with significantly more energy. Research showed that 20 minutes of deep relaxation can be as powerful as 8 hours sleep! Deep relaxation also improves your intuition, thereby enhancing your intuitive decision making. Hence the reason Harvard Business Review stated that "intuition and meditation (deep relaxation) are the two most important tools in business in the 21st century." I believe deep relaxation daily is a powerful tool for winners in business and sport. Begin with 5 minutes a day and build it up every week for four weeks. Winning habits create winning performances.

Twenty minutes of deep relaxation has a powerful affect on intuition and energy.

The less stressed you are the more energy you have got.

The more relaxation you do during the day, the less sleep you will need during the night. Which will give you more time! To work, train, learn, have fun or relax!

"Research has shown that 20 minutes of meditation can be as powerful as 8 hours sleep." - Gita Belin

Meditation benefits

Deep relaxation like meditation has super benefits like increasing energy and intuition. The advantages of meditation are;

1. More energy
2. Enhanced intuition
3. Reduce stress
4. Improve memory, problem solving and creativity
5. Increases feelings of happiness and self esteem
6. Improve overall health (mental and physical)
7. Improves relationships
8. Speeds recovery from disease and illness
9. Compact mental issues like anxiety, depression, insomnia

The deep relaxation techniques suggested in this chapter are like meditation and as powerful as meditation.

Deep Relaxation boosts

The benefits of having a few minutes of deep relaxation every day have already been outlined. The best techniques for deep relaxation are the same as some of the techniques for short relaxation "brain breaks" already outlined.

If you get one 20-minute period of deep relaxation (or two 10 minute periods) a day expect your energy and intuition to jump dramatically!

Sit yourself comfortably somewhere quiet and close your eyes. The brain and body associate lying down with sleeping so sitting is best. For a few minutes or twenty minutes (a day) do one of the following;

1. Breathing; Big and slow breaths, count 1-7, and then restart.
2. Body; Relax your body from head to toe very slowly. E.g. consciously relax your head, then forehead, then neck, then ears, then eyes, then face, etc all the way to your toes and then work back up your body slowly (breathing slowly as well of course!)
3. Boring; Repeat a word like 'relax' over and over with your eyes closed. Silently or aloud. Slowly!
4. Boring; Hum the word 'hum' slowly and for as long as you can without straining. And then do it over and over again. Slowly!
5. Bach; Put on a relaxing piece of music (2-20 minutes long) (classical composer Bach is said to be ideal) and then sit and just listen to the music. Listen.

These techniques are very relaxing. Positively verbalise that you will relax for twenty minutes and then become alert and fresh. If you need to you can set an alarm and put it under a cushion or pillow (set it for 22 minutes to give yourself a few minutes to relax). These techniques are all powerful. You can use one, a combination or ideally start with number 1 and work down to number 5 and then start again.

1-5 Deep Relaxation Technique
Put on some relaxing music. First take 7 slow deep breaths, then relax from head to toe, then repeat the word 'relax' 7 times, then hum 7 times, then listen to the music for a few moments and then go back to number 1 again! Do it once, twice or as many times as you like! Sit with a friend and talk them through it (especially relaxing head to toe) and then swap after 10-20 minutes. You will make many grateful friends if you give (and teach) them some deep relaxation! You will be teaching yourself at the same time.

Note
You will be relaxed so expect some thoughts to occasionally pop into your head! Let any 'useless' random thoughts go but take a short two-word note of any useful thoughts (preferably have voice recorder to hand and you can keep eyes closed). Secondly, there is no right or wrong way to do it and you may find it easier or more difficult to do than you expect (we are all different!). It always gets easier. Never give up! Thirdly, it's useful when developing any new habit to build some routine into it than do it randomly. It helps your memory if you use the same place, time, music and routine. Fourthly after this exercise you'll be in a relaxed state of mind so it's a great opportunity to view some mental movies, repeat some mantras or talk to your passengers! But one thing at a time!

To develop new habits adopt a routine
rather than adopt them randomly.
You may need to write a reminder to yourself initially.
We teach what we most need to learn.

It's amazing how surprisingly easy it is to waste time
and how surprisingly easy it can be to make time.
Rome wasn't built in a day.

Practice
Initially when I began doing the 20 minutes of relaxation I would use a soft alarm clock set for about 22 minutes and put it under a pillow so I knew when 20 minutes was up and I didn't dose off into a deep sleep. Now I actually seem to 'know' when twenty minutes is passed and don't need the alarm. The relaxation is powerful, but it took a few goes to get used to.

Relaxation makes a BIG difference
To people who are very stressed 20 minutes of relaxation makes a big difference. I know one stressed business guy that began doing around 20 minutes of meditation a night and found he was able to cut down from 20 to 3 cigs a day! He said he had no will power! He also stopped eating chocolate or sweets! He found that when he has the choice of a bar of chocolate or an apple he chooses the fruit. He said "My body seems to know what's good for it."

ACTION!
Deep Relaxation 1-5
Do this exercise once now just to experience how good a few minutes relaxation feels and how powerful it is. If you are unable to put on some soft classical music or classical radio do it without sound. Take 7 slow deep breaths, relax from head to toe, repeat the word 'relax' 7 times or hum 7 times, listen to the music for a few moments and then go back to number 1 again! Do it at least once.
GO!

STOP!
Long term Relaxation
Short-term relaxation is essential in sport and business. So too are periods of long-term relaxation. Take several weeks off work every year like Sir Richard Branson and Lance Armstrong. Winners need it and deserve it! Many like Bill Gates work 7 days a week the rest of the time! These long brain breaks will improve your performance and motivation during the rest of the year. This time off is also likely to be when you come up with your best ideas and best visions of the future. You cannot afford not to take time off. Don't wait until you have the time! You won't find the time, just take the time. The time off does not have to be a 'relaxing' two weeks by the pool. A change is as good as a rest. Anything away from work for a few weeks every year will benefit the weeks at work every year. It also benefits your mental and physical health!

Spending time away from work is a great investment.
Time is money. You cannot afford not to take time off.

Improve your business; take a holiday
Gerry McKenzie is the owner of award winning company McKenzie Biscuits. He told me that he works 7 days a week. He didn't take holidays for the first 10 years in the business. He has taken holidays for the last 14 years, ever since he got divorced. He married again and takes 5 holidays a year. He says, "For the last 14 years business has improved." I asked him if he ever came up with ideas on holiday and he said, "It's a brilliant time for that." His longest holiday is five weeks. He takes his notebook, digital tape recorder and guitar with him and

writes songs and often comes up with brilliant business ideas. Gerry's business has improved in the last 14 years. It could be the holidays or it could be the divorce, he doesn't know! I'll let you make up your own mind and take your own lesson from the story.

A tulip survey of millionaires done for the BBC found that two thirds take three or more holidays a year and one in five take six holidays a year. I've noticed people are at their most productive before they go on holiday! They have so much to do and so little time to do it that they have to become more effective. More decisive, less waste. Therefore the more often you go on holiday, the more effective you will be! And the more great ideas you will come up with! Founder of Richer Sounds Julian Richer only works every second week for Richer Sounds and he admits he is forced to be effective! The other week he does consultancy work.

If you want to improve your business; take a holiday!
If you want to be more effective; take a holiday!
If you want to come up with ideas; take a holiday!
If you want to improve your self, improve your health.

Ideas are king. Actions are making.

Two out of three millionaires take three or more holidays a year
and one in five take six holidays a year.
I've never met a stupid winner. I've never met a
stupid self-made millionaire.

Relaxation is not just useful it's essential

Relaxation keeps you away from the energy enemy, which is stress! Reducing stress keeps you away from the stress enemy, which is depression. But avoiding depressions take a few things and one of them is holidays! Winners take holiday's. Often they have to force themselves to take them or they are forced to take them (family or business related) but nevertheless the top performers don't just take time out every day, or time out of every week, they take time out of every year to recharge.

Relax or else (performance dives)

Ask a golfer what happens when they focus for 14 holes non-stop. Their concentration dives for the last 4 holes. They must relax between shots during a 3 hour game of golf. You must relax during a 12-hour workday. Or your concentration and performance will dive. Increase performance by increasing energy; reduce stress and increase relaxation.

Time out

Time out benefits mental and physical health. I've noticed how powerful it can be. We are humans not superman. We need to take time out. Every 'winner' in business I know takes holidays and I woke up and realised that I need to do the same too. Every person is different. Knowledge is power. I now follow all of the advice in this book. Long-term brain breaks weren't in the book until I learnt my lesson! Destiny. Our biggest mistakes are always some of our biggest lessons.

You don't <u>have to</u> do anything you don't want to do.
The things you choose to do and not do will shape your future, as well as provide great lessons.
Big Mistakes provide big lessons.
The 'teacher' arrives when I was ready to learn and I rarely make mistakes twice.
Some things are meant to be. Destiny
Everything happens for a reason.

Muscle memory

Your muscles have 'muscle memory'. Your mind and muscles always remember how to ride a bike. A sportsman you will <u>not</u> lose their touch by not playing regularly. They just lose their confidence! As the saying goes 'you never forget how to ride a bike'. I worked with pro Paul Arthur at the start of the golf pre-season training and he normally took months to 'get back into it' but after a one-hour lesson he gave me the testimonial at the front. If you are a winner you NEVER lose your winning touch. If you think you can you can. Your muscle has memory. It's like any knowledge you learn. EVERYTHING you have ever seen and done is in your memory. You just have to tap into it.

Confidence is key to be a winner.

Holiday helps win

US Masters Champion Phil Mickelson won $1 million at the PGA Grand Slam of Golf in Hawaii in 2004 after taking a holiday! Only four players were in the tournament. The four major winners in the world. U.S. Open Champion Retief Goosen, British Open Champion Todd Hamilton and PGA Champion Vijay Singh in a two-day, 36-hole stroke-play event. While everyone else did 'practice preparation' Phil did 'relaxation preparation' and never touched a club for TWO weeks. He won.

"It was certainly unexpected. I didn't hit it great today and somehow I shot 59. So go figure. It just all kind of came together. I just went out and just kind of played and today, the ball went in the hole. I don't really have an explanation for it. I made everything. It was a great feeling to see the ball go in the hole. Awesome." - Phil Mickelson

You don't have to be perfect.
Winners are never perfect
They just do better than everyone else.
Strikers miss.
Batters miss.
Golfers miss.
They get over it, get on with it and go and win it!

EVERY game of golf I have watched I have seen the winner make a big mistake. But they won. You don't have to be perfect to win. You just have to get over it. And play better than everyone else. Business winners are not perfect. But if they make a mistake they get over it! And they become better than everyone else.

Phil was asked, "Taking a couple weeks away from golf and having your friends and family here, do you think that actually helped you?"

Phil said, "Very possibly. Very possibly. I think that and not having much expectation. You know, I see Vijay out there practising so hard, knowing I haven't touched a club in a couple of weeks, and he's played so great all year, and thinking it's very unlikely that I'll be able to play two rounds at that level. But a lot of things kind of came together. I kind of freewheeled it. I think the fact that there wasn't much wind allowed me to keep my misses a lot smaller and get around the course. And it came down to a putting match, and I was able to out putt everybody."

One lesson

I think following the example of Chris Gorman would have benefited me and certainly the example of Sir Richard Branson would have helped me and my motivation over 12 months. Chris Gorman's one piece of advice to people is finish work at 4pm on a Friday and review your week on Sunday night and then plan your week ahead. Sir Richard Branson takes one month off every year to spend with family and friends on his Island in the Caribbean. Few entrepreneurs will 'work hard, play hard and rest hard' like top entrepreneurs.

Top entrepreneurs take time off, bottom entrepreneurs don't.

Be a business 'athlete'!
Look after your mind and body like a business athlete and you'll have athletic energy and be able to give an athletic business performance.

Short term (minutes), medium terms (hours) and long term (weeks) relaxation is essential for being healthy mentally and physically and for being a winner.

Quality not quantity.

"I feel brilliant after a long weekend doing some sailing and drinking. I actually feel better after a long weekend sailing than sitting on a beach for a week."
- Colin Howie, Partner, Laurie and Company

Why is taking a month off better than working 12 months on?

1. Mental and physical health
2. Motivation is maintained during the other 10-11 months you work.
3. Time off is a conscious *and* subconscious motivator to be more productive and get things done. Makes you focus on VIP tasks. 80/20 tasks.
4. Necessity is the mother of invention and motivation. In the weeks and days before a holiday you'll complete twice as much work (not far off what you would have done if you hadn't taken the holiday)
5. One idea can change your life and your business. A holiday is THE best time for business people to come up with ideas. The holiday pays for itself!
6. The time spent away makes you happy and the people you love happy. The time invested keeps everyone happy for the other 10-11 months when you'll be working 6 or 7 days a week! If you are happy you work better.

Anything is possible

In extreme circumstances people can perform well mentally for hours, days, weeks on end with little sleep and no 'brain breaks'. Anything is possible. Can I positively suggest that you cannot be superman every day of the year? I gave it a go. I failed. I discovered I am a human that needs 'long brain breaks' every year or even just 'weekend brain breaks' occasionally! If I didn't discover this while writing this book 'long brain breaks' would probably not have featured in this book. My 'teacher' arrived in perfect time, as they always do. It was destiny that it is in this book. I hope it is useful advice for you. You may be able to work every day of the year, you may be better than me. I don't think it's worth the risk! Just assume you need 'time out' occasionally.

Don't be a hero. Don't work hero hours all the time.

Hero hours, horrible results

During the war people were acting like brave heroes every day for years. However, in a factory in Britain which supplied ammunition for use in the war they found that people were working heroic hours every day and never taking time off. Over time the mistakes being made were increasing and a lot of end product was useless. The factory started to make time off compulsory as well as limiting the maximum number of working hours per day for everyone. Efficiency went up and mistakes went down. No hero hours.

Working hero hours all the time gives horrible results. Don't be a hero.

Long term Relaxation in Sport

Relax before and after training and performances. Long-term relaxation will differ from sport to sport. Time off will benefit every sport. Through visualisation you can actually improve when you go back to perform. Find a winner in your sport and find out when they train and when they relax and when they take time off during a full year. Sports vary. Winners vary. Phelps trains everyday. Armstrong takes a break after the Tour de France.

Winners in sport and business

Winners in sport and business are different. A huge part of the routine of a winning athlete is relaxation outside performing and training. Gold medallists prepare four year plans for an Olympic games and month long holidays are not part of the routine! A business winner works long hours 5 to 7 days a week therefore needs the time off to return to peak performance whereas a sport winner relaxes daily and needs to remain in peak physical condition (use it or lose it), so can't take extended periods of time off. A medium term 'brain break' of a day or several hours a week greatly benefits a business performance. Chris Gorman takes Friday night, Saturday and most of Sunday off every week but admits in the early days of setting up DX he worked 80-100 hours a week.

Short, Medium and Long Relaxing Brain Breaks

Short, medium and long brain breaks will improve your performance, positivity, creativity, motivation, decision-making and mental and physical health. Time is money. You cannot afford not to relax. Looking after your mind and body is a wise investment. Make time.

Healthy body, healthy mind.

Very fast Summary
Stress is the enemy of energy.
A little stress when we are excited or stretching ourselves is good.
A lot of stress either mental or physical is not good
There are 9 ways to increase or decrease energy
Stressed thoughts make you feel stressed.
Relaxation is essential. Relaxation increases energy.
Positive thoughts create positive people.
Stimulation is not relaxation.
There are 9 easy ways to stress your mind and body. Most people do 8.5
Keep your sanity and positivity with exercise. No excuses
Exercise is not a "waste of time." It's an investment of your time.
Time is money. You cannot afford not to relax or exercise. Make time.
Invest in your health and invest in your future wealth.
Your health is your wealth.
Exercise keeps the mind razor sharp.
Healthy body, healthy mind. Healthy mind, healthy body.
Increase your energy <u>and</u> improve your sleep and you'll double your time!
How you spend your time will dictate whether you win or lose.
Winning preparation creates winning results.
Winners reduce stress by looking after their mind and body.
Laughter is the best medicine.
A happy worker is a good worker.
Being stressed helps performance. Being over stressed affects performance.
Winners handle pressure and stress using their mind.

Many entrepreneurs and sports winners have a supportive partner, which keeps them healthy, happy and relaxed.

<u>Everything</u> you do <u>everyday</u> of the year affects your performance.

"I don't drink alcohol. I eat healthily. All the benefits of a hard training session can be lost by munching the wrong food afterwards so I choose not to eat sweets, biscuits or chocolate. I also steer clear of fast food."- Jonny Wilkinson, 'My World'

"Visualisation, mental rehearsal, stress management, and intuition are as much a part of an athlete's training regime as diet, exercise, and sport specific practice." - Lance R. Miller, International Shooting Coach; 1995, USA Shooting, Coach of the Year.

Spend your time wisely. It's the most important investment you will make.

When it comes to work, relaxation and exercise the key is quality not quantity.

Increase your energy and you increase your time. Time is money. You are given 1,440 minutes or 24 hours to spend every day. How you invest it, will relate to how you profit from it.

"The fight is won away from the arena."- Mohammed Ali

Not all situations are of your choosing, but all your thoughts are. Control your thoughts and you control your stress.

Sleeping helps Olympic performance.

"The two best physicians of them all; Dr Laughter and Dr Sleep." – Dr Gregory Dean

Be prepared

If you want to improve your performance; take a holiday!

Don't be a hero. Winners take short and long term 'relaxation brain breaks'. Take a few minutes out every day, a few hours out every week and a few weeks out every year.

If you want to perform as well as a formula one car, you need to take some pit stops. You won't win the race if you don't pit stop.

Don't find the time. Make the time.

No excuses!

Chapter 7.5
ENERGY (Positive Energy)

Very Fast Summary

Long term; Healthy Winners need positive energy and happiness not stress and sadness. Positive energy is good for the mind or body. Negative energy is not. Healthy mind, healthy body.

Included in this chapter;

Importance of Maslow's Magic 5 to performance
Happy athletes make winning athletes
Happy entrepreneurs make millionaire entrepreneurs
Being happy is great for performance
Our mental, emotional, social and physical needs
A lot of energy is used up by trying, resisting and negative thinking
Negative thoughts and fears create a lot of physical problems.
Be positive; mentally, physically, emotionally & socially
If you are mentally positive you will be physically positive
If you are mentally negative you will be physically negative
Negative thoughts injury your body
You need a healthy body to have a healthy mind
You need a healthy mind to have a healthy body
How negative emotional stress impacts performance
How having a positive life outside work improves performance
How physical stress damages performance and damages the body
If you are relaxed and happy you will have more energy
Being healthy mentally, physically, emotionally & socially
Negative thoughts can hurt you
Aiming anger at yourself will hurt
Laughter is the best medicine
Love provides a lot of energy.
People who are happy are full of energy.

'Healthy body, healthy mind'

'Healthy mind, healthy body'-Phil McNally

Love is positive energy.
Fear is negative energy.

"You don't cure the body with the body,
you cure the body with the mind."-Plato

Winners focus their energy on their dream

Because winners are happy they have lots of energy for their dream. Because successful people have got the Magic 4 they can chase their dream (part of Magic 5). They focus almost all their time and energy on chasing their dream. They don't have to worry about not loving themselves, fearing for their life, finding food for the table, finding a loving partner. They are happy at the same time as chasing their dream.

Maslow's 5 Magic needs and motivators are;

5th Need- Self Fulfilment; Realising potential using creative talents.
4th Need- Self Esteem; Achievement, recognition & success.
3rd Need- Belonging; Love, belonging, affiliation & acceptance.
2nd Need- Safety; Protection against danger, freedom from fear & security.
1st Need- Physiological; Survival needs; Water, food, clothing, shelter & sex.

Here are other useful words to represent Maslow's 5 Magic needs. As humans we have the natural need for;

5. Purpose and goals and creativity and stimulation
4. Feeling significant and giving and receiving attention
3. Intimacy with someone and connection with others
2. A sense of control (security)
1. Fulfilling the physiological requirements of our mind and body

Two things humans must get for mental and physical health; quality sleep and exercise.
As humans we naturally need some relaxation, calmness and quiet time in our life. Our mind and body are not designed to cope with excessive stress, especially over long periods.

Winners have got the Magic

Almost all winners have got their Magic 5 needs fulfilled so they can focus your energy and motivation on achieving their dream. Summary of the Magic 5 are;
Goal love
Self Love
People love
Mind love
Body love
The Magic 5 cover four areas of needs; mental(2&5), emotional(3&4), social(3), physical(1)

'Love is all you need'
- John Lennon and Paul McCartney

Not all stress is equal
Stress researcher H. Selye identifies four different types of stress;

1. Eustress - exciting things like watching sport, roller coaster rides or 1st dates
2. Over stress- stretching your ability e.g. in sport, life or business
3. Under stress- boredom, not using your ability,
4. Distress- fear, anger, or unresolved anger

OR to put it another way;
1. Positive stress
2. Stretching stress
3. Bored stress
4. Negative emotion stress

Negative emotion stress (distress) is the most damaging to our mental and physical health.

Stress is negative thinking.
Calm is positive thinking.

NES lands you in a mess
Negative emotion stress happens when we think negatively. A negative mind creates a negative body. Fear, anger and past hurt as well as any other negative thought can cause negative emotion stress (NES).

The fight, flight or freeze response has kept us alive since the cave.
Fear is an essential emotion for human survival.
But don't use it up too much. It not good for you.

Stress is 'negativity' and it uses up energy
When someone asks you to do something you don't want to do and you do it <u>you</u> will create resistance, tension and stress in your body. Imagine a young boy playing his computer and the hours fly past so quick before he realises the time. His Dad is shouting "Time for bed". The first answer is "no!" And so are all the answers after that! How many minutes does it take? How much energy does it take? How much stress is there? The answer to all these questions is "LOTS"! The son is full of resistance. When playing he was doing something he wanted to do, he was in the zone! Time flew past, his energy and concentration high and he performed superbly.

How about someone watching TV being asked to take out the rubbish! Same thing happens. Resistance! How many minutes does it take? How much energy does it take? How much stress is there? The answer to all these questions is LOTS! What happens when you "try" to lose weight or "try" to get to a party or "try" to remember to do something? Resistance! You don't really want to do it, if you did you would do it not try to do it!

Time flies when you're having fun.

When you go WITH the flow time flies,
energy is plentiful and stress is negligible.

When you resist the flow, time slows,
Energy drops and stress climbs.

Don't try to succeed or try to win. Do it or don't it. Don't try.

Love the actions you hate.
Or pretend to and things get done in less time,
with less energy and less stress!

Walk out your front door as yourself and walk in the back door as a cleaner and you will be amazed at what you get done!

Don't do anything you don't want to do.
It creates tension.

There are things you like to do and things you don't.
There are things that must be done and things that don't.
Spot the difference. Do what must be done and
decide to enjoy doing it!

Resistance is like washing dishes

If you resist washing the dishes and put it off after dinner or do it but resent it, it can takes hours sometimes days before you wash the dishes. Meanwhile you have used up all this energy resisting doing it. It's always on your mind, often subconsciously. When you do it for fun it –it IS fun and takes no energy time at all!

Go with the flow. Time flies when you are having fun.

Avoid a fight

Rather than resisting, Dan Millman in his book 'The Inner Athlete' suggests being non-resistant like some fighters. It's used in martial arts in Brazil and Japan. He states, "The Aikido approach can also be applied to potential verbal confrontations. On such occasions, instead of verbal tussling—trying to prove a point, win an argument, and overcome another with reason— just side step the struggle. Simply listen, really listen, to your opponents' points; acknowledge the value of what they are saying. Then ask gently if there isn't some validity to your view also. In this way, you can learn to blend and apply non-resistance not only to "attackers", but to all of life's little problems and difficult situations. Remember that you create the struggle in your life; you create the collisions. You can dissolve struggle through non-resistance."

"In Judo, he who thinks is immediately thrown. Victory is assured to those who are physically and mentally non-resistant."
-Robert Linssen

"You create the struggle in your life; you create the collisions. You can dissolve struggle through non-resistance."
- Dan Millman, Author of 'Inner Athlete'

Loser Talk
Here is a list of tasks and words used by losers;
I try to diet
I try to win
I try to score
I try to lift up the pen
I try to focus
I try to get up early
I try to be positive

The word 'try' is associated negatively with things we don't really want to do.

Playing or trying?
Regardless of whether you play golf or not consider this picture. A one to one competition with your best friend. You both have to make the same 10-foot putt and if one gets it in and the other doesn't, the loser has to do a silly dance for 30 seconds! Now lets play the same game against a serious competitor and if you make the putt you win around a month's salary, if you miss you have to give them your month's salary. The tension is a bit different isn't it! You are trying harder! There is tension whereas before you were relaxed! Other than pretend if you miss the putt you have to do a silly dance I have found the following approach useful when considering options and actions.

Give yourself a choice
When considering ANY action give yourself a choice. "OK Phil you can get up early and get to work on your dream or you can sleep all day if you like and you will never achieve your dream". Then I decide what I WANT to do, not what I SHOULD do or have to do. Just like I do everyday before I have my cold shower are training! Here are a few situations with choices;

Do it or don't do it

Eat an apple and get a healthy and energetic body and mind or eat those crisps and put on weight and get a tired and unhealthy mind and body.

Go out and train the hardest you have ever trained and become a champion or take it easy today and achieve nothing.

Pick up the phone and make the difficult call or avoid making the call and avoid being a success and let the competition win.

OK. You get the idea. Give yourself the option. To do or not to do that is the option! Visualise the impact of both. When you consider the future consequences of 'doing' or 'not doing' it's usually enough to encourage you to take action. You can't kid yourself.

"There is 'do' and 'do not'. There is no such thing as 'try.'"
- Yoda, The Empire Strikes Back

Carrot or Stick

There is a story about a donkey. The owner found he could encourage and motivate the donkey to go forward either by enticing it with a carrot or by threatening it with a stick. Humans can be motivated by "carrots or sticks" in a metaphorical sense. Not many humans would go forward for an actual carrot. But if the 'carrot' was a gold medal or a cash prize that's different! If the 'stick' to go forward was a fine of several of our hard earned pounds that could be motivating for most people!

Internal Carrot and Stick

What I have found is that we have to be motivated internally and not externally. We like to do what we want to do. We don't like to do or be told to do what other people want us to do. Which is why Alfie Kohen says that "performance pay doesn't work" and he has researched by the truckload to prove it and Jim Collins says "when you get the right people you don't have to motivate them with ra ra sessions". Couldn't have said it better myself!

The external 'carrot or stick' does not work.
The internal 'carrot and stick' does work.

External Carrots and Sticks don't work

Alfie Kohn comments "Have your ever noticed that the people who love what they do, do a terrific job?" Yes! Great point! Alfie Kohn is the Author of the ground breaking books 'Punished by Rewards' and 'No Contest'. He states, "Numerous studies have shown that when people are asked what is most important to them about work, the top answers are factors such as interesting work to do, or good people to do it with, or a chance to have some say about what one does. What matters about the idea of carrot-and-stick control is how it feels to the people to whom it's done, not what new versions - or rationalisations -- consultants are able to come up with to justify the concept. It's particularly interesting to ask folks who have worked at organisations that don't use rewards at all, those that pay people a decent salary and then help them create interesting tasks, a sense of community, and an opportunity to participate in making important decisions. These people, in my experience, rarely choose to return to a place in which employees receive patronising pats on the head or other goodies for pleasing the boss. They want to be paid, not "incentivised"encouraged, not praised; offered respect, not reinforcements." He uses the teaching profession as a good example. He found the same finding with kids. Reward systems and contests do not make for great performing schools or kids.

No praise

Praise is like a verbal 'carrot'. You get a 'praise carrot' if you do this, you don't get a 'praise carrot' if you do that. It's an external motivator. Kids and adults need to be internally self-motivated. And not motivated by verbal or physical 'carrots' or 'sticks'. When people do things out of curiosity, passion and enjoyment, the best results are achieved.

No praising; just discussing

If an abused child paints a picture a trained psychologist will NOT praise the painting or the child. They will discuss the painting with the child. They will talk about the colour or the choice of picture. Attachment to praise creates needy poorly performing kids.

Happy Worker

Three things make for a happy worker according to Alfie Kohn;

1. Interesting/enjoyable job
2. Good Team/Colleagues
3. Opinion and ideas heard; make a difference (Listening & acting company)

Happy

Although this book is about 'Winning Mentality' and not 'life balance' I have discovered that a lot of the BEST business people and sport people are those who are "happy" (or "very happy") and have a balanced life e.g. enjoy what they do, have high self esteem, have a long term partner (sometimes with kids), take 3-5 holidays a year, have a hobby, keep fit and eat healthy.

Successful people get two benefits from having the Magic 5; being happy with their life means that they have more energy and less stress physically and mentally and secondly they can focus almost ALL of their energy and motivation on their big goal/dream.

Whereas those that are unhappy or aren't positive in the Magic 4 areas don't have as much focus and motivation towards their goal. And they are more likely to have stressful or negative thoughts which will affect energy, motivation and physical and mental health. Athletes who are happy with all aspects of their life rarely have injuries. Sports people who are under significant mental stress, worried about their future or angry about their past, get injured.

Winners who have Maslow's Magic 4 needs can
focus their energy on their dream.

"When I'm happy I run better."- Paula Radcliffe,
World Marathon Champion

Being happy is great for performance

Those that are happy with their job are more committed and perform better according to a study by the Corporate Leadership Council. They found that those committed to their job and therefore happy with their work performed 20% better than others. They were also 87% less likely to leave that job.

People who love what they do, do it brilliantly.
Find a job you love and then find a way to make money!

Fun and Friends

When International England footballer Paul Gascoigne was living in Italy and playing football for an Italian Football Club he paid money for his best friend Jimmy to go and hang out with him. Paul wanted more than football and money, he wanted fun, friendship and happiness!

Friends are forever but they change over the years.
You meet who you need to meet on your journey.
Choose your friends carefully. You are only as successful as the people you hang around. Avoid spending time with "the wrong crowd".

"No matter how great an entrepreneur you are, unless you have the right people around you to challenge you and help you along the way, it's still not going to work." –Chris Gorman, Great Entrepreneur

Surround yourself with great people and funny people.
The person that has the most fun wins. Work hard, play hard.

If you're not having a good time, change your attitude.
The party and the people will improve.

Choose your attitude. With a good attitude you can have a good time on a rainy day at a bad party. With a bad attitude you won't have a good time on a sunny day at a good party. (Been there done that!)

Take your life and your goals seriously. But have some serious fun

Happily Married

Napoleon Hill interviewed 500 wealthy men before writing his book on how to be successful called 'Think and Grow Rich'. It states in the book "It seemed quite significant to the author when he made the discovery that practically every leader with whom he had the privilege of analysing was a man whose achievement were largely inspired by a woman". In many cases a modest wife who the public were unaware of.

Recent research in the UK revealed;
Seventy five percent of millionaires have a partner.
Most of them have been married for over 10 years.

Happiness leads to greatness

World Marathon Record holder Paula Radcliffe has her husband as her coach and she states that on race day his main priority is to "make sure I'm happy. If I'm happy I'll run well". Paula is the fastest marathon runner in the UK bar none. The men cannot keep up with her!

If you are happy you will do a great job even if it's not the job you are happy about! After England Football Team's win to take them through to the quarterfinals in 1996 productivity in English factories went up by 250%!

Happiness leads to greatness!

Unhappiness leads to not greatness

If you are happy and positive you will perform better. British Long Jumper Jonathan Edwards won a gold medal at the 2000 Olympics in Sydney and admitted that he had "things going on at home at the time" and even when he watched his jump 4 years later he described his gold medal-winning jump as "not great"!

Unhappiness leads to "not great" ness!

Hosts Happy with Advantage

The country that hosts the Olympics always does better than at any other games. America, Australia and Greece can testify to that. When France hosted the World Cup in 1998 they won it. When Portugal hosted Euro 2004 they got to the final. When Australia hosted the Rugby World Cup they got into the final and almost won it. Why do home countries do so well? I believe hosts do better than non-hosts because the players or athletes are 'boosted' by 4 factors;

1. They are likely to be happier being close to family and friends.
2. They are very proud, passionate and motivated to compete and win in front of lots of their fans/family (carrot)
3. It is more painful to lose and let family and fans down (stick)
4. They receive and feel the positive thoughts and energy from thousands of their fans.

Home fans provide an advantage

The team on the field can feel the positive energy of fans in the stadium. Thinking some positive thoughts about someone sends them some positive energy. If lots of people are thinking or visualising positive about a person or team that person or team will feel lots of positive energy. Just ask any rock star!

Our thoughts are full of energy.

Motivational Carrot

We are motivated to do something either to avoid pain (physical or emotional) or to achieve pleasure. The former can motivate us more than the later. I like to describe these as a 'Motivational Stick' and a 'Motivational Carrot'. When you set yourself goals for the day, week or year it can be productive to your focus if you have a 'Motivational Carrot' like a reward to motivate you (e.g. dinner! cinema! sex! clothes! holiday!). These are rewards as you work towards your big goals. One way to motivate yourself daily is to view your 'mental movie' of your goal or to look at your 'dream advertising' to inspire you. A 'carrot' I sometimes give myself if 'taking lunch' after I have finished a task. I've often ended up having lunch at 4pm but I worked very productively and achieved great work and focus from giving myself the challenge.

Happy holiday

I have noticed for some time that it is periods before I go on holiday that I am most efficient and effective. I remember a time when I wasn't actually on holiday but my Mum was and travelled to Australia to see me. I had negotiated two days off on the understanding that "there's nothing urgent left on your desk". During the first three days that I was in the office I also met my Mum for lunch every day and did some tourist sight seeing or lunch. I remember on one of the days I ended up having a 3-hour lunch break but I returned to work relaxed and without any guilt because I had my priorities in my life and work in order and would not claim for the un-worked hours. It was not until I went away that my family priority went up. You don't miss something until it is gone.

People are more effective under deadlines that don't over stretch (stress) them. People are more effective before they go on holiday. Take regular holidays and long weekends and you will become more effective. Time flies when you're focused.

Controlled employees watch the clock

"Clock watchers" are impassionate, unmotivated and ineffective people. They often arrive 'just in time' or a few minutes late and leave exactly on time and not a second more! They are resisting and rebelling against the 'external stick' of management which tells them what hours to do. People don't like to be told what to do. If 'management' isn't looking they will waste time at work or leave early! They are not internally motivated to do a great job or work the agreed hours.

"Clock watchers" are the worst workers.
Controlled employees watch the clock.

Employees in control forget the clock

Employees will resist and rebel against the 'external stick' of management, which tells them what to do. The more in control people are the better the results are. When employees are involved in the decision making over what they will do and when the will do it they perform better. Lack of control leads to resistance or stress.

People don't want to be controlled, people want to have the controls. Winners are control freaks. Winners control the input to get control over the output. The more in control they are the better the results are.

Choose your hours

Microsoft and St Luke's are two leading companies and they don't ask employees to work 9 to 5. They ask them to do a job and do whatever hours they want. Work early, leave early, work late or arrive late, they don't care as long as you do a great job. You then become internally motivated to do a good job and the responsibility and trust you are given to choose your hours means you focus on the job not on the time. If you finish early, you leave early. If you need to work late, you work late. If you don't care, you won't last long.

St Luke's does not use a 'stick' to get you to work 9 to 5.
As a result the employees are internally motivated.
Controlled employees work against the clock.
Employees in control work round the clock.

Hungry for success?

One time management tip I remember hearing was to set a small reward for yourself for completing any activity you choose, but especially those tasks you dislike or have been putting off. I have followed this advice often and set a goal and reward. I sometimes set the reward as lunch and have often ended up working until 5pm and missed lunch altogether! Hungry? Yes. Focused? Yes. I believe that people who succeed are hungry for success; metaphorically and physically. They don't take a one-hour lunch break. An hour every day is five hours a week that could be used to make money or work towards goals. They arrive early, leave late and take a short lunch. However I do believe that a working lunch is actually an ineffective way to do two things. Work or lunch. Don't work lunch. A short lunch is more effective than eating lunch at your desk. The same goes for dinner. Research shows that eating dinner while watching TV is not as healthy as not.

Every morning do the hardest thing first.
Everything else after that is easy.

Motivational stick

We are often motivated to do something to avoid pain (physical or emotional). We can be motivated because we want to or have to. The latter can motivate us more than the former. A smoker may be ill and unable to smoke and have to give up. They all do it because they have to but might not necessarily want to!

Necessity

For example a parent with a newborn baby may only get 1 hours sleep and still go to work the next day. A farmer may stay up all night if a cow is about to calf. A smoker may be ill and unable to smoke and have to give up. They all do it because they have to but might not necessarily want to!

Chosen Necessity

We can also be motivated because we have chosen to make a commitment to something and do not want to let people down or be embarrassed. For example a woman may choose to run her first ever marathon for charity and have to train in pouring rain and snow in order to prepare for their run. An entrepreneur may have to work 7 days a week for months in order to deliver a contract they have won.

We can also be motivated to do something because of an experience we have had in life. For example a man may change his unhealthy lifestyle after having a heart attack. A woman may take a self-defence class after being followed home one night. We can also be motivated through choice like exercising 3 times a week or leaving a company after a fall out to set up a business. We may also be motivated in a non-positive way like to get back at someone or prove someone wrong.

Mental Stick

One mental 'stick' to motivate you is to view a mental movie of where you will be/what will happen if you do not change. For example with an unhealthy body or habit you may die early therefore picture in your mind the funeral and the people you will leave behind. That is likely to motivate you to stop. Another method is to picture someone that may think you can't do it or want you to fail. Picturing competition can motivate you.

We are often motivated to do something to avoid pain (physical or emotional). We can be motivated because we want to or have to. The latter can motivate us more than the former.

Another motivational 'stick' is to stretch yourself to a commitment beyond your comfort zone, which you are not yet, capable/able to deliver. Make a promise. Then you have to deliver it! Necessity is the mother of invention and motivation.

What picture might motivate you? What question might motivate you? What thoughts would motivate you? What experience would motivate you?

Enough pain; enough motivation!

We have all had times in our lives when we have had "enough" or said, "enough is enough" and taken some action which we had put off previously. When there is enough pain there is enough motivation to take action. When the pain of remaining the same is greater than the pain of change then change will come. We change when we want to change.

It often takes a lot for us humans of habit to change our ways.

A lot of motivation or a lot of pain.

It's easy to change our ways when we want to, it takes a lot of pain before we change our ways when we don't want to.

'When the pain of remaining the same is greater than the pain of change, then change will come.'

Painful image; powerful motivation!

A friend of mine visited me in Australia. After returning he saw a picture of himself in Australia (weighing 16st). He looked at his Company ID pass taken 6 years ago when he weighed 12st and he decided 'enough was enough' he was going to lose weight! After four months he lost 4 stone in weight! Painful picture; powerful motivation!

Smoking is a pain in the ear!

An ex-smoker I met in Australia told me that one of the things he thinks would motivate smokers to give up smoking was hearing the question "Do you love your family? If you do, you'll give up". Painful question! Powerful motivation!

Near Death experience

I met an author called Greg Barnes in Australia and I discovered the reason he was motivated to write his book 'The Genie Within' was after his third near death experience. He had a fear that he might die before being able to talk to his 4-year-old son Callum about "life, the lessons learnt and the secrets to success and happiness". So he wrote a book of great advice for his son! Painful thought; powerful motivation! What thoughts would motivate you?

If you want to appreciate something, imagine it is lost.

Sweet Revenge

The great coach Sir Alex Ferguson was embarrassed and angry after being given the boot from the club he supported as a boy (Rangers Football Club) when he was a player! The boot motivated him when he got into coaching and took the managers job at Aberdeen Football Club. He got his revenge by beating RFC on many occasions. Alex took AFC through their 'glory days' to win the European Cup Winners Cup. His painful experience was powerful motivation!

Socially Happy (Magic 3)

Our Magic 3 need is for "belonging, love, affiliation and acceptance, intimacy with someone and connection with others". Dr Andrew Weil in his book '8 Weeks to Optimum Health' agrees. In his book he states, "Human beings are highly social, communal animals. We are meant to live in families, tribes, and communities and when we lack those connections we suffer. I do know for sure the connectedness is necessary to well being. You can eat as much salmon and broccoli as you can, take antioxidants for the rest of your life, breathe terrifically and walk all over the earth, but if you are disconnected, you will not achieve optimum health."

One patient had a back problem unsolved after visiting a long list of practitioners over the years. He had injured his back playing tennis 10 years before and had been bothered with it ever since! No previous treatment, advice or doctor had helped him (he was becoming a bit of a boomerang patient always going back to a doctor). Dr Weil, suggested that his back pain and fatigue was due to the fact he was 'disconnected' and he believed some 'social medicine' was in order. He gave him "a number of suggestions for changing his life". These included seeing a therapist to discuss his lonely lifestyle, finding a hobby, getting a puppy to love and care for and doing some volunteer work (Helping himself by helping others. Givers gain).

Don't change a winning game

Open Winner Paul Lawrie played on the European Tour and won the Open in 1999. He went to play on the US Tour while his family continued to live in Aberdeen, Scotland. He got injured. He returned home and now only plays on the European Tour and is able to spend lots of time with his family again. He returned to fitness again! He hasn't gone back to the US Tour and he hasn't gone back to being injured.

You need to spend time with your partner and family to be happy.
(Magic 3)
If you keep happy you will keep fit.
You need to be fit to be a winner!
Keep the Magic 5; keep fit.
Return to doing and thinking what you did when you were winning and you will return to winning.

Home fans support away team!
There are few occasions when home fans want the home team to get beat. Such a thing occurred when Rangers FC fans wanted their manager Alex McLeish to get sacked after a series of embarrassing defeats. In their next first home match during the losing run many of the home 'supporters' wanted their team to get beat so they could have additional 'evidence' to voice their opinion to RFC directors "McLeish must go" style.

John Robertson was the manager of Caledonian Thistle Football Club at the time who were playing against Rangers in the game. He said, "It was a strange feeling. You could feel the home fans wanted us to beat them". The fans felt another defeat would get Alex McLeish sacked which is what John 'felt' most of them wanted. Rangers won the match. It turned the team round and they began a winning run of matches! Which saved the manager from further negative abuse from fickle fans who wanted him sacked. Alex went on to win the Scottish Premier League Manager of the Month award!

A team on the pitch can feel the energy of fans in the stand.
Our thoughts are full of energy.

Our body is full of energy
A lot of our heat and energy leaves our body through our hands. When we place our hands near someone they can feel our energy. Test it! We can send energy from our hands to someone. It can increase their energy and if they are unwell it can help their body heal. When you rub your hands together you generate more energy into your hands from your body. To help yourself or others heal, rub hands, rub your hands and then point the energy towards the area. To feel your own energy rub your hands together. Hold hands apart. Point fingers at other palm and aim from the top to bottom of palm and feel the energy.

Our hands are full of energy.
Our hands are healing.

Make a Wish
A young girl was dying from leukaemia and the Make a Wish charity got in touch with her to find out what she would really like to do with her wish. She did not choose Disney Land or anything like that as expected. She wanted to go to a talk by the speaker Mark Victor Hansen. He was introduced to the girl before the session began and he too was surprised that she had chosen to come and hear him speak over anything else. As he got to the end of his presentation he started to talk about energy and how we all have healing energy in our hands and 5% of people have a healing energy so powerful they could make a living from it.

By rubbing our hands together we charge up our hands and we can direct our energy towards someone by pointing at, towards them or hovering near them. There were a few hundred people in the audience and he asked them to raise their hand if they wanted to help a young girl in the audience who had leukaemia. All hands went up. He asked the little girl onto the stage and then got the audience to rub their hands and point towards the young girl. A few months later Mark received a note from the girl to say that she no longer had leukaemia, was completely healthy and has amazed and baffled her doctors!

"We all have healing energy in our hands."
– *Mark Victor Hansen, co-author, Chicken Soup for the Soul*

Chicken Soup for the Soul is a great book filled with 101 amazing stories. It's so inspiring and motivating that every human from 3 to 103 years old must read. Read one story every night. It will be the best 3 months of your life!

Mark Victor Hansen, co wrote and compiled Chicken Soup for the Soul with Jack Canfield. Great team work. The book and the 'Chicken soup for the Soul' series have sold over 85 million copies! They had both written several other books before but 'Soup' made them famous. Fifty percent of something is better than one hundred percent of nothing. One idea can completely revolutionise your life.

Magic Mechanic
A good friend of mine Duncan had been having trouble with his neck for years. Through a friend he found out about a man who had this ability to help heal people with his hands (the man is in the magic 5% of people which Mark Victor Hansen mentioned with strong healing power). Duncan told me (and assured me) that he was definitely not normally someone who would either believe or try this approach! However he was in some pain with his neck and his movement had been restricted for years.

Desperate times call for desperate measures!

Duncan visited the man's house and arrived before he got home from his work as a mechanic. They were invited into the house and when the man arrived he went to wash the grease from his hands before working on Duncan. He asked what the problem was and Duncan explained. The man felt his neck with his hands and then moved along his shoulder. The man seemed to find a spot where he said "ah there it is" and held his hands in the area for a short period. Duncan felt a warm heat in the area. The man removed his hands and his neck was back to normal. As Duncan thanked and talked to the man, Duncan also revealed a problem with his knee. The hand went through the same process and found a spot on his shin that he worked on and then cured Duncan's second problem. The man refuses to take payment for helping and believes that if he did so he might lose his gift. The mechanics' brother does not have the same gift but his Dad does. Duncan told me that he would not have believed it if someone had just told him about it.

Seeing is believing.
If you don't believe anything you read in this book test it!
Or come and hear me speak and see it!
Hugging is healing

Hugging

Intimacy, connection and the need for human contact is a NATURAL human desire since birth. We all need hugging. It's a physical need (Magic 1) and a emotional need (Magic 3). Babies get hugs just for being alive, not as a reward for doing anything good or bad. Children give and receive hugs with affection 10-20 times a day and are SO much happier than us adults! Most adult's get 0 hugs a day! Where have all our hugs gone??!

"Hugging can lift depression, enabling the body's immunization system to become tuned up. Hugging breathes fresh life into tired bodies and makes you feel younger and more vibrant."- Dr Harold Falk

Dr Bresler at the UCLA pain clinic gives hug prescriptions - "get your hug in the morning, a hug at lunchtime, at dinner, one before bed and you'll feel better."

"The haemoglobin in the blood increases significantly when you are touched and hugged." Helen Colton - The Joy of Touching

" Being that it's the haemoglobin that carries the vital supplies of oxygen to the brain, heart and through the body, hugging begins to look very important". - Andrew Mathews

"Hugging is healthy. It helps the body's immune system, it keeps you healthier, it cures depression, it reduces stress, it induces sleep, it's invigorating, it's rejuvenating, it has no unpleasant side effects and hugging is nothing less than a miracle drug. Hugging is all natural."
Mark Victor Hansen and Jack Canfield, 'Chicken soup for the Soul'

Hugging is free! Hugging is good for you and good for me!

Hugging is loving.
Hugging is healing.

Why wait? Before it's too late.

Mental and Physical
There is a strong link between the mind and body. Physical symptoms are often related to the emotional feelings. Here are a few examples;

What a person said	What they got
"My head is spinning with so many things to do."	Headache
"I'm really heart broken."	Heart problems
"I'm under a lot of pressure."	High Blood Pressure
"I'm a bit tense about the whole situation."	Muscle Tension
"This job is a real pain in the neck."	Neck Pain
"I've got a rigid and set way of doing things."	Stiff Arthritis
"It made my stomach turn."	Stomach problem

"Your body may express the tension from holding on to repressed emotions through physical symptoms and disease."
- Dr John Gray, psychologist and author 'What you feel you can heal'

Positive Players?
A fascinating study was done at a Scottish University on one of the top Professional Football Teams in Scotland a few years ago. The study examined the diet, training and mental approach of the players. As part of the study a few of the players were asked to keep a detailed dairy. The unhealthy diet of the players was criticised in the study. However, the amazing discovery of the study was the finding that when a player was unhappy, unmotivated, worried or had problems at home (in other words had thoughts on his mind) they got injured soon after it was first recorded in the diary! Whereas players that were positive, happy and motivated during the period of the study did not get injured! The study concluded by suggesting that players were monitored in some way mentally and if appropriate a player is taken out of training and games to be given a suitable period of physiological coaching. Players are then reintroduced to training and games with a great state of mind after a few hours or few days (or weeks) where appropriate.

Thereby avoiding an injury and potentially spending weeks or months out of action. A final copy of the study was given to the club concerned and completely ignored! The 'teacher' had arrived too early for the sceptical club who didn't believe the lesson!

Positive players can play. Negative players can get injured.
Negative emotions cause injuries.
Mental problems cause physical problems.
"If at first the idea is not absurd, then there is no hope for it."
- Albert Einstein

Unhealthy mind, unhealthy body
It was not until years later, when I discovered a book by Louise Hay, that I was able to gain a better understanding of the mind body connection and the findings of the football study. Louise Hay is a metaphysical teacher and her books titled 'Heal your body' and 'You can heal your life' explain that our mind is very closely linked with our body.

"I believe we create every so called "illness" in our body. The body, like everything else in our life, is a mirror of our inner thoughts and beliefs. Every cell within your body responds to every single thought you think and every single word you speak."
-Louise L. Hay, author of 'Heal your body' and 'You can heal your life'.

Healing the body with the mind
Louise Hay was able to put the 'Healthy mind, healthy body' theory to the test herself when she was diagnosed with cancer. Every physical problem has a corresponding mental problem. The physical problem area and the corresponding mental 'problem' area are shown below;

Physical Problem;	Mental 'problem'
Eyes;	dislike what you see, worry about past, present or future
Ears;	not wanting to hear, stubborn, anger
Throat;	swallowed anger, stifled expression
Neck;	stubbornness, inflexibility
Shoulder;	carrying a burden
Arms/hands;	not able to handle/ hold current challenges
Back;	lack support, love or money
Legs;	fear of future
Upper legs;	holding onto past
Lower legs;	fear future
Knee;	stubborn ego and pride, fear, inflexible, won't give in
Foot;	fear of future, fear of security, change
Injuries;	angry with yourself, feeling guilty

Overweight;	fear, need for protection, insecure.
Cancer;	deep hurt, long standing resentment from past
Depression;	anger you feel you do not have a right to have
Fatigue:	lack of love for what you do, resistance, boredom

(For a full list see the book 'Heal your body' or 'You can heal your life' by Louise L. Hay)

After finding out she had cancer Louse realised that she had deep anger and resentment about her past experience when she was abused as a child. She started by releasing her anger and aggression positively (a pillow is good for that!). Louise then put herself in the shoes of her parents and began to understand the past they may have had. Louise then started to actively repeat positive mantras about her past every day and she stunned doctors who re-examined her to discover the cancer had gone. By identifying her negative thoughts she chose to repeat positive opposite thoughts.

Heal your body with your mind.
Heal your mental problem and it will heal your physical problem.
"A sour mind creates a sour body." - Andrew Matthews
"There are no such thing as accidents; just physical, mental or emotional discord." – Dan Millman

Sport Injury
You can make up your our mind on the 'healthy mind, healthy body' metaphysical theory. If you want to keep doing and thinking what you've always done and thought, and getting what you've always got. Like the top Scottish Football Club that ignored the University study. If you don't believe it, test it!

Carrying responsibility
One very important player in any rugby team is the kicker. Jonny Wilkinson is one of the best kickers in the World and as part of the England Rugby team was a crucial player in the 2003 World Cup tournament. Their coach Clive Woodward and Jonny himself were aware of that especially going into the final against Australia. Therefore kicking phenomenon Jonny was under a lot of pressure. In the final he picked up an injury which put him out of the game for eight months.

Injured again
Jonny has played little rugby due to injury since the World Cup in 2003. The pressure and stress *before* the World Cup final wouldn't have helped his physical body *during* the final (where he picked up the injury). And the negative emotions since the World Cup wouldn't have

helped his physical body. Below are some of his comments since the World Cup.

"More negative than anything else has been my encounters with the paparazzi. I don't know how these people can look themselves in the mirror. I know everyone has to put bread on the table for their families but there are choices to be made in life. No one is forced to do that job. Experiencing the flip side of fame since the World Cup has made quite an impact on my life. It has created negative energy out of what should have been an entirely positive experience."

"I felt uptight, angry, depressed."

"I'm asked: have you ever known pressure like we had in Australia a year ago? My answer is yes; the injury afterwards has been harder. The World Cup surely is a more positive pressure; you're winning, you're looking ahead to the next game, the semi- final, the final. With the injury, you're working so hard just to come back and play and the pressure is on when you do because everyone's looking at you, scrutinising you, thinking: "Is he the same player?" Give me the World Cup any day."

"Not playing does odd things to your head.
It is funny how quickly you can begin to doubt yourself."

Having a lot on your mind

The area of Jonny's most recent physical injury is his shoulder. The mental 'problem' according to Metaphysics is "Carrying a burden". Note for simplicity of understanding I use the word 'mental problem' in a different context to the medical one. Have a 'mental problem' in the context of this book is having a mental issue or challenge (like fear of failure) which is causing stress and needs to be resolved. There are no 'problems' only 'challenges'. I smile at challenges.

If you have a mental 'problem' on your mind,
you'll soon have a physical 'problem' with your body.
Responsibility can put a lot of weight on your shoulders.
Having 'a lot on your mind' is not a lot of good for your body.

Fearless footballer

One international England Football player played a key part in Euro 2004 in Portugal. England teenage sensation Wayne Rooney was England's star of the tournament from the moment he won a penalty against France in the opening group match and followed up with doubles in the 3-0 win over Switzerland and the 4-2 victory over Croatia. It was at this time the whole of the UK and Europe 'discovered' Wayne and he was called "the next Pele" by England's coach Sven-Goran Eriksson and then by Pele himself! Can you imagine the pressure the 18-year-old boy was under for the next game?

Fearful footballer

Wayne may or may not have read all the press reports about him but I'm sure he knew the team, the media and the nation were almost relying on Wayne to score and win the next game for them and get them to the semi-final. In England's quarterfinal game against Portugal, Wayne went off injured in the first-half and was out for several weeks afterwards. Sven said at the time, "His injury is pretty serious, it appears to be the same as David Beckham suffered in 2002 and could see him out for several weeks. I would say if Rooney was on the pitch we should have won the game but I don't want to use that as an excuse." He added that the four-goal hero was taken off 5 minutes after a soft "innocent-looking tackle" by a Portuguese defender. The physical problem? Broken metatarsal bone in his right foot. The mental problem according to Metaphysics? Fear of the future.

'A chain breaks at its weakest link and so do we.'
'Healthy body, healthy mind'
is widely believed and followed by winners.
'Healthy mind, healthy body'
will become widely believed and followed by winners.

Recurring Injury

The term 'recurring injury' is so regularly used in sport that it is almost a cliché. Time and again players go from month to month or year to year and pick up the same injury. Some players can go for years without major injury. It is the same with amateur sports people and with no sports people. The same physical problems come back because the mental problem has come back (or in most cases never went away). Recently a Highland Football League goalkeeper broke his leg in his first season for club Cove Rangers. It was the second time he has had the same injury. He also broke his leg less than two years ago in his first game for Inverurie Locos Football Club. If you think the same thoughts you get the same results.

The reason injuries reoccur is because the physical problem (the effect) was 'fixed' but the mental problem (the cause) was not fixed.

A man with the same mental thoughts will get the
same physical problems.

If you keep thinking the same way mentally,
you keep hurting the same way physically.

Getting cancer twice

It is not uncommon for people to get cancer twice. Norman Cousins cured himself of cancer through humour and then got cancer again. The former England player and manger Sir Bobby Robson said, "I've had cancer twice. When I was at PSV (Eindhoven) in 1991 I discovered I had cancer of the bowel which was caught early, thank God. It was operated on and removed and I've led a full and active and healthy life since." Bobby also had cancer a few years before that. The physical problem (effect) was 'fixed' but the mental problem (cause) was not fixed. A person with cancer has a mental problem of "deep hurt or long-standing resentment from past" (according to Metaphysics).

If you don't cure the mental problem you
won't cure the physical problem.

"You don't cure the body with the body,
you cure the body with the mind."
- Plato

Positively proactive

'Healthy mind, healthy body' is good advice for those in sport and business. If we resolve problems with our mind we can resolve problems with our body. When occasions occur when there are 'things on our mind' it's useful to think these issues through rather than 'bottle them up'. Where it's felt appropriate professional help is a valuable investment rather than a costly long-term injury or health problem.

Be proactive rather than reactive!

"I think all players should have a mind coach like you."
-Kevin Davidson, Sports Agent, K.W.A.D.

"Be proactive." – Stephen Covey
'The 7 habits of Highly Effective People'

Fear is a question. Your answer is often silly scary.

Positive actions

Where "dis-ease" does occur it's worth using the mind to resolve them, otherwise they keep reoccurring. To cure myself I think positively about the area of "unhealthyness" and then target my body with healing mantras e.g. "I am fully fit" or "Every day it gets better and better". Within a day of starting mantra's I notice a difference. However I am only solving the physical problem. I need to consider the mental problem, which is at the root of the physical problem. I look at the great advice within Louise Hay's book 'You can heal your life' to be able to do this.

If we don't change mentally we get the same problems physically. For example if a car tyre is deflated, we may solve the problem by pumping it up with air but the problem will reoccur if the root of the problem is an unresolved puncture. The cause is the puncture the effect was the flat tyre. We need to treat the cause not the effect.

We can pump our bodies with cures or we can
cure our problems at the root.
We need to treat the cause not the effect.

We can cure a punctured tyre by repairing it but the problem will
reoccur if we haven't solved the cause of the
puncture and cured the road of nails!
If you stay the same, you get the same results.

To change your results, change yourself.

Love or Fear

When we feel stressed it's due to fear. Hate and anger are fear. Every emotion falls into the category of love or fear. Our body responds to fear by setting off the 'fight, flight or freeze' response. This uses up a lot of energy if we are fearful or stressed all the time. However, a little bit of stress can help stretch our performance.

Cause

Negative feelings have a cause. To solve your negative feelings you have to deal with the cause. Your feelings are giving you a message. If you don't deal with the cause of your feelings your body will then give you a message through dis-ease. If you still don't deal with your feelings your body will keep the dis-ease or keep repeating the dis-ease.

If you don't make changes, you don't see changes.

Negative minds; negative body

In a scientific experiment where blood samples were taken from people experiencing intense fear or anger and injected into guinea pigs they have killed them in less than two minutes. Imagine what these emotions are doing to the human body.

"The toxins that fear, anger, frustration and stress produce not only kill
guinea pigs but kills us off in a similar manner. It is impossible to be
fearful, anxious, irritated and healthy at the same time. Your body's
health is a reflection of your mental health."
-Andrew Mathews, author, 'Being Happy'

Your mind is the weakest link
Imagine the body like a chain. If you put the chain under stress it will break at its weakest link. The body is similar. It's the 'weakness' in the mind not the body that makes the body 'break'.

Stressed Mind, Stressed Body.
Stress affects our body.
'A chain breaks at its weakest link and so do we.'

How NOT to cure our negative emotions
It's clear from the evidence above that we need to cure our fear, anger, frustration and stress to be healthy. An unhealthy mind will eventually mean an unhealthy body. The mistake most people make (like all of the sport stories above) if they're ignoring their emotion, surpassing their emotion or controlling their emotion.

"Most people try to "control" their feelings and the way they do this is usually to move through the four R's and resist, resent, reject and repress. Repressing your feelings does not eliminate them. Feelings never die. It takes a tremendous amount of emotional and physical energy to hold down your emotions." –Dr John Gray

"What we resist persists. The more we resist, the more stuck we become. And what we refuse to feel never goes away. When we summon the courage to release that resistance, we find joy."
– Raphael Cushnir, author, 'Unconditional Bliss: Finding happiness in the face of hardship'

Controlling your emotions is a painful mistake
A survey of cancer patients found the majority admitted that they hadn't expressed strong emotions such as crying or anger for years and they "controlled" their emotions.

Time is a great healer (not)
The theory 'Time is a great healer' is completely untrue in many cases. If NES like anger or hurt are not expressed at the time a person will be affected in some way sometime. Anger is like a time bomb. If it is not defused properly (through external expression) at the time, it will tick away inside, eventually causing physical or mental damage to the 'anger owner'. Of course it's difficult to spot "anger owner's" because they have bottled up their anger and it's ticking away inside them.

Instant forgiveness doesn't work.
Time doesn't heal.

Anger (one letter short of danger)

Anger that is not expressed can lead to physical dis-ease like cancer or mental dis-ease like depression. Dr John Gray makes the point well in one of his great books;

"If you are not able to fully express your anger (in a non-destructive way, of course) you may be walking around afraid, hopeless or depressed most of the time. Depression is not intense sadness –it is suppressed anger that has been directed at yourself. Depressed people usually feel tired and lifeless because they are using up their vital energy to keep that anger and rage from coming out. If you are very depressed, you need to work on healing your old relationships, first by expressing your anger for others, then your anger at yourself, working your way back through all the other emotional levels until you arrive at the love and forgiveness." (Dr John Gray, author 'What you feel you can heal')

The 'Santa Claus effect' <u>does not</u> work if you are depressed. Depression can decrease motivation. Someone depressed may stop finding the desire to work, to socialise, to have fun, to exercise or to eat healthily.

'The angriest people I know are the ones with the most hurt inside.'
-Dr John Gray, psychologist and author 'What you feel you can heal'

If anger, initially directed at other people, is turned and directed at yourself the long term effect is not pretty; depression.

Going onwards and upwards when you are down

I have been mentally 'down' once in the last 12 months for the first time in over 5 years and only the second time in my life. The first time was over a woman and the second time was (I thought) over work. I thought the cause was work, work, work. It was - partly. I took one week off in 12 months and worked 7 days a week for the latter 6 months working over 12 hours a day, before 'it' hit me. In those 6 months I was only stopping working for meals, exercise, sleep and a few hours time out a week. That was before I gained REAL knowledge about the error of my ways. Yes, lack of 'long term' relaxation time out like two weeks off was not wise. It was unhealthy and unproductive long term. But unknown to me the real cause was anger. (Anger that turned out to be with others, but mainly anger directed at myself). When I realised I was 'down' (writing my book didn't motivate me anymore and I no longer slept for just 6 hours I slept for almost 12 hours!) I was so angry with myself for making a mistake that cost me my motivation.

I am a highly motivated person normally so I was devastated and disappointed to lose my motivation and find myself no longer excited about my dream (writing a book) and find myself sleeping for 8 or 10 or

12 hours. That to me was wasting 4-6 hours of my life and 4-6 hours I could have been writing this book and chasing my dream. I made a mistake and it cost me. I was angry at making the mistake.

When you look back you have to laugh. Firstly because the cause of depression is being angry at yourself. And secondly when I discovered I was depressed the first thing I did was get angry at myself for becoming depressed! That was before I gained REAL knowledge (wisdom) and realised my anger was the first thing I had to deal with. In hindsight, it happening to me was a good thing. I learnt about the negative affects of anger. And I realised how important medium and long-term time out can actually be for mental and physical health. It was destiny.

It was good for me and I hope it was good for you (that I should learn that lesson). I never thought it would happen to me. You live and learn. I won't make that mistake again. I hope you never make the same mistake. Learn from your mistakes and learn from the mistakes of others.

I don't class 'time out' for a few minutes every hour as wasted time. And now I don't class long term and medium term 'time out' as wasted time either.

Sometimes I get angry with myself for wasting time. It used to be practically all the time now it's just sometimes and I'm a lot healthier mentally!

How to cure our negative emotions

We have to deal with our negative emotions by expressing them. We must express our negative emotional stress in order to maintain mental and physical healthiness.

Emotions must be expressed externally not suppressed internally.

You use up a lot of your energy if you hold down your emotions.

Ways to express NES

Feelings must be expressed. You can express your feeling through talking, writing, visualising or physically expressing (as long as the method is wise and doesn't get you into trouble with the law!).

Talking

It's good to talk. One of the reasons talking is so good is because it gets us to actually say aloud what is on our mind and we hear our thoughts. After we hear our thoughts and problems out loud we either feel better or we solve the problem ourselves. We just needed someone else to listen.

Having a chat with someone is a great opportunity for you to solve your problems out loud while someone else listens to you do it! But if they weren't there and you didn't talk through your problem out loud you probably wouldn't solve it for ages!

Speak your mind. It's good for you.
When we talk through our thoughts we can
process our problems better.
A wise loving friend is the greatest coach to chat to and listen to you.

Imaginary friend
Using your imagination you can pretend to discuss your challenges with friends, family, therapists or of course your heroes and passengers in your car.

Willing Well
To direct your future positively and positively solve challenges, imagine a wishing well beside your imaginary car and as you sit in the driving seat looking at the cinema screen of your future see your positive instructions dropping into your 'willing' well. For example 'I will wake up with the solution', "I am happy, the disagreement is sorted out" or "I am happy and relaxed now about everything". Speaking in this way actually builds a picture in your mind so it can see your goal and help you achieve it. I like to describe the mind as a bit like a waiter and you get what you order. So be careful what you wish for!

Whisper Worry
When you are in bed at night your subconscious is more active therefore you are more creative therefore if you think any non-positive thought or worry your subconscious will creatively work on it and increase the size and intensity in the worry. Most worrying is done at night hence why many people have sleepless nights! If you need a solution write the challenge on your Idea pad or Journal. Use this 'Whisper Worry' tool to reduce your worry and increase your sleep! Alternatively whisper your worries to a teddy or toy or doll and 'sleep on it'. You will sleep soundly and in the morning the worry will have gone.

Any opportunity to talk about the problems on your mind is productive
even if it's only your teddy that is listening!

Writing
Writing your feelings down is a good way to become aware of your feelings and then resolve them. One of the reasons writing is so good is because it slows down your thought process to the speed at which you can write which can be useful. (Joanne Rowling says that she is glad she didn't have a pen and paper when the idea for Harry Potter

first "popped into my head" because it would have slowed her thoughts down.)

Whether our feelings relate to thoughts about yourself or others writing them down is useful. A great way to do this is to write a letter. One of the best methods of writing a letter of your feelings is suggested in Dr John Gray's books 'What you feel you can heal' and 'Men are from Mars, Women are from Venus'. Dr John Gray's great 'Love letter' goes through the five main emotional levels;

1. Anger, blame and resentment
2. Hurt, sadness and disappointment
3. Fear and insecurity
4. Guilt, regret and "I'm sorry"
5. Love, forgiveness, understanding and intention

Forgiveness cures many of life's problems.
Forgiveness cures many physical problems, even cancer.
Forgiveness cures anger. Forgiveness cures cancer.

John suggests you write a love letter by going through each of the 5 levels and expressing your thoughts to paper. Very powerful. Very useful. Here is a simple way to remember his advice when you don't have this book or John's book to refer to and you want to write a quick 'feelings letter' to yourself or someone else;

1. Anger
2. Sadness
3. Fear
4. Sorry
5. Love

You may find it easy to remember as; A.S. F.S. Love

Writing the letter is the most important step. But don't share it. If the 'feelings' in the letter are about an issue with someone else, don't give the other person the letter and within days you will be amazed when the person seems to change their behaviour and you have a great friendship, relationship, or partnership, whatever is relevant.

If you intuitively feel it would be advantageous to share the letter and the issue involves your partner you may wish to follow John's advice and give them the letter. But let them read it alone. When you are very angry with someone it's better to talk on the phone than face to face. If you look at the person you are angry with while you are angry it will create an angry memory ('anchor') in your mind which means that when you next see them you automatically feel angry even if the issue was resolved. If you're angry it's better to talk to a partner back to back than face to face. You only want to look at each other when you are happy and full of love and not angry (and full of fear).

Forgiving is a present you give to yourself.
Forgiving is good for your health.

"It is always our choice whether we get on with our life and live in the now, or whether we chain ourselves to grudges and upsets of the past. People think that if they won't forgive their mother for being nasty, it is their mother's problem. It is not their mothers' problem; it is theirs! When we withhold forgiveness, WE suffer."
- Andrew Matthews, author 'Being Happy'

Special occasions
I am not suggesting that you need to write a letter every time you get angry, annoyed or a little emotional or negative! We might end up writing letters every single day! This technique is for when you really need it. Special Occasions. When you are on a roll, a winning streak and life is great you won't need this letter. Sometimes, after a big major win, you will. (After you have celebrated of course). The letter will keep you on the winning track and winning habit. The letter will also be useful in times when you really are not that impressed with yourself. Times like that are good to stop and assess what you need to do and do it.

Sometimes anger has to be let out before the humour is brought out. For big issues or major mistakes. Start expressing, forgiving, laughing and then forgetting. You will intuitively know when you need to do a 'AS FS Love' letter. Sometimes you need to do a 'AS FS Love' letter to "get over it". Other times like when you are angry over a 'silly subject' or minor mistake, you will intuitively know you just need to change your state of mind and switch to the comedy channel to change your mood. Laugh about it and forget about it! That will get you over it.

Once you have dealt with the subject, change the subject.
Change your thoughts and change your mood.

Quick letter to yourself
With practise you can write a short letter or even go through AS FS Love letter to yourself quickly in your head. "Phil I'm angry you didn't take more action today, I'm disappointed with you and it makes me sad, I'm scared you won't achieve your goal, sorry I am always on your case I just want you to win and succeed, I love you and forgive you and accept you are not perfect". Use the letter a few times just for fun and get comfortable with it. Use it or lose it.

AS FS Love in your head
I was angry with someone I care about so I went through 'AS FS Love' in my mind for the first time to see if it would work. It did! I was able to go from angry into saying "sorry" to the person I was upset with within

minutes. Any man saying "sorry" to a member of their family is a big thing! For me it was huge. It was a big moment for me. I think this technique will save me a lot of energy and a lot of time from going in "moods". And it will maintain my relationships with the people I am closest to and love unconditionally. It will also help me in dealing with other people that upset me or let me down. Instead of "losing it" with anger and causing a heated argument like I normally do this technique will channel it and release it. Don't get me wrong I had plenty of reason to be angry but after I went through "AS FS Love" I decided that I would forgive them for not being perfect. Instead of pointing out their faults or mistakes and solve their problems like I normally do (Mars men solve problems, Venus women talk about them) I would let them be themselves and if they decide to change in the future great. If not I'll accept it. It wasn't a big thing. Unconditional love means loving without "conditions" e.g. you must do this or I won't love you. Good family and friends who love each other unconditionally will remain loving whatever people do or say.

Often the hardest word in the world to say is "sorry"!
The biggest mistake most people make is instant forgiveness.
Skipping to forgiveness will not work.
You must release your anger, express your sadness, identify your fear, say you're sorry and state your love.

A hug at the end is good too! And good for you.

Why? AS FS Love
If you or someone you know is angry go through the five questions below with them. If it's a couple who are angry I suggest they sit back to back and go through the questions or do it over the phone or by letter. If driving I think stopping the car is a wise and wonderful idea. Face the front!

Do the following questions in your head it's amazing the first time you use it! Which will create problems not solve problems. Unless you let them see all 5 points. Doing the 5-point face-to-face is dangerous and damaging to any relationship. Even if it's the bank manager!

Emotions Questions EQ
1. Why are you angry?
2. Why are you sad?
3. Why are you fearful/scared?
4. Why are you sorry?
5. Do you love them?

The more aware you are of emotions the higher your EQ.
The 'emotions questions' will release your angry and increase your energy and love! Happy days!

When "love in the air" you can feel it. Love is energy.
When there is "tension in the air" you can feel it. Anger is energy.

I highly recommend using the AS FS Love questions on yourself and others. You'll be happier, healthier and you won't "throw your toys around".

'AS FS Love' is great for getting along with people.
'Put yourself in their shoes' is great for understanding people.
'Who? Why? What? Where? When? How? Are my good friends.'

Visualising

One great way to resolve emotion is to visualise it being resolved on the big cinema screen. You can imagine talking to anyone (Even yourself) and make your feelings (and anger) known and imagine they respond in a way in which you would like. Visualise positively and then be surprised by the effect it has on the other person, as well as on yourself. One of the best times to go through this exercise is preferably while they are sleeping or relaxed and more open minded. Either way the most important thing is that your emotions and feelings are expressed and not repressed. Trust yourself with what to say and what they say. You can go through it with yours eyes open or closed. The main thing is doing it. If you want to go through the same five levels of emotion you can (Anger, Sadness, Fear, Sorry, Love).

Healing Questions

The following technique uses the visual and touch senses. The healing questions are amazingly powerful for curing or reducing most types of physical or emotional pain, pressure, unease or negativity.

For example, it can be used for headaches, stomach pain, slight physical injuries, illness or emotional upset. Where physical injury is serious (like a broken arm) the questions can be used to assist healing and pain relief. (The questions won't cure a broken arm!)

Instructions;

Close your eyes. Scan your body for a sensation, pressure, pain, tightness or block. Ask yourself or have someone ask you the following;

Healing Questions;

1. Where is it?	(Area of body with pain)
2. What shape is it?	(Round, oval, square, flat, shaped like a....)
3. What size is it?	(Exact measurement)
4. How deep is it?	(On the surface of skin, skin deep, couple of inches deep)
5. What colour is it?	(Use imagination, if in doubt guess)
6. What texture is it?	(E.g. hard, hot, soft, wet, smooth)

7. On a scale 0 to 10, what number is it now? (If 10 is the worst)

Repeat the 'healing questions' 1-7 again. Continue for a few minutes. Results are amazing!

Goodbye pain

While working in Australia one of my colleagues was in severe pain. The man had recently had "the snip" and had been told by his doctor it was common to have "some pain afterwards but there is nothing I can do". I asked how much pain he was in on a scale of 1 to 10 and he said "10"! He could not even move from his office chair! I asked if he wanted to try something and he said, "I'll try anything if it works". We went through the questions about 4 or 5 times and the pain reduced to "0" and disappeared! He was both amazed and happy and immediately said, "Give me a copy of the questions"!

Goodbye sickness; hello tears

I was able to help someone else who told me she was so upset about something that she felt sick in her stomach. I went through the questions a few times and the area moved up from her stomach and out her mouth. The sick feeling disappeared, she felt much better and I could tell she released a few tears afterwards (I was on the phone with her at the time).

Expressing emotion physically

Another natural way to express emotion is physically. Women love to talk! However sometimes men and women express themselves physically and feel much better after doing so. Here are a few highly recommended methods for expressing your emotions.

Punch Bag

Spend some time with a punch bag! If it is not possible (anything is possible!) use some pillows. This punch bag technique is for releasing anger (stress) and is useful in two situations. When you are angry with yourself (perhaps over a mistake!) or when you are angry at someone else (perhaps over a mistake!).

If you may have been angry with a person for years it is not good for your mind, body or effectiveness. Get hold of a punch bag or get some pillows against a wall and kneel down. Think of the person(s) you are angry with and imagine you are punching them when you punch the bag. It is even more powerful if you do some kicking as well. This is especially effective if the anger is due to someone sexually mistreating you. Take a full 60 seconds with arms and legs and use full force. It is possible to move towards forgiveness of other people and yourself after using this exercise. It is not effective to instantly forgive someone when they have really hurt you. The 'Punch Bag' or 'Letter' must be used first. To release tension punching a bag (pillow) is essential. It is also very effective after a 'challenging' or stressful day.

Scream and Shout

Screaming or shouting is a good way to release emotional and physical tension. We feel better almost instantly after doing it, because it is good for us to release emotion. It can feel instinctive and natural to scream or shout. It's unnatural and physically and psychologically unhealthy to bottle up emotions. It can lead to physical and psychological difficulties. Every now and them it's good to scream and shout and 'let it all out'. Especially if you are angry or stressed. Do it in the shower. Do it in your car. Do it under a pillow. Do it for fun.

Scream and shout, let it all out. Don't bottle it all up.

Say it and feel better

I talked to a senior fishing association official who told me that their meetings with fishermen are quite heated and the meetings "might not achieve anything but they get to raise their voices and that makes them feel better". I think he's right.

Scream and shout, shake it all about

One of my clients told me that during a tense bowling match there was a winning shot which made him initially cheer and clench his fist. The ball kept rolling and was not in fact a winning shot but he said the tension he felt was released and he felt more relaxed thereafter and it helped his performance. Football managers often jump, shout or chew gum to relieve their tension. Celtic Manager Martin O'Neill jumps higher than most managers!

People that get involved in "Road rage incidents" have expressed their anger in an aggressive and dangerous way. It's possible to scream in the car effectively and non-aggressively! The punch bag, sofa, pillow or mattress can be used when you get back home!

Don't suppress it, express it.

Angry exercise

I have used the punch bag exercise on many occasions and feel that it is a great way to release anger as well as relieving stress and keeping me sane.

Lots of energy and lots of orgasms

A woman I met told me that as a child a relative had once inappropriately touched her on her vagina. The relative told her not to tell anyone and threatened her and she never did. Although she could achieve orgasm by herself, since she started having sexual relationships with men she was never able to achieve an orgasm with a man and had always faked it. She attended a workshop where all past anger towards people was directed at a pillow (using her hands) and then a mattress (using her feet). She was encouraged to unleash all her physical and verbal energy in the exercise.

The first part of the exercise involved sitting upright and punching. And for the second part she was lying on the floor and kicking. She was told by a woman who had a similar experience in childhood that she had found that after doing the kicking exercise on a previous workshop she soon became able to experience an orgasm with her partner. So the woman went through the two exercises and even did the kicking exercise twice “just to be sure”. After she finished the second time she turned to the other attendees and said “multiple orgasms here we come”. Within a few days she had achieved an orgasm with her partner. She also found that she had an incredible amount of energy afterwards and one reason for this is that the energy she had previously used to suppress past hurt was no longer required.

Crying

Crying is a way of expressing emotion. The male myth “real men don’t cry” is not only completely wrong but also completely unhealthy. People always feel better after crying. Crying is physically and psychologically healthy. As long as it’s not for hours and days on end. Not crying is physically and psychologically unhealthy. Repressing tears and emotions uses up more energy than expressing tears and emotions. Repression causes physical and psychological problems. Repression can lead to depression.

Research has shown that certain types of people are more likely to get cancer and heart disease. The mind affects the body.

Sir Edmond Hillary is quoted as saying that he firmly believes his Everest climbing partner “died of a broken heart” a few years ago after being forgotten about by his country and no longer treated like a national hero for being the first to climb Everest.

Singing is healing

Dr. Richard C. Moss runs workshops that are based on healing through singing and his book ‘The Black Butterfly’ is about how he healed himself and others of serious illness through singing. The following quote is taken from his amazing book. "It was the second day of the conference. For several hours Laura had been singing a childhood hymn, repeating it over and over. Suddenly the quality of her singing changed. She felt as though she were no longer singing. She was the song. She found herself lifted to her feet, her arms raised toward the sky, her head arched upward. She said her hands did not end at her fingertips, but continued into the air and sky. The air and sky were alive, and she and they were the same. Her feet seemed to disappear into the earth. Earth, feet, body, arms, sky, song, singer – all were one living being. Laura did not consider what was happening, it just took her. She was the experience. The next day her terminal liver cancer was gone."

Do not underestimate the therapeutic and healing power of singing. Uplifting songs are uplifting.

For thousands of years humans have gathered in groups to talk, laugh, sing and dance. It keeps us healthy and happy. Keep it going to keep yourself going. Don't change a winning game!

Talking, laughing, singing and dancing are powerful for relaxing, expressing and healing ourselves.

Keep talking, laughing, singing, dancing and hugging!
They are great for your health!
Your health is your wealth.

We may look different and wear different clothes but our basic human needs are not different from 2000 years ago.

Awareness, Understanding and Dealing

Be aware of your emotions. Emotions are audible in our words, visible in our actions and sensed in our feelings. When we feel, hear or see negative emotional stress of some kind understand it and then express it. What is making you angry, fearful, stressed or hurt? Discover it and destroy it! Get it out. Express it using one of the methods above. Then identify the route cause of your negative emotional stress (either using your intuition, using this book or using the book 'You can heal your life'). When you identify it, change how you look at it.

If we think what we've always thought, we get what we've always got! If we ignore mental messages in our emotions, our body might send us a physical message. If we ignore the physical message and keep the same mentality we will get the same problem returning to our body physically.

Be aware of your emotions. Understand your emotions. And deal with the cause of any negative mental emotion. If you don't deal with negative mental emotion you will soon have to deal with a negative physical problem.
Healthy mind, healthy body.

Emotional Messages

Our mind may send us a message about our current emotions through our dreams.

Reading dreams
The 'hidden' message in dreams is not always easy or obvious to read. Using a dream book or online dictionary can help you identify the message in your dream and become aware of your emotions.

Falling
Falling dreams are an indication of insecurities, instabilities, and anxieties. You are feeling overwhelmed and out of control in some situation in your waking life. This dream may be reflecting a loss of control, which may parallel a waking situation in your life.

Flying
Dreams in which you have the ability to fly and control your flight is representative of your own personal situation and sense of power. If you are flying with ease and enjoying the sights below, then it suggests that you are on top of a situation. If you feel fear when you are flying or you feel that you are flying too high, then it suggests that you are afraid of challenges and of success.

Obstacles
When you come across barriers or obstacles in your dream these represent a particular obstacle or person who is standing in your way in your waking life. You need to identify who or what is hindering you and resolve it to go onwards and upwards.

"I smile at obstacles." –Tiger Woods

Nightmares
Nightmares are said to be an indication of a fear that needs to be confronted.The nightmare is a message from our mind to acknowledge it and deal with it.

Recurring Dreams
Dreams that reoccur could be positive ('good dream') or negative ('nightmares'). Nightmares may recur because the message from the dream has been ignored and the route problem remains unresolved. Once the message/problem has been resolved the recurring dream may cease. Good dreams also have a message (positive message) and the dreams reoccur because the positive situation is sit apparent.

Recurring nightmares are like recurring injuries. The route mental problem has not been solved so the 'message' will return in the form of a nightmare dream or nightmare injury.

Listen to our emotions
If we ignore the message in our emotions and message in our dreams our mind will send us a message through our body. If it does don't miss the message! Or it will keeping coming back.

Emotion Examination
One way to assess how positive we are emotionally is to look at the Magic 5 areas of our life and note our thoughts and feelings about each. When you do the next exercise feel free to look back at the full description used by Maslow given above. Write down your feelings, positive or negative for all 5.
GO!
Goal love (job, interests etc)

Self Love

People love

Mind love

Body love

You need the Magic 5. The Magic 5 fulfil our needs in four ways; mentally, emotionally, socially and physically. When you have love and positivity in all Magic 5 areas you can focus your energy and motivation on achieving your dream.

It is not just current emotions that affect our physical health and energy. Feelings and emotions about the past that have been suppressed and not expressed. are damaging to our physical health and energy. Any thought you have will either be about the Past, Present or Future. Write down any thoughts which come to mind. Trust yourself. Explore these three chapters of your life and write down your thoughts for each.

GO!

Past;

Present;

Future;

Journal of your journey
Having personal 'awareness' e.g. being aware of your characteristics and emotions is common in great people and uncommon in average people. Keeping a diary develops and maintains awareness (many successful people do). Also it's useful to record a short log of your emotions in your diary. This process is a good way to 'monitor' your positivity (like the top Scottish football players did). Keeping it short and simple is fine (KISS). When negative emotions are strong it would be very wise to write an 'A.S.F.S. Love' Letter as suggested by Dr John Gray.

Life is a journey. Take notes.

Where you feel it necessary (perhaps due to particularly challenging or emotional period of your life) organising a session with a qualified psychologist is a wise investment. Use your intuition to do what is right for you (as well as pick advisors that are right for you). Talking to a wise friend is good but there is only so much a friend can know and say (and a friend can often tell you what you want to hear and not what you need to hear).

A powerful letter writing technique that is beneficial to adopt (weekly, monthly or at least annually) along with your daily journal notes is explained later in the book.

Assess and monitor your positivity.
You do not have to be positive all the time, just most of the time.
Choose positive thoughts. Choose a positive attitude.

"The only thing you ever have any control over is your current thought."
– Louise L. Hay

Be a FORD
After dealing with your NES get back to being a winner and FORD ASAP!

FORD's; Funny, optimistic, really enthusiastic, driven, smilers!

Be Positive not non-positive
A study at Yale University shows positive thinkers live on average seven and a half years longer than their more negative peers. Are you positive? Good for you.

You must be joking
Winners have a good sense of humour. A lot of healthy people do. People who are positive and funny are rarely ill, people who are negative and rarely laugh are often ill. Laughter stimulates the body's natural painkillers and 'feel good' enhancers, called endorphins, helping relieve stress.

Laughter is the best medicine. Laugh a lot!
A good sense of humour is essential.

One minute of solid laughter provides up to 45 minutes of subsequent relaxation. An adult laughs on average 15 times a day whereas a child laughs an average of 400 times a day!

I've had a funny day
Norman Cousins believed his serious approach to life was one of the reasons he gave himself cancer; given only months to live he used humour to cure his cancer. His book 'Anatomy of an Illness' book where he cured himself of terminal cancer by; checking into a hotel, reading comics and watching comedy videos. After six months of laughter 'medicine' he amazed doctors by being completely cured. The film about the doctor 'Patch Adams' depicts the real life doctor of the same name who set up a humour hospital in the USA who mainly administers large doses of fun and humour to every patient that goes there. The research and doctor have inspired 'clown doctors' in the UK and Australia. Laughter truly is the best medicine.

Take your life seriously but have some serious fun!

"Do not take life too seriously. You will never get out of it alive."
-Elbert Hubbard

Four great healers are; love, laughter and
positive thinking and visualising.

A study of cancer patients who visualised their body fighting and winning a war lived longer than patients who didn't visualise. One doctor has told a story of a kid that imagined a star wars fight and recovered from a terminal illness completely.

The MAGIC 5 is good for you

Being happy, in love and motivated is good for your health. Scientific Research has shown that being in love boosts the immune system and helps people fight potentially fatal diseases. Love conquers all.

People with pals and pets live longer. Fact. Pets are proven to improve the health of owners. 'Patient Pets' tour hospitals visiting patients to improve their health. Retirement homes with animals allowed have healthier residents.

Goal love; goals are good for your health. You live longer. A goal gives you a job to do whether it is running a family, a business, a marathon or a garden allotment. If you love you're job you do a better job and you are happier.
Self Love; self-esteem is the start of self-belief. People with high self-esteem have less negative thoughts about themselves and look after themselves.
People love; all we need is love. All we need is someone to love and someone to love us. Even if it is a pet! People with pets live longer. Fact.
Mind love; we all need to live with love and not live with fear. Negative emotional stress must be released and not repressed or we use up lots of energy and create mental or physical problems. A little stress keeps us going. Over stress makes us unhealthy. We need a healthy mind to have a healthy body.
Body love; we need to have a healthy body to have a healthy mind. We need to give our mind and body the 'food' they need. As detailed extensively in the previous chapter. Any way that reduces stress will increase energy. Which is why I have included 9 ways to increase energy and many 'stress reduction' suggestions in the chapter!

Being one of the PEGS is great for you

Being Positive, energetic, goal driven and Intuitive is good for greatness. PEGS go from good to great eventually. Positive belief gets positive results and positive people live longer! Energy is needed to take action and achieve what you believe. The relaxation 'time out' helps your performance and keeps you healthy mentally and physically. Setting goals is the first essential step to achieve goals and it gets results and helps you live longer! Making intuitive decisions with your sixth sense will make you pick the right path for your performance and for your long-term destiny.

How to improve yourself mentally and emotionally
Get the Magic 5 and live it – you will be happy and motivated.

Learn the 7 Winning Mentality tools and use them – you will be one of the PEGS

You will be fit and not injured.
You will be healthy, happy and motivated.
You will be stronger mentally and physically.

A study of 2,000 people who did regular meditation (relaxation) found that compared to a control group of non mediators they were hospitalised 87% less for heart disease and 55% less for cancer, than the group of non mediators. Healthy mind, healthy body.

If you're happy you're healthy. A study in Aberdeen found that blue collar council workers were off sick 11 days a year, whereas teachers were off sick 5 days a year. Why? I think this is for two reasons. Teachers love their jobs and 'workers' hate their jobs. Love always wins.

If you're happy you're healthy. And vice versa! Teachers are healthy because they are happy. Secondly, teachers are more committed so they have a better performance and better attendance!

There are some exceptions
Not every physical problem is caused by a mental 'problem'. If I wear new shoes and they cause the heel of my feet to bleed I don't have a mental problem or fear of the future, I just have a shoe problem. The physical problem was caused by a 'school boy error'! If I had put tape on my heel for the first two weeks to 'break in' the shoes they would not have caused a problem. If a pregnant woman puts on weight during pregnancy it is natural, it is not because they have a mental 'problem' or feel insecure.

Making a 'school boy error' can cause problems'!

What you 'know' can make a big difference. But it is not what you know that makes that difference; it's what you know and what you do with what you know that makes the difference.

Very Fast Summary

Winners are healthy and happy
Healthy mind, healthy body.
Have supporters around
Negative thoughts can hurt you
Positive thoughts can heal you
Love or Fear
Aiming anger at yourself will hurt
Laughter is the best medicine
Love provides a lot of energy.
People who are happy are full of energy.
Be positive mentally, physically, emotionally & socially
Negative thoughts injury your body
You need a healthy mind to have a healthy body
You need Maslow's Magic 5
Behind every great man is a great woman. And vice versa.
Happy athletes make winning athletes
Being happy is great for performance

You need the Magic 5. The Magic 5 fulfils our needs in four ways; mentally, emotionally, socially and physically. When you have love and positivity in all Magic 5 areas you can focus your energy and motivation on achieving your dream.

We have to deal with our negative emotions by expressing them. We must express our negative emotional stress in order to maintain mental and physical healthiness. Negative thoughts will hurt your success, dream, business and results. Negative thoughts will hurt your body.

If we ignore the message of our emotions, our mind may send us a message through our body or through our dreams.

What are you thinking? Positive or Negative? Love or Fear?
The five 'emotions questions' will release your angry and increase your energy! (+Improve your relationships and increase your love!)

The seven 'healing questions' will release tension, headaches and pains. Improving health and energy!

We may look different and wear different clothes but our basic human needs are not different from 2000 years ago. Keep talking, laughing, singing, dancing and hugging! They are powerful for relaxing, expressing, healing and health. Your health is your wealth.

"Man's greatest motivating force is his desire to please woman!"
– Napoleon Hill, 'Think and Grow Rich'

Love is a positive energy.
Fear and hate use up our energy.
Every minute of anger is a waste of 60 seconds of happiness.

Heal your body with your mind.
Heal your physical problems by healing your mental problems.

"Fear is behind failure, sickness and poor human relations."
-Dr Joseph Murphy

"There are no such thing as accidents; just physical, mental or emotional discord." – Dan Millman

Positive or Negative. You choose.
Love or Fear. It's your choice.

If you think what you've always thought,
you'll get what you've always got.

Change your mind, change your body.

'The mind is a great healer.' – Hippocrates

A famous mantra in times of difficulty is "this too shall pass".

Smiling on the outside is great, smiling on the inside is greater.
Unless you wake up with a smile on your face or go to bed with a smile on your face –you have a problem to solve.

"If you think you understand everything that is going on, you are hopelessly confused." – Walter Mondale

It's not what is on the outside that causes injury, accidents and stress.
It's what is going on inside someone's mind that counts.

"There are only two emotions love and fear." - Michael Leunig

Fearful thoughts create a fearful person.
Loving thoughts create a loving person.

Positive thoughts create a positive person.
Confident thoughts create a confident person.

Negative thoughts create a negative person.
Angry thoughts create an angry person.

Healthy mind, healthy body.

CHAPTER 8
ACTION – WINNING MENTALITY

Very Fast Summary

Use the 7 tools everyday. Winners have winning habits. Be one of the Winners and PEGS

Including in this chapter;
Use your car everyday
Follow your intuition. Decide decisively.
Talk to yourself daily.
Keep dreaming and believing
The 7 tools
Guard your positive mind
Be a warrior
Be a winner
Create winning habits
Be hungry

Winners do the winners work.

Winning Mentality- Positive Mindpower Tools

I hope you begin to apply the tools now! The car is a way to represent and remember the information visually. The car is what you will use to drive towards your goals with the 7 Positive Mindpower Tools.

Tool	Winning Mentality	Visual Tool
Goals	Dream, Goals, Motto	Destination Sign
Hero Talk	Sixth sense (Intuition)	Passengers
Mental Movie	Positive Visualisation	Movie Screen
Directing	Positive Verbalisation	Director Chair
Mantra	Positive Belief	Car Mirror
Switch	Positive State	Switch
Brain Break (5 B's)	Energy (Relaxation)	STOP sign

Read any book on memory recall and you'll read the same advice; use a visual, rhyming or K.I.S.S type representation for information where possible. Enter my visual "car" and the keep it simple "P.E.G.S." idea. However, you might come up with a better idea! Use what you feel comfortable with and what works best for you and your memory.

You are in control of your destiny. Where you go is up to you.

Winning Mentality
If you need to have a dream to achieve a dream.
If you've got goals you'll get goals. And vice versa.
Follow your intuition. Decide decisively.
Talk to yourself daily.
Believe in your dream.
Picture it in your mind. And get a picture of it.
Verbally WILL it. "I WILL..."
Stop negative thoughts with red light and 'cut' and put in bin
Mantra, mantra, mantra. "I am....."
Switch into a positive state. If you act like a great, you will become great.
Time out
Relax. Relax. Relax.
Every hour take a minute or two out.
Every week take some hours or days out.
Every year take a few weeks out (min is; 1 x 2 week break, not 2 x 1 week)

Winning sport man > winning business man
Many great sports people have gone on to great things in business. David Murray, Jackie Stewart and the late Mark McCormack to name but three. Their competitive and positive 'winning mentality' mind set them up well for going into business with the same attitude. Did these

successful sports people have any "qualifications" to suggest they had any right to feel they could succeed at running their own business? No. Did they let that stop them? No! They are winners. Obstacles are for jumping over, knocking down or running round! Did they succeed? Yes!

"Getting to play at that level takes discipline. You're only going to achieve it through hard work. I'm convinced those characteristics are carried forward into business success." – Denys Shortt, CEO, DCS Europe

Denys Shortt set up DCS at 28 after retiring from international hockey and in the first year his turnover was £5M which shocked his bank manager!

Winning sport man> winning business man> Winning sport man

Clive Woodward is perhaps one of the most famous rugby players that set up and run a successful business and then returned to rugby as England Rugby manager. The rest is World Cup history. Clive puts much of his success as manager down, not to what he learnt playing for England himself, but what he learnt in business. Clive had a fortunate history and created history. Now that is destiny.

"The best experience I've had for this job is having to run my own company. In business every decision is your own and so is your money. You learn very quickly not to waste time as every second of the day is money."
-Clive Woodward, England Rugby Manager, World Cup Winners 2003

Does he boss the players around? No. The external stick is not used. They internally motivate themselves by discussing and deciding on training and tactics. The communication is so significant that a camera crew which filmed a documentary on a range of team sports were shocked when they saw how much talking England did. Winning communication and motivation. Winning results. Their methods are uncommon which could be one reason why their success is uncommon.

"If you make a wrong decision you change it immediately. If you make a mistake you hold your hand up and admit it. We pride ourselves on concentrating on why we've been winning. We're always trying to move the benchmarks up. If you get the odd set back it's not time to over react."
-Clive Woodward, England Rugby Manager, World Cup Winners 2003

Clive has been inspired by two great sources. Dr Paddi Lund is a dentist in Australia and he was close to breaking point in the 1980's and decided to cut 95% of the clients at his surgery while retaining the 5% whose company he enjoyed and asked them to refer their friends to him. Being happy is everyone's goal. His other inspiration like most people is the SAS.

"You wouldn't call the SAS chokers. They are the best prepared and have the right investment. As a result, they're the best in the world. Our businesses are the best in the world. And I don't think we're chokers in sport."
-Clive Woodward, England Rugby Manager, World Cup Winners 2003

Winners have got the Magic
Keep your Magic 5 to fulfil your human needs and focus your energy and motivation on achieving their dream. The Magic 5 are;
Goal love
Self Love
People love
Mind love
Body love

Got
Write a list of the things you have in your life NOW, that are important to you. That way you can focus on your goal but not take your eye off the ball and lose sight of the Magic 4 things that make you happy. E.g. Health, Home, Energy, Happy, Talent, Fun, Partner, Friends and Family.

Decide to pick things that are important to you, make you happy and perhaps remind you of your achievement to get to where you are now. It's important to have a goal. But it's also important to be happy on your journey and when you get to your goal destination. Choose your sacrifices. Be ruthless with your time. But keep your Magic 5. Be healthy and happy and get there in one piece. With your Magic 5 photos or list with you everyday you will be reminded of the things worth keeping when making decisions. Keep hold of you're family and you will keep hold of your happiness.

I recommend getting photos of these important things in your life and displaying them somewhere would be good, just like your Top 7 dreams your advertising. You need the Magic 5 to cover you physical (1), mental (2&5), social (3) and emotional (4) needs.

Having a picture of the Magic in your life will enhance your health, happiness and motivation! It will make you smile. (as well as enhance your memory of the Magic 5). It's easy to forget the ball when your so busy focusing and working day in day out on your dream goal.

I must admit I have written a list of my friends to remind me who they are. It's not that they are not important it's just that I focus on my goals and fill my mind with necessary information. It's easy to miss birthdays and lose touch with people if you do not have a list and use a calendar and diary. It takes seconds to send a text or email and a minute to write a postcard which will ensure you keep your friend, family and partner.

'All you need is love.' - The Beatles

Goal setting has one danger. It's easy to focus on what you haven't got and 'forget' what you have got.

Pick a motivating dream
Pick motivating goals in all areas of your Magic 5

Outside Motivation
One past client would do his "winner work" the night before our coaching session 'just in time'. In order not to be embarrassed he took action just before our meeting. I was metaphorically an external "stick" that motivated him. After our planned sequence of sessions stopped the client stopped doing the "winners work" and stopped using the tools. Profits did not increase.

Inside Motivation
Another client put his "winners work" as a top priority and actioned it urgently. He would often do it right away and have 6 days of experiences of using a technique to share with me. He was self-motivated internally to do the work and use the tools and achieve his dreams and great things. After our planned sessions stopped the client kept doing the "winners work" and using the tools EVERYDAY. He tripled his business turnover. Took on one extra employee. Wrote a best selling book. Moved into a new house. Swam with dolphins and other fun goals. Improved his health. And become well known as a "marketing guru". People who knew him before I worked with them (I didn't) told me they were amazed and impressed with how changed he was, telling me he came across as much more confident, relaxed and humorous (I'll take their word for it). One person was actually unaware I was coaching him and happened to mention the increase in my client's confidence and fearlessness.

Picture yourself achieving your goal regularly. It gives you motivation to take action and focus on what must be done to make it happen.

Picture yourself not achieving your goal occasionally. It gives you the motivation to focus on what must be done, not what might happen.

"I only think of what must be done, not what might happen."
-The Village

Winners live by their own rules.
Which are always tougher than everyone else's!

No one forced Paula Radcliffe to run for 10 miles in pain and create a world record. She forced herself! (No one could get near her!) Winners go solo and get so high.

Morning motivation

Three things can get you up early in the morning; excitement, hunger or necessity. Desire is like an internal hunger. I think this is best demonstrated in the story about the cyclist whose hunger to win earned him the nickname from the media and fans of 'the cannibal'. Unsurprisingly he was a winner on many occasions.

Chris Gorman and Richard Emmanuel left good jobs to set up a shop called DX Communications to sell mobile phones. The 'D' stands for desire and the 'X' stands for expectancy. Expectancy means 'expect to succeed'. Belief! And they did. They became self-made millionaires when they sold a share of the company to BT and multi millionaires when they sold their entire stake.

"It's a good thing that it still really hurts when I don't win. That shows the desire is still there. I'm a winner and not doing everything I can to win tournaments is not an option." - Paul Lawrie, 1999 Open Golf Champion

When you achieve one dream, chase another one.

"It's been a journey. I've fulfilled my material needs. Then I've thought 'What is the point?' And the point is this (The Hunter Foundation). I'm more invigorated. It's made me more determined and ruthless in business. I'm just as determined to make money as I always was. But the motivation is the foundation." - Tom Hunter, Millionaire Entrepreneur, founded The Hunter Foundation with £100M, to fund education related projects in UK and outside.

Tom Hunter's hero and inspiration is Andrew Carnegie.

Necessity is great for productivity

It's amazing how productive we are to finish necessary jobs on the week before we going on holiday for a weekend away. It's amazing how productive we are to finish necessary jobs on a Friday when we are catching a flight for a weekend away. Go on holiday. Improve productivity.

External Stick (rules ruin results with employees)

I found an employee working a weekend once because her boss was back on Monday and she had done few of the things agreed while he was away. She admitted she had approached the work with an "all in good time" laid back attitude and ended up getting little done. Her guilt got her. She went in at the weekend to get things done when she would normally be spending it with her boyfriend or out with friends. It's amazing how much she got done on 'her time' when she was motivated. I had met her on many occasions chatting to friends in a nearby office and arriving at work, 15 minutes late!

St Luke's is like university. No one will tell you what to do and chase you up. If you turn up late or fail to turn up some days it's your choice. No sick notes and excuses are needed. If you fail to do the work you fail. You are out the door.

Most employers are like school. They tell you what to do and when to turn up and they chase you up if you don't keep to time. If you turn up late or fail to turn up some days you will get a verbal and written 'stick' motivating you to do what they say. Sick notes and excuses *are* needed.

Don't give kids 'stick'

I read about a successful person recently and he was not keen on school and was looking for an incentive from his Mum to pass exams. His Mum told him "If you want to fail your exams and waste your life it's your choice". (He took that as a "no"!) It did him no harm and was ultimately good for him. Give kids choice. No stick. Give employees choice. No stick.

Guard your positivity

Let only positive stimulus 'feed' your mind during the day. Especially in the morning but before sleeping is as important to see, hear and read positive things. The last thing you watch, read or hear at night affects your sleeping thoughts, mood, dreams, sleep and waking thoughts.

Listen to inspiring super songs

Copy Phelps and Kouros who use music to motivate them and keep in positive state. Sad music makes you sad.
Listen to the same track before performance everyday and create an association. Change track when you feel like it.

Music ideas;

Theme for rocky, superman, gladiator, star wars, etc
OR great tracks which make you happy
Louis Armstrong -beautiful day, Pavarotti -Nessun Dorma, M people-Search for the hero, u2 -Beautiful day
OR any artist tracks you fancy
Foo Fighters, Prodigy, The White Stripes, Oasis, Blink 182, Jamiroquai, Chemical Brothers, Beastie Boys, Eminem, Dido, David Gray, Travis, Franz, The strokes, The Beatles, Red Hot Chilli Peppers etc

Dream song
Pick a song you have no association with but is a track you would like. Perhaps a new song. Listen to the track several times and while you do so visualise yourself achieving your dream. Any time you need a boost, play the track. A great idea suggested by Michael Cheney.

Read one quote a day
Open this book randomly at one page for one month. Read 1 quote.
Collect good quotes and good stories.
Read a book a week (50 books a year means 500 books in 10 years!)
Put quotes on your walls for a month. Then change.

Watch Positive TV
Even good stuff you don't normally watch.
I don't do skateboarding , in line skating or BMX'ing (yet) but I find watching them and listening to them very inspiring.

Watch Positive Movies
Rocky, Pay It Forward, When we were Kings, Forest Gump, Dead Poet Society (see web for other inspiring movies)

Positive motivation
Nodding your head
Smiling
Talking (shouting loud is good!)
Clapping the hands
Standing tall (chin and head up)
Punching the arms
Pacing the floor

Are all motivating moves to get you moving!
Use them to get you going.

Keep healthy body, healthy mind
Keep healthy mind, healthy body
Exercise
Relaxation
Nutrition
Look after your 9 energies

Release fear and anger and converse energy.
Take a few minutes out every hour,
a few hours out every week and a few weeks out every year.
Achieve greatness with health and happiness.

Grow Knowledge
Knowledge is power. Inspiration and motivation is very powerful.
Fill your mind with useful. Disregard useless. Copy Bruce Lee.
Information you need will find thee. Trust destiny.
The more you know the more you grow.
Learn to speed read

One of the best book you can read is the one called Your Life. You need to write it and live it everyday.

"I wish I knew what I know now when I was younger." – Rod Stewart
Sharpen the Saw. Be a sponge of knowledge.
"He was like a sponge." – Butch Harmon on coaching Tiger

When you meet a challenge or
When you meet adversity
Keep believing
Keep dreaming
Keep smiling
Keep nodding
Keep chin up
Accept every day and every challenge with a smile and a nod. Tell yourself "This is easy. I can handle it. I can do it."
Never doubt
Never give in
Believe and achieve.
People who frown are likely to get ulcers. So keep smiling. Smiling is contagious. If you see someone smiling it's actually difficult not to smile back! If you see someone without a smile give them one of yours.

Plan A to a positive feeling (mood) is; Think Positive > Feel Positive.
Plan B to a positive feeling (mood) is; Act Positive> Feel Positive.

Positive body language creates positive mind language.

"Body language is an unconscious outward reflection of inner feelings so, if you feel positive or affirmative, your head will begin to nod as you speak. Conversely, if you simply start nodding your head intentionally, you will begin to experience positive feelings."
-Allan and Barbara Pease 'The Definitive Book of Body Language'

Keep an open mind
Leaders are open-minded. Leaders are keen travellers. They explore new places and don't go the same place every year. If you are looking to become great in business, travel round the world. That will teach you everything you need in business. Travelling will take you to the top. Several leaders I know have done extensive non-business travel usually a year round the world. John Calcutt is one former round the world traveller who returned from travelling and within one year the company he set up 'Sky Signs' was sold for £1M. He now runs a company that works for airlines like Virgin, which is an industry that has had the most challenging 10 years in industry. Is John

complaining? No. His company Watermark had a value of £1.5M in 1995 and in 1998 was already worth £37M and growing.

What is the best-read magazine by leaders around the world bar none? National Geographic

Keep an open mind on your travels.

Be random and patient

Occasionally read 'useless' stuff. You may be intuitively interested to look at something and find out it gives you a great idea! If it doesn't you may find that in a few years time it comes in very handy. Like I have found.

'Winning Mentality' as taught by Scotland Coach Rainer Bonhof

1. Competitive fighting spirit

Fire in heart, ice in the mind. Be hungry to win, be cool under pressure.

2. Always keep winning mentality

Statistically, a team are most likely to concede a goal immediately after they've just scored because when they go ahead there is a tendency to change mentality from trying to win, to 'defending a lead' and thus becoming more negative! 'Kill teams off' by going for the throat instead of becoming negative and defending a lead. Ahead or behind always keep winning mentality.

3. Belief

Before matches relive winning memories. Watch a videotape of all the goals scored to date and all the victories to ignite team spirit and belief. Or watch them in your mind. Then create your future mental movie; future history. You achieve what you believe.

4. Never say die attitude

Remain calm even when losing, fight till the death. Every minute and every second counts.

Think BIG! Be BIG! Get some fire inside you and go and win.

"I don't like losing." -Jean Claude Killy,
Winner of three gold medals in 1968

"I play to win, whether during practise or a real game. And I will not let anything get in the way of me and my competitive enthusiasm to win!"
-Michael Jordan

"If you don't hate your competitors, you're not very good." –Tom Hunter

Trust Intuition and destiny

Trust your intuition when it comes to plans, preparation and performing. And finding ways to help you win. Stand beside a bookshelf and tell yourself you will find a useful book. Put your hand out and pick up the first book your mind has drawn you to. Then open at a random page and you will be surprised how useful it is. More difficult to do on the Internet but it can be done! Use the technique for films and music. Close your eyes and pick from a list. Use the technique for holidays and day trips. Close your eyes and pick from a local or world map. Use it for sitting a dinners and meetings and buses. Trust your intuition and you get great luck and a great destiny!

This is all 'winners work'.

Warrior

Here is one website that I found by luck when searching for a General Patton quote. I happened to also have a copy of Ross's great Book. He has helped my healthy destiny in many ways. But he is also an inspiration and as wise as he is strong like Geoff Thompson and Arnie. Leaders are great readers in sport and business. They all read books and love quotes. Here is a cracker from Ross below.

"I choose the name warrior for its relevance to life. A warrior is any person engaged in some struggle or conflict. This definition encompasses the entire population. We are all faced with obstacles and struggles, which we must overcome in our pursuit for success and triumph. If you stop to observe the world around, you will quickly realise the struggles and hardships faced by all. Life is no picnic. There will be good days and bad days."
- Ross Enamait, author of 'The underground fitness guide to warrior fitness' and founder of warriorforce.com

"The warrior does not search for the easy way out."
Ross Enamait, author of
'The underground fitness guide to warrior fitness'

The Warriors Creed (Ross Enamait)

I will train with the utmost intensity, dedication and desire.
I will turn obstacles into opportunities to demonstrate my power and strength.
No feat is beyond my reach, I write my own destiny.
The hell with genetics, I will determine my physical prowess and strength.
I am an action taker not an action faker.
I am a leader, not a follower.
There are no magic pills. My strength and power originate from my intensity and devolution.
There are no shortcuts to the top. The warrior's journey is never ending. I will surge forward improving myself each day
I will rise to the top, overcome all obstacles and destroy my enemies
Excuses are weak, warriors are strong. I am a warrior.

Winning Mentality Creed (Phil McNally.com)

I am a winner. I am number 1. I am the greatest.
I chase my dreams and my goals
I am very hungry to win and hate to lose
I bravely take action in spite of my fear. Fortune favours the brave.
I visualise every dream, goal and action positively in my mind
I think and speak only positive thoughts
If I think I can I can. If I believe; I will achieve. Anything is possible.
I imitate, copy and follow my heroes to achieve greatness.
I look after my mind and body and feed it with only positive 'food'
I use every second of my time and energy wisely. Every second counts.
I follow my heart and intuition and make decisions quickly
I smile at all challenges, including failure. Adversity is an advantage.
I never give up. I get up. Success is a numbers game.
I am in control of my destiny. Every thought and action creates my results.
I will do everything to win. Whatever it takes.

Very Fast Summary of Winning Mentality

If you had could do anything what would you do? Go for it!
If you had no fear what would you do? Go for it!
If you won the lottery what would you do? Go for it!
What are you waiting for? Chase your dream. Jump after it.
Shoot for your goal. If you don't shoot, you don't score. 100% guaranteed.
Winners have Guts and Goals.
You must be highly driven (motivated) to win or you won't win.
Great people make great decisions and great mistakes.
Knowledge is power. Imagination and intuition are super power.
If you think you can you can.
Believe and achieve.
Fear is like a hurdle on the path to your dream. Get over it.
You won't reach your destination with your hand on the handbrake.
Everything is a choice. Your thoughts, actions, attitude…future.
Zero action equals zero results.
There is a risk and reward to every action and inaction.
Stop thinking and Jump!
You can build your wings on the way down.
Necessity is the mother of motivation.

Winning is simple but not easy. Do better than the others.

Choose a big goal that motivates you. Create a positive mental movie of you achieving your big goal. Make decisions with your intuition. Listen to the advice from your heroes and yourself in your head. Write down steps and goals. Visualise each action and goal positively in your mind. Direct your future using positive words and thoughts. Repeat your mantra to build up your belief fuel tank. Flick your switch and become a brave hero. Take action. Never give up. Take time out. Regular brain breaks will improve performance. Hourly, weekly and yearly 'time out's. Relax deeply for a few minutes every day. Exercise and feed your mind with positive mental and physical food and you will always think positive and feel energetic. Take several hours off every week and several weeks off every year.

Today will be a great day. Don't delay. Seize the day.

Anything is possible. The sky's the limit.

CHAPTER 8.5
ACTION

Very fast summary

In two words; Do it!

Included in this chapter;

Winning Mentality is not enough to win.
PASS.
Action.
If you take no action; you get nowhere. You don't want to go there!
Sacrifices, risks and hard work.
Preparation and luck make dreams come true.
Made the most of the opportunity.
Conceive, believe, act and achieve your dream. Never give up.
Get up.
You were a winner when you were young.
You can be a winner now.
Smile every time you fall.
Every time you fail, you are one step closer.
Use your capabilities beyond imagination.
Take your chances, give it everything you have got and you'll have no regrets.
You are in control of your thoughts, actions and time.
You can decide your destiny. Achieving your dream is a choice.
A journey of a thousand miles begins with a single step.
Jump.

Dream it and begin it

Winning Mentality is the first and most important "ingredient" of winning. Then is second most important. The skills and strategy you will ONLY acquire if you begin your journey to your goals. You grow as you go. It's amazing what you can do when you commit yourself. Ben ran the sand marathon. Branson ran set up an airline in a few months with no relevant experience from running his record company! Rocky was written because Stallone began his journey and he kept hungry and did not stop. He then found the idea to make him an actor and achieve his dream. Dream it and then begin it!

The "ingredients" of winning

The formula of winning is;
PxAxSxS = Success

P =Positive Belief aka "Winning Mentality"
A =Action
S = Skills
S = Strategy

P is essential
A is essential
S is attainable
S is simple

You can and will acquire skills and you can and will discover strategy but first you have to do something. Take action.

Winning Mentality is not enough to win. You need action!

Winning Strategy

After taking action you learn or 'find' a winning strategy. Usually from taking lots of action and making lots of mistakes! Bill Cullen got no response from his first 736 job applications. When he changed his strategy (changed the home address on his application) he got the first job he applied for. Chris Higgens got beat by Australian Brad McGee in the Commonwealth Games in 2002 who took the gold. He changed his strategy (advice from Chris Boardman) and beat Brad McGee at the Olympics in Athens 2004 and took the gold. The best strategies are normally very simple.

"The secret of business success? Sales up, costs down, cash in."
– Geo Benedetti, Millionaire Entrepreneur

"It might take you a while to work it out but
profit is the most important thing."
- Graham Thom, millionaire founder, Grampian Freight International

"Chris (Boardman) looked at my training and my mental approach and simplified the pursuit for me and it has brought me success."
– Chris Higgens, Gold medal World Champion Cyclist

Winning is simple but not easy.

Winners like business legend John Calcutt of Watermark and cycling legend Chris Boardman's admit to having a simple strategy. Them and other winners like him have simple strategies and stick to it.

"There are two old mottos we have here; never sell anybody what you want to sell them, sell them what they want to buy and never make anything but money". – John Calcutt, CEO, Watermark (and friend of Virgin founder)

Winning Skills
Walking is a skill that takes months to master. It requires practice. Falling over looks like failure but actually cleverly disguised 'practice'. You only become great at anything with lots of practice.

To become supremely skilful you must be a great student and have a great teacher.

To become great requires a great amount of practice. There are few exceptions.

"Champions have to have the skill and the will. But the will must be stronger than the skill. When I was boxing I would set a goal for myself to demonstrate to other people what could be done, and to prove to myself that anything was possible when I set a goal then worked to achieve it. We create our own realities according to our thoughts and beliefs." Muhammad Ali, 'The Soul of a Butterfly – Reflections on Life's Journey'

"It is not our abilities that truly define us - it is the choices we make". "Harry Potter And The Chamber of Secrets" by J K Rowling (1998)

"When we were younger, Kim supported everything I did. The older we got, the more reality started to set in. She's one of those people that's really down to earth, like "Hello! You're living in fantasy land. These things don't happen to people like us." I was always the optimist, like, yo, I'm gonna make this happen." -Eminem, Platinum selling music artist, married to wife Kim

*"Nothing in the world can take the place of persistence.
Talent will not. Genius will not. Education will not.
Persistence and determination alone are omnipotent."
- Calvin Coolidge*

*Omnipotent means invincible!
You are invincible is you are hungry and never give up!*

*"I think a lot of teams can go all the way. It depends on how badly you want it." - Richie Byrne, Professional Football Player,
Aberdeen Football Club*

"Always listen to experts. They'll tell you what can't be done, and why. Then do it." - Robert A. Heinlein

Necessity is a great teacher
You only learn when you have to. I'll admit that my baking and cooking skills were basic when I was living at home. Just before I went to live in London I was like a sponge watching my Mum and wanting to learn. It's amazing how well you can learn and survive when you have to or want to. I had no fear of it. I went for it. Everyone can do it even young kids but only when you have to. It's easy to get Mum to do it!

It's amazing how much you can do when you have to. It's like leaving home and learning to cook, wash and iron for yourself within a week. Your Mum always thought those 3 tasks were impossible to you, but you kept them nicely hidden! Necessity is the mother of learning.

*It's not important if you have the skill to achieve. What's important is if you dare to believe. And if you don't believe, you still dare to begin.
Winning starts with beginning.*

*"I don't think there will be a female Prime Minister in my life time."
– Margaret Thatcher MP, a few years before she did the 'unbelievable'*

*"One only gets to the top rung on the ladder by steadily climbing up one at a time, and suddenly all sorts of powers, all sorts of abilities which you thought never belonged to you- suddenly become within your own possibility and you think, 'Well, I'll have a go, too.'"
– Lady Margaret Thatcher, Europe's first female Prime Minister!*

*"What this power is I cannot say; all I know is
that it exists and it becomes
available only when a person is in that state of mind in which they
know exactly what they want and are determined not to quit."
-Alexander Graham Bell*

Child Prodigy

Have you ever noticed how quick children learn new skills compared to adults. They don't let thinking get in the way. Sometimes what looks like 'no fear' is actually 'no thoughts'.

Child Prodigy's actually put in lots of hours to become great and 'naturally talented'. However a Child Prodigy will learn in a faster time than an adult during the same practice and getting the same coaching because of their mind. They don't start off with the belief 'this is going to be difficult'. They "just do it" and have less fearful thoughts.

Tiger Woods was an overnight success. If playing golf since he was 3 years old and hitting thousands and thousands of golf balls classifies as 'overnight'!

Most success looks like it happened 'overnight' but is actually down to hard work for years out of sight.

Keep going

Barbara Taylor Bradford has written 19 best selling books over 25 years and now at the age of 70 years old she still writes! She earns about £8m a year and is worth £95m. She has talent, she has a passion and she has motivation! Why stop? She has a winning game going. Wise woman. Do what you love, do it well and you will be paid well.

What would you do if you did not know your age?
What age would you be if you did not know?
Age means nothing. You're old if you think you're old.
After 21 forget your age! Women rarely do, they just don't tell you!

Stop thinking; start doing

Major winners Sandy Lyle and Tiger Woods started playing golf when their Dads gave them clubs at three years old. Lyle's Dad cut down normal clubs and gave him a bag so he could play golf with him. Tiger is said is have had the perfect swing at three years old! Why? Because he wasn't thinking he was doing! They both took over 15 years of 'doing' before they won their first major. Well-done Tiger. Well-done Sandy.

The only way a child becomes a winner early in life is by starting early in life.

Jonny and Jordan were no good

Michael Jordan and Jonny Wilkinson were both knocked back from their local teams for not being good enough. Coaches thought they weren't skilled enough! Hard to believe! But it helped them achieve. It was a great internal motivational stick to drive them to greatness. Great experience helped them become great.

"When I got cut from the varsity team as a sophomore in high school, I learned something. I knew I never wanted to feel that bad again. I never wanted to have that taste in my mouth that hole in my stomach. So I set a goal of becoming a starter on the varsity." - Michael Jordan

"In hindsight, I think having what I perceived to be a rough ride was good for me. A lot of players who achieve success early find it hard to maintain their inner drive at senior level. Because I wasn't handed the chances I thought I deserved, I fought all the more to earn them." -Jonny Wilkinson

No skill, no strategy

You don't need skill. Maggie never knew she had it in her. You don't need strategy to begin. You find the winning skill and strategy on your way. But you must have winning mentality and you must begin! Action!

Action

For something to happen action is essential. For nothing to happen inaction is essential. Action is one of the essential "ingredients of winning" along with skill, strategy and winning mentality. Without the 'action' there is no success, no results, no 'birdie', no 'eagle' and no 'par'!

P.A.S.S. to win.

No Action Man

In 2000 I set over 30 goals and a year later I had made progress on one of my top goals because I took action. But I hadn't yet achieved any of the 30 goals yet. I thought to myself "If goal setting is so effective why didn't I achieve any?" The answer popped into my head instantly like a slap on the face. The answer was ACTION! No action, no results. I hadn't taken action towards many of my goals and hadn't used the 7 winning mentality techniques. The lesson for me was; mental and physical actions are essential to achieve goals. The four lessons were; take mental action (use winning mentality techniques), take physical action and focus on your dream goal before working towards the others. I also realised that some goals take years not months or weeks or seconds to achieve! Don't be over optimistic!

To achieve any dream requires mental and physical effort.
No action, no dream.
You don't need to take action towards all your goals,
just the ones you want.

"It is a hard event and requires a lot of physical and mental preparation."
-Paula Radcliffe on running a marathon

Cooking Action
Imagine a chef dreams up a great recipe for your dinner and then goes back to sleep. You'll go hungry. Next time you eat, be grateful for the 'action'!

Sweaty Action
In the words of Colin Powell; "A dream doesn't become a reality through magic; it takes sweat, determination, and hard work." Next time you dream, remember you need to sweat. Next time you sweat; remember you're working on your dream body!

Executive Action
Research was done on the emails sent within a company. (I bet they made for some interesting reading!) They did make an interesting discovery. Middle managers sent emails, which had very good grammar, very good spelling and were very long! Whereas directors and executives sent very short (mistake filled) emails! Speedy success at the top. Next time you take action, remember it doesn't have to be perfcet.

It takes action (not perfection) and sometimes years of sweat to reach your goals. But without action you'll go hungry!

Champion Action
To go from good to great takes a lot of action. Ask Open Champion golfer Paul Lawrie. In his junior teenage days I have been reliably informed that he was a good golfer but not a great golfer. He played at Kemnay Golf Course and competed against the best North East (Scotland) boys, rarely winning competitions. He turned pro with a handicap of 5, which is below the great standard of normal pros (handicap of 0). Twenty years later and he beat the best golfers in the World at Carnoustie. Next time someone else beats you, give yourself a few years.

What do you want? Go get it

Succeed like Stephen
Stephen Gallacher's years of patience and motivation finally paid off after he won his first European Tour title at his 188th attempt! After playing and losing in 187 title competitions he won the Dunhill Links Championship at St Andrews, the Home of Golf in 2004. Stephen is 29 years old and said "I've been knocking on the door for so long and to do this at St Andrews is like a dream come true. I must have played

here over 30 times. My past performances here haven't been all that great. I can't remember doing any good round here." Over 30 losing performances and 187 unsuccessful attempts and Stephen never gave up! He beat the best golfers in the world to win! Players included, World number one Vijay Singh, World number three and European Number 1 Ernie Els, former World number one Ian Woosnam, World number four and US Open champion Retief Goosen, former Masters champion Fred Couples and Ryder Cup hero and European Number 1 for 7 years Colin Montgomerie. The Scots are good at golf!

Never give up and you're dreams will come true.
Succeed like Stephen!
Achieving your dreams takes years. Keep dreaming!

"Winning isn't everything--but wanting to win is." -Vince Lombardi

Success takes years

Former World number one Ian Woosnam turned professional in 1976. However, it took him three attempts to quality for the tour and he only won £6,000 in his first five years! He travelled around Europe in a camper van competing in tournaments and in 1982 won the Swiss Open (six years after turning professional). It wasn't until 5 years after the Swiss Open, in 1987, that he achieved great success winning 8 tournaments and topping the money list on the European tour with US$1m in a season. It took a motivated and determined Ian eleven years after turning professional to achieve that! In 1989, he came second in the US Open and in 1991 he was World Number 1 and won the US Masters. Fifteen years after turning pro and over 25 years after he started playing golf!

Becoming world number one takes years of work.
It can take years of losing before you start winning.

"There is no substitute for hard work." --Thomas Edison (1847-1931)
Edison often worked more than 40 hours straight!

Success takes years. Success takes sacrifices.

"You make goodness knows how many sacrifices." – John Madejski

Buy expensive; You get what you pay for

Don't skimp on your time and money when it comes to achieving your dreams. The latest lesson I've learnt is paying cheaply and poorly with your time and money gets you cheap and poor results. The original book cover design for 'winning mentality' would have made you laugh. I would have laughed to when I saw it, if I wasn't so appalled and mad! I learnt a good lesson. I then decided to invest some good time and money (mine) into the cover and I hope you agree I got a great 'winning' result. There are no short cuts to great results. Just take the right path in the first place. Fast. Stick to it and only change if it's certainly not right. If it's not right, change it fast.

If you pay poorly with your time and money to achieve your dreams you'll get poor payback and results.

Cheap effort today, cheap payback tomorrow.
Great effort today, great rewards tomorrow.
Cheap cars give cheap results
Cheap trainers give cheap results.
Cheap meals give cheap results.
Cheap computers give cheap results.

'A man that buys expensive cries once.
A man that buys cheaply cries many times.'

"You have to pay the price - but if you do you can only WIN."
-Frank Leahy

You get what you pay for!

Spare no expense. You have to pay the price for success.
Are you paying enough?
Those that pay richly will be rewarded richly tomorrow.
You get out what you put in.
GIGO. Garbage in; garbage out. Gold in; gold out.

World Number One

Vijay Singh from Fiji is just the twelfth player to achieve World Number 1 status in golf in the last 18 years. Some of the other players to have been World Number One include Seve Ballesteros, Ernie Els, Ian Woosnam and Fred Couples. Two players though have held the spot for over 12 years! Tiger Woods held it for a record 334 weeks and Greg Norman achieved 331 weeks. Lots of golfers and only a few great winners.

Winners pay the price for success. No expense spared.

No excuses

This whole book packed with amazing stories and amazing techniques. If it proves anything it's that anything is possible! It also proves there can be no excuses for not chasing and achieving dreams and goals. Time, money or skill will not stop winners.

Go for your goals and if you have no excuses you'll have no regrets.

Anything is possible.

"Building alibis with which to explain away failure is a national pastime." - Napoleon Hill

"Lack of persistence is one of the main causes of failure." – Napoleon Hill

The only person you can cheat is yourself.
The only person you can let down is yourself.

"Give it your best shot everyday. If you don't, if you loaf or coast, you are cheating only yourself." -Michael Burke

"Some of us will do our jobs well and some will not, but we will be judged by only one thing-the result." - Vince Lombardi

Read the following powerful poem;

The Man in the Mirror

When you get what you want in your struggle for self
And the world makes you King for a day
Then go to the mirror and look at yourself
And see what the Man has to say.

For it isn't a man's father, mother or wife
Whose judgement upon him must pass
The fellow whose verdict counts most in his life
Is the Man staring back from the glass.

He's the fellow to please, never mind all the rest
For he's with you clear up to the end
And you've passed your most dangerous, difficult test
If the Man in the glass is your friend.

You can fool the whole world down the pathway of years
And get pats on the back as you pass
But your final reward will be heartache and tears
If you've cheated the Man in the glass.

The story behind this poem is about two men on death row in California, just about to be executed, the prison guards were cleaning the cell that both prisoners had shared the night before - their last night on earth. To the guards' amazement, they found this poem inscribed on the cell wall.

Are you proud of yourself?
Look in the mirror and see what the person has to say today.

Regret gives you no sleep. Pride gives great sleep.

"The destination is not always the one we would like but there is a bizarre pride even in a losing dressing room if you have given everything." - Jonny Wilkinson

Give it everything you've got and more. Do whatever it takes.

Look in the mirror

IF you can look in the mirror at the end of everyday and be happy with the effort of the person in the mirror, a life of greatness and happiness will be yours. Give yourself a CRC performance report card every night. Mark yourself out of 7. Your goal is to be happy every night. You can't lie to your mind! Honestly is the best policy.

If you get up every morning and go to bed every night with a smile on your face you are doing well. In both senses of the word.

The only person you have to please is yourself.
A winner is very honest with themselves and if they perform badly they will say "I let myself down."

Seve Ballesteros once denied himself a meal after failing in a golf competition because he told himself "you don't deserve to eat".

No one can criticise the methods of someone who is getting GREAT results. You can learn from it! Great methods gives great results.

Learn from the methods of someone who is getting GREAT results.
Don't learn from the methods of someone
who is getting POOR results.

" Regret for the things we did can be tempered by time;
it is regret for things we did not do that is inconsolable."
- Sydney Harris

"I live my life as if a twenty -four hour surveillance camera is trained on me. At the end of my days, I want to be able to hand over and sign away the video." - Jonny Wilkinson

A day in the life of…YOU!

Something I realised a long time ago when I began skiing and then snowboarding and then swimming is that it's easy to spot other people's faults but it's more difficult to spot your own. Two options.

Use imagination. Watch yourself performing in your mind and talk to your passengers and your future self. Option two; video your performance from when you wake to when you go to bed. Then review your performance and pick out the positives and negatives. Do a CRC. Commend, recommend and commend. You will spot very quickly where you could make improvements in yourself, your life and your performance. Or imagine a camera is on you all the time. I love Jonny's great idea and I am using his idea. I have an old camera on me now that I set up to remind me of the message. Pretending is powerful. How often do people tidy up when people come round or run faster down the street when people look round. Put in a great effort everyday.

Record a 'A day in the life of...ME!' every year and keep your results.
It's easy to criticise; it's better to construct.
You can only be aware of your mistakes when you are aware of them!
Ignorance is useless for performance.
Knowledge is powerful for performance.

Dream, Believe, Plan, Act, Achieve

This year's winner at Wimbledon of the women's final was 17-year-Old Russian Maria Sharapova. Before the final she said, "I've just been going out and just believing in myself that I can do it. It really doesn't matter who I play. It's unbelievable. I'm in the final. It's absolutely crazy. It's my favourite Grand Slam. I never in the world expected to do so well here, so early. I'm amazed." She has achieved a dream early! Note- she used the word "early" indicating that it was a dream goal! It goes without saying that she was hungry and motivated to achieve her dream. Maria is Russian. Have a look at the match history of a winner in any sport and you will see a history of losing! Lucky they never give up.

"I've just been going out and just believing in myself that I can do it."
-Maria Sharapova, 17-year-old Russian, Wimbledon Winner 2004
Maria's mentor is tennis great Martina Navratilova! Great advice! She spotted her at a young age when Maria was hitting a tennis ball against a wall and was amazed at her ability. Great advice; great results.

Keep dreaming and believing and you'll achieve them.
Sometimes dreams are achieved earlier than you expect!
Sometimes dreams are achieved later than you expect.
Sometimes dreams are achieved just as you expect!
But keep dreaming and believing or the dream will never be achieved.
If you don't chase or believe in your dream,
don't ever expect to achieve it.
Chase your dream even if you don't believe it.

You can do it
Most people fear failing so much they fail to take action. But failing to take action guarantees failing!

Delaying all decisions is the wrong decision.

Think now
You can think about the past, the now or the future. Visualising the future now will impact upon your future. But only your thoughts of what to do now will impact upon your results now and in the future. Learn from the past and then forget it. Picture the future and remember it. Decide what to do now and do it.

The power of NOW
You cannot take action in the past or the future. You can only take action now. You can't do everything at once, but you can do something at once. Take action NOW.

Vision without action is just a dream.
Action without vision is just a nightmare.
Vision and action achieves a dream.
We can always do something or we can always do nothing!
Do something.

You are in control of your destiny
What you think and do now, today will decide what you achieve tomorrow. You are in control. You have the power. Where you go is up to you.

You are in control of your thoughts, actions and time.
Therefore you are in control of your future.
You can decide your destiny.

Achieving your dream is a choice.
Spend your time wisely. It's the most important investment you will make.

"I am a bit of a control freak, which is probably why I'm such a good squash player. I control my life, my training and my diet and the routine is very strict and I'm very hard on myself. What I don't like is giving my power over to other people." -Peter Nicol,
World Number 1 Squash player for six years

Winners have self-control, losers don't.

"Entrepreneurs are usually a controlling-type of person."
- Tom Hunter, founder of Sports Division, which he sold to JJB Sports

You have the controls. Choose your thoughts. Choose your attitude. Choose your actions. Choose your future. Your decisions create your destiny.

There is great power in your thoughts, words and actions; they are like stones thrown into a pond - the effect is seen not immediately, but eventually.

"Destiny is no matter of chance. It is a matter of choice." - William Jennings Bryan

"It is very difficult to control your own destiny but I think you can do it up to a point. My life will change depending on the decisions I make and the destiny I choose." -Jean Claude Killy, French sport and business legend, winner of three gold medals in 1968 and successful entrepreneur and business man

Commitment

When you choose the path to a big goal, expect big challenges. Only the committed pass all the challenges. Lot's of interested people go to a gym in January, but only committed people will be in a gym in December. A survey of 7500 workers found that those 'committed' delivered 112% returns to shareholders over 3 years. Those 'not committed' delivered only 76%.

You can quickly spot someone that is motivated and committed. And you will soon spot the difference in the results.

"There's a difference between interest and commitment. When you're interested in doing something, you do it only when circumstance permit. When you're committed to something, you accept no excuses, only results." - Art Turock

Running in the sun shows interest.
Running in the snow shows commitment!

Sacrifices

Sacrifices are essential. Great achievements require great sacrifices. Pursuing your dream is a risk and gamble and the path has many hurdles and difficult choices and sacrifices. Stephen Henry and Jonny Wilkinson are two of many winners who readily admit that throughout their teens they spent all their time practising and not socialising.

To get the reward you need to take the risk. Risk and reward. Sacrifice, risk and work hard. Speculate to accumulate.

"Decide what you want, decide what you are willing to exchange for it. Establish your priorities and go to work." HL Hunt, American Oil Magnate

"I've chosen a narrow passage through life, trading my youth to challenge myself to become the best rugby player I can be. I haven't missed the hangovers." - Jonny Wilkinson MBE, Newcastle and England Rugby Player

"There is not a lot of time for hard partying if you are pursuing greatness."- Les Brown

"It's easy to have faith in yourself and have discipline when you're a winner, when you're number one. What you've got to have is faith and discipline when you're not yet a winner. There's only one way to succeed in anything, and that is to give it everything." -Vince Lombardi

No pain, no gain

Paula Radcliffe ran so fast in the London Marathon in 2004 that her pace maker couldn't keep up with her for long. She won the race in a World record setting time and it was interesting to hear her interview after winning the London Marathon. As she started to say the words "It was painful for the last..." I thought to myself "last mile? Two miles?" Her words were "..10 miles!" Paula was in pain for the last 10 miles! Can you imagine? No, me neither. For almost half the race and almost an hour Paula was in pain! Wow. Wonder woman.

Winning is simple but not easy. No pain, no gain.

"I hated every minute, of the training, but I said, "Don't you quit. Suffer now and live the rest of your life as a champion." -Muhammad Ali

Hard man Lance Armstrong

Six times Tour De France winner Lance Armstrong says, "I train harder than I race." Apart from one section of the Tour de France where he was so angry at a broken pedal, which cost him a few seconds, he said, "that was the only time I raced harder than I trained."

Anger can be a great motivator!

Train Hard. Work Hard.

Winning basketball player Michael Johnson is well known for saying, "I train harder than I play." So when it comes to a match he can mentally and physically cope with a hard game.

Be prepared.

"Preparation is power." -Jonny Wilkinson

"Winning gold medals today is down to the quality of an athlete's physical and mental preparation, not the quantity of training." -Sylvester Stein, World Champion Runner, gold medallist and Chairman of Peak Performance Newsletter

Winning training, winning execution

SAS are world renowned for their ability. Why? They are very highly trained. It's not an accident that the SAS is called upon to deal in hostage situation and they do so very successfully; they train to deal with hostage situations! An SAS soldier is trained to cope with pain and stressful situations. BP.

Today's work. Tomorrow's rewards.

Overnight Success Takes 10 Years

Most overnight successes take 10 years. Danny Williams UK heavy weight champion beat Tyson in 2004 to become another overnight success; his boxing match was at 1am UK time. Danny had in fact been boxing for years and has boxed in the heavy weight division for 9 years. He firmly believed he was going to win. Few did. And if you saw the match you'll know he was lucky to stay on his feet for the first 2 rounds. Round 3 and Danny landed 30 punches unreturned on a tired Tyson. Tyson went down and never got up. Danny was fitter and better in round 3. Being defeated could motivate Tyson to increase his fitness beyond 3 rounds. Scott Harrison was World Champion and in 2003 got beat. He admits he got too complacent and expected to win but never trained as hard as he used to. The defeat was a huge 'blow' literally to his ego and it hurt. So much that he trained harder than he has ever done before and began hill running! Walking up a hill is hard enough.

What will get you to take action? ….

Overnight Success Takes 10 Years.

Microsoft first year sales in 1975 were $16,005!

Kelly Holmes

Kelly Holmes became a British Olympic hero after winning the Gold medal for the 800m in Athens 2004. She then had the 1500m qualifiers a few days later and got through to the final, which was to be her sixth race in nine days. She won Gold! Kelly said that she pretended that she hadn't won the 800m gold medal when she ran in the 1500 final! Consciously or subconscious she knew it would increase her desire and hunger to win a second Gold. The technique obviously helped! She won her second Gold Olympic medal just days after winning her first.

You have got to be very motivated (hungry) to win.

After the 1500m win she said, "I don't know what got me through it but I think it was guts and tunnel vision. It's so surreal; I'm just so exhausted. A lot of things have happened this week that made me believe that fate was with me. But it was difficult to focus mentally and physically after everything I have achieved this week. The hardest thing was pretending I hadn't won it. I looked at the medal this morning and I had a tear in my eyes. I had one but I wanted another one. I just stayed focused and ran my own race. I knew I had to relax through the first 800m and then use my strength and hang on. I don't know what got me through it but I think it was guts and that tunnel vision. This had been a psychological battle because I knew this was my one chance ever. I genuinely just can't believe it's happening to me and I'm too tired to even think at the moment. But to be mentioned in the same breath as Coe is unbelievable. He was my idol for absolutely years and he was my inspiration."

Stay focused and run your own race.
Winners have idols who inspire them.

It's the first time in seven years Kelly has been able to train throughout the winter and come into a major championship. She only decided to run in the 800m the day before the first day of qualifying. Kelly said, "I kept expecting something to go wrong, something always goes wrong but when it didn't I started to grow in confidence and I really just tried to believe in myself."

Believe in yourself.
If you expect things to go wrong they usually do.

Kelly is 34 years old and achieved her dreams after working towards her dreams for 21 years! She took her chance, "I knew this was my last chance of achieving my dreams and the 1500m was the one I was always going to take part in, so winning this is brilliant beyond my wildest dreams. I'm so in shock I really can't explain how I feel except that I'm so bleeding knackered. I had nothing left at the end, I'm just glad that neither did the others. If you'd told me I would have to run that fast to win or get a medal, I just wouldn't have turned up. The 1500m is such a psychological battle for me because it means so much to me and any athlete will tell you that's the biggest battle." In order to win she had to call upon a powerful performance she never knew she had. Necessity is the mother of motivation. Kelly Holmes is a former army sergeant and the kind of mental toughness found in any female or male soldier was required to win her gold medals. Past experiences help you succeed. Good or bad. Everything happens for a reason. Everyone is born for a reason. Make your destiny.

Achieving your dreams can take 21 years.
Never give up. You only fail if you give up.

"I've been dreaming about this every day since
I started running at the age of 13."
- Kelly Holmes, 34, after winning Olympic Gold at Athens 2004.

Dreams are motivating. Keep dreaming. Dreams can come true.
'The first bite is with the eye.'

It's good to have heroes. In fact it's essential.

Take your chances and give it everything you have got,
you'll have no regrets.

The difference between ordinary and extraordinary is that little extra.

Go for Goal

One of the best examples of exactly what it takes to succeed is the story of Chris Hoy. In the 2004 Olympics in Athens cyclist Chris Hoy won Gold with an amazing performance in the 1km event. Chris Hoy's story is an inspiring one. Here is a summary of the relevant steps to achieving his dream;

1. Good role model growing up (Father Dave Hoy is a keen cyclist)
2. Got good advice and coaching from young age
3. Set GOLD medal as a goal at 13 years old (achieved it at 29)
4. Made sacrifices
5. Trained with winners
6. Got winning advice from Queally, MacLean and Boardman
7. Was inspired by Gold medal winner Jason Queally in 2000 Olympics
8. Believed he could do it (if Jason could do it)
9. Trained hard and raced hard (in harsh Scottish winters)
10. Visualised winning race for years including receiving Gold medal
11. Relaxed before race
12. Risked winning and risked losing
13. Made the most of the opportunity

Gold Medal Story

Ray Harris was Chris's first coach at the Dunedin Cycling Club when he joined at 13 years old. He taught him the benefits of setting short, medium, and long term goals. Chris went home that night and wrote down his goals in a diary. The list included his long-term goal of the Olympic gold in 2004! Bingo, it worked. Sixteen years after setting the goal, at the Athens 2004 Olympics at the age of 29 Chris Hoy won a gold medal in the one kilometre time trial.

Focus on your performance (not the competition)
Teammate Craig MacLean set the fastest time with just six men left to ride. The last four broke the Olympic record and put pressure onto Hoy.
"The times were so fast. Everyone was phenomenal tonight. I knew I had to focus on my own ride, and not anyone else's' because it can be very off putting when you see such quick times. The crowd was fantastic. Every time I passed the line they pushed me on."

Visualise your dream
"To win the gold medal for Britain after Jason in Sydney is just a dream come true. I'd visualised the night in my mind for so long that when it actually happened it didn't feel real."

Surround yourself with eagles, success takes 8 years
"It was weird, half an hour before I won my gold medal, Craig MacLean and I were reminiscing. Nowadays we are team mates and peers but in the early days, he was like a coach to me and we were laughing about the days when we were training through the harsh Scottish winters, having to wear thermal gloves as we tried to perfect standing starts. And there we were eight years later in the heat of the Olympic Games in Athens contesting one of the most amazing and high class finals ever." Chris's attitude and effort in training was noticed by Dave Brailsford, performance director, British Cycling who said "it's his attitude that is so inspirational to others in the team. His is a tireless trainer, a guy who doesn't know the meaning of the taking things easy."

A good coach, a good attitude and years of hard work.

Inspiration, belief, sacrifices, some help and luck
"It was Jason Queally who inspired me four years ago in Sydney. I remember getting really emotional when he was getting his medal and thinking 'Hell, if he's up there then there is hope for me as well', because I trained with the guy and knew he didn't take drugs. It made me realise that you could be clean and still win an Olympic gold medal. He's an inspirational guy and although he has had some difficult times he had always been encouraging and there for the other riders. On Friday night (before race day) he was definitely there for me. I feel so fortunate that so many people have been there supporting and inspiring me all the way and I can't help but wonder how different

things would be if I hadn't met even one or two of those people. I might not have an Olympic gold in my collection and that's unthinkable now. I could not have done this without so many people. I thank them all. I don't count anything a sacrifice. Not tonight with this gold medal."

Choose your mission and make the most of the opportunity
"Sydney was my first Olympics, this time I came here with a mission. I had a job to do and that was to win Olympic gold. It wasn't just about the Olympic experience it was fulfilling an ambition and making the most of the opportunity."
The steps to success are relevant to business or sport;

1. Found something he enjoyed
2. Set dream goal and worked on it for 16 years
3. Got good advice, coaching and help
4. Made sacrifices
5. Took a risk on his dream
6. Surrounded himself with eagles, believers and supporters
7. Through 'luck' met people who helped him achieve dream
8. Trained with winners and got advice from gold medal winners
9. Was inspired by friend who achieved the same dream
10. Had strong belief he could achieve his dream
11. Worked hard and took action
12. Visualised his goal
13. Relaxed before race
14. Made no excuses
15. Made the most of the opportunity

Dreams are hard work. But don't attempt to achieve your dream "the hard way." Take the "sweaty way." Use your head and your heroes to decide the best route and then you've taken the sweaty route.

Work up a sweat thinking it through,
then work up a sweat following it through.

'Dream. Believe. Plan. Act. Achieve.' – Walt Disney

'Luck is only preparation meeting opportunity.'- Oprah Winfrey

Be prepared.

"The more I practice, the luckier I get." – Gary Player, legendary golfer

You are in control of your thoughts and actions.
You <u>are</u> in control of your destiny.

"It's not easy. You must have self-belief, a real appetite for hard work and a lot of energy. If you just put in enough to get past, that's all you'll ever do." - Tom Hunter, Self Made Millionaire, founder of Sports Division and West Coast Capital

Lucky opportunity

The story about Chris Hoy and the quote from Oprah make an important point. When you have a dream, work on it and when the opportunity occurs to achieve it you can grab the opportunity and achieve it. If Chris Hoy had not prepared for the Olympics he would not have won gold at the Olympics. You have to work on your dream and be prepared for dream opportunities. Whether you believe you can do it or not, take action! The opportunity will arise if you follow winning mentality and follow lucky mentality. Take action and keep positive!

'Before everything else, getting ready is the secret to success.' -Henry Ford, hard working, positive & enthusiastic Inventor of the motorcar

If your mind isn't aware of your goals,
you won't be aware of the opportunities.
If you fail to give up you will never fail.

Sony failed on their first two products. Then the Sony founder had a problem. He wanted to listen to classical music on the golf course. He solved it by inventing the Sony Walkman. The rest is history. Lucky Sony never gave up.

"Daring ideas are like chessmen moved forward;
they may be beaten, but they may start a winning game."
-Johann Wolfgang von Goethe

Lucky assistance

A second element of luck is mentioned in Chris's story and is mentioned by almost every great person. After they set their dream goal and got to work on it, they were lucky to receive help that was crucial to their success. Chris comments that a few people helped him achieve gold and without their help he wonders if he would have achieved it. He's not sure! I know exactly what he means. To write and publish this book I needed help (see Authors Thanks) and without many of my 'helpers and believers' as well as mind teachers' I would not be writing this 'Winning Mentality' book and would not be publishing it. It's not just people but any lucky events that 'assist'. For example I only found out about my book publisher after walking into my Dad's office and noticing a letter from a local book company lying near his desk! (By the way I phoned 10 different big publishers based in

London and either failed with them first time or was unimpressed. They were not very hungry and their 'action' time was slow. Only one company was keen to receive it but they were going to take 6 weeks just to look at my book summary!

"I feel so fortunate that so many people have been there supporting and inspiring me all the way and I can't help but wonder how different things would be if I hadn't met even one or two of those people."
-Chris Hoy, Gold medal winning cyclist, 2004 Olympics in Athens in 1Km

If you have a list of goals your mind will spot anything relevant to those goals and make you consciously aware of it.

Trust your intuition and you get great luck and a great destiny!
I have followed my gut so many times and it's the only way I have achieved a lot of my goals. Whether it is books, people, holidays or films trust your gut!

Lucky events

Third element of luck that is important to success is lucky events that do not relate to goals or dreams but create future success. For example it wasn't until I went on holiday with my cousin Andy and asked if I could read his book about the mind rather than the book I had taken that I discovered the power of the mind. A very lucky event! I have always been positive so I have always been lucky! I was lucky my cousin took a book on the mind with him and lucky he allowed me to read it! (The business books I had taken with me to read were of no interest to him at the time!). I wasn't till after reading the book and I took a huge interest in the subject and I wanted to help other people use their mind. Furthermore I did not have the goal or the dream to write a book until (luckily) I happened to meet a 21-year-old student by chance in Australia who inspired me. I did not have an idea or the knowledge how to write a book but it didn't stop me setting it as a goal. Then the ideas and skills were 'attracted' to me by my mind in order to achieve my goal.

The author of the book 'Bridget Jones Diary', which got made into two films, had the idea suggested to originally as a newspaper column by a newspaper editor. Now she is an author and millionaire by taking action with one idea! She was a writer for the newspaper and not an author at the time. I went on to read over 100 books on the mind and thousands of pages on successful people. Graeme Obree set the goal of the one-hour record after he watched Chris Boardman achieve gold at the 1992 Barcelona Olympics! He achieved the one-hour record the following year and won the World Championships. He achieved them both using a bike that he had made himself and the bike included a piece of medal tube that he happened to come across while out training! Lucky bit of assistance!

Lucky people have lucky life changing moments
that benefit their future.
Unlucky people have unlucky events throughout their life.
Negative mind, negative future!

Lucky events only happen to lucky people. That is people who believe they are lucky. People who don't, don't get lucky.

Lucky people will have a good life and destiny.
Hard working lucky people will have a great life and destiny.

Being relaxed and confident, believing in luck, following your intuition and being positive even after 'bad' events, gives you a very lucky life.
I know that for sure! I am very lucky!

Lucky Experiment

Professor Richard Wiseman found that when lucky people looked through a newspaper they found his notice 'STOP COUNTING. TELL THE EXPERIMENTER YOU'VE SEEN THIS AND WIN 150 POUNDS' but when unlucky people looked through it they never saw it! Why? They are not relaxed and confident people. Being nervous affects your sight. Secondly they BELIEVED they were unlucky so their mind often saw the notice but ignored it because their mind wanted them to achieve what they believe!

If you are relaxed, confident and lucky you will spot lucky opportunities.

If you are nervous and unlucky you will miss lucky opportunities.
You achieve what you believe.

Open to opportunity

Being relaxed and open to new experiences affects your ideas and your luck. Unlucky people are stuck in routines. They don't do anything new. Even sitting or parking somewhere new is not for them. Lucky people always want something new. They're prepared to take risks and relaxed enough to see the opportunities in the first place. I am lucky and always sit somewhere different in large meetings and I often just trust my intuition where I will sit. It's always profitable in some way.

Confident, relaxed and focus (but not too focused)

In his ground breaking scientific research into 'luck' Professor Richard Wiseman made an important and counter intuitive discovery revealed in his book 'The Luck Factor'. If you focus with tunnel vision all the time or 'try' hard it's possible to miss opportunity.

"We are traditionally taught to be really focused, to be really driven, to try really hard at tasks. But in the real world, you've got opportunities all around you. And if you're driven in one direction, you're not going to spot the others. Unlucky people, if they go to a party wanting to meet the love of their life, end up not meeting people who might become close friends or people who might help them in their careers. Being relaxed and open allows lucky people to see what's around them and to maximise what's around them."
- Prof Richard Wiseman

Be open-minded, have fun and don't have too much tunnel vision on your goals. Watch your rules. Like rules for fun. People who have fun in the rain have no rule that says 'raining is no fun'.
Kids don't have that rule!

Four tips for being lucky

1. Maximise chance opportunities
2. Listen to your intuition
3. Be Positive
4. Put bad experiences into perspective (Be Positive)

Maximise Chance Opportunities

"Lucky people are skilled at creating, noticing and acting upon chance opportunities. They do this in various ways, including networking, adopting a relaxed attitude to life and by being open to new experiences." ('The Luck Factor', Prof Richard Wiseman)

Think about it

How did Duncan get his job just by thinking about it? Four things; he maximises his opportunities by keeping in touch with ex colleagues who offered him his job, he is a relaxed and confident guy; he believes I quote "I am very lucky" and fourthly; he had a goal!

Everyone you meet helps your journey in some way

I can recall meeting two people who recommended books to me. One recommendation years ago was 'Men are from mars, women are from Venus' which I bought and read almost immediately to impress this woman and it turned out she had bought it and never read it! The book and the author had a great impact in my development and wisdom especially his later books on what he has learnt and the stories he has received since then. My book would not be as useful without my introduction to Dr John Gray several years ago.

The second person last year recommended 'Good to Great' which I initially decided not to read (while writing this book I imposed an almost complete ban on reading more books unless absolutely essential). Well what happened was I visited an office that had a copy, which I spotted, tucked away high up on a shelf (I am lucky I am tall!). I flicked through the book and saw how great it was. I could not memorise all the points I wanted to remember- so I knew I needed a copy! I then borrowed the book from my friend and the insights have improved my book with information and inspiration. All because of a chance recommendation of 'Good to great' and then a chance sighting. Interestingly the woman who mentioned it had not yet read it! But she was recommended she read it by entrepreneur legend Richard Emmanuel (that was good enough for me. But only enough initially to 'flick it'. I did not want to read it due my writing time at the time. That was how strict I was being on myself over reading and not writing. I love to read good non-fiction books!)

Everything happens for a reason. People you meet, events that occur and opportunities that arise. If can take a few years to work it out.

Trust your intuition. Follow your intuition.
If you get good vibes; go for it.
If you get bad vibes; watch it.

The latest person recommended a book of which I admired but had never read (yet) called 'The monk who sold his Ferrari'. I fully intend to read that book. But I need to finish writing his book first! I have some great quotes from him.

"Never sacrifice happiness for the sake of achievement. The real key to life is to happily achieve." -Robin S. Sharma, robinsharma.com (The monk who sold his Ferrari!)

"Number 1. Sleep less. This is one of the best investments you can make to make your life more productive and rewarding. Most people do not need more than 6 hours to maintain an excellent state of health" -Robin S. Sharma,
'The Top 200 Secrets of Success and the Pillars of Self-Mastery'

When you have got a dream you need a team

No one achieves success on their own. Especially in business. Richard Morris, Chris Gorman and Andrew Carnegie among others have all said that you need to surround yourself with great people. So great in fact they actually state "surround yourself with people better than yourself". Great advice. Carnegie said eloquently before his death when he suggested his own epitaph should read;

"Here lies the man who was able to surround himself with men far cleverer than himself." - Andrew Carnegie
But not braver than himself!
It's the brave people not the brainy people that win.

Surround yourself with people better than yourself.
Even if you are a one-man band. Find eagles.

<u>Your</u> luck and assistance

When your set your dream goal and get to work on it you will get lucky assistance and help to help you achieve your goal. You will also spot the opportunity to achieve your dream goal. But only if you are prepared will you succeed like Chris and Oprah. The lucky event for you was buying this book!

Never give up!

Sahir Hashemi and her brother Bobby Hashemi of Coffee Republic were rejected by 22 banks before they got a "yes." It's been written that Walt Disney was rejected by over 900 banks! He was told he had a "crazy idea that will never work." Both ideas succeeded. Many didn't believe it.

Your goal is a vision not everyone sees or believes.
"You just can't beat the person that never gives up!" -Babe Ruth
CNN Anchor newsreader Aaron Brown phoned the news director of King TV every Thursday morning at ten for four years. Didn't miss one! Then KING TV gave up saying no so gave him the worse job they had and he loved it! Now look at him on CNN!!

Come back King

Sports history is filled with teams who have come back. Manchester City Football Club made one of the most famous comebacks in English football 2004. Man City played 17 games and won only one. During there 18th game against Tottenham Hotspur FC they were getting beat by 3 goals after 45 minutes. In the second 45 minutes of the game they scored 4 goals and won the game! What did Man City Manager Kevin Keegan say to his players at half time? I don't know exactly. What I do know is what he said made the players believe they could do it and made the players not give up.

Never give up. Believe you can do it and you can do it.
Be careful of using negative labels. When you say, "this is tough", "I am crap", "I am tired", "not bad" or "it is a nightmare" you have already instructed the mind to achieve what you believe. You will give yourself a tough, crap, tiring, not great, nightmare day! Use positive labels. Remember to say everyday "I can handle it. This is easy. I can do it." "I am winning", "good to great", "energy break", "tiny challenge for a winner" and the day will be a great day

Winners never quit and quitters never win

Paula Radcliffe spent years known as the “unlucky loser” after missing out on medals and wins for years. In 2002 she became the world record holder for the marathon. Lucky she never gave up.

You never gave up. Learning to walk and talk.
You kept doing it until you got it!
Get back up.
"The most important thing is that you rise every time you fall."

Faith no doubt

Admiral Jim Stockdale was a prisoner of war for eight years in Vietnam after being shot down in 1965. He was tortured severely twenty times during that time, so much so that he has a permanent limp and abnormal walk. He was the highest-ranking officer captured in Vietnam so he was looked to for leadership from all the prisoners, as well as given harsh torture by his captors. He survived those 8 years and went on to thrive after his release.

“I never lost faith. I never doubted not only that I would get out, but also that I would prevail in the end and turn the experience into the defining event of my life, which, in retrospect, I would not trade.”

Optimism’s Dangerous

In an interview with author Jim Collins, Admiral Jim Stockdale was asked, “Who didn’t make it out?” and his reply is interesting important and almost counter intuitive. “The optimists.” Jim explained that, those that were over optimist kept thinking they would be “out by Easter” and then “out by Christmas” every year and it never happened. After a few years “they died of a broken heart.”

“This is a very important lesson. You must never confuse faith that you will prevail in the end- which you can never afford to lose- with the discipline to confront the most brutal facts of your current reality, whatever they might be.”- Admiral Jim Stockdale

Being Overly Optimistic is Dangerous.
I used to be OOD myself! Don’t be OOD!

People are like teabags. They don’t know how strong they are until they get into hot water.

Mandela’s Dreams

Although in jail for nearly 30 years Nelson Mandela believed and dreamed of being released one day. However, if he had been optimistic and believed he would be released within 20 years he may not have survived AND thrived for almost 30 years before achieving his dream! If Nelson had been over optimistic he wouldn't be here today!

Adversity is the best thing that could happen to you.

Challenges build character.

You must chase your dream and be patient for it to arrive. If you patiently wait for your dream, like a bus you will catch it but only if you are patiently waiting for it to arrive. Good things come to those who wait. Dreams take their time!

"Difficulties are just things to overcome."
-Sir Ernest Shakleton, survived for a year at the Pole and never lost one man

Onwards and upwards!

"Mental toughness is essential to success." -Vince Lombardi

"Mental toughness is many things and rather difficult to explain. Its qualities are sacrifice and self-denial. Also, most importantly, it is combined with a perfectly disciplined will that refuses to give in. It's a state of mind-you could call it character in action." - Vince Lombardi

Adversity is an Advantage

The 'International Committee for the study of Victimisation' did a study of people who had suffered adversity like prisoners of war (POW), cancer patients and accident victims. They discovered that people usually fitted into three categories; people who were permanently dispirited by the event, people that got their life back to normal and those that used the experience as a turning point in their life that made them stronger.

When you meet adversity you have three choices; get over it, let it get you down or let it inspire you to great things.
If this book proves a turning point in your life or even a point in your life at which you went 'onwards and upwards' from,
I will be a very happy man.

"Where there is adversity there is opportunity. There's been 9/11, the downturn in the world economy, an ongoing threat of terrorism, the war in Iraq and SARS disease. It's like a boxer who's knocked down and just as he gets up again there's another great smack on the nose, and down he goes again, he staggers to his feet trying to recover and in comes another. If we hadn't of changed we wouldn't have survived."
-John Calcutt, CEO, Watermark

Rocky never gives up

Sylvester Stallone, the American actor, was turned down time and time again as an actor. But he kept dreaming and then one day his mind put an idea in his head and showed him a way to become an actor; write a script! In March 1975 he watched the real 'Rocky' fight Ali and the fight changed his life. He went home and wrote his screenplay for three days straight using caffeine tablets to stay awake. When sending studios his screenplay he was offered a lot of money for the screenplay but they didn't want him to star in it. He knocked back s thousands for just the script and says his inspiration was the story he wrote! Eventually someone said "yes" and he was allowed to star but at a much-reduced payment for the script. Just over 18 months later the film was released! The rest is history.

Often you have to take a step back financially to move forward one step closer to your goal. Like Rocky. Like Chris Gorman. Eventually someone will say "yes" to you. If you keep on asking.

Over 900 banks turned down Walt Disney when he was looking to finance Disneyland. KFC founder Sanders had a similar experience as he drove across America looking to sell his recipe to restaurants. Billionaire Mary Kay Ash sold less than $2.00 worth of cosmetics at her first beauty show! American President Lincoln failed at two businesses and lost six elections before becoming president.

Success is a numbers game. If you don't ask, you don't get. Quality counts but only where there is a high count of quantity.

Winners are failures

Golf Champion Phil Mickelson succeeded after failing 46 times to win a major championship. He became a major winner when he sunk a downhill 18-foot birdie putt on the 72nd hole. Phil made a great come back to win with a stunning 31 on the last nine holes to win by one shot! Featuring birdies on five of his final seven holes. Necessity. That gave him a 69, and a winning total of 9-under-par 279, for his 23rd career victory.

"It almost feels like make believe. My first thought was, 'I did it! I finally did it! I knew I could, but I finally did it. I can't believe this is happening. This is the fulfilment of dreams. I'm just proud to be a champion here." - Phil Mickelson, 2004 Masters Champion

"Success is connected with action. Successful people keep moving. They make mistakes but they don't quit. That's why I'll never quit." - Conrad Hilton

Losing and Winning
Michael Jordon didn't make his high school basketball team.
Jonny Wilkinson didn't make his county rugby team.
Abraham Lincoln didn't succeed initially in business or politics.
Walt Disney didn't succeed in his first business.
Chris Hoy didn't win gold at his first Olympics.
Sir Roger Bannister didn't succeed at his first Olympics.

Best thing that ever happened to them!

Failure makes you hungry for success.
Losing makes you hungry for winning.

When you fail, come back thinking bigger!
"To me, the most remarkable thing is how every time Lincoln failed at something, he was soon trying for something even bigger. When he loses his seat in the state legislature, he runs for the national congress. When he loses a bid for the Senate, he tries to become vice president and when he loses the Senate race again, he winds up President of the whole country.

Lincoln saw himself as a leader long before anyone else did and this is the first key to his leadership genius. He may have failed many times, but somehow he always failed upward. He was propelled by a sense of mission, and he was willing and able to do whatever it took to get that great mission accomplished. Lincoln saw himself as a leader long before he was one." - Dr. Tony Alessandra, 'Secrets of Ten Great Geniuses'

"Every time you get rejected, say: 'Next!'"
- Mark Victor Hansen
Rejected by 32 publishers for 80 Million selling
'Chicken Soup for the Soul'!

Identify the most important use of your time and energy
NOW and do it!
You can do it. Quality not quantity.
Quality counts and so does the quantity.
Success is a numbers game.

Start at the 'top' priority everyday and you will get to the top. If you work on the 'top' priority every minute of everyday you will get to the top. The best use of that minute might even be taking a 'time out' and relaxing for a minute.

Talking, walking and riding
You have achieved amazing goals already. You are a great person! You are a hero and a winner. You can talk, walk and ride a bike!

These are difficult 'impossible' goals but you achieved them because you believed you could do them! Other people inspired you. You failed the first time you did them. You failed the second time you did them. You failed over and over again but you never gave up! You achieved great things because you took action over and over again. You did not fear failure. Even now you still fall sometimes and you've been doing it for years! Get back up.

Success is a numbers game

I spoke to a friend recently and she said her son fell off his bike about 20 times learning to ride before he got the hang of it. And he still falls! Kids never give up! A friend of mine Craig has a young 10 month old baby girl called Kira and he told me that she falls down at least 20 times a day learning to stand and walk and it will take her months before she can walk! Which means she will fall over 100 times a week for months before she can walk! So did you! In just 8 weeks she will fall over 1,000 times! Which means we 'fail' over one thousand times before we learn to walk! Lucky we never gave up and always get up! Success is a numbers game! Even after we achieve our goal and can walk we still sometimes fall! I watched Kira in action and she actually smiles when she falls over! Wow. An inspiring and very memorable lesson from a young baby! A class with Kira!

Some people fear failure, some people success and some people fear both! Are you one of them? Do not fight fear. You will only beat yourself up. Fear helps humans survive. Accept and face the fear. Overcome it with a positive mind.

"We are afraid of failure. We want to win but we are afraid to lose."
- Rene Carayol

"Success is not forever and failure isn't fatal. This was my favourite quote when I was head coach for the Miami Dolphins.
It drove a great deal of my behaviour during my long career."
- Don Shula, ex-Miami Dolphins coach, 325 wins between 1970-1995

As a kid you were a brave winner. While learning to stand and walk you fell down over 1,000 times before you achieved your goal!
Be a brave winner. Success is a numbers game.
Keep believing, keep standing and you will keep achieving.
When you fall, you haven't failed. You just haven't succeeded yet.
Every step you take is one step closer to achieving your goal.

"If you haven't made any mistakes lately you must be doing something wrong."- Susan Jeffers

"As you watch a child learning to stand you cannot be anything more than impressed by the dedication and perseverance of that child even when faced with fall after fall they just keep on trying. They have not learned that failure is an option-it is only as we grow old and 'become' or are 'told' of our weaknesses that we 'learn' of our option to fail and give up. This is proven with one great lesson with children. If a child falls while learning to walk you can tell it off and even though it cannot talk it will understand the message and give up trying. But offer it your hand and that same child will grasp it eagerly and on having a cornerstone, encouragement, trust and love will smile and automatically move forward to now try and take its first step. Be a cornerstone for your child and your loved ones and release capabilities beyond imagination. Let us not give up and lose a generation." - Craig Bunyan, father of Kira and author of 'Arran and The Stonehaven Giant'

Smile every time you fall. Do not give up. Get up.
Do not fear failure. Every time you fail,
you are one step closer to walking.

Do not fear success. It's better than you think! Succeed.
You can handle it!

Are you a born salesman?
We all are but few people think they are. Sales is like getting married. You do a lot of looking, a lot of talking and when you find a match you do some asking and eventually someone says, "Yes". You won't get married or get sales if you don't go out looking and asking! You are a born salesman!

Are you a born dreamer?
We all are but few people think they are. Finding a dream is like getting married. You do a lot of looking and eventually one day you find a match that says "Yes" to you! You won't find a dream if you don't go looking!

Are you a born winner?
We all are but few people think they are. IF you think you are you are. You are a born winner! Never give up.

"The way to succeed is to double your failure rate."
-Thomas J. Watson, founder of IBM

As IBM got bigger it was beaten by a better winner, failure and risk taker Michael Dell. His company Dell Computers sells more PC's online than anyone else in the world

Talent and knowledge is over rated
You could read 1,001 technical tips on playing sport or doing business but it WON'T help you very much! The real way to learn is by "DOING"! Just like how you learnt to walk, talk and ride your bike! You didn't read a book to learn how to walk. You just did it! You watched a few people and then went for it! You fell down several times (over 1,000!) but you got back up. It's the same with sport and business. You don't read a book to learn how to do it, you do it! Get out there and do it. Walk on.

We learn by 'doing' not by reading. So start 'doing'.

Winners win at night
I was having a meal one evening in a local golf club and the golf course was deserted and so was the practise ground, except for a young boy hitting balls down a fairway. I knew I was looking at a motivated kid. Actions speak louder than words. I went out and gave him some advice and several months later I was asked by his Dad to give him some coaching for his golf and for his forthcoming exams. I did and I didn't have to guess if he would use my advice, I knew he would because I knew he was motivated. I got an email within days telling me he played great in his local medal competition and his handicap had been cut! Ewen's comments are at the front of the book.

Winners win in the dark.
Winners are the first to arrive and the last to leave.
Winners do more, so they achieve more.
Winners do the things that losers don't.

The only people you'll find doing any sport in the dark is winners and kids. Or should I say the only people you'll find doing any sport in the dark is winners and winners.

Dreamers
Keith and Michael Spence are young winners and future golf champions. They are also very clever. So after getting their grades from school you would think they'd be off to University like everyone else they know. Not the dreaming Spence brothers! They are both working in the evening stacking shelves! They work on their golf and fitness during the day, every day. Luckily they have parents that believe in their dream!

The Spence brothers are working on their dream during the day and their money during the night!
While everyone is sleeping, winners are 'doing'.
Winners work on their dream day and night.

"The gent who wakes up and finds himself a success hasn't been asleep." – Wilson Mizner

While winners are working, losers are sleeping.

ACTION
Daily Motto
Winning habits make winners win. Use your 'I am a hero' switch. Imagine you have achieved your dream, ask your future self 'what things do I have to do everyday to achieve my dream?" Daily habits, goals or rules. Write the answer down now!
GO!

STOP
These can be the basis of your daily 'motto'. Like Daily 'rules' or 'creed' or 'goals'. Have no more than 7 and change them if you wish. Put them where you will see them! Now you have a mantra and a motto! Here is mine.

My Everyday Motto (Goals)
I WILL;
Seize today and use every second.
Make and create a fun day.
Be positive, brave, urgent and focused.
Act like my heroes.
Dream, laugh, learn, love, smile, exercise and play.
Be helpful and grateful (remember what I've got)
Do what's important not urgent. Invest and create my future now.
+ *Live today like there is no tomorrow! Today will be a great day!*

Winners live by their own rules.
Which are always tougher than everyone else's!

"I have a set of long term goals. I wrote those down too…..To play at my very best in every match-not just the big ones…..To train at my very best in every session. Never accept that bad days just happen. To make every day a good day…" – Jonny Wilkinson, 'My World'

Top athletes trust their body and often set their goals for the day based on how they feel or their heart rate. Past research on Olympic athletes has found that setting daily training goals was one ingredient that separated winners from losers.

"We must make automatic and habitual, as early as possible, as many useful actions as we can."-William James

"I wasn't afraid of much. I made a promise to myself. I was very lucky. It is very difficult to control your own destiny but I think you can do it up to a point. My life will change depending on the decisions I make and the destiny I choose." -Jean Claude Killy, Gold Medal Winning Skier and now very successful business man

"Whatever you do, if you do it hard enough you'll enjoy it. The important thing is to work and play hard." - David Rockefeller

"People who lead a satisfying life, who are in tune with their past and with their future — in short, people whom we would call "happy" — are generally individuals who have lived their lives according to rules they themselves created."- Mihaly Csikszenthihalyi, American psychologist

Action everyday

Every day use your intuition or imagination and ask yourself "What do I have to do today to achieve my dream? What is the best use of my time and energy?". Write the answer down. Then Do it! Even if the answer is take the day off! Quality not quantity. Another question to ask everyday 'If I had no fear what would I do?' Take those actions. Never give up. Get up. Conceive, believe, act and achieve your dream.

Imagine you have achieved your dream and talk to your future self. Ask yourself 'What actions do I have to take to achieve my dream?' Take those actions.

Asking a great question gets a great answer. The opposite is also true.

"My all time favourite question, "What do you know for sure?" – Oprah

Daily talks (to yourself)

Remember daily and weekly communication with yourself reaps rewards. Reviewing reaps rewards. Remember the New United Motor Company. Winning Habits;

1. <u>Weekly</u> team meetings, for one hour
2. <u>Daily</u> meetings
3. <u>Monthly</u> meetings
4. <u>Regular</u> performance progress reports
5. <u>A weekly</u> newspaper (written report!)

Results;

1. A <u>100%</u> increase in the first year, 20% the second
2. Faults down 56% in first year
3. A reduction of 50% in costs
4. An increase of 33% in machine uptime
5. Ten times more ideas

Thinking and talking is an investment of your time.
Unless you keep tracking your path to your goal, you lose track.
Winning teams communicate.
To win have a communication –with yourself.

If no meetings were allowed in team sport all teams would be less effective.

Meetings are magic.

Are you doing what is important or what is urgent?
Are you working on your problems today or working on solutions for your future tomorrow? Are you putting out the fire every day or are you letting it burn and inventing a better solution for your future. You are doing what needs to be done or what you like to do? Every action you take fits in one box.

Urgent and Important	Not urgent and Important
Urgent and Not important	Not urgent and not important

Winners work in only the first box and the second box; what is urgent and important plus what is not urgent but important. Losers do all the urgent things today and get beat by the competition who dream up a new strategy or product tomorrow. Winners lead their life, losers manage their life. Are you leading or managing?

'Management is like straightening deck chairs on the titanic.'
Leadership is finding a better boat for your future.

"Leaders are made, they are not born. They are made by hard effort, which is the price which all of us must pay to achieve any goal that is worthwhile." - Vince Lombardi

Are you surviving or thriving?
"Survival is not enough." – Seth Godin

Do what's important not what's urgent.

Fitness is important but not urgent.
Dreams are important but not urgent.

Your future may not be urgent but it's important.
Make time to think about it and do something about it.

"Why do so many men never amount to anything?
Because they don't think." -- Thomas Edison
Ask yourself "What is the best use of my time?"
When you ask a good question you get a good answer.

Do the right stuff everyday
Time management can be useful 'knowledge' to have if you use it! But it would be more useful to have an occupational psychologist watch you 'using your time' and see which behaviours are helping and which are wasting your time. OR analyse your time yourself. How are you spending your time every day? You do not need time management when you spend time doing the right stuff every minute of every day. Think 80/20. Only 20% of your actions are giving you 80% of your results. Only 20% of your fun activities are giving you 80% of your fun. Only 20% of the things you do are giving you 80% of your energy. Only 20% of the things you do are using 80% of your capacity. Think 80/20 for everything just to get you thinking! I have made these all up. (However, I've heard the book 80/20 is a good read- I do a lot of my learning just by reading titles or quotes from books! Quick Lessons! Give it a go sometime. It's a great start to the day. 'Nothing is Impossible' – superman Christopher Reeve.).

80/20 thinking can get you thinking! And acting!
"The real question is, once you know the right thing, do you have the discipline to do the right thing and, equally important, to stop doing the wrong things" – Jim Collins, 'Good to Great'

VIP Time
One of the most important things I've learnt is the importance of my time. - Bill Gates

Use ALL your time
Don't say you don't have enough time. You have exactly the same number of hours per day that were given to Helen Keller, Pasteur, Michelangelo, Mother Teresa, Leonardo da Vinci, Thomas Jefferson, and Albert Einstein. - H. Jackson Brown

Make time
You will never find time for anything. If you want time you must make it. -Charles Buxton

It takes time
It takes time to build a castle.
-Irish Proverb

Don't waste time
A man who dares waste one hour of time has not discovered the value of life - Charles Darwin

NOW is the time!
There is only one time that is important - NOW! It is the most important time because it is the only time that we have any power. - Leo Tolstoy

Organise all the time
Late to Bed, Early to Rise, Keep the Faith and ORGANIZE!
-Lisa Sullivan, founder of LISTEN Inc.

Lazy time
There are no lazy people, just lazy goals. - Anthony Robbins

Idea Time
Must take time out to think and talk.

Can't buy time
You can't buy more time.

Invest ALL your time
24 hours a day. 1,440 minutes a day. 86,400 seconds a day. Every second counts. Time is money.

Watch your time
Your time is ticking. Watch your time!

Heart Time
Put your hand on your heart. That pulse is your clock. Time is ticking.

Action time
Take action. It's like driving. It's the only way you get anywhere.

French Time
One marketing and business Guru who I rate very highly is Seth Godin, author of several great books, including 'Permission Marketing' and 'Idea Virus'. He told a story recently in the brilliant American business magazine 'Fast Company'. He said that when Jerry Buckhiemer wanted to get a film done efficiently and cost effectively, in a short time not a long time he used 'French Time' rather than

'Hollywood time'. Seth described the Hollywood approach to film making as being very effective and smoothly run but very lengthy. The main reason is the power of the Unions, which represent the employees who work in the studios. The Unions ensure that every worker gets sufficient breaks, an hour for lunch and works 8 hours a day and not a minute more. Not unreasonable but it means that films take months not weeks to 'shoot'. In contrast French films are made over short periods because the workers are happy to put in the hours necessary to get the film done. They work hard over a short period and then relax! Therefore films made in 'French time' can be made more cheaply and be released more quickly than Hollywood movies.

"'French time' is very good for short projects.
But you can't work in 'French time' all the time." – Seth Godin, Author

To get things done quickly and effectively set short term project goals and do whatever it takes to get there. But take time out afterwards.
There are people chasing a dream and people living a dream.
Everyone else is just helping them.

Every 1 counts
1 year counts; ask a footballer or entrepreneur
1 'half year' counts: ask a 3-month pregnant mother
1 month counts; ask a sport or business team
1 week counts; ask a tendering company
1 day counts; ask a company away day
1 hour counts; ask a student or salesman
1 minute counts; ask a sports team
1 second counts; ask a runner
1 millisecond counts; ask a swimmer
Every 1 counts!

ACT! Take Action!
You have to start somewhere.
Every action you take is one step closer to your dream.
Don't just stand there do something!
Focus and action is the key to quick results.

Focus
Focus on the step in front. Focus on one step at a time. Focus on one thing at a time. Studies show that multi tasking is often more time consuming and more stressful than focusing on one thing at a time. Focus on the most important thing you have to do. Get in the zone. Go with the flow. Ignore distractions. And temptations!

It does not matter how slowly you go,
so long as you start and do not stop.

"One great cause of failure is lack of focus." – Bruce Lee

"The good to great leaders were able to strip away so much noise and clutter and just focus on the few things that would have the greatest impact."
- Jim Collins, Author, 'Good to Great'

"I speak to people a lot about "focus" because I think in business it is SO important to remain focused and not go off on tangents ~ sell, sell, sell! However, focus in my view is difficult without being positive, particularly where there are setbacks and there will always be setbacks ~ what you have to be is positive in your own ability and it will come good. My 2005 mantra is therefore "Positive Focus" (as well as Monsieur Bon-Chance 'Mr Lucky')."
-Steve Cook- Entrepreneur, sold his first company for £3M

Steve Cook is a very successful business person that has used my services. He didn't 'need' me to succeed in business. But he did use my services and I expect him to be even more successful as a result. (His great mantra will be a great help.)

"If you chase two rabbits, you catch none."

Positive Mantra in mind

I had one mantra on my last snowboarding trip which helped me succeed and stopped me falling. After visualising and psyching myself up, I approached and completed every jump with one mantra in mind "Land it" and it was amazingly successful. I kept upright when I had no right to be.

Always finish on a high everyday. Like making three sales or putts in a row. It might take you a half day or all day. But you can look in the mirror with pride. Quality not quantity. Remember 80/20. 20 percent of your actions are getting you 80% of your results. Focus on the right areas and actions and your performance will jump dramatically.

Remember 'muscle memory'. Once you are highly skilled at something the skill becomes automatic, sometimes called unconscious competence. Like walking, driving and cycling. As a results of 'muscle memory' you can decrease the quantity (even go on holiday!) and you will still have automatic competence. But for competence you need confidence. Like driving a car. Every one has the skill when they sit a driving test but it is only those that are confident under pressure who display their competence.

At the highest level in golf, preparation time is more effectively spent focusing on fitness and confidence, than skill. Phil Mickelson winning the Grand Slam of Golf in 2004 after a two-week holiday proved that. It the same with any task under pressure. Like public speaking. Everyone can talk! But under pressure few can talk to an audience.

Competence is important but confidence is most important.
You never forget how to ride a bike!

Your mind and body have a memory! Once you acquire knowledge or skill, it will always be there in your mind and body.
If you are relaxed and confident!
You need to cope with pressure to be competent and confident.

Winners force themselves to keep positive and keep believing, even when they are behind, so they keep achieving.

"You know, I see Vijay out there practising so hard, knowing I haven't touched a club in a couple of weeks, and he's played so great all year, and thinking it's very unlikely that I'll be able to play two rounds at that level. But a lot of things kind of came together. And it came down to a putting match, and I was able to out putt everybody."
- Phil Mickelson, Winner of Grand Slam of Golf 2004

Funny Focus
Apart from changing the negative label of "cold calls" to "calls to future customers" or "calls to future friends" one suggestion I give to clients is Giving yourself a fun mantra and goal for your mind. Focus on fun. Like playing a game of tennis and the objective is to get a rally going with questions and answers or laughs. If you get 4 you win the game and if you get more than 5 minutes you win the set!

When I work with players on their putting I get them to think less technical. It hinders performance. They imagine themselves as a clock. The rhythm of the old pendulum is their hands and putter. As they swing back they actually say "tick" at the top of the back swing and "tock" as they connect. Their mind is filled with only helpful thoughts and concentration and no doubts can enter and no fears can disturb. There is no fear because regardless of the size of putt the task I have given them is easy. Tick-tock. Anyone can do and say that. Easy! They putt brilliantly.

Humming while you work
I often get players to hum while they hit a shot. It helps them relax and also gives them a focus; listen to their breathing and tension. The pitch of the hum must to relaxed with little pitch difference.

Singing while you work
One golfer I know played his best golf when "The best I ever played was when I was really happy and I was singing a song all the way round". It worked wonders. By chance Jonny Wilkinson found himself

humming the Oasis song 'Married with Children' before taking his kicks in an England international and discovered it helped him to relax. It works wonders!

'I am happy because I sing. I don't sing because I am happy.'

Whistle while you work

Whether in sport or business 'whistle while you work' is a good philosophy. You can always spot a happy worker; they whistle! Like painters working on your house.

Phil Mickelson had winning mentality and a holiday and won!
Vijah practised for hours and lost.

Direction

When you are up and running it is easier to change direction than if you are standing still. You may be moving in the wrong direction at times but if you're not moving you'll never go in the right direction. When you have a dream you have a destiny and you will be surprised how many 'wrong' paths and mistakes turn out to work in your favour. Trust destiny. Everything happens for a reason.

If you <u>are</u> going in the wrong direction, running faster does not get you to the right destination! So STOP to think and check to ensure you are going in the right direction (and taking the right actions) to get to your dream destination. Do what is best not what is easiest. If being a winner was easy we would all be winners.

Successful people do what unsuccessful people don't.

Winners will do whatever it takes to be successful.
Some things they like. Some things they dislike.

Winners have winning habits.

"A goal is not always meant to be reached; it often serves simply as something to aim at."- Bruce Lee, Martial art legend

"Where you are headed is more important than how fast you are going." - Stephen Covey

Are you expecting to win or expecting to lose?

What do your actions say about you? Are you dressed for success? Are you ready to win? Have you got someone to sponsor the soles of your feet for when you fall over in front of the cameras? Have you booked a hotel for 3 nights for a five-day tournament? Have you invested in your future success? Or are you cost cutting your tools in case you fail? Are you taking a risk to get a reward?

Walt Disney told his brother 'everything all right' and when he got off the train a day later he was right! Tosh made a promise he'd score to his newborn baby and on the pitch he did. Chris Gorman took a gamble on himself and he became a millionaire at thirty like no one else. Are you not spending money because you don't believe you will make money? You need to spend money to make money. I don't mean regularly blowing away all your profits for the week or month. I mean a few presents to yourself every year and a few investments (presents) to your future. When it's done rarely, it sends a clear message to your mind that you expect to succeed and expect to make money this month! You need to speculate to accumulate. There is a saying 'The man that buys expensive cries once. The man that buys cheaply cries many times'.

Are you preparing to win or preparing to lose?
You can't kid yourself. Your mind will know if you don't believe in yourself. Actions speak louder than words.
Have you prepared for failure and not for success?

Expect and prepare to win. If you are expecting to lose, you will lose.

Don't kid yourself.

If you have already prepared your 'funny celebration' you will score.

I have a motto 'If you are behind never give up,
if you are ahead never let up.'
- Ken Doherty, World Snooker Champion at 28

Under promise and over deliver.

"You've got to search for the hero inside yourself."– M People

Are your actions telling your mind you are a winner?
In sport and business there are competitions. Act like a winner. Arrive early leave late. If you book an early fight home you will get your early exit home from the tournament. Lack of belief gives you lack of achievement. Your actions speak louder than words.

Positive actions demonstrate positive belief to your mind.
With positive results. Burning the bridge brings success.
Negative actions demonstrate negative doubt to your mind.
With negative results. Preparing to fail makes you fail.
You wait for a bus because you expect one to arrive.
Your actions speak for the thoughts and beliefs of your mind.
You can't lie to your mind with your actions!
Actions speak louder than words.
You can 'lie' to your mind with positive thoughts and words.

Positive words give positive results.
Negative words give negative results.
Don't even utter a negative word as a joke!
Your subconscious mind can't take a joke! You'll get negative results!

Push yourself!

Even eagles need a push. So says author David McNally in his book 'Even eagles need a push'. He reminds us of the story of a baby eagle who does not yet know he can fly. His mother knows he can and pushes him out the nest. The young eagle is forced to use his wings and of course realises he can fly. A bird is safe in the nest but that is not what birds are for. It's only when they attempt to fly that they realise they have got wings.

Come to the edge.
We can't. We're afraid.
Come to the edge.
We can't. We will fall!
Come to the edge.
And they came.
And he pushed them.
And they flew.
- Guillaume Apollinaire

100%

Some people say, "give 100%." After all that's the most you can. Some people say, "give 110%." How can you give that? What do they mean? I think Olympians know what they mean. When you watch someone going for gold in a sprint you can see on their faces they are giving everything. And squeezing a bit beyond what is comfortable. It might even hurt a bit. Winners go beyond their "comfort zone" and endure the pain. Paula Radcliffe hurt for the last 10 miles of the London Marathon! She's the fastest marathon runner in the UK male or female!

"There's only one way to succeed in anything, and that is to give it everything." --Vince Lombardi, Hall of Fame football coach

"I love pushing myself to the limit. I'd like to die feeling I've done as much as I can. I've never wanted to be cautious.
Life is too short." – Angelina Jolie

"It's amazing how many matches I've been able to win throughout my career by giving 100% out there. Yet again, it gets me through another big match, having to forget about my body out there and just tough it out." - Lleyton Hewitt, Tennis Champion, not feeling 100% but giving 100% and winning!

"Push yourself again and again.
Don't give an inch until the final buzzer sounds." - Larry Bird

100 % gets gold

Interestingly cyclist Chris Hoy who won gold in the 2004 Olympics says, "If you win you don't feel anything afterwards. If you lose you hurt all over." To go for it, give for it. Give it all you've got and you'll sleep soundly at night. John MacLean is an Australian legend in my book. John is a disabled endurance athlete & record holder, has no use of his legs, competes in Ironmans and has swam the English Channel! Words of motivation that he was given when in pain during the last leg of his first Hawaii Ironman were "The pain won't last forever but the memory will."

Go for it.

"There are no limits" – Motto of World Champions
Australia Women's Hockey Team
The following quote helped me finish a marathon;
"The pain won't last forever but the memory will."- John MacLean,
Record Holding Channel Swimmer, Australian Triathlete, Hawaii
Ironman Hall of Fame (and paralysed below waist)

"Today you must do more than is required of you. Never think that you have done enough or that your job is finished. There is always something that can be done – something that can help to ensure victory. You cannot let others be responsible for getting you started. You must be a self starter. You must possess that spark of individual initiative that sets the leader apart from the led. Self-motivation is the key to being one step ahead of everyone else. Always be on the lookout for the chance to do something better. Never stop trying. Fill yourself with the warrior spirit – and send that warrior into action."
-General George Patton

Winners give 100% and get 200%

Robert Morris of Morris Furniture told me that things were so bad at one-point years ago they had to cut staff and went from 60 people to 29. He told those that remained. We need to do the work of 60 people to keep our jobs. They did! Everyone gave a full 100% and they did two jobs each 200%!

If you give a full 100% you can do the job of two people.
You get out what you put in.
What you do today, is your pay tomorrow.

"The credit belongs to the man who is actually in the arena; whose face is marred by dust and sweat and blood; who strives valiantly; who errs and comes short again and again; who knows the great enthusiasms, the great devotions, and spends himself in a worthy cause; who, at the best, knows in the end the triumph of high achievement; and who, at worst, if he fails, at least fails while daring greatly, so that his place shall never be with those cold and timid souls who know neither victory nor defeat." -Theodore Roosevelt

"You don't know what your limits are. You're ready to drop into bed and then something happens up on deck and you're up there for four hours. And four hours ago you thought you were at your limit."
- Emma Richards, first women and youngest ever person to sail solo round the world.

The Running Man; The Journey
The spirit of the Greeks is inspiring. Greece born ultra runner Yiannis Kouros is another great Greek who has been a legend for 20 years when he shocked the running community by winning his first race as an unknown competitor. He became well known after that! Why is Kouros so amazing? Kouros has set 152 world records! He competes in races like Athens to Sparta and Sydney to Melbourne! He runs in 1,000 miles races and 6-day events! He has run 1000km in 5 days, 100 miles in 22 hours and 50 miles in 6 hours! He beats competitors by hours and sometimes days in events! He has written a book and has recently had a real film (documentary style) made about him. If only he as well known as Tiger! His actions and his words below are inspiring.

"The verb 'endure' is not a physical verb, it's a spiritual one. Endure means to withstand…you must be patient and then do solid training. Without patience, you will never conquer endurance. I practice a couple of hours morning and evening with many breaks.
I disagree with speed and quantities;
I do quality training with rhythm depending on the race's needs."

"We are racing against nature, clock, time, distance…your body cannot carry you…to run for 24 or 48 hours or 6 days.
No one completes the race via his body but via his mind."

"I eat every 20 min. I drink every 15 min in cold, 10 min in normal and 7 min in heatwave. All this while moving. When I run the 24 hrs, I never sleep; I hardly sleep on the 48 hrs unless I have an incredible need to, I sleep for only 10 min on the second night.
I'll rest for 10 min…no longer…I cannot afford to lose more time.
I change my T-shirt every half-hour whilst running, without a second's delay. When I pause it is for the bare minimum time waste."

"I ask for music on two occasions: When tired and need inspiration or when high and wish to be higher. When you are at your lowest, exhausted, having nails missing, knees blown up and a sore back you try to inspire yourself and overcome these obstacles.
The day after the race, you feel like death itself."
"The rational in doing such a sport, is to experience the extraordinary moments of 'exceeding'. You cannot experience them in normal life. There is nothing more dear than your health, your life, and of course your family."

" I'd like to think myself as a messenger.
I want to inspire, give the message that something is doable, it is not improbable…everything is possible as far as
I am concerned as long as you go for it."
- Yiannis Kouros, World Record Holding Endurance Athlete

As you go on your journey let Kouros inspire you!
It's a marathon journey not a sprint to achieve your dream.
I ran a marathon in 2003 and told myself
"If you can do this you can achieve your dream."

(I also told myself 'The pain won't last forever but the memory will'!)

Burn the bridge
There is a famous story about an army general. He brought his army by boat to fight a battle in which his army would be out numbered at least 3 to one. After they came ashore they had to climb a hill. When they got to the top of the hill the general stopped the army. He told them they would be outnumbered in the battle and asked them to look back down at the boats on the beach. The boats were burning. He told them there was no going back now. The army went on and won the battle. They had to.

If you want to drive towards your dream you need to cross the bridge.
Then you need to 'burn the bridge'.
Necessity is the mother of invention and motivation.
"A thousand mile journey starts with one small step."
-Lao-tzu, The Way of Lao-tzu, Chinese philosopher (604 BC - 531 BC)

Certainty
Sometimes you have a dream and you have belief in your dream long term. In the short term that dream is like a prayer. You hope it comes true but you cannot be 100% sure. However you know that you must take action or you will be 100% sure to fail. You must jump and take action. Take your chances. Even if you are not certain, chase your dream. If you do not chase your dream you are certain to fail.

Stop thinking. Take action. Jump.
There comes a point when you need to stop thinking and start doing.
That point is 60 seconds after you had a choice to make!

"Don't be afraid to take a big step when one is indicated.
You can't cross a chasm in two small jumps." - David Lloyd George

"Five frogs are sitting on a log. Four decide to jump off.
How many are left?
There are still five - because there's a difference between deciding and doing." - Mark L Feldman & Michael F Spratt 'Five Frogs On A Log'

Stop thinking and jump!

"First you jump off the cliff and you build your wings on the way down."
- Ray Bradbury

"To accomplish great things, we must not only act, but also dream:
not only plan, but also believe" - Anatole France.

"Great love and great achievement require great risk."- Dali lama

"The brave may not live forever, but the cautious never live at all."
- Timothy Luce

Travel 1st Class

No journey is started without a dream. No dream is achieved without the journey. It is not the most intelligent or skilful or rich or fastest person that succeeds but the person that walks there the quickest. The difference between a 1st class letter and 2nd class letter is not that the 1st class letter is more intelligent, stronger or more skilful, the difference is that a higher price was paid to go 1st class and get there the quickest. Note, sometimes it's a faster route (strategy) but often is the same route as second class but 1st class gets there quicker by going directly there without stops or de-tours) Imagine your dream is like a 1st class parcel and you have to get up every day and 'deliver the parcel'. You do not have to be faster, stronger or more skilful to beat the competition to your dream you just have to pay a higher price by taking action using the quickest route every week. One day you will get to open the parcel. But no parcel is delivered without action. Get a 1st class stamp on your TOP 7 goals and start delivering it! Remind yourself that actions achieve dreams.

Get up every day and deliver your dream. Take the 1st class route!
Go slow, fast or steady or stop but don't stop for long.
Before you begin a journey each day do two things.

Make sure you are going the right way and make sure your laces are tied. Prepare yourself. BP.

Commit and Begin

"Until one is committed, there is hesitancy, the chance to draw back, always ineffectiveness. Concerning all acts of initiative, there is one elementary truth, the ignorance of which kills countless ideas and endless plans. That the moment one definitely commits oneself, then providence moves too. All sorts of things occur to help one that would never otherwise have occurred. A whole stream of events issue from the decision, raising in one's favour all manner of unforeseen incidents and meetings and material assistance which no man could have dreamed would come his way. I have learned a deep respect for one of Gothe's couplets; "Whatever you can do, or dream you can, begin it. Boldness has genius, power and magic in it."
-WH Murray, The Scottish Himalayan Expedition.

Begin your journey

Regardless of whether you feel you have the skill or the strategy or the time or the money begin your journey. Chase your dream. Find a way or make a way, as you go on your way. Either way if you begin your way you will find a way. Obree found the parts for his bike on his journey and achieved his dream. I found the parts for my book on my journey and achieved one of my dreams. You will find the parts for your dream on your journey and achieve your dream.

Dream, Believe, Plan, Act and Achieve.

Plato said, "The beginning is the most important part of the work."

Do you REALLY want it? WHY?

Why do you want your dream? Do you REALLY want it. If you have a big enough 'why?' you can overcome ANY 'how?' You must start towards your dream goal before you actually know 'how' and then when you find the 'how', overcome it.

'Who? Why? What? Where? When? How? Are my good friends.'

Dreamer with no 'how'

English man Ridley Scott, director of Alien, Gladiator, Platoon, Thelma and Louise graduated at 19 with a degree in graphic design. How would he get into his dream of film making with a graphic design degree?! He didn't know either!

"By the time I was 19 I'd seriously begun thinking of becoming a film director, even though I was still drawn to advertising and set design. I didn't know how I'd become a director but figured I'd be one step closer if I could get a job designing sets at the BBC, because then I'd be working alongside directors. Which is exactly what happened."
– Ridley Scott

Facing fear and beginning the dream
His film making experience began due to him bolding travelling to New York with no job! He went to New York, walked into the top advertising agency and showed them his work and got a job! However he wasn't satisfied with just focusing on the ad industry and wanted to see if he could gain experience for his dream "film making".

"I decide to drop advertising for a while and pursue the two best known documentary film makers of the time. I didn't know how to get to Pennebaker and Leacock, but I knew where their offices were and I knew what Leacock looked like. And it's funny , but when you're on your own and you've got no one to ask and no one to help, you do all kinds of outrageous things. So one day I just stood around with my portfolio in the lobby of the building where these two guys worked and in came Leacock and Pennebaker. They were headed for an elevator. So I shuffled in behind them, waited until the doors closed and started my pitch. I got a job." - Ridley Scott

Ridely Scott had no fear and no help.
Just like Ridley you must do what you have to do and ignore fear. Begin your journey. You will meet some great teachers and by chance or destiny you will have some great experiences, opportunities and ideas! Grab them. Chase the dream!

"Every great teacher changes your life.
Every great love affair changes your life."
–Alan Lightman MIT Professor and writer

"I know for sure that life is a gift to be treasured –and that we must always live it to the fullest." – Mattie Stepanek

Dreaming never stops
I tell you none of my personal stories to impress you but to impress upon you the importance and significance of each of the points. Share my journey that got me here. There are similarities with my experiences, challenges and lessons and those of great people in sport and business and life who have chased and achieved their dream. I wanted to share how someone ordinary achieved something extraordinary. This book has revealed how I discovered, chased and achieved my dream. But the next dream is bigger and more important.

My goal was to write a book so good that if I picked it up in a book store myself I would have to buy it. A very high bar. I am ruthless about reading rubbish. I wouldn't waste money on recycled ideas. I can re-read my existing books. It must have something my other books lack. A powerful and simple user guide that works. Amazing information with inspiration, clarity and simplicity.

Getting my book published was my dream and I have achieved that today. Tomorrow it means nothing. A book is useless if no one buys it and reads it and uses it. If no one buys the book AND reads it AND benefits from it I will throw it in the bin myself. Writing it means very little to me now. Selling it means everything. It is my big dream to be a number 1 best seller. There is nothing vague about my target and dream.

Now I have published my book it is like getting to the Olympics. It was a battle to get here but now I have come to the arena to fight the thousands of competitors in the book market, my Olympic book games. But I didn't come here to go home without a gold medal. I came her to win.

Let the games begin

I am here to win. To be number one and receive my gold medal and achieve my dream. No one goes to the Olympics Games to come second. I didn't either. I am here to be a winner not a loser. I did not come here to get second and be a nobody. I came here to be a somebody. To be somebody that shakes the hand of my competitor and then crushes them. I will let nothing get in the way of my success, NOTHING! I will never give up. I have no time for fear. I have a job to do. I will dare to win and take my chance - for it would be a bigger regret to waste this opportunity. Regret would keep me up all night. I will not give myself sleepless nights with regret. I will sleep soundly with pride as my pillow. I will unleash all the power within me and no one will get in my way. No one can match the hunger and fire inside me. I will stagger from this field with my scars, my blood, my sweat and my tears and have nothing left to give. For I will give everything today and I know I will leave with something. I will leave the field today with a face that does not hide in shame, but can look with pride in the mirror. There is no shame and no regret when you give everything. In preparation and in battle. Not many will achieve that face today. But I will. Today is gonna be my day. Let the games begin.
Phil McNally.com

Very Fast Summary

Find something you enjoy, have a dream, write the dream down with a deadline, get good advice, make sacrifices, take risks, work hard, surround yourself with winners, find someone who has achieved your dream, believe you can do it, work hard, take action, visualise it, relax and make no excuses.

Preparation, positive thinking and luck make dreams come true.

Made the most of the opportunity.

Conceive, believe, act and achieve your dream. Never give up.

Get up.

You have capabilities beyond imagination.

Dreams are motivating. Keep dreaming. Dreams can come true.

It's good to have heroes. In fact it's essential.

You're your imagination and intuition.

The most powerful habit you can adopt is talk to your heroes & your self!

Take your chances, give it everything you have got and you'll have no regrets.

You are in control of your thoughts, actions and time.

You have the controls of your future. You can decide your destiny.

Achieving your dream is a choice.

Until you cross the bridge and burn it, there is a chance to go back.
Once you are committed to a goal
you will be amazed at what you achieve.

Spend your time wisely.
It's the most important investment you will make.
Time is money. Start investing your time and stop wasting your time.

" Regret for the things we did can be tempered by time;
it is regret for things we did not do that is inconsolable."
-Sydney Harris

"Dream. Believe. Plan. Act. Achieve." – Walt Disney

Be a brave winner. Do not fear failure.
Success is a numbers game. Failure isn't fatal.
Smile every time you fall. You are one step closer to walking.
Do not give up. Get up.

"What I know for sure is in your lifetime you will hear the word 'no' much more than you will hear the word 'yes'. What have I learnt? That secure people say yes much faster than people who operate out of fear. If you keep saying 'yes' to yourself one day someone might say it to you." -Nia Vardlalos, screenwriter and actress 'My Big Fat Greek Wedding' (refused by several film studios before getting 'yes')

*"Whatever you can do, or dream you can, begin it.
Boldness has genius, power and magic in it." – Gothe*

When you have a dream you have a destiny. You will be surprised how many 'wrong' paths and 'mistakes' turn out to work in your favour. Trust destiny. Everything happens for a reason.

*Fear less, act and think more.
Stop thinking and jump! Seize the day.
Take action NOW!*

We are very motivated to do things that give us pleasure! But only if they won't give us pain! No hero achieved a painful dream.

One of the most powerful things you can do is talk to your self!

*"In order to win, you have to risk losing."
- Matthew Pinsent, 4 time Olympic Gold Medallist*

*"Indecision and delays are the parents of failure."
--George Canning (1770-1827) British statesman*

"If I have the belief that I can do it, I shall surely acquire the capacity to do it even if I may not have it at the beginning." – Mahatma Gandhi

"Your will be no better than the plans you make and the action you take. You are the architect and builder of your own life, fortune, destiny." – Alfred A. Montapert

"Genius is 1% inspiration and 99% perspiration." – Thomas Edison

The only thing that ever holds us back is ourselves.

*"A man can be as great as he wants to be. If you believe in yourself and have the courage, the determination, the dedication, the competitive drive and if you are willing to sacrifice the little things in life and pay the price for the things that are worthwhile, it can be done."
-Vince Lombardi, Green Bay Packers Coach, NFL Hall of Fame*

*"If everything seems under control, you're not going fast enough."
- Mario Andretti*

Now you know what to do, do it

This book is just 'The Beginning of your adventure'. Where you go is up to you. Your hands are on the steering wheel. Where are you going?

Now is your chance to start dreaming, stop fearing and begin winning. If you could do anything what would you do? Write your BIG goals down and have a picture of your dream. If you're looking for directions use your intuition and trust your internal conversation. Visualise the first step and jump. Keep the voice positive and you'll keep the results positive. Look in the magic mirror and see your biggest fan. Repeat your mantra. Switch yourself into a positive state. Become a hero. Switch off every day. Smile every time you fall. Do not give up. Get up. Achieving a dream is like learning to walk again. Never give up. Success is a numbers game! Take 4 weeks off and celebrate.

Remember; you're in a car. You have the power. Where do you want to go?

Start your great adventure now! Take your hand off the handbrake. Stop thinking and start driving. Follow the PEGS!

Be a winner!

Fantastic Phil

PS. Let me know when you get there. (…I believe in you, do you?)

Dream it. Believe it. Plan it. Action it. Achieve it.
Be brave. Start walking. Smile every time you fall.
Never give up. Get up. Keep walking. Keep smiling.

"You've got to have a dream. If you don't have a dream,
how you going to make a dream come true?" - D. Rascal

"All of our dreams can come true,
if we have the courage to pursue them."
– Walt Disney

Don't delay. Seize the day.

Anything is possible. Shoot for the stars. The sky's the limit.

7 Positive Mindpower Tools TM for Sport

GOALS

Have one dream goal that motivates you and work on it. Set 7 big goals and write them down. Look at the list twice a day. Get a picture of your big goals somewhere. Subliminal Goal advertising! Before every performance set yourself goals. The winner who wants to win the most will win the most. If you play a stop-start sport like golf, pick your target before every shot. Be positive. If you aim close, you hit close. If you aim for the hole, you hit the hole.

PASSENGERS

Choose a hero you admire to guide, motivate & inspire you. Imagine conversation. You will make winning decisions. When you are unsure of a decision during performances talk to your hero in your head to make decisions. Imagine you have achieved your big goal. What advice would your future self give you and what actions do you need to take to succeed? Take those actions. Sometimes you use this tool before you decide on your goals.

MENTAL MOVIE

Imagine each performance in your mind, like a movie, before you perform. Visualising years before, weeks before and minutes before a performance will all help build belief. Mental movies are powerful. Use your mind to 'see, hear and feel' the performance. Use your imagination to create a 'Mental Movie' of what you want to happen and what you want to achieve. You are the movie director of your future. If you play a stop-start sport imagine each shot in your mind before you play it, like a movie.

DIRECTING

Choose positive thoughts and words and you'll get positive results. Today will be a great day! I will play amazing! Use 'will' power and 'direct' verbally what you want to happen in the next few seconds and the next few years. Like a movie director directing the next scene. Be careful what you wish for! People who are successful are always positive! If you think you can or say you can, you're right. STOP any negative thoughts, them with a red Traffic light, CUT them from your mind and your movie and put them in the Garbage bin. Go green! Negative thoughts give negative results. Stop negatives with "STOP" & "CUT". If you play a stop-start sport before each shot say where you want it to go e.g. "this is in the hole!" Even when a shot does not go to plan keep positive! Look at mistakes positively! You need to be positive for the next shot. Few sports need perfection to win. Some of the biggest mistakes in golf are made by the eventual winner!

MANTRA

Say "I am a winner" and "I am lucky" every day. Remember Mohammed Ali said many times "I am the greatest", before he got there! The suggested mantra will increase your success and luck and build your confidence, belief and performance. Say it while you are performing as well. Write this mantra down and have it where you will see it daily. Get into winning habits! Believe and achieve. A mantra is a verbal version of visualisation. It creates a picture. You can also use a mantra for during a pressure shot or play. Helps focus. Have a Funny Focus like 'tick tock', 'bounce hit', 'head up' or 'humm'!

SWITCH

The switch is very powerful. Say your magic 'word' and switch on your positive bubble so you feel positive and give a positive performance. The bubble is negative proof so any non-positive comments, thoughts and energies bounce off. Or press your switch and act and think like your hero now. You will give an amazing performance. Imagination is more important than skill, knowledge and strategy.

RELAXATION (Brain Break's)

Relaxation boosts positivity, intuition, concentration and mental and physical energy. Essential for winning. Relax before every performance using one of the five 'B's; 1. Breathing slowly. 2. Banter; have a laugh. Have a banter break! If you're laughing, you're relaxing. Laugh by yourself if you have to. 3. Body moving; dancing, singing, playing, walking and smiling relaxes you. 4. Boring; Repeat the word 'relax' over and over with your eyes closed or sit and relax yourself from head to toe slowly 5. Build belief by repeating your mantra several times or writing it out several times. For golf you need to relax between shots therefore use the technique(s) during performance. After every sport performance; the better the relaxation the quicker the recovery. Note- Alcohol is a depressant and a very poor nutrient. Relax between training and performances. Find a winner in your sport and find out when they train and when they relax, during a full year. Phelps trains everyday. Armstrong stops training after the Tour De France.

7 Positive Mindpower Tools TM for Business

GOALS

Have one dream Big Goal that motivates you and work on it. Set 7 big goals and write them down. Look at the list twice a day. Get a picture of your 7 big goals somewhere. Subliminal Goal advertising! Every day, every week and every year set yourself goals.

PASSENGERS

Choose heroes you admire to guide, motivate & inspire you. Imagine conversation. It is very useful and effective to have a diverse range of advisors with different skills, sex, experience and personality. The more often you use this tool the more comfortable you become with it. You will make winning decisions. Imagine you have achieved your big goal. What advice would your future self give you and what actions do you need to take to succeed? Take those actions. Sometimes you use this tool before you decide on your goals.

MENTAL MOVIE

This is a very powerful tool. It can be used with your eyes open or eyes closed. Picture yourself achieving your goals. Use your imagination to create a 'Mental Movie' of what you want to happen and what you want to achieve. You are the movie director of your future.

DIRECTING

Choose positive thoughts and words and you'll get positive results. Today will be a great day! Use 'willpower' and direct what you want to happen in the next few seconds and the next few years. Be careful what you wish for! People who are successful are always positive! If you think you can or say you can, you're right. STOP any negative thoughts, then with a red Traffic light, CUT them from your mind and your movie and put them in the Garbage bin. Go green! Negative thoughts give negative results. Stop negatives with "STOP" & "CUT".

MANTRA

Say "I am a winner" and "I am lucky" every day. Remember Mohammed Ali said many times "I am the greatest", before he got there! Believe and achieve. A mantra is a verbal version of visualisation. It creates a picture. The suggested mantra will increase your success and luck and build your confidence, belief and performance. Write this mantra down and have it where you will see it daily. Get into winning habits. You can also use a mantra for during a pressure call or presentation. Helps focus. Have a Funny Focus like 'back forth', 'bounce hit', 'head up' or 'humm'!

SWITCH

The switch is very powerful. Say your magic 'word' and switch on your positive bubble so you feel positive and give a positive performance. The bubble is negative proof so any non-positive comments, thoughts and energies bounce off. Or press your switch and act and think like a hero now. You have super power. Imagination is more important than knowledge.

RELAXATION (Brain Break's)

Relaxation boosts positivity, creativity and intuition, as well as increasing concentration and mental and physical energy. Take a few minutes break to give yourself a brain boost using one of the five 'B's;

1.Breathing slowly.

2.Banter; have a laugh. Have a banter break! If you're laughing, you're relaxing.

3.Body moving; dancing, singing, playing, walking and smiling relaxes you.

4.Boring; Repeat the word 'relax' over and over with your eyes closed or sit and relax yourself from head to toe slowly

5.Build belief by repeating your mantra several times or writing it out several times.

Powerful exercise! Take several short brain boosts and one longer relaxation break every day. Take several weeks off work every year like Sir Richard Branson. These short and long brain breaks will improve your performance, positivity, creativity, concentration, motivation, decision-making and mental and physical health. Time is money. Invest it wisely. Not relaxing or exercising is costly. Make time to take time out. Take a few minutes time out every day, a few hours out every week and a few weeks out every year.

Recommended (not) Reading

You've got work to do!

'Stop reading about it and start doing something about it'

Be an action man who occasionally reads not a reader who occasionally acts.

Don't become addicted to reading.
Become addicted to doing.

Knowledge gets you nowhere without action.

The clever man reads a book and gets another to feed on.
The wise man reads a book and gets a move on.

Imagination is more important than knowledge.

For one month absorb only this book and adopt the 7 Positive Mindpower Tools as habits. It will take one month. Take a few minutes everyday to preview goals and then review goals at night. What does the mirror have to say? Monitor your CRC and emotions. Read only your motto every morning.

Thereafter take bites out of great books every week.
Read a quote a day..
Reading is rewarding. Knowledge is power.
The books mentioned in this book are all good.
Trust destiny. You don't choose a book, a book choose you.

Stop and sharpen your saw every week. But don't over do it.
Trust intuition.

Recommended Actions

EVERYDAY

Use the 7 Positive Mindpower Tools + stop –ve's with "STOP"& "CUT!"
Wake up using Mental Clock.
Look at Dream Board with pictures of goals.
Look at the list of TOP 7 big goals and 7 hero qualities you need.
Look at the list of TOP 7 happy goals and 7 qualities you have got.
Display happy goal pictures (things you have got)
Keep a diary or journal (Like Branson, Hunter, Churchill and Kennedy)
Ask your future self "What do I have to do today to achieve my dream?" and "What is the best use of my time and energy?" (write answers and do it!)
Focus on one big step at a time.
Write goals every morning for that day, visualise and direct.
Take a pen or voice recorder everywhere!
Relax and exercise daily.
Review time invested every night noting actions, lessons, positives & ideas.
Write a short note to yourself from your future self.
Preview goals for next day every night.
Make decisions with your heroes and your future self.
Start investing your time and stop wasting your time. All the above takes minutes but gives you more time, energy, effectiveness, creativity, awareness, intuition, positivity, belief, success and luck.

EVERY WEEK

Review week at end of every week.
Write a short note to yourself.
Preview goals for following week every Sunday with heroes and future self.
'What actions do I have to take to achieve my dream?" What is the best use of my time and energy?"
Read, watch, talk or listen to a winner/hero every week.
Spend time with eagles.

Re-read this page every week.

EVERY MONTH

Check you are using 7 tools. Check progress. First weekend every month.
It takes 30 days to adopt a habit into 'automatic'.

Find someone else as motivated and positive as you. Coach each other.
Meet once a month; discuss 1 lesson, 1 mistake and 1 quote each.
Find great people to learn from. Ask questions!
Your friends will change along your journey.
You meet who you need to meet.

EVERY YEAR

Re-read this book in one year's time. The more action you take the more amazed you will be. You need to stop and look back to see progress.

How to make knowledge easily recalled
How to Remember the 7 tools;
Use them everyday and you will. Use it or lose it.
How to remember any knowledge;
Use it. Repeating means remember! Use it or lose it.
How to remember non-skill knowledge;
Read it as follows;
One day later, one week later, one month later, six months later and one year later. (This is proven in research.)

Re-read your notes or the areas of the book you have highlighted at least in one year's time. Get a diary for next year!

To achieve your dream you need to use the PEGS and work on your PASS. Use it or lose it. Take action now! You know what to do, now do what you know.
GO!

Recommended Action

ACTION! (One of the most powerful exercises in the book!)

Write a letter to yourself
Instead of talking to yourself and 'coaching yourself' as recommended in the book as one of the 7 tools, this method is to write to yourself. Which I'd like you to do now and I hope you use it many times in the future (daily, weekly, monthly or yearly –your choice. Or never again if you choose!)

Listen to yourself; the wisest and greatest person you can listen to is yourself!
Listen to me; one of the best habits you can adopt is coaching yourself!

What advice can that wise and wonderful person give you right now? Write a letter to yourself now before you close this book. Write a short note to yourself daily. Re-read this powerful letter in a year. This will only take a few minutes to write but it is the most effective and powerful minutes you will spend. However, you will only realise that in 12 months time! There is no right or wrong way to write this letter. You are a VERY wise person! You need and deserve this letter. This exercise has only been shared with a few clients and everyone that has read their letter one year later has been amazed. Words like "I've done almost everything in the letter" are common. The person that taught me this exercise was reading her one-year-old letter and had also (subconsciously) taken all the advice in her letter and it brought tears to her eye. I saw the power in it immediately and I thought, "that is very powerful…I've got to let people know about it". I just have.
GO!

SEIZE TODAY – ACT(ION) NOW!

1. Write a list of every ACTION you KNOW you have to take
(Write the list below. It may be a long list!
Use back pages if necessary)
2. Prioritise that list and write date beside each ACTION (don't go OOD)
(Decide decisively! 60 seconds is too long!)
3. Write down a list of actions. Put the word 'I should' at the top. Read the list out. Cross out should. Should; should never be used. Should is a shit word. Any "I should" about the future rarely happens. Any "I should have" about the past beats you up. Now put the word 'could'. Read the actions out. Now you have a choice. Life is about choices. The choices you make right now, create the results you get from now on. Your choices every 'yesterday' created your today. Your choices every 'today' create your destiny every 'tomorrow'. What will you choose to do? Decide decisively. Put 'I will' beside any action you WILL do. Alternately if you want to cross out 'could' and put 'WILL' in capitals. Writing or saying your 'wills' makes a positive statement about what you WILL do. Now do it. Your mind is listening to your every word and watching your every action. When you make a commitment helps you make it happen and keep your promises.
4. Identify the most important use of your time and energy NOW and begin the 'winners work'!

Useful Information

Sign up to my FREE 'Winning Mentality' e-mail sent every Monday
www.pownow.co.uk/newsletter
See website for great quotes and information.
Extras for you for buying the book.
www.winningmentality.co.uk/winners

Charity
To encourage kids and adults to dream.
(Inspiration, education and support)
Dreamers Charitable Trust.
www.dreambelieveplanactachieve.com

Self Esteem Information
www.self-esteem-nase.org

Enhance Your Performance
Watch and Learn, Question and Experiment, Read and Play.
Keep open minded.
Best teachers are; quotes, life, nature, kids, history, war and animals.
Sport and business are great teachers.
Keep a diary;
Use mind maps for ideas and info (www.mind-map.com)
Keep list at back of actions, lessons, ideas, compliments, success, bottle

Winners are Readers
Read books on winners and heroes.
Interview winners.
Research winners.
Biography Books (and Biography Channel)
Growing Business, HBR and Fast Company Magazines.
www.gbmag.co.uk
harvardbusinessonline.hbsp.harvard.edu
www.fastcompany.com
Look outside your field occasionally.

Winners and Heroes
www.bornwinners.com
www.guinnessworldrecords.com
www.yianniskouros.com
Search for your heroes
Book, mags, press, films, music, radio, tv, internet, talks, sport events

Nutrition
www.chrisfenn.com
www.patrickholford.com (Consider a personal evaluation –we are all different)
www.mynutrition.co.uk
www.vitaminshoppe.com (Click on 'free health info')
www.glycemicindex.com
www.mentalhealthproject.com

Health and Fitness
www.pponline.co.uk (Peak Performance)
www.ultrafit.com
www.menshealth.com (Good Advice for Men and Women)
www.mensfitness.com (Good Advice for Men and Women)
www.bbc.co.uk/health/complementary/
www.bbc.co.uk/health/
www.google.com (Search web for what you need)

REAL Natural Products with no chemicals (rarely found on the high street)
www.naturalscfactory.com
www.simplysoaps.com
www.greenpeople-organic-health.co.uk

World Famous Aberdeen Alpha
Email myself if you want to network with business 'winners' in Aberdeen. You need to be motivated. Meetings start at 7am!
www.aberdeenalpha.com

Business Networking FORD's only
Find Business Winners to network with near you
www.bni.com

Creativity Guru
Dr John Park
www.emusicproductions.com

Develop Succeed Prosper
Successful business Strategy from a successful business millionaire
www.dspconnect.com

Performance pay doesn't work
www.AlfieKohn.org

Personality Profiles;
Buy the ingenious Four Personality Cards or 'The Genie Within' by Greg Barnes
gcb@optusnet.com.au Ph: 61-8-9481-2788 Fax: 61-8-9481-2755
Profits from book donated by author to Multiple Sclerosis Society
Or look up 'Insights', 'DISC' or 'Myers Briggs' using internet
or Contact local library or Human Resources company

Helpers and Heroes
Find yourself some supporters, helpers and advisors.
Focus your time. Time is money. Get winning team.
Only do what you must do. Get others to do rest. Pay the price.
I use a Personal Assistant

Find information on anything (seek, ask and knock)
Do your detective work
Seek and ye shall find, ask and ye shall receive, knock and the door will open.
Library, bookshop, magazine, Internet or ask someone!

Be an action man, not a reader man.

(Note; none of the products or people mentioned in this book have paid for me to mention them. I only mention or endorse products, companies or books that I have read, used or personally recommend.)

Authors Thanks

Thank you for buying this book and helping me achieve my goal. I know this book will help you achieve your goal. I'm happy you're happy. I'm winning if you're winning.

BIG thanks to those who made the book possible, the 'believers'. The people 'behind' the book. Without them it would not have happened.

Firstly without the physical, emotional and financial support of my Mum and Dad none of it would have happened. Thanks for loving me and supporting my dream. My brave parents live their dream life due to love, belief, hard work and taking risks. Without that inspiration there may not have been a Fantastic (Brave) Phil. My sister and brothers who assisted with great stories and ideas and Paul and my parents who provided a great sounding board. Big Stephen for being the first person after myself to believe in my dream and told me four years ago ("Phil, you're gonna be big"), Andrew at Winninggolf.net for using my services for his golf clients which shaped the book, Magic Mike for inspiring and helping (a lot!), Jason who made me believe I can do it, Jack Black who told me I could do it, Joanne and Rick at Looking for Inspiration and Mark also for their design help, Simon for kindly suggesting that the original title wasn't snappy enough and made me come up with a better one, Sam and Hailey Fowler, Sarah Morrison for all the books she gave me - she was throwing them away after reading another book called 'cut the clutter'! Ironic!, Lipstick Maria a publishing gem and winner, Caron Slessor my PA for proof reading final version, mum and dad for reading and helping along the way and Steven Kerr and John Petchey at Royal Bank of Scotland who 'made it happen'. Finally but most importantly I want to thank the first person that believed in my writing and twenty years on I still remember her saying "You're a great writer, I think you're going to be a journalist when you grow up" after reading my letters I sent to her when I was very young; Gran Hoy :) She was very close! A writer, speaker and coach.

The book contains a little piece of many people who have been behind me, met me, used me and helped me create the book and create some of the stories.

My Clients; My biggest teachers

Thanks to all the open minded people who have used my services. Especially in the early days. In particular clients and inspirations; Valerie (attended 1st POW seminar), Mark (attended 2nd POW seminar), Lucky Stephen Burt (1st POW coaching client), Andrew Smith, Mike Cheney, Paul Williams, Brian McNally, Dunlaw Engineering, Keith and Michael Spence, Simon Lynch, Tiger Tommy Mitchell, David Skene, Joanne, Jen, Anni, Kemnay Academy, Frances Jones, Campbell Robertson, Hazlehead Academy, Carolyn Nicol,

Peter Grossi, David Naylor, Jenny McLovely, Nicola Johnston, Ian Buchan, John Thornton, Doug Whyte, Colin Armstrong, Steve Cook, Graeme Ross, Mavis Mbe, Alan J, Helen Crighton, Ian Crighton, Lawrence of Kemnay, Norman Lawrence, Stephen Walker, Mike Bain, Brian Sinclair, Mike Robson, Mark Rushton, Chris Oliver, StoneyWood Dyce Cricket Team, Inverurie Locos FC, Wendy Geddes, Steve Judge, Donald Smith, Alex and the Club Class Bus team, Mike Glaire and Edinburgh Training Centre team, Ron Emerge, David Christie and all the many many golfers and pros.

Email subscribers; Thanks to all those who are Monday 'Winners' and get my email every Monday. Your positive feedback has been 'fuel' for my belief tank and the comments and ideas food for thought. Thanks to everyone who reads them, replies to them or forwards them on (if you do all three great!). It means a lot to me.

Family;

Cath, Paul, Brian, Mum and Dad. Grandmother McNally. Gran Hoy and Granddad Hoy and McNally. Thanks for the love and thanks for raising such great kids!

Supportive Relatives; Simon, Andy, Martin and Andy Lynch, Aunt Margaret, Ronnie and Marjorie, Robert and Anne, Uncle Jim, Anne Lacey, John, Frances, Mag and Stephen.

Friends;

Mark, Mike, Rick, Craig, Bruce, Dave Ridal, Writer Jason, Genie Greg, Vic Baxter, Johny "Great day to be alive" Conway, Maddy, Duncan, John Wils, Graeme Pyper, Graham Watt and my Friends/ Coaches/ Counsellors! Emma and Nicola. All my friends and business contacts who believed in me (you know who you are-I love you). Including the BNI members especially World Famous Aberdeen Alpha (www.aberdeenalpha.com)

Thanks

Adrian Innes, Ian McDougall, Willie Skene and Vic Baxter (one of my second role models and first mentors after my Dad). Thanks also to Dr Sheila and Dr Ian McDonald for the use of their tranquil house, which gave me quiet time to finalise some ideas.

Big helpers and fans;

Mark Smith, Rick Carney and Joanne Sim.

Inspirational authors (inc. first mind teachers)

Jack Black, Tony Robbins, Joseph Murphy, Napoleon Hill, Andrew Mathew, Louise Hay, Geoff Thompson, Jeffrey Gitomer, Greg Barnes, Paul Hanna, Chuck Spezzano, Dr Robert Holden, Lou Tice, Paul Wilson, Gita Belin, Beth Mende Conny, Dr Christine Fenn, Prof. Dennis Tournish, Mike Cheney (future best seller) and Jason the 21 year old 'teacher' who inspired me.

Teachers
I have no friends, I have no enemies, only teachers.
To those that didn't believe in me, the non believers, the closed minds who said 'no', ignored me or rejected me (it's a long list). Thanks. You've been more help than you'll realise!

This book is dedicated to the dreamers who went for it (you inspired me) and the dreamers reading now who are going for it (you will inspire me).

Authors Goals

By sharing my dream goals with you I am putting my goals in 'stone'. Carved in this book. I believe and will achieve;

TOP 7 (without my dates and detail)
Bestselling Book UK, Eur, USA, Aus,
Beautiful Partner
Make Book and Business Profit
International Coach and Speaker
Dream House
Dreamers Charity
£1M

Have book translated into French, Spanish, German, Greek, Dutch, Swedish, Danish, Norwegian, Portuguese, Chinese, Japanese and Indian.
Write Books for; Kids, Football, Golf and on Winning Mentality Stories (If you have a story for these books, they would be gratefully received)
Raise £1M for Dreamers Charity; Inspire and raise self esteem and belief in adults and kids and cut depression and suicides in young, especially artists and musicians. (There are physically healthy young people dying in this country!)
Number 1 Best selling CD & DVD
Radio and TV programme- UK, USA, AUS
Meet all my heroes (All the people alive mentioned in this book)
Work for my heroes
Coach;
Paul Lawrie, Stephen Henry, Tiger Woods, Kelly Slater, Tony Hawk, David Coultard, Peter Nicol, Chris Hoy, Jonny Wilkinson, David Beckham, The highlander, Aberdeen Football Club, Manchester United FC, Scottish and British athletes, business people and kids, Scottish Football Team, Scottish Rugby Team, French Football Team, 2004 British Olympic Winners, 2008 British Olympic Team, Army, Navy, SAS, SBS, MI5, Diplomats world wide, Prime Ministers, Presidents, Councils, UN, Arnold Schwarzenegger, Bill Clinton, Oprah, Pierce Brosman, M. Night, Jerry Bruckheimer, Virgin, Southwest Airlines, emergency services workers, Doctors, nurses, teachers, inventors, musicians, actors, influencers, MP's and SMP's and many others.
Coach winners and 'losers' in every sport and every industry.
Do world tour for;
Royal Bank of Scotland, Nike, Microsoft, Virgin, Sony, Ferrari, Dell, Honda, BP, Quicksilver, Burton, Pixar, Apple, U2, Rock Band, Dance Act, Mediacom, St Luke's, Universities, RGU, MIT, Harvard, Schools, UN, Red Cross, VSO and many other organisations I admire.

Be Number 1 'winning mentality' mind coach in the World.
Be inspiring, funny and as well known as my heroes
Be known as a winning and 'come back king' coach

And many other goals.

(Any assistance to help me achieve a dream goal welcome!)

"Outstanding! The principles have had a profound effect on my business!" – Michael Cheney, Founder of Seniority.co.uk and Author of 'The Website Marketing Bible'

Business Testimonials for 'Winning Mentality' Seminar

"I have witnessed Phil excite, enthuse and empower his audiences. Here at PSYBT our clients have ideas, goals and dreams, with his techniques and encouragement Phil McNally lets them turn them into reality!"
-Simon Fraser, PSYBT Aberdeen Regional Manager

"Brilliant. Absolutely fantastic. I'm absolutely delighted. 10/10"
-Mike Robson, Marketing Director, Mearns and Gill

"Great session! I got a lot from it personally and the sales team have been using the tools with great success!"
-Gavin Chalmers, Sales Director, Lawrence of Kemnay, Ford Car Retailer

"Hit the spot, well paced with solid content. Thought it was refreshing, highlighting the benefits of positive thinking needs to be a continuous process. Unfortunately it is too easy to drift back to the perceived comfort zone of negativity. Have focused on (my) 7 goals and my "Mantra" Good + Lucky = GREAT. Best comment was 'Be careful about what you wish for, it may come true'. Personally I feel better about myself and what we're chasing as a team."
-Andy Skinner, Business Development Manager, Red Spider Technology

"I was very sceptical before you started out but gradually everything you said seems to make sense. Thanks for opening my eyes."
- Brian Mullen, Engineering Manager, Technip

"Put us in your diary for next year! I spoke to the pupils you talked to a year ago and they still remember your talk!"
-Frances Jones, Guidance Head, Kemnay Academy

"Very interesting and thought provoking. I focus on the positive rather than on the negative and feel a bit more positive than usual (am a very positive person anyway)."
- Claire Kennedy, HR Development Manager, Baxters Food Group

"Generally, I feel more upbeat during the day. Reading my mantra, remaining positive, when I would normally have felt disillusioned. Best bit was; Convincing the audience to allow only positive thoughts, and the "board room." "
-Tony Leitch, Product Assurance Manager, Hydro Group plc

"Absolutely brilliant! Mind-opening, life changing and inspiring. Has changed my whole way of thinking in life, business and personal terms.

Now feel I can, and will, achieve anything I set my mind to in life. Made me re-evaluate myself and all areas of my life. What did I learn? How to get more from my life, control my destiny, think positively and basically aim high and achieve whatever I want! 10 out of 10 for being useful, understandable, fun and enjoyable. I now achieve a two to three fold increase in new business every week. We are on target to hit a 3 fold increase in company turnover in October. I will also meet a personal financial goal I set for myself in May. I've got more energy, I get an extra days work from my week which is massive. It's very significant when you multiply that over a month and year."
-Michael Cheney, Founder of Seniority.co.uk and Author of 'The Website Marketing Bible'

"I'm very driven now. I don't surf the net at work, call friends, or take work home. Before it was foggy. Now it's very clear where I am going. I feel I'm back on track. 'Power hand' is very powerful. In my opinion the sessions have now opened up areas of thought that I hadn't previously harnessed – whilst everyone is aware of the power of the mind, few take the risk of opening themselves up. Phil will open up huge opportunities and improve their business and well-being. If anyone has had the experience of going to the optician and getting glasses/lenses for the first time – as is amazed by what they can see. This is exactly what the session did for me"
- Stephen Burt, Founder and Managing Director, Motion Software

"Thanks. I really enjoyed your course! I feel positive. I have been using some of the tools. All in all I feel a lot more positive and feel a lot less stressed everyday. Sales are booming, I feel really confident."
-Nicola Johnston, Sales Manager, Escape Business Technologies

"I asked a girl out on a date. When I asked Michelle out I took your advice and thought "what have I got to lose?" If I hadn't spoken with you I might not have had the confidence to ask her. We have since got engaged and are expecting a baby. Thanks again for your help."
-Phil Anderson, Senior Mortgage Advisor, The Mortgage Shop, Aberdeen

"I am sleeping a lot better now - which is a relief! So thanks very much for your help!"
-Wendy Geddes, Business Advisor, Royal Bank of Scotland

"Very interesting and a lot of fun. Good team-building. Loved the idea about banter breaks! (Noticed results) Has reflected in the teams working attitude. 9/10"
-Debbie Rose, Business Manager, Edinburgh Training Centre

"Absolutely awesome!"– Adrian Walley, MD, Natural Skincare Factory

Sport Testimonials for 'Winning Mentality' Coaching

"I am now Junior Club Champion and Men's Club Champion and I am only 13 years old."
-Tommy Mitchell, North East Under 14 Champion 2004 and Junior and Men's Champion Longside Golf Club 2004

"A **win** after a 5 week drought was great. The spirit of the guys on and off the pitch was great and I'm sure a lot of that was down to your chat in the morning. We had five losses till Saturday. Thanks again on behalf of the boys."
- David Lamb, Stoneywood-Dyce Cricket Club (five wins in a row after session)

"(My) Golf has improved quite a bit. I even won my first tournament!"
-Benoit Vidick, Schlumberger Well Services

"I am more confident and a lot more relaxed. Phil has helped me become a winner. I have won several bowling competitions. Thanks for all your help."
-Phil Anderson, Aberdeen Silver City Triples Bowling Champion

"What a difference. It's bizarre. I'm actually hitting the ball as well now as I did when playing every day last year (after months of pre season training). I find it a lot easier to hit shots....fades, draws, etc. With putting it's made a vast difference. I'm actually hitting some shots with my eyes closed."
– Paul Arthur, Aberdour Golf Course PGA Professional (Tartan Tour)

"I've just won my first tournament the Tetra Masters, thanks to following your advice. I often as a high handicapper dismiss my chances but not any more!
For the first time I tried the techniques you taught earlier in the year, I felt more relaxed and comfortable with my golf and will be adopting this on future outings."
- Graeme Ross, Business Manager (and golfer), Royal Bank of Scotland

"Very helpful. Especially to focus the mind and work out goals. (The coaching) Gives confidence. I am more confident and believe in myself. All good. Been a really good help and turned me around not physically but mentally. 9/10"
- David Skene, Aberdeen Football Club, U16

“I’ve been using two of the techniques which I like. Golf is 99.9 percent mental.”
-Gary Forbes, PGA Professional, Murcar Golf Club

“I was 1ST at Oldmeldrum Junior Open, equalling the junior course record (3 under) and retaining my title from last year. I won the Royal Aberdeen Junior Open retaining my title from last year as well. Cheers for all the help.”
– Michael Spence, Kintore Golf Club, Kintore Golf Club Champion 2003

"I just thought I would tell you that on the first day of trying this new mental approach I shot a 77 a net 68 off the men’s medal tees in the medal on Friday and my handicap has been cut already because of that. Thanks”
-Ewen Noble, Golfer, Kemnay Golf Club

“You’re the man!”
-Simon Lynch, Preston North End Football Club, Scottish U-21 International

Authors Details

The best way to contact me is by email;
Phil@pownow.co.uk

Other details;
Tel: +44 (0) 1467 641635
Fax: +44 (0) 1467 641185

POW
Thainstone Business Centre,
Inverurie,
Aberdeen,
AB51 5TB,
Scotland, UK

I would be very grateful for feedback on using the tools in the book, stories on your results and any amazing stories of people's achievements that you hear of. Real stories are as powerful as unreal stories. Rocky and Superman are powerful stories with good heroes to model.
(If using mail please include contact details e.g. address, phone, and email.)

To discover what I have learnt since this book was written; read my weekly emails, come and hear me speak at an event or book my services. See web for details of events.
Q. Why use my coaching services?
A. Winners use coaches.
Average Golfer has 0 coaches. Tiger Woods has 7 coaches!
Winning Mentality Coaching *will* improve your performance.
Or I will give you your money back.

POW Services;
Winning Mentality Coaching
Winning Mentality Seminars
Winning Mentality Corporate Talks
Winning Mentality for Caddies, Coaches & Physio's
Winning Mentality and Physicality for Sports Professionals*

**Proactive and Reactive service for increasing fitness time and reducing injury time.*

Published by Lipstick Publishing
Scotland.UK
www.liptickpublishing.com